1978

In Memory of

Selma Loeb
Sanders

SISTERS
OF
THE QUILL

by

Alice Anderson Hufstader

DODD, MEAD & COMPANY

NEW YORK

1 2 3 4 5 6 7 8 9 10

Library of Congress Cataloging in Publication Data

Hufstader, Alice Anderson.
Sisters of the quill.

Bibliography: p.
Includes index.
1. Women authors, English—Biography. 2. Authors,
English—18th century—Biography. I. Title.
PR113.H78   828′.009 [B]   78-2642
ISBN 0-396-07544-4

This Book Is Dedicated
in Loving and Grateful Memory
to My Husband
Robert Hufstader
1907-1975

ACKNOWLEDGMENTS

During the nineteen fifties and sixties, I gave a series of talks on diarists and letter-writers at the Public Library of Winter Park, Florida. We ranged from Mme. de Sévigné of the early 17th century to Alexis de Tocqueville of the 19th. We explored such disparate figures as Samuel Pepys, Clerk of the Acts to the Navy of Charles II; David Garrick of Drury Lane Theatre; that inconsistent preceptor, Lord Chesterfield; and the four women of Georgian England who, with their friends, constitute *Sisters of the Quill*.

I am grateful to the Friends of the Winter Park Library, under whose aegis these lectures were given, for the incentive and inspiration they provided. I also thank Charlotte Moughton, now Mrs. Ernest Brunoehler, Librarian, for her help and encouragement.

Paul Henry Lang, when he was editor of *The Musical Quarterly*, encouraged me to write on musicological subjects. One of the resultant articles, *Musical References in Blue-Stocking Letters*, suggested *Sisters of the Quill*. I am deeply grateful for his making possible these publications.

I am also indebted to Thomas Scherman for including in his *Beethoven Companion* an excerpt from another of my *Musical Quarterly* articles, *Beethoven's Irische Lieder: Sources and Problems*.

Sylvia Hilton and the late Helen Ruskell of the New York Society Library have been kind and efficient in fulfilling requests for photocopies and in mailing books. Their assistance is deeply appreciated.

Mollie Sands Jaquet, of London, author of *Invitation to Rane-lagh*, has sent me prints and photocopies from the British Museum and other English sources. I very much appreciate her willingness to act for me, to say nothing of her inexhaustible knowledge of Georgian social, musical, and theatrical history.

I also appreciate Joyce Hemlow's reply to my inquiries about Fanny Burney's musical enthusiasms.

My cousin Thomas O'Conor Sloane has been unfailingly generous with his time and professional advice. For his loyal support, I am most grateful.

Dan Wickenden very kindly read the manuscript. I am grateful for his help and suggestions.

Elizabeth Riley's vast experience in publishing has been invaluable. For her willingness to counsel me, I can never express adequate thanks.

I am deeply grateful to Louise Talma for her kindness in helping me with proofreading.

My late husband, Robert Hufstader, died shortly after this book was finished. It is dedicated to him. Without his help it could not have been written.

In conclusion, I thank our sons, Peter and Dom Anselm Hufstader, for continuing the assistance given by their father.

—ALICE ANDERSON HUFSTADER

August 4, 1977
Edgartown, Massachusetts

CONTENTS

Sisters of the Quill

1

THE ENTRANCE

"Evelina"

1778

IT WAS COMPOSED in "secresy" and written in "a feigned Hand." *
Two aunts, three sisters, and a younger brother were in the author's
confidence. The latter conspirator, acting as agent, carried the manuscript to the well-known publisher, Dodsley, who refused to print an
anonymous work. The committee of siblings reconsidered the matter
and at random selected Mr. Lowndes of Fleet Street, who stipulated
only that the last volume be in existence prior to the publication of
the first volumes—a precaution the writer deemed "priggish punc-
tilio."

Worn out by the nocturnal toil of writing a clandestine novel,
the author suffered prolonged illness, and after months of seclusion
awoke to unexpected acclaim.

Edmund Burke sat up all night to finish the story. Dr. Johnson
claimed for the work qualities not to be found in the novels of Richardson or Fielding or, for that matter, in the poetry of Pope. Sir
Joshua Reynolds could not put it down and vowed to give fifty
pounds to discover the identity of the author. Some of the "ton" believed the writer to be a man, others thought a woman. Mr. Lowndes,
who had bought a best-seller for the meager sum of twenty pounds,
was quite certain that the anonymous author was "a gentleman of the
other end of town."

* NOTE: Archaic and occasionally eccentric spelling, punctuation and grammar have
been retained throughout as they appear in the originals of quotations.

Evelina, or A Young Lady's Entrance into the World was published in January of 1778. The following June Dr. Charles Burney's twenty-six-year-old daughter, Fanny, was by benevolent betrayal catapulted into fame. Not only had she written a best-seller; she had established the woman novelist.

Evelina has been called a minor classic. Fanny's characters exemplifying, as they do, extremes of loftiness and coarseness, leave so flattering an evaluation in doubt. Of *Evelina*'s significance as a turning point in the respect accorded to female talent there can be, however, no question. Like most turning points, it had been a long time in the making.

Prior to the late Renaissance, women's attainments depended largely upon hereditary station or force of circumstance. Queen Elizabeth was born great. Joan of Arc had greatness thrust upon her. It was not until later years that the less dramatic achievement of greatness was permitted to women. This distinction is not to deny the possession of exceptional gifts to a princess like Marguerite de Navarre or a saint like Teresa of Avila, but rather to point out that the professional path to female fame rather than that of inheritance or inspiration is, in terms of history's span, recent.

Women entered the professional world by two principal avenues, performance and hospitality. The stage attracted talented women of the workaday world. The salon provided women of the upper classes with an opportunity to exert through social skills a profound influence on philosophy, politics and letters.

These two spheres of feminine prestige came into being in the 1600s. During Shakespeare's career it had been boys with unchanged voices who declaimed to the Globe's Groundlings "Out, out, damned spot" and "The quality of mercy is not strained." With the development of the masque, most notably in the casting of *The Siege of Rhodes*, female roles were played by women. The Restoration theatre, as patronized by the Merry Monarch, smiled upon feminine talent, especially the talent of the "Protestant Whore," Nell Gwynn. When Händel became composer-impresario to the first two Georges, such legendary stars as the rival "Queans" Faustina and Cuzzoni embellished his operas with virtuoso "divisions" (coloratura passages), not all of them vocal. Fanny Burney's youth saw David Garrick, actor and manager, at the peak of his career. In his theatre in Drury

Lane were to be applauded Peg Woffington, Kitty Clive, and the versatile Susannah Cibber, who excelled both as an actress and a singer.

The careers of these Restoration and Georgian actresses and singers were safeguarded by the fact that they represented, in person and voice, womanhood, a natural phenomenon that playwrights and composers were no longer willing to entrust to male children. Their origins were almost always humble and sometimes shady, their liaisons dubious, and their skill and ambition impressive. They had their way to make by virtuoso performance; by wiles, professional and personal, they hoped with luck to scout out a "protector." In France, actors and actresses were automatically excommunicated. The "polite" society of England contented itself with deeming them, often accurately, as no better than they should be.

The woman of intellectual curiosity and literary ability faced more complex problems. She was of necessity well-educated and therefore of the aristocracy, or perhaps a clergyman's daughter or niece. To the inhibitions of gender, especially in England where a girl may still be warned against "braininess," were added those of class.

The intellectual ladies of France had, almost a century before *Evelina,* found hospitality the answer to scholarly cravings. The salon, like opera, had crossed the Alps. A clever hostess surrounded herself with stellar guests who vied with one another in wit, profundity, philosophical theories, criticism, and, in the opinion of Molière, absurdity. Conversation was not only cultivated, it was studied and, one sometimes suspects, rehearsed. Letters and journals which are, in essence, written conversation, reached a degree of excellence associated today only with professional authors. Despite this medium for the exercise of the mind, publication of a book by a woman (unless it were anonymous) remained the sign of "female usurpation."

"Inspire, but do not write," commanded LeBrun. He was obeyed. Catherine de Vivonne, Marquise de Rambouillet, inspired the hostesses who were her successors. Blind Mme. du Deffand, until Julie de Lespinasse took him away from her, inspired d'Alembert and in her turn was inspired by Horace Walpole, her junior by twenty years. Mme. d'Epinay inspired Rousseau, and Mme. du Châtelet, experimenting with the theories of Newton, inspired Voltaire. When the Paris salon had, in Fanny's youth, inspired the coteries of London, Bath, Tunbridge Wells and Streatham, we meet Mrs. Montagu holding court in her feather-upholstered drawing room, Mrs. Chapone coaching Samuel Richardson in decorum and, most celebrated of all, Mrs. Thrale pouring tea for Dr. Johnson.

The salon, viewed in the light of today, suggests a brilliant social occasion. Such an impression misses the essence of these gatherings, which was that of a nimbly led seminar rather than a glittering "At Home." The success of a hostess was determined by her skill in causing her guests to shine, rather than in shining herself. She presided over a chamber orchestra of conversationalists, each participant being chosen to sound a distinctive timbre in the ensemble. Mlle. de Lespinasse, estranged niece to the blind Mme. du Deffand, leaves us the following description of such an evening:

"M. de Marmontel proposed to me to come last Wednesday and read me his new comic opera. He came; there were some twelve persons present. Behold us in a circle surrounding him, and listening. . . ."

Those who listened were expected to proffer comment, to pose stimulating questions, to debate matters of taste and to form judgments. By these means conversation, and for our purposes most significantly, correspondence became what they no longer are, literary forms.

For all its hothouse quality, there can be no questions of the contribution of the salon to feminine influence and literary skill. Women may, in fact, be said to have conversed their way into literature.

In the matter of publication by women, England again tarried behind France. More than a century before *Evelina*, Elizabeth Pepys, the diarist's wife, had refreshed herself with the leisurely chronicles of Mlle. de Scudery. Mme. de Lafayette had published her *Princesse de Clèves* but, as befitted a patrician, she claimed to have no idea who the author was.

Thus, the acknowledged authoress was a newcomer to the literary scene. The same was true of the novel itself.

Fanny's masculine predecessors were, of course, Fielding, Sterne, Smollet and Richardson, whose long-winded stories were so much admired by the hectic Mlle. de Lespinasse. Nor was Fanny the earliest of "female pens." She was the first, however, to make authorship popular for a woman. Years earlier, the playwrights Aphra Behn and Susanna Centlivre had prospered in the production of the well written comedies of ill-conduct required by the Restoration theatre. Mary Manley had sunk lower. In *The New Atlantis* and other *romans à clef,* she had marketed thinly disguised scandal, Lady Mary Wortley Montagu being an eager customer. These women, for all their undeniable ability, operated far more in the uninhibited worlds of Drury Lane and the Haymarket than did the letter writers and conversationalists who must be viewed as *Evelina*'s forebears.

More than a century of warfare did not prevent the Age of Enlightenment from being an age of travel. English authors, among them Hume and Gibbon, studied at first hand the theories of the rights of man which were being hammered out in the Paris salons. French philosophers, principally Voltaire, came to England to admire the then-supposed practice of these rights. The Grand Tour was a requisite for the sons of parents able to afford the luxury of international polish. Travel, in that it supplies novelty, news and distance, has always been a powerful stimulant to letter writers. Mme. de Sévigné, most fanatical of mothers, was prompted by an absent daughter to communicate herself into immortality. That chilly peer, Lord Chesterfield, an equally fanatical, if somewhat more irregular, parent, found it advisable to badger by post Philip Stanhope as he plodded from capital to capital in search of worldly perfection. Lady Mary Wortley Montagu, absent in Turkey with her husband and, without him, in France and Italy, wrote out her brilliant tragedy to Pope and later to her daughter, Lady Bute. Mary Granville Delany sent home to England her delightful accounts of life in Georgian Ireland; Mrs. Montagu, as her interests and health dictated, vibrated between London, Tunbridge Wells, a farm in Berkshire and coal mines in Yorkshire. She wrote and received letters that are numbered in four figures. Among those with whom she corresponded were Elizabeth Carter, scholar and translator of Algarotti and Epictetus; Hannah More, dramatist and friend of Garrick, and chronicler in verse of the English Blue Stockings; and Hester Chapone, whose *Letters on the Improvement of the Mind* were held by Mrs. Delany to rank close to the Bible in sublimity. Two centuries ago distance was a commodity easily available. It played an essential role in stimulating virtuoso epistolary performances by both sexes.

Fanny Burney, loyal to the tradition of the amateur writer, confined herself in girlhood years to keeping a diary and writing letters. Her *Early Diary* is addressed in part to an imaginary confidante called, reasonably enough, Nobody. The principle of absence was also in her case to operate as an incentive. We read letters to distant relatives, in particular to her favorite sister Susan and to an elderly friend who lived an invaluable fifteen miles from London.

During these years of artless outpourings, Miss Burney the novelist was, perhaps without knowing it, at school.

The reader of the *Early Diary* will note that there is a pronounced falling off of entries for the year 1776. Evidently Fannikins was preoccupied. This was indeed the case; she had two projects in hand.

The first was her father's monumental *General History of Music*. Helped by her sisters, Fanny served as copyist.* This daughterly task done, she was free to toil by candlelight, her shortsighted eyes forcing her to "murtherous stooping," upon her second project. She was writing what she knew and what she imagined of a "Young Lady's Entrance into the World."

The world into which Evelina entered was very largely Fanny's world as she recorded it in the *Early Diary* and as she was to continue to record it during an eventful life. She utilized her knowledge of public and social London, populating her story with characters that recall Hogarth in their simplicity. Her heroes and heroines are without blemish and her fops and oafs never deviate toward propriety.

Fanny Burney, in *Evelina,* served as foothill to the heights of such youngers and betters as Jane Austen, the Brontës and George Eliot. *Evelina* remains, however, of another significance. It is an epistolary novel. Versed, as were the ladies of the Age of Reason, in the writing of narrative letters, Fanny gave new direction to what had been heretofore a purely amateur medium. Her first novel occupies a double role in the annals of English literature; *Evelina* is both a point of departure and a culmination. Fanny Burney opened the door to women novelists and, in so doing, climaxed the generations of women letter writers who were her spiritual forebears.

The following chapters will explore this inheritance as it is exemplified by four "Sisters of the Quill."

---

* Hence the feigned hand in which *Evelina* was written.

2

THE REBEL

Lady Mary Wortley Montagu

1689-1762

LADY MARY WORTLEY MONTAGU is chronologically the first of Georgian "female pens." She is also first in terms of literary skill. We will not meet her equal until the emergence of Jane Austen. She was a rebel; she had far more in common with the feminists of today and yesterday than had her gentler successors. It was to remain her cast-iron conviction that life is a bad bargain, and that women have the worst of it.

Although she is the best remembered of English amateur authoresses, she is also the least understood. Her complex character has undergone drastic distortions at the hand of Alexander Pope, with whom she recklessly quarrelled. Those who did so were assured a negative fame. As "Sappho," Lady Mary is a member of the company of caricatures that includes "Atossa," "Sporus" and "Atticus" *; it was a lofty, rather than comfortable, society. In poem after poem Pope described her as promiscuous, averse to soap and water, and afflicted with venereal disease. The name he gave her adds the titillating suggestion that she was "gay." Nor was her husband, stodgy Edward Wortley Montagu, omitted from the slanderous campaign. His large fortune had been augmented by habits of thrift, which Pope promoted to avarice.

It was a systematic persecution. Because of it posterity has sup-

* "Atossa" was believed to be the Duchess of Marlborough or the Duchess of Buckingham; "Sporus" was Lord Hervey; and "Atticus" was Addison.

posed, without a shred of impartial evidence, that this highly gifted woman was a filthy freak whose amorous favors endangered the health of her admirers.

We do not know why Lady Mary and Pope quarrelled. Was it an anticipation of Thomas Mann's *Little Herr Friedemann,* the story of a hunchback who makes love to a beautiful woman and is spurned? Friedemann committed suicide; Pope lived, if not to tell the tale, to take revenge upon the woman who, if it is to be believed, had mocked him. Enmity being to his Muse what beauty was to Keats's, he made her immortal.

The long supposed mystery of her wanderings on the Continent has added to the sum of her eccentricities. Over and over again the questions have been asked: Why did she go? Why did she remain away for twenty-two years? Had she quarrelled with her husband? Was she running away from Pope? Robert Halsband, her recent biographer, makes obsolete these questions. Letters, somehow "lost" by her family, reveal that she had fallen in love with Francesco Algarotti who, as a favorite of Frederick the Great, had distinctly other fish to fry!

There can be no doubt that Lady Mary relished being the smoke that, to reverse an adage, causes fire. She was no more averse to notoriety than was Byron. Brilliant, restless, arrogant, romantic and inconsistent, she preferred incurring scandal to living within the confines of Georgian ground rules.

She was born Mary Pierrepont in 1689, the eldest of four children, with two sisters and a brother. Heredity had, in terms of literary talent, favored her: a kinsman on her father's side of the family was John Evelyn; through her mother she was a cousin of Henry Fielding. Her father, Evelyn Pierrepont, following the deaths of his older brothers became the Earl of Kingston in 1690. Thus it was that the infant Mary became Lady Mary. This worldly advancement was by no means an unmixed blessing to the precocious child. The England of William and Mary and of Anne, despite the presence of female sovereigns, did not give to clever women of patrician status the encouragement which France offered to Mme. de Sévigné or Mme. de Maintenon. The Great House tolerated cuckoldry but not learning. Lady Mary's gifts would have been better nurtured in one of the modest parsonages that sent forth Jane Austen and the Brontës.

Lady Mary Wortley Montagu

Lady Kingston did not long survive her husband's patrician progress; she died while her children were still in the nursery. Lord Kingston made over his three daughters to their grandmothers, to an aunt and to governesses. A major part of the year was spent at Thoresby, a great mansion in Nottinghamshire. Fortunately for the ambitious Lady Mary, Thoresby housed a splendid library. Here, interrupted by little more than lessons in the carving of gargantuan roasts, she scrambled herself into erudition and evolved her ambivalent nature.

The child was mother to the woman. In her earliest writings we find the conflict between romance and reality that was to remain the touchstone of her character. She lived in the world of Rousseau and Voltaire. Long before she could have known of the existence of either, she exemplified in herself something of their contradictory philosophies.

There remains among her unpublished juvenilia an "Autobiography." From it we receive a bitter view of her neglected childhood, a view that was to color her later life. She opens her autobiography on a romantic note: "I need say nothing of the Pedegree of the unfortunate Lady, whose Life I have undertaken to write. 'Tis enough to say she was daughter of the Duke of Regiavilla" (the carving lessons had been accompanied by instruction in Italian) "to inform my reader there is no nobler descent in Portugal." Abandoning fiction for fact she continues, "Her first misfortune happened in a time of life when she could not be sensible of it. . . . I mean the death of a noble Mother, whose virtue and good sense might have supported and instructed her youth, which was left to the care of a young Father, who, tho' naturally an honest man, was abandoned to his pleasures, and (like most of his quality) did not think himself obliged to be very attentive to his children's education. Thus was the unfortunate left to the care of an old governess, who, though perfectly good and pious, wanted a capacity for so great a trust."

This reproach was to darken Lady Mary's potential for happiness. Modern psychology tells us that a girl's attitude to men is usually conditioned by her father, or a father figure. In this relationship Lady Mary had been damaged, and she knew it; Lord Kingston had let her down. It would therefore follow that she could expect no justice in a male-oriented society. Marriage was to pall, friendship to sour, a would-be affair to dwindle. Most crucial of all, Lady Mary was to prove a total failure as mother to the son whom she came to hate.

There was another traumatic consequence to her solitary studies. She came to believe that excellence isolates rather than unites. By her own efforts she had amassed a considerable store of knowledge, and, as a result, thought that most of her contemporaries were fools. It is not an uncommon delusion among the self-made. Upon this confident note her chronicle sweeps on: "Laetitia [as she called herself] had naturally the strongest inclination for reading, and finding in her Father's house a well-furnished Library, instead of the usual diversions of children made that the seat of her pleasures, and had very soon run through the English part of it. Her appetite for knowledge increasing with her years, without considering the toilsome task she undertook, she began to learn herself the Latin grammar, and with the help of an uncommon memory and indefatigable labour, made herself so far mistress of that language as to be able to understand almost any author."

Not one, despite her protestations to the contrary, to hide her light under a bushel, "Laetitia" tells us that "This extraordinary attachment to study became the theme of public discourse."

Lady Mary next reveals her penchant for intellect as weapon. "Amongst the girls of her (Laetitia's) own age was Mlle. ——. She had a large fortune which was enough to draw after her a crowd of those that otherwise would never have thought of her. She triumphed over Laetitia when she related to her the number of her conquests, and amongst others named to her Sebastian [Mr. Wortley Montagu] as he that was most passionately her servant and had made the most impression on her heart." Mlle. —— rashly arranged a party of basset to which Wortley Montagu and Lady Mary Pierrepont were invited. Sebastian was to be cast in the role of lover, and Laetitia as that theatrical commodity, the confidante. It didn't quite work out that way:

"Tea came in before cards, and a new play being then acted, it was the first thing mentioned, on which Laetitia took occasion to criticize in a manner so just and knowing that he"—Mr. Wortley Montagu—"was as much amazed as if he had heard a piece of wax-work talk on that subject. This led them into a discourse of Poetry and he was still more astonished to find her not only well read in the moderns but that there was hardly any beautiful passage in the classics that she did not remember; this was striking him in the most sensible manner. He was a thorough scholar, and rather an adorer than an admirer of learning. The conversation grew so eager on both sides neither cards nor Mlle. were thought upon, and she was forced to call on him several times before she could prevail on him to go towards the table. When he did, it was only to continue his discourse with Laetitia, and she had the full pleasure of triumphing over Mlle. who was forced to be silent while they talked about what she could not understand. This day put an end to his inclination ever to see her again, and his admiration [for Laetitia] was so visible that his sisters (who are generally ready to make court to an elder brother) made all sorts of advances of friendship to Laetitia, who received them very obligingly, and the acquaintance was very soon made."

This meeting probably took place in 1708. Four years and seventy-seven letters later, Lady Mary Pierrepont and Edward Wortley Montagu eloped.

Of the seventy-seven letters, eight were written to Anne Wortley, one of the above-mentioned sisters. They too must be accounted love letters. It was unthinkable, in 1708, that a spinster should under any circumstances correspond with a bachelor, let alone express affection. It was, however, entirely suitable for her to tell "Mrs." Wortley that she was entirely hers, that she would run mad if her letters went astray and that she esteemed her above all the world. Since the elder brother was the true recipient of these letters, it was desirable that, in the course of them, his bride-to-be should tell her future husband something of her philosophy of life. Her scholarly tastes must be emphasized. She preferred a life of retirement; she would not be extravagant. As perhaps something of a come-on she told her beloved that she was deep in dictionaries and grammars but uncertain whether "it be possible to learn without a master." Continuing on this new note, she wrote, "I am not certain (and hardly dare hope) I shall make any great progress; but I find the study so diverting, I am not only easy, but pleased with the solitude that indulges it. I forget there is such a place as London and wish for no company but your's."

The next passage is Lady Mary at her romantic best: "You see, my dear, in making my pleasure consist of these unfashionable diversions, I am not of the number who cannot be easy out of the mode. I believe more follies are committed out of complaisance to the world than in following our own inclinations—nature is seldom in the wrong, custom always—."

This, in 1709, was avant-garde indeed. Already the world was too much with her.

Lady Mary was perfectly sincere in presenting herself as one devoted to solitary studies; witness her years of retirement in Italy. However, the Lady Mary who was to write *The Town Eclogues* and to regale her sister, Lady Mar, with malicious gossip was also at hand. A specimen of her "alter ego" was the letter written to an older neighbor, Mrs. Hewet. From her father's house in London she dispatched the following down-to-earth, not to say salacious, tattle: "Next to the great ball, what makes the most noise is the marriage of an old Maid that lives in this street, without a portion To a Man of £7,000 per Annum and they say £40,000 in ready money. —But with all this glory, never Bride had fewer Envyers; the dear Beast of a Man is so filthy, frightful, odious and detestable I would turn away such a footman for fear of spoiling my Dinner while he waited at Table. They was marry'd friday and came to church en Parade Sunday. I happen'd to sit in the pue with them and had the honnour of seeing Mrs. Bride fall fast asleep in the middle of the Sermon and snore very comfortably, which made several women in the Church think the bridegroom not quite so ugly as they did before. Envious people say 'twas all counterfeited to oblige him, but I believe that's scandal, for she's so devout, I dare swear nothing but downright necessity could make her miss one Word of the Sermon."

A few months before Lady Mary described this honeymoon idyll, Anne Wortley had died. The lovers were now without a go-between. Characteristically, it was Lady Mary who took the plunge. She had written earlier that she could "never allow even prudence and sincerity to have anything to do with one another. . . . And being devoted to the one, had never had the least tincture of the other." On March 28, 1710, she acted upon this principle. She and Wortley must have discussed marriage at some previous time, otherwise she would hardly write, "Give me leave to say it (I know it sounds Vain): I know how to make a Man of sense happy, but then that man must resolve to contribute something towards it himselfe. I have so much Esteem for you I should be very sorry to hear you was unhappy, but for the world I would not be the Instrument of makeing you so, which (of the humour you are) is hardly to be avoided if I am your Wife. . . . You distrust me. I can neither be easy nor lov'd where I am distrusted, nor do I believe your passion for me is what you pretend it; at least I'm sure, was I in love I could not talk as you do, . . . I don't injoin you to burn this Letter. I know you will. Tis the first I ever writ to one of your sex and shall be the last. You must never expect another. I resolve against all correspondence of this kind. My resolutions are seldom made and never broken."

Thus opened a long and bickering courtship. Marriages at this time were based on considerations of family, politics and money. If bride and groom were not actually averse to one another it was all to the good, but that they should be in love was by no means necessary to the matching of estates and party prejudice. Lady Mary Pierrepont and Edward Wortley Montagu were in these essentials well met. Both came of noble families that boasted, as noble families cannot always do, of intellectual distinction. As grandson to Lord Sandwich of the Restoration Admiralty, Edward was a distant relative of Samuel Pepys, friend and fellow diarist of the Pierrepont's John Evelyn. The Montagus were of East Anglia; their seat was Hinchingbrooke Park in Huntingdonshire. Their wealth was derived from the coal mines of Yorkshire where they maintained, not far from Thoresby, Wharncliffe Lodge. Edward was, in his own right, a man of parts. He was a lawyer and, during most of his career, M.P. for Huntingdon, the borough dominated by his family. He had distinguished friends, among them Addison and Steele. Both families were committed to the Whig cause. This preference had seen, in 1706, the erstwhile Evelyn Pierrepont advance from Earl of Kingston to Marquess of Dorchester. It was to prove a useful affiliation when Hanoverians replaced Stuarts in 1714.

Despite their shared literary tastes and social origins, Edward and Lady Mary were temperamentally ill matched. By her own admission she could suspend caution in favor of emotion. He could not. If she wrote affectionately he snubbed her, going so far as to insinuate that her ardor might lead to gallantries. (To her regret he used a coarser word.) If she removed her heart from her sleeve, it was because she had tired of him. Relapsing into her concept of herself as a victim of injustice, she wrote that "Prudent people are very happy; tis an exceeding fine thing, that's certain, but I was born without it, and shall retain to my day of Death the Humour of saying what I think."

It was, however, on material rather than emotional grounds that so apparently suitable a match led to elopement. Lord Dorchester proposed that his future son-in-law settle, prior to marriage, a sum upon a non-existent son and heir. He would not, he declared, have his grandson a beggar. Edward demurred. Why not wait and see how the boy turned out? A period of clandestine maneuvering ensued. The seesaw correspondence in which it was carried out does not encourage hopes for the lovers' domestic happiness.

To break off negotiations, Lord Dorchester sent Lady Mary to his property in Wiltshire, where she would be less accessible to her frugal suitor than in London or Thoresby. Under such circumstances, her vaunted preference for a life of rural retirement failed her. "Yes, yes, my dear," she snapped to the friend to whom she complained of the happiness of the prudent, "Here is Woods and Shades and Groves in abundance. . . . Tis not the place but the solitude of the place that is intollerable. Tis a horrid thing to see nothing but trees in a wood, and to walk by a purling stream to ogle the Gudgeons in it."

A recent and severe case of measles could hardly have cheered the lovelorn girl. After reproaching Edward for his part in creating her exile, she struck a terminal note. "My sicknesse was more dangerous. than you think it. I have not liv'd very long in this world but begin to be weary of it and in the situation I am in, am very sorry I recovered."

Lady Mary, despite, or because of, her unhappiness, advanced in literary excellence. During the summer of 1710 she wrote a significant letter to Gilbert Burnet, Bishop of Salisbury. It has to do with women's intellectual rights, a subject that was to be of lifelong concern. The elderly prelate, all of Lady Mary's theories to the contrary, played mentor to his clever young neighbor. Under his guidance she translated from a Latin version, the Enchiridion of Epictetus. She sent it to him with a splendid letter in which she thanks him for his condescension in teaching her. This, she declares, is the way things should be and are not. "My sex is usually forbid studys of this Nature, and Folly reckon'd so much our proper Sphere, we are sooner pardon'd any excesses of that, than the least pretentions to reading or good Sense. We are permitted no Books but such as tend to the weakening and Effeminateing the Mind, our Natural Defects are every way indulg'd, and tis look'd upon as in a degree Criminal to improve our Reason, or fancy we have any. We are taught to place all our Art in adorning our Outward Forms, and permitted, without reproach, to carry that Custom even to Extravagancy, while our Minds are entirely neglected, and by disuse of Refflections, fill'd with nothing but the Triffling objects our Eyes are daily entertain'd with." Lady Mary concludes that this sorry state of affairs worsens at the top of the social scale where are to be found "Women of Quality, whose Birth and Leisure only serve to render them the most uselesse and most worthlesse part of the creation."

This is the stuff of which reformers are made. This is Seneca Falls and here, more than a century before their time, approach Lucretia Mott and Elizabeth Cady Stanton. In Lady Mary's lament we have a prefiguring of the Nineteenth Amendment and of Women's Liberation. It was her misfortune to possess the mind of the nineteenth and twentieth centuries during the reign of Queen Anne and the first of three Georges. She was to be haunted all her life by ideals that the factors of time and society made inaccessible.

Even if Lady Mary had lived when women entered the public forum, it is difficult to see in her a Florence Nightingale or a Harriet Beecher Stowe. She was, as they were not, gifted with humor and handicapped by cynicism. Those who go on crusade do so out of a sense of human perfectibility. They exemplify the Christian precept of hating the sin while loving the sinner. This was hardly in Lady Mary's deistic, not to say agnostic, character. Reformers usually have one-track minds; Lady Mary's was a four-lane highway. She ardently desired a life of intellect. She craved a social framework that awarded to female intelligence the recognition bestowed on less challenging charms. There was a reverse side of the coin; she was in love with a coldly correct statesman who, as "Laetitia" had boasted, admired her wit. It is one thing to prefer brains to basset, another to marry them. It was early on in the long-winded courtship. Lady Mary did not know in 1710 whether "Sebastian" would select for his wife a strong-minded woman *avant la lettre*. She thought it advisable to adjust her ambitions to the preferences, real or supposed, of her older, scholarly suitor. Thinking not only of the bishop to whom she was writing, but also of the member for Huntingdon whom she wished to marry, she beat a hasty retreat: "I am not now arguing for an Equality for the two Sexes; I do not doubt God and Nature has thrown us into an Inferior Rank. We are a lower part of the Creation; we owe Obedience and Submission to the Superior Sex; And any woman who suffers her Vanity and folly to deny this, rebells against the Law of the Creator and indisputable Order of Nature."

In a letter already quoted, Lady Mary had favored following nature rather than convention. Here she reversed herself. She forsook her proud and independent personality in search of the principle of feminine subservience. She rehearsed the clinging vine, a role in which she was ill cast. She accepted, if only on paper, a premise by which she could not live. It followed, "as the night the day," that a union based on well-meant deception was in trouble before it took place.

The courtship had another two years—not to run, but to jerk. The final partings, reunions, dissensions, reproaches and reconciliations would have tried the skill of a Beaumarchais. Steele came forward as the sympathetic friend necessary in such a tragi-comedy. He expedited forbidden letters and lent his house, as did Sir Godfrey Kneller, for clandestine meetings. He even, presumably at Edward's urging, wrote articles for *The Tatler* in which mercenary marriages were opposed. It was to no avail. Edward would not invest in an unborn son. Lord Dorchester would not give his consent under any other circumstances.

By the summer of 1712 Lord Dorchester sought to strengthen his case by bringing forward his own candidate for Lady Mary's hand. She wrote Edward that she would thrust the desired extremity into flames rather than bestow it where she hated. "I have," she wrote in June, "made all the opposition in my power; perhaps I have carried the opposition too far. However it is, things were carry'd to that height, I have been assur'd of never having a shilling except I comply. . . . By this real and sincere Account of my Affairs you may see I have no design of any Engagement beyond freindship with you, since should we agree," (agreement was still in doubt) "'tis now impossible, my fortune only following my obedience." In other words, if Edward married Lady Mary, he married her penniless. This deprivation was vexatious at two sensitive points, the groom's purse and the bride's self-respect.

The dowry was, in Lady Mary's world—and remains in many others—a legal part of the marriage ethic. It conforms to the modern feminist principle of financial responsibility being assumed by both spouses. A man who married a portionless woman did her, as Mr. Collins later suggested to Elizabeth Bennett in *Pride and Prejudice,* a favor. Such a woman was a liability rather than an asset. As Lady Mary had two years earlier admitted, all women were submissive to their husbands. A wife who had arrived empty-handed at the altar was doubly so, and must compensate for her poverty by obedience and gratitude. Neither of these attitudes was second nature to the mettlesome Lady Mary.

July and August was a period of agonizing doubt and suspense. Lady Mary proved herself the larger spirited of the balked and still reluctant lovers. She was honest, generous and unfailingly (as Edward was not) prepared to lose gracefully. She loyally supported his refusal to settle money on a hypothetical son, cost her what it might. She wrote within a month of the elopement, "I confesse I am entirely of your Mind. I reckon it among the absurditys of custom that a Man must be oblig'd to settle his whole Estate on an eldest Son, beyond his power to recall, whatever he proves to be, and make himselfe unable to make happy a younger Child that may deserve to be so."

Lady Mary gave Edward every opportunity to end the tottering love affair. In her first letter to him she had offered to bow out rather than cause him unhappiness or even anxiety. She repeated these assurances during the few remaining days before marriage, especially as regards the sacrifice of her dowry. We may, I think, take with a grain of salt her pretended ignorance of the Montagu wealth. Since the match hinged upon finances, it seems highly unlikely that she would not have known that her cautious suitor was extremely rich. On August 1st she wrote with more coyness than candor, "I do not very well understand how your Circumstances are, or how far they may be impair'd by marrying a Woman without a Fortune." Perhaps (horror of horrors!) Edward thought she was courting "The Prince of the Coal Pits" for his money. Characteristically, she bade him another of her numerous adieus. She wrote on August 6th: "I now set you free from all your Fears, which your late letters have evidently shewn you have been under, that I should accept of your Offer. I will not accept it without a probability of makeing you happy; however I thank you for the generosity of the proposal. I hope this shews you I had no design upon your Fortune, which you seem to imagine in your last. . . . I go next Monday; probably I shall see you no more. . . ."

A wild two weeks ensued. By good fortune the marriage contract that would have committed Lady Mary to him whom she loathed had to be rewritten. This blunder afforded the panicked lovers time to scheme of a carriage at a garden door, of stealing onto a balcony, and of evading the rage of Lord Dorchester, whose temper was in no wise sweetened by having laid out four hundred pounds in "wedding cloaths" for his pig-headed child. The climax of this comic opera was reached when both Lady Mary and Edward unknowingly put up at the same inn. From it Lady Mary wrote her last farewell; it was in a different context. "Adeiu. I am entirely yours if you please."

This final acquiescence was penned on August 20, 1712. Sometime soon thereafter Lady Mary Pierrepont became Lady Mary Wortley Montagu.

She soon discovered that she had replaced a neglectful father with an indifferent husband. Upon the conclusion of his successful suit Edward exchanged the mantle of Young Lochinvar for that of a minor Whig whose fortunes turned on the approaching Hanoverian takeover.

Lady Mary had written within a few days of her flight that the scheme she favored was "living in an agreeable Country with a man that I like, that likes me, and forgetting the rest of the world as much as if there was no other people in the world, and that Naples were the Garden of Eden." Such a removal, had it been taken, might have saved the precarious marriage. Both spouses loved travel and Lady Mary was, in much later years, to discover that she had an affinity for Italy. It is tempting, at this point in their story, to see the uncongenial husband and wife reconciled in the exile to which the wife eventually took her solitary way.

Edward agreed to this plan on one condition. He replied, "I had rather live in any part of Italy than in England and shall never wish to be here unless my affairs suffer too much by my absence." The condition was conclusive. Queen Anne was entering upon her last illness. The succession was in dispute between the Tory-favored Stuarts and the Whig-favored Hanoverians. It was no time for an ambitious man to be out of sight.

At thirty-four, Edward was a veteran in matters of state. As a husband and father-to-be, he was insensitive. Lacking the castle in Italy he had encouraged his bride to build, he should have made her a part of his London life and career. He dispatched her instead, on his favorite motive of economy, to live at the Montagu county seats. The girlhood of Lady Mary had been spent rattling around Thoresby. The wife now rattled around Hinchingbrooke and Wharncliffe Lodge—and she rattled alone. Thoresby's loneliness had, in large measure, been mitigated by its library. At Hinchingbrooke Lady Mary's chief literary refreshment consisted of an "old Trunk of papers" containing letters exchanged by Edward's grandparents, the Lord and Lady Sandwich of Pepys's diary. Money seems always to have been a Montagu enthusiasm; Lady Mary wrote to her absent and thrifty bridegroom that she was much edified by finding in the family correspondence "the most extrodinary Lessons of Oeconomy that ever I read in my Life."

Perhaps these lessons prompted Lady Mary to suggest that Edward remain in London for Christmas rather than incur the costly hospitality expected of newlyweds upon ancestral acres. She seems to have found this a depressing prospect. Her letters of December make no secret of her melancholy or of the adverse effect her emotions might have upon the child to be born in May. At an earlier time, it will be recalled, she had espoused the cause of woman's education. She now took a bolder step; she gave thought to the frustrated writer she knew herself to be, and in a roundabout fashion hinted to Edward that she could hold her own with *The Tatler* and *The Spectator*. After apologizing for intruding upon a man of "busynesse" she projected herself as journalist. She wrote banteringly, but she meant every word of the following lines: "Idleness is the root of all evil. I write and read till I can't see, and then I walk; sleep succeeds; and thus my whole time is divided. If I was as well qualified all ways as I am by idleness I would publish a daily paper called the *Meditator*."

Although Edward deprived his wife of affection and companionship, he always did justice to her intelligence. His response to her journalistic stirrings was generous and, for him, imaginative. He set her a literary task.

In 1713 Addison's tragedy *Cato* was being readied for staging. Like many other members of his circle, Lady Mary had read the controversial play when it was still in manuscript. Remembering, perhaps, that it was "Laetitia's" critical sallies that had first charmed him, Edward proposed that she sublimate loneliness and the moodiness of pregnancy into a critique of the new play. The resultant essay survives among her unpublished papers with the catty comment, "Wrote at the Desire of Mr. Wortley; suppressed at the desire of Mr. Addison."

In setting up as a critic worthy of Mr. Spectator's suppression, Lady Mary declared her literary ambitions. Her endorsement served to remind any chance reader of the limitations placed on the exercise of female wit. Opinion was still a man's affair; its theatre was the coffeehouse and the club. Its avenues were supplied by innumerable pamphleteers. Lady Mary proposed to crash the party and to claim as colleagues not only her friends Addison and Steele, but also her dangerous admirer, Alexander Pope.

Lady Mary thought the love interest in *Cato* forced. Dr. Johnson, when he came to write his chapter on Addison in *Lives of the Poets,* was of the same opinion. His comments provide an interesting insight into Addison's creative process, a process in which suggestibility played a considerable part. Concurring with the future Sappho, he wrote, "The greatest weakness of the play is in the love scenes which are said by Pope to have been added to the original play in compliance with the practice of the stage." Whose practice, one wonders? Lady Mary considered Addison's verbiage too folksy for Roman heroes. She especially objected to having every character exclaim "believe me." Addison, her pique notwithstanding, weighed her opinions and, at her suggestion, fortified his lines by increased use of that Augustan staple, the rhymed couplet.

Two years later the suppressed critique proved having been worth the writing. It was the custom of Addison and Steele to publish in *The Spectator* unsigned articles by their friends. Pursuant to this policy, they printed, just before Queen Anne's fateful death, an essay by Lady Mary. Robert Halsband identifies it as number 573. She was in print, albeit anonymously.

Pope, who wrote the prologue to *Cato,* believed the play more suited to the library than to the stage. Here spoke the poet rather than the impresario. He could not have been more mistaken. Great Anna's three realms seethed with party malice. Cavalier and Roundhead passions were mirrored in Tory and Whig contentions. A war, a treaty and a succession were in dispute. A tragedy which depicted these dilemmas in terms of Roman history was, in the year before the Queen's death, a sure sell-out.

Contested crowns made the history of the last Stuarts and first Hanoverians. The year before Lady Mary's birth saw the "Glorious" Revolution inaugurate a struggle between Catholic James II and his Calvinist son-in-law, William of Orange, for the English throne. It was a deeply divisive campaign, involving not only the royal succession but religious and family loyalties as well. The Whigs, including Edward Wortley Montagu, favored the Protestant line, while the Tories were divided by their preference for the Jacobites and their aversion to Popery.

It is customary to speak of the period between 1688 when James fled to France, and 1714 when George lumbered in from Hanover, as the apotheosis of double-dealing and intrigue. It is hard to see how it could have been otherwise. Open covenants openly arrived at is a very recent principle. A statesman with concern for his head, his freedom and his lands kept in with opposing contenders. Rapid reforming of party allegiances involved all of society, with the most prestigious of authors serving as pamphleteers to advance or retard Whig and Tory aims.

The spirit of factionalism was greatly increased by the War of the Spanish Succession which followed hard upon the victory of William of Orange. While the exiled James and his son, James Edward, conspired at St. Germain-en-Laye, their mighty cousin, Louis XIV, claimed through his wife, Marie Thérèse, the Spanish throne for their grandson, Philip of Anjou. In thus extending Bourbon power, *Le Roi Soleil* was said, like faith, to have moved the Pyrenees from his southern boundaries. England, allied with Holland and Austria, waged under the tremendous generalship of Marlborough a bloody and disputed war to keep Philip at Versailles rather than at the Escorial.

The War of the Spanish Succession had a divisive effect on English opinion. It was the mercantile and, in Stuart terms, liberal Whigs who promoted and profited from Marlborough's dazzling campaigns. The conservative Tories of church and county agitated for, and secured a negotiated peace that left, for more than two hundred years, the Bourbons on the throne of Spain. Marlborough fell from his role of warrior-patriot to that of despoiler of his country's treasure and blood. He went into exile as the Whigs, among them Edward Wortley Montagu, went out of office. The Tories, under the contentious leadership of Harley and Bolingbroke, swept into power and the Treaty of Utrecht was ratified in 1713, within days of the presentation of *Cato*. It was a separate peace by which England not only gratified Bourbon ambitions, but also abandoned her allies. The battles of Blenheim, Oudenarde, Ramillies and Malplaquet were virtuoso victories, but in history's terms they could be said to have been fought in vain. A century later Robert Southey commented on this irony in a poem familiar to generations of schoolroom orators. Old Kasper (after his work was done) tells us that

> It was the English . . .
> Who put the French to rout;
> But what they fought each other for
> I could not well make out.

The topical impact of Addison's *Cato* anticipates that of Gay's *Beggar's Opera* of a generation later. The theatre-goers of 1728 were to identify Gay's highwayman as Sir Robert Walpole with his hand in the till. *Cato* favored liberty over military despotism, an unoriginal preference that could be levelled against Marlborough of the present, Cromwell of the past, or even the believers in the Stuart doctrine of the Divine Right of Kings as they temporized at St. Germain-en-Laye. Whigs and Tories were seated at the theatre by party. At each utterance in which freedom was extolled both groups responded with collective applause to claim the virtue as their own. Bolingbroke made doubly sure that Cato voted the Tory ticket. He summoned to his box during the intermission Booth, who played the hero, and in the presence of the audience rewarded him with fifty guineas for his eloquent portrayal of a hero.

Lady Mary was in London for the tumultuous run of *Cato*. She had come to town to await the birth of her baby, an event that might, or might not, have ruled out play-going. Because she and Edward were for a brief time together, there are no letters to him to tell us what she thought of the play in performance and its effect upon possessive Whigs and Tories.

On May 16th Edward Wortley Montagu Junior was born. Fatherhood made no addition to Edward Senior's small stock of emotion. When the baby was six weeks old he went for a period to

Hinchingbrooke whence Lady Mary had so recently come. It is hard to understand how he could have resisted the passionate letter sent by the lonely new mother who, by now, was well aware that her husband would have preferred reticence to tenderness. "I shall passe the whole Evening in my chamber alone, without busynesse but thinking of you, in a Manner you would call Affection, if I should repeat to you. That Refflection brings me back to remember I should not write my thoughts to you. You will accuse me of Deceit when I am opening my Heart to you, and the Plainesse of expressing it will appear Artificial. I am sorry to remember this, and check the Inclination I have to give a loose to my tendernesse, and tell you how melancholy all things seem to me in your absence, how impatient I am for the End of this Week, and how little possible I find it would be for me to live without you. . . ."

"Tuesday. My first News this Morning is what I am very Sorry to hear. My Brother has the Small pox."

Lady Mary's only brother, William Evelyn, had come into the Kingston title when their father was created Marquess of Dorchester. There remain among family papers two letters that suggest a winning young man with a flair for writing not unworthy of his older sister. During the months when Lord Dorchester was forbidding Lady Mary to marry the correct, if economical, Edward Wortley Montagu, he was promoting the union of his only son and a bastard heiress. It was perhaps affection, or perhaps a sense of justice, that prompted young Lord Kingston to defend the Wortley Montagus. Securing Lord Dorchester's forgiveness kept pace with political ambition on the agenda of the rejected bride and groom. Lord Kingston played a vital part in mollifying Papa. Suppose he should die! "I hope he will do well; I am sure we lose a Freind, if he does not."

Three days later the situation worsened. The sick man was attended by Pope's friend, the fashionable Dr. Garth. We will meet him again when Lady Mary suffers the same dread disease. She comforted herself with the theory that he was an alarmist. On June 25th she wrote, "Dr. Garth says 'tis the worst sort and he fears he will be too full,* which I should think very foreboding if I did not know that all Doctors (and particularly Garth) love to have their Patients thought in Danger."

---

* Garth meant that the extent of the eruption made recovery doubtful.

Lord Kingston died a week later. He was not yet twenty-one. Lady Mary, once more in prudent rural exile, was profoundly saddened by the loss of her loyal brother and the spectacle of his forlorn young family. She wrote on July 3rd, "I am afraid of every thing. There wants but little of my being affraid of the Small pox for you, so unreasonable are my fears, which, however, proceed from an unlimited Love. If I lose you—I cannot bear that If, which I blesse God is without probability, but since the losse of my poor unhappy Brother, I dread every Evil.

"Satterday. I have been to day at Acton to see my poor Brother's melancholy Family. I cannot describe how much it has sunk my Spirits."

The dynastic uncertainty that hung over the kingdom was also dispiriting. All England marked time and intrigued until it should be known whether the dying Queen's successor would be her Protestant cousin, George, or her Catholic half-brother, James Edward. The Tories, in large part Jacobites, were more numerous than the Hanover-committed Whigs. Had they been as united they might have succeeded in setting aside the German claimant in favor of the Stuart line. In modern parlance, the Tories were split. Their leaders, Harley and Bolingbroke, quarrelled in the Queen's presence and the failing woman, worn out with dissension and divided loyalties, bestowed the staff of office elsewhere.

A more vexatious problem (because it was more delicate) was James Edward's religion. His father had given England three years of inept administration marked with bigotry. Under the son's regime, would there be further Bloody Assizes? Most of the supporters of the Divine Right of Kings desired that this Divinity be invested in Canterbury rather than Rome. In vain did Jacobites remind James Edward that his great-grandfather, Henri Quatre, had said *"Paris vaut bien une messe"* (Paris is well worth a mass). Could the Pretender not reverse his ancestor's acceptance of Catholicism and exchange the Roman Missal for the Book of Common Prayer? No, he could not.

Among those charged with catching the conscience of the king was Lady Mary's future brother-in-law, Lord Mar. He was a highly placed Jacobite and had served for several years as Secretary of State for Scotland. It will be recalled that Lord Dorchester, like his estranged son-in-law, Edward, was committed to George I. In marrying his daughter, Frances, to one who, under the circumstances, was virtually an enemy, he again proved himself to be a capricious parent. Thomas Burnet (son of the Bishop who had tutored Lady Mary during her Wiltshire exile) quipped, "My Lord Marr is marry'd to My Lady Frances Pierpont, so that there is a good Whig *marr'd* by taking a Scotch Jacobite for her Husband."

James Edward refused with heroic loyalty to compromise or dissemble. To those who urged him so to do he wrote, "I neither want counsel nor advice to remain unalterable in my fixed resolution of never dissembling my religion, but rather to abandon all than act against my conscience and honour, cost what it will. . . ."

Ecumenism, in the France from which these sturdy lines were written, was as remote as it is in the Belfast of today. The curtain thus rose upon thirty years of the futile Jacobite mystique. It was to be marked by clappings into the Tower or into exile, intrigue at home and abroad, and the irresponsible sacrificing of dedicated lives. Of the dreary struggle, nothing remains but a few historical novels and a handful of glorious songs.

It must have been thoroughly galling to the ambitious and inquisitive Lady Mary to be forced to sit out these exciting months in Yorkshire. After weeks of house-hunting she settled with her child at Middlethorpe Hall. Here she worried about her baby's health, her husband's career and the paucity of letters from London.

Like so many of our infant forebears, young Edward suffered from rickets, a deficiency disease that should have been treated with vitamins, but instead was supposed to respond to plunging in a cold well. The more serious deficiencies inherent in a tragic parent-child relationship were still in the future. Little dreaming that she would one day regret being mother to such an "animal," Lady Mary wrote in July of 1714, "I am in abundance of pain about our dear child. Thô I am convinc'd in my reason tis both silly and wicked to set one's heart too fondly on any thing in this world, yet I cannot overcome my selfe so far as to think of parting with him with the resignation that I ought to do. I hope and I beg of God that he may live to be a comfort to us both . . . the cold Bath is the best medicine for weak children but I am very fearful and unwilling to try any hazardous Remedys."

Lady Mary had long complained of the indifference of her fiancé and spouse. She now charged the preoccupied Edward with neglect of their child. On July 30th she wrote, "You mention your little boy with so slight a regard I have no mind to inform you how he does." Anxiety, however, got the upper hand. Two days later she reported to the unconcerned and absent father that "this cold agrees very much with the child and he seems stronger and better every day." Remembering perhaps Dr. Garth's diagnosis of the gravity of Lord Kingston's illness she continued, "I should be glad if you saw Dr. Garth if you ask'd his Opinion concerning the use of cold Baths for young children."

It seems unlikely that either physician or parent had thoughts to spare for little Edward's "bignesse in his joynts." Lady Mary's letter was written on August 1st. It was the moment upon which Tory and Whig fortunes turned. Queen Anne was dead.

Characteristically, the Senior Edward let Lady Mary learn of this sudden change from others. On August 3rd she went to York to see history made. "I went with my Cousin to day to see the King proclaimed, which was done, the Archbishop walking next the Lord Mayor, all the Country Gentry following, with greater Crowds of people than I beleiv'd to be in York, vast Acclamations and the appearance of a genneral satisfaction, the Pretender afterwards dragg'd about the streets and burnt, ringing of Bells, bonfires and illuminations, the mob crying liberty and property and long live King George."

For members of both parties there followed a period as crucial as the Restoration of a half-century earlier. The approaching struggle for position or pardon found the Pierrepont sisters in opposing camps. "Bobbing John" Erskine, Earl of Mar, was, as his name implies, skilled in the deceptions he had recommended to James Edward. His naïve bride believed that his Jacobite history would be overlooked in the scramble for office and that he would remain persona grata under the new regime. To her lonely sister, still vegetating in Yorkshire, Lady Mar wrote "of nothing but living in London, fine preparations for the Coronation etc."

Lady Mary, like many another woman before and since, now sublimated her own ambitions in Edward's career. In letter after letter she badgered him with political advice. His father, doubtless elated with Whig prospects, replaced him as candidate for the family borough of Huntingdon. Although Lady Mary considered this piece of self-service "prodigious," it cleared the way for a loftier post than that of M.P.

Lady Mary was accustomed to chide Edward with coldness and neglect in domestic relationships. She now complained of the same lacks in the steps he took, or failed to take, in political advancement. George I arrived to assume his distasteful duties on September 18th. Less than a week later Edward had not stormed the fortress. Lady Mary fumed in an exceptionally spirited letter that he must get the better of his conservative tendencies. "No modest man ever did or ever will make his fortune. Your freind Lord Halifax, Robert Walpole and all other remarkable instances of quick Advancement have been remarkably Impudent."

Better was to come. "The Ministry is like a play at Court. There's a little door to get in and a great Croud without, shoveing and thrusting who shall be foremost; people that knock others with their elbows, disregard a little kick of the shinns, and still thrust heartily forwards. Your modest man stands behind in the Croud, is shov'd about by every body, his Cloaths tore, almost squeez'd to death, and sees a 1,000 get in before him that don't make so good a figure as himself."

At this time, nepotism was by no means the suspect engine it is today. The Montagus had long been a powerful clan. Charles Montagu, the "impudent" Lord Halifax of Lady Mary's recent letter, was more than a friend; he was a cousin. Early in October he was rewarded for his fidelity to the Whig cause; he was made First Lord of the Treasury. He offered Edward Wortley Montagu the post of Junior Commissioner, a position the latter accepted with reluctance because he correctly believed the office to be of short duration. Lady Mary was quite equal to attacking such procrastinations. She wrote on October 12th, "Your Letter very much vex'd me. I cannot imagine why you should doubt being the better for a place of that consideration, which 'tis in your power to lay down whenever you dislike the measures that are taken. Supposing the Commission lasts but a short time, I believe those that have acted in it will have the offer of some other considerable thing."

She was, of course, quite right. Had Edward not served under his elderly cousin he would not have become Ambassador to Turkey, the Embassy Letters would not have been written, and the science of inoculation would have journeyed west under another aegis.

With Edward once more blessedly in office, Lady Mary's marking time was at an end. London beckoned and, to crown their good fortune, Lord Dorchester forgave the errant pair. Early in January of 1715 Lady Mary drove south to new scenes and new troubles.

Not only was Lady Mary's life and environment changed; so was she. The months of solitude and rejected affection had done their work. The passionate girl who had risked her father's enmity and sacrificed her patrimony was replaced by a cool and wary observer of society. The connubial tête-à-tête that "Laetitia" had envisioned with "Sebastian" was too long postponed. Edward had proved himself entirely able to dispense with her company, wit and beauty. She now proposed to display these assets where they might be better appreciated.

During the following months the annals of court, basset table and theatre take precedence over those of home and nursery. She was at last in the presence of her husband, if not perhaps in his mind or in his heart. Thus, she was at liberty to transform her recent epistolary activity to topical satire. It was a medium in which she proved herself dangerously adept.

Addison, Steele, and Congreve were old friends. Lady Mary soon added to her circle Pope and Gay. Like them, she brought to the proper study of mankind the predominating faults and virtues of the Age of Reason. She was skeptical, sure-footed and sharp-tongued. She relished contention and excelled, as did most of her contemporaries, in having the last word. She was devoid of hypocrisy and cant. She shared in the prevailing respect for form, workmanship and grace.

At this time John Gay was anticipating the highwayman symbolism of *The Beggar's Opera*. Using the language and style of Virgil's *Eclogues* or *Pastorals,* he described the routines of fashionable London. This was a project suited to Lady Mary's tart talents and to those of her new admirer, Alexander Pope. Working sometimes alone and sometimes with her fellow poets, she wrote a series of six satires which she called *Town Eclogues.*

Never one for half-measures, Lady Mary opened her lampoons

with the new royal family. Peeresses desirous of court appointments buzzed around the Princess of Wales because, as we shall later be reminded, Sophia Dorothea, King George's wife, was imprisoned on a charge of adultery. Hostility between monarch and heir was a characteristic of the reigns of the first four Georges, with courtiers entrusting their careers to father or son in very much the previous Whig and Tory pattern. Edward Wortley Montagu was progressing in the King's favor because he could speak French to a Britannic Majesty who had no English. Stimulated by the open secret of rival courts, Lady Mary composed *The Drawing Room,* in which we have "Roxana" and "Coquetilla" vying for preferment. This contest gave Lady Mary an opportunity to describe Princess Caroline as given to filthy plays, surrounded by lewd companions and, worst of all, accessible to tradesmen. But for the care of "Roxana":

> . . . and daughters standing in a row,
> To all the foreigners a goodly show!
> Oft had your drawing room been sadly thin,
> And merchants' wives close by the chair been seen,
> Had not I amply filled the empty space,
> And saved your highness from the dire disgrace.

This satire with two others fell into the hands of the disreputable printer, Edmund Curll. He specialized in slander and obscenity, always best-sellers but especially when identities are in doubt. Under the title *Court Poems,* he published, in addition to *The Drawing Room, The Basset-Table* and *The Toilet.* He included an "advertisement" in which some claimed the poems to be "the productions of a lady of quality," another proclaimed "that Mr. Gay was the man," while a third umpire wrote, "Sir—Depend upon it these lines could come from no other hand than the judicious Translator of Homer" who was, of course, Pope.

Lady Mary, to her regret, was no more than a frustrated authoress. Gay and Pope were professional men of letters who could ill afford royal disfavor. Pope has told us himself how he revenged himself on Curll. He offered him a glass of wine in which he dropped an emetic; the results are luridly described in *A Full and True Account of a Horrid and Barbarous Revenge by Poison, on the Body of Mr. Edmund Curll, Bookseller.*

Town Eclogues were assigned to the six weekdays. (Even in a secular society it seems that satire rested on the Seventh Day.) The three poems pirated by Curll were subtitled Thursday, Monday and Friday. The remaining three were *St. James's Coffee House* for Tuesday, *The Tête à Tête* for Wednesday and for Saturday a somber note, *The Small-Pox.*

Lady Mary had earlier expressed her fear of this general scourge. It had cost her brother's life and it was to deprive her of beauty. She caught the disease in December of 1715. Her convalescence is the subject of the last of the *Town Eclogues.*

As a poem *The Small-Pox* is similar in style and skill to its companion verses. However, it has an extraliterary value because it gives us the woman who could see herself and her disfigurement not only with objectivity, but with humor as well. Dr. Garth, who had feared for Lord Kingston's life, encouraged Lady Mary to believe she should "again be well, again be fair." As regards the second part of his prediction, he was wrong. Her pretty face was scarred and her dark eyelashes gone. Calling herself "Flavia" she reversed her mirror and shunned "the face she sought before."

It is not everyone who can find comedy in his own disappointment. Lady Mary's most attractive quality was her ability to abide by the results of misfortunes and mistakes. She was preeminently of the "never complain, never explain" school. In her closing lines she bade the world what was to be a mercifully brief farewell:

> Plays, operas, circles I no more must view!
> My toilette, patches, all the world adieu!

While Lady Mary was taking leave of looks, her brother-in-law, Lord Mar, was embarked upon the double-dealing that led to his taking leave of home and kindred. He "kissed hands" at the court of King George on August 1st, 1715. Immediately thereafter he hurried to Scotland to rally armed support for "King James III." Here was bobbing with a vengeance! The same December days that saw Flavia avoid her mirror witnessed the landing of the Pretender to claim his father's throne. The resultant insurrection was soon put down. James Edward's supporters were easily scattered, while he and Lord Mar escaped to France. Neither Prince nor Earl ever returned to England.

Lady Mar, because of her father's unimpeachable record as a

loyal Whig, was at liberty to remain in England or to share her husband's exile. Thus did the fortunes and misfortunes of party allegiance separate the Pierrepont sisters, a circumstance to which we owe a brilliant succession of the elder's letters.

The Wortley Montagus' departure for Turkey followed close upon the defeat of the Jacobites. Edward's appointment as Ambassador to the Porte (the Ottoman court) was made official in April, 1716. His was a complicated assignment. In addition to a diplomat's duties, he was charged with negotiating a peace between the Austrian and Ottoman empires. It was an undertaking in which he was to prove unsuccessful, perhaps because of inexperience in foreign affairs, perhaps because of ignorance of the Eastern mind.

Lady Mary's *Embassy Letters* were published in 1763, a year after her death. They are the best known (although not in every opinion the best) of her voluminous correspondence. They cover in statistical, philosophical and picturesque detail the twenty-seven-month period between the landing of the Wortley Montagus at Rotterdam during the summer of 1716 and their return to Dover in the fall of 1718. They are addressed to a new set of correspondents. Among them are Lady Mar, Alexander Pope, the Abbé Conti, Princess Caroline and several figures of fashion who might have been culled from *Town Eclogues.*

Lady Mary was skilled in varying subject matter and style to suit her friends' interests and tastes. Lady Mar, struggling with political misfortune and soon to succumb to melancholia, received the major part of the *Embassy Letters.* For Pope, toiling in London's "Smoak and Impertinencies," Lady Mary played Scheherazade rather than Sappho. In reply, she was pursued by borderline love letters that paved the way to hatred. Abbé Conti, an Italian savant who had been recently welcomed by the Prince and Princess of Wales, brought out the philosopher in Lady Mary. At his request she wrote essays in letter form on Mohammedan and Christian tenets. Princess Caroline (who had apparently forgiven *The Drawing Room*) received an account of the rigors of travel, in which Lady Mary claimed with more brio than accuracy that the ambassadorial journey to Constantinople had "not been undertaken by any Christian since the Time of the Greek Emperours. . . ."

The easiest route to the East would have been by land to the

Mediterranean and then by sea to Constantinople. Austria and England were still allies, despite the inequities of the Treaty of Utrecht. Diplomatic decorum demanded that the Ambassador's conciliatory mission open with Emperor Charles VI at Vienna rather than the latter's enemy, Sultan Achmet III. Accordingly, the train of coaches, postillions, baggage vans and outriders travelled overland all the way from the shores of the North Sea to those of the Bosporus. Allowing for delays and detours, the journey required seven months.

The Ambassador's retinue was large and varied. There were twenty servants clad in secondhand liveries that had cost an aching one hundred ten pounds. There was young Edward, now three years old, and his nurse. The Wortley Montagus' meager spiritual needs were in the care of a chaplain, and medical emergencies, which were to include inoculation against smallpox and the birth of Lady Mary's daughter, were entrusted to Dr. Charles Maitland.

Lady Mary's letters from Holland and Germany gave her correspondents the realist rather than the romantic. She was delighted with Rotterdam's clean streets, the canals that permitted ships to penetrate to the heart of the city, the absence of beggars and the well-stocked shops. Every prospect pleased and only religion was vile. She fortified her insular, if skeptical, allegiance to the established church by deriding both Dissenters and Catholics "because speaking disrespectfully of Calvinists is the same thing as speaking honorably of the Church." The former favored melodramatic preaching, while both Lutherans and Papists venerated relics. At Cologne she was particularly diverted by the heaped-up skulls of St. Ursula's 11,000 virgins. If she saw the cathedral she did not think it worth describing. The "Gothick" in 1716 had not returned to favor.

The antiquities of Nuremberg were also matters of indifference. She was, however, struck by laws that required the citizenry to dress in accordance with their rank. She wished that "these Laws were in force in other parts of the world. When one considers impartially the merit of a rich suit of cloaths in most places, the respect and the smiles of favour that it procures, not to speak of the Envy and the sighs it occassions . . . one is forced to confesse that there is need of uncommon understanding to resist the temptation of pleasing freinds and mortifying Rivals." Thinking doubtless of the laced liveries that trotted at her side, Lady Mary concluded on a wistful note: "These Refflexions draw after them others that are too melancholy."

The final stage of the Ambassador's journey to Vienna consisted of a passage down the Danube by "wooden House." The vessel which was boarded at Regensburg supplied, as houseboats still do, every domestic comfort. It was rowed by a crew of twelve, and moved with great speed. Lady Mary wrote to her sister within a few days of her arrival at Vienna of her delight in the voyage: "in the same day you have the pleasure of a vast variety of Prospects and within a few Hours space of time one has the different diversion of seeing a Populous City adorn'd with magnificent Palaces and the most romantic Solitudes which appear distant from the commerce of mankind, the Banks of the Danube being charmingly diversify'd with woods, rocks, mountains cover'd with Vines, Fields of Corn, large Citys and ruins of Ancient Castles."

Here, as in her campaign for women's intellectual integrity, Lady Mary was in advance of her time. The 18th century preferred its landscapes tamed and its solitudes peopled. It was the Lady Mary of Rousseau, rather than of Voltaire, who had written years earlier that "nature is seldom in the wrong, custom always. . . ." It was this same Lady Mary who now found solitudes enchanting and who was not disposed to see in "horrid" mountains a threat to man's dominance over his environment.

Baroque Vienna was in every way an excellent preparation for Constantinople. Emperor Charles VI, stung by the Hapsburgs' loss of the Spanish throne, consoled himself with magnificence. Conspicuous consumption reigned at court, in architecture and the theatre. Patrician families outdid one another in lavish entertainments. In accordance with this spirit of competitive formality, Lady Mary's presentation at court was postponed to allow the running up of a new gown, none of her London clothing being deemed worthy of imperial hospitality.

While the Ambassador opened his peacemaking mission, his wife was received at the "delicious" palaces of such persons of quality as Count von Schönborn. There passed before her delighted, if puzzled, eyes a wealth of painting, sculpture, tapestries, masterpieces of the applied arts and domestic comforts spurned by stiff-upper-lip England. Lady Mary was especially impressed by the porcelain stoves that heated her hosts' apartments and permitted the cultivation of "vast Orange and Lemon Trees in Gilt Pots." She complained, in writing to Lady Mar, of England's indifference to so practical a device: "I am surpriz'd we do not practise in England so usefull an Invention. This refflection naturally leads me to consider our obstinancy in shaking with cold 6 months in the year rather than make use of stoves . . . so far from spoiling the form of a Room, they add very much to the magnificence of it when they are painted and gilt as at Vienna. . . ."

Nor were the pleasures of the table neglected. While awaiting her court costume Lady Mary was "entertained with 50 dishes of meat, all serv'd in silver and well dress'd, the dessert proportionable, serv'd in the finest china; but the variety and richnesse of their wines is what appears the most surprizing. The constant way is to lay a list of their names upon the plates of the guests along with the napkins, and I have counted several times to the number of 18 different sorts, all exquisite in their kinds. . . ."

In describing to her friends these opulent scenes, Lady Mary formed the exotic style that was to prove so successful in letters written from the gorgeous East. They are, however, the observations of a storyteller rather than a connoisseur. Like most Georgians, she had narrow notions of scholarship. Knowledge consisted of philosophy, history, language and literature. These disciplines were found in books and illustrated by the passing social pageant. The arts had little to do with learning and were habitually undervalued. She was to live for twenty years in the London of Händel and Hogarth without mentioning either of them. I doubt that, in driving across Europe, she gave more than a superficial thought to the painters, the composers and the craftsmen who created the Baroque. It sufficed that a room be "Gay by Pictures"; her correspondents did not necessarily learn by whom they were painted. The Liechtenstein Collection, which is still to be visited, was dismissed as consisting of "modern" statues (Bernini perhaps?), and "pictures not of the first hands." The Emperor's Treasure had, at least, the prestige of size. Here Lady Mary spent five hours. She saw "a few of Corregio" but, disappointed with the jewel and coin collections, she omitted "the catalog of the rest of the Lumber."

The Emperor, in defiance of Bourbons in France and Spain, spent vast sums upon theatrical productions to rival those of Versailles. In her first letter to Alexander Pope, Lady Mary wrote a charming description of "Alcina" in which she detailed the spectacular effects of machines, rapid scene changes and "2 fleets of little gilded vessels that gave the representation of a naval fight." She did not find it hard to believe "that the Decorations and habits cost the Emperor £30,000 Sterling." Characteristically she ignored the composer and misquoted the opera's title. We owe to the editor of her letters, Robert Halsband, an identification of the opera and its creator. Lady Mary, although she did not think the matter worth chronicling, had assisted at *Angelica Vincitorice di Alcina* by Johann Josef Fux.

Thus opened Lady Mary's correspondence with the first poet of the age. She wrote to Pope in the same enthusiastic, narrative and, when the subject required it, earthy style she employed in letters to Lady Mar and other friends. Because he was a poet, she sent him an example of Turkish love poetry, just as she described Mohammedanism to Abbé Conti because he was a priest. There is nothing in her letters to suggest that she had designs on his unstable emotions.

Pope's letters to her tell a different story. Lady Louisa Stuart, Lady Mary's granddaughter and quasi-biographer, wrote the "Introductory Anecdotes" for *The Letters and Works of Lady Mary Wortley Montagu*. In this delightful essay she attempted to reduce Pope's outpourings to the level of empty compliment. It will not do. Although Lady Mary did not reply in kind, she probably knew Pope's letters to be those of a man required by physical misfortune to "talk upon paper" of the passions he could not otherwise express. The humiliation, to which a deformed dwarf in love might be subjected is, at all times, an unpleasant theme and one unsuited to the preferences of Victorian readers. It has remained for modern scholarship to set aside Lady Louisa's well-meant hypocrisy and to discuss Pope's frustrated sensuality with candor and compassion.

The early stages of the friendship of Lady Mary and Pope were deeply flattering to both participants. The lady, recently released from Yorkshire stagnation, craved intellectual recognition. The misshapen genius fed her not inconsiderable vanity while gratifying his weakness for fashionable society. Had it not been for the embassy to Constantinople such a hostess-poet pattern might have played out its familiar routine. Absence not only made the heart grow fonder; it made the ink run warmer. Pope early proposed to take advantage, in a literary sense, of Lady Mary's travels. He wrote soon after the

Wortley Montagus' departure that "The unhappy distance at which we correspond removes a great many of those punctilious Restrictions and Decorums that oftentime in nearer Conversation prejudice Truth to save Good breeding. I may now hear of my faults and you of your good qualities without a Blush on either side."

As regards his handicaps, rather than his faults, Pope did not spare himself. "Not a feature," he assured his beloved-in-fancy, "will be softened, or any advantageous Light employed to make the Ugly thing a little less hideous, but you shall find it in all respects most Horribly Like." His erotic reveries were, in addition, stimulated by the fact that Lady Mary was bound for a polygamous land; delicious perversions suggested themselves. "I am capable myself of following one I lov'd, not only to Constantinople, but to those parts of India, where they tell us the Women best like the Ugliest fellows, as the most admirable productions of nature, and look upon Deformities as the Signatures of divine Favour. . . . If, instead of Hungary, you past thro' Italy, and I had any hopes That Lady's Climate might give a Turn to your inclinations, it is but your sending me the least notice, and I'll certainly meet you in Lombardy, the Scene of those celebrated Amours between the fair Princess and her Dwarf."

Vienna, in the meantime, had its own titillations. To Lady Rich, whose giddy mind was obsessed with looking younger than she was, Lady Mary sent encouraging news of the amatory prestige of aging women. "A Woman till 5 and thirty is only look'd upon as a raw Girl and can possibly make no noise in the World till about forty. I don't know what your Ladyship may think of this matter, but tis a considerable comfort to me to know there is upon Earth such a paradise for old Women, and I am content to be insignificant at present in the design of returning when I am fit to appear no where else."

This *Rosenkavalier* state of affairs turned upon a polyandrous commodity, the *cicisbeo* or *cavaliere servente*. Lady Mary explained him to the doubtless fascinated Lady Rich as she continued her letter. "I have not seen any such Prudes as to pretend fidelity to their Husbands, who are certainly the best-natur'd set of people in the World, and they look upon their Wives' Galants as favourably as Men do upon their Deputys that take the troublesome part of their busynesse off their hands. . . . In one word, 'tis the establish'd custom for every Lady to have 2 Husbands, one that bears the Name, and another that performs the Dutys. . . ."

Lady Mary, "raw girl" as she was, being not yet thirty, was soon urged to comply with this triangular luxury. A young man about town suggested that her stay in Vienna merited "a little affair of the Heart" and, upon her refusing his cooperation in the project, offered to secure "who you like best amongst us." She concluded her letter on a note of indifference toward the Christian marriage ethic that Pope may have found useful when he embarked upon slandering his erstwhile friend: "Thus you see, my Dear, Galantry and good breeding are as different in different Climates as Morality and Religion."

Lady Rich, who was a member of Pope's circle, may have shown him this letter or, as it has been surmised, Lady Mary may have written him another account. He replied that, "The Court of Vienna is really very edifying: The Ladies with respect to their Husbands seem to understand that Text very literally that commands us to *Bear one another's Burthens.*" If Vienna tolerated such promiscuity, what might not be hoped from Constantinople! Pope judged the time had come for what contemporary criticism would call phallic symbolism. "I shall look upon you no longer as a Christian, when you pass from that charitable Court to the Land of Jealousy, where the unhappy Women converse with none but Eunuchs, and where the very Cucumbers are brought to them Cutt."

The voyage to the East promised a slackening of moral values; Pope found it an encouraging topic. "You have already (without passing the bounds of Christendom) out-travl'd the Sin of Fornication, and are happily arrived at the free Region of Adultery: In a little time you'll look upon some other Sins, with more Impartiality than the Ladies here are capable of. I reckon you'll time it so well, as to make your Faith serve out just to the last Verge of Christendom; that you may discharge your Chaplain (as humanity requires) in a place where he may find some business, and not be out of the way of all Trade."

Pope, who was—at considerable cost to fortune and favor—a practicing Catholic, now permitted himself vicarious reveries having to do not only with sensuality, but with sensuality's regulator, religion. The following overheated lines almost justify Lady Louisa's dismissal of his letters to her grandmother as "expressive neither of passion, nor affection, nor any natural feelings whatsoever; tissues of far-fetched conceits and extravagant compliment." Amorality would be further hastened, Pope mused, if Lady Mary accepted the supposed Mohammedan tenet that women have no souls. After suggesting that the Ambassador inaugurate a drift toward Islam by undergoing circumcision, he luxuriated in the license enjoyed by those who are not inhibited by notions of divine reward or punishment. "I shall hear," he wrote on, "how the very first Night you lay at Pera, you had a vision of Mahomet's Paradise, and happily awaked without a Soul. From which blessed instant the beautiful Body was left at full liberty to perform all the agreeable functions it was made for."

This is hardly a new idea and, in addition to its banality, it was, in Pope's case, insincere. The poet who wrote *An Essay on Man* was, by his own definition, a moralist. His was a code against which he constantly offended by acts of malice and vindictiveness; nevertheless, it was a code. The amorality which he so superfluously recommended to Lady Mary was totally foreign to his passionately committed character. She was indifferent to distinctions between vice and virtue. He was profoundly conditioned by a Christianity to which he did frequent and ugly violence.

In his feverish imagination, having set Lady Mary free from the custody of the soul, Pope now considered his own spiritual destiny in terms of the Apostles' Creed. The doctrine of the resurrection of the body seems to have posed problems to the sufferer of "that long disease, my life." He continued, "But if my Fate be such that this Body of mine (which is as ill match'd to my mind as any wife to her husband) be left behind in the journey, let the Epitaph of Tibullus be set over it."

> Here stopt by hasty Death, Alexis lies
> Who crost half Europe, led by Wortley's eyes.

The Ambassador and his lady remained in Vienna from September until November. They were then summoned to Hanover, where the King was refreshing himself with his native air and the company of his favorite mistress, Countess von Platen. Here, Edward received additional documents and, doubtless, gave his sovereign a *viva voce* account of the Viennese phase of his negotiations.

This diplomatic detour was, of necessity, hurried. To save time and to avoid the dirty inns of rural Bohemia, the Wortley Montagus travelled continuously for three days and nights from Vienna to

Prague. Lady Mary, no matter how fatigued, could never sleep on the road. Others, as she learned to her peril, could. Writing from Leipzig to Lady Mar she was once more the compelling storyteller. "We pass'd by moonshine the frightfull Precipices that divide Bohemia from Saxony, at the bottom of which runs the River Elbe, but I cannot say I had reason to fear drowning in it, being perfectly convinc'd that in case of a Tumble it was utterly impossible to come alive to the bottom." It was fortunate that Lady Mary was awake. The postillions were not. Her letter continues, "I perceived by the bright light of the moon our Postillions nodding on horseback while the Horses were on a full Gallop and I thought it very convenient to call out to desire 'em to look where they were going. My calling wak'd Mr. W. and he was much more surpriz'd than my selfe at the Situation we were in, and assur'd me that he had pass'd the Alps 5 times in different places without ever having done a road so dangerous. I have been told since it is common to find the bodies of travellers in the Elbe; but, thank God, that was not our destiny; and we came safe to Dresden, so much tired with fear and fatigue, it was not possible for me to compose myself to write."

Lady Mary here sounded new notes. Although her letters to Wortley can be numbered in the hundreds, she rarely described him to another correspondent. Her picture of the swaying coach and the frightened couple within is not only exciting, but it also contains a sense of companionship that is usually lacking in her first-person-singular comments on scenes and mores. The exclamation "thank God" is so uncharacteristic of her cool agnosticism as to leave no doubt of its sincerity. A day's rest was required to restore her to her usual spirits. Once more the tart observer, she was equal to detailing the mannerisms of Saxon ladies and, by the time Hanover was reached, she believed herself to have made "the Tour of Germany."

New Year's Day of 1717 found the Wortley Montagus again in Vienna. It was now time to prepare for the journey east. Lady Mary, as well she might, found it a formidable prospect. The Danube, down which she had travelled so happily in September, was frozen, and deep snow lay on the ground. Her new friends, among them Prince Eugene of Savoy, warned her against the hardships of overland travel "through desart plains cover'd with Snow, where the cold is so violent many have been kill'd by it." These fears were, of course, increased by the presence of young Edward. His mother, writing to his aunt, Lady Mar, confessed that she needed all her courage to face the icy journey. "Adeiu, Dear Sister. This is the last Account you will have from me of Vienna. If I survive my Journey, you shall hear from me again. . . . I have long learnt to hold myself at nothing, but when I think of the fatigue my poor infant must suffer, I have all a mother's fondness in my Eyes and all her tender passions in my Heart."

To Pope, who had at an earlier time warned against the Spartan journey, she bade an even more emotional farewell. In addition to the rigors of a landlocked winter, there were brigands and bands of marauding Tartars. To guard against the latter, the Wortley Montagus travelled in an armed convoy. Lady Mary was never one to play down a dramatic situation; she wrote to her distant admirer of the perils of an attack: " 'Tis true we shall have a considerable Escorte, so that possibly I may be diverted with a new Scene by finding my selfe in the midst of a Battle. How my adventures will conclude I leave entirely to Providence; if comically you shall hear of 'em."

Two weeks after these leave-takings, the Wortley Montagus arrived in comfort and safety at the fortress town of Peterwardein. Their journey might be said to have ended comically, in that Lady Mary laughed heartily at the exaggerated warnings given her in Vienna, warnings which were, she wrote to Lady Mar, "wholly owing to the tenderness of my Vienna friends and their desire of keeping me with 'em for this Winter." Upon this confident note, Lady Mary embarked upon a "short journal" of the *winterreise* which had led across the snows of Hungary to what is now the interior of Yugoslavia. The journal covers seven printed pages and marks an advance in its writer's descriptive and narrative skills.

In her letters from the East, Lady Mary suspended the sarcasm with which she so expertly satirized Western society. As she approached the Ottoman frontier, she addressed herself without mockery to an unknown culture. Her disapproval of the contrasts between extremes of opulence and barbarism that characterized Moslem life was expressed with a frown rather than a sneer. It is this tone of sincere inquiry that sets apart her *Embassy Letters* from her familiarity-breeds-contempt vignettes of London, and makes them more, or less, favored, depending upon their readers' tastes.

The *Embassy Letters* have a more important worth. They are letters of fulfillment. Lady Mary, during much of her life, battled with boredom. The Duke's daughter,* the M.P.'s wife, the wit, the scholar and the diminished beauty all clamored for recognition. During the mission to Turkey she was in a prestigious position. She was also in a new environment, which supplied daily stimulus to her curiosity and literary talent. Her life, past and future, contained many bitter and frustrated pages. Here was a propitious period when the riches and lore of the Osmanlis were hers, to explore and transmit for the dazzling of friend or foe.

Lady Mary now added to her habitual enthusiasm for sightseeing the scholar's touch; she no longer confined herself to visual impressions. Lady Mar learned not only the exhilaration of travel by sleigh, of the hospitality of government officials, of Hungary's great plains and forests, but also something of the bloody history of the regions traversed. Characteristically, Lady Mary had done her homework. Armed with Rycaut's *History of the Turks,* she explained to English friends the complicated contest of cross and crescent.

The Ottoman Empire in 1717 extended to what are now the northern parts of the Balkan states. Consequently, the Wortley Montagus entered Turkish territory after leaving Peterwardein and, at an appointed village, nervously exchanged the armed escort furnished by Emperor Charles VI for the brutal janissaries of Sultan Achmet III. A long stay at Belgrade ensued while the Ambassador awaited the Sultan's pleasure. From Belgrade Lady Mary detailed to Alexander Pope the contrast between frightfulness and refinement that was characteristic of the Osmanlis and their institutions.

Lady Mary was understandably afraid of the janissaries who were charged with the safe conduct of the ambassadorial party. Originally a superbly disciplined corps of soldier-slaves, they had, during the previous century, degenerated into a mutinous force living off plunder, and were quite capable of murdering those who incurred their ready displeasure. The governing pasha of Belgrade, Lady Mary wrote Pope, lived in a condition of blackmail. "He takes all pretences of throwing money amongst the garison and suffers them to make little excursions into Hungary where they Burn some poor

---

* The former Lord Dorchester had been rewarded for his loyalty to the Whigs by being created Duke of Kingston-upon-Hull in 1715.

Rascian (Serbian) Houses. You may imagine," she continued not un-reasonably, "I cannot be very easy in a Town which is realy under the Government of an insolent Soldiery."

Still more sinister were the perils awaiting the luckless brothers of the Sultan. The imperial succession could, by an abominable edict of Mehmet II, be simplified by the slaughter of Princes. "The majority of my jurists have pronounced," he stated, "that those of my illustrious descendants who ascend the throne may put their brothers to death, in order to secure the repose of the world. It will be their duty to act accordingly."

Polygamy assured a generous supply of sibling rivals. One of Achmet's predecessors did away with nineteen brothers, while another contented himself with five. Such superfluous heirs were strangled by bowstring to obviate the spilling of Osmanli blood. The assassins who performed these dynastic murders were mutes and so called because, to assure discretion, their tongues had been removed.

Nor were the Sultan's ministers more secure. They, too, could be cut down subject to court or harem intrigue. They frequently incurred the wrath of the janissaries or the mob. Lady Mary, with an eye to the bisexual mores of the Middle East, thus described the terrors of a political career: "When a minister here displeases the people, in 3 hours time he is dragg'd even from his Master's arms. They cut off his hands, head and feet, and throw them before the palace Gate with all the respect in the world while that Sultan (to whom they all profess an unlimited Adoration) sits trembling in his Apartment and dare neither defend or revenge his favorite. This is the blessed Condition of the most Absolute Monarch upon Earth, who owns noe Law but his Will."

The gentler aspects of Islam were exemplified by Achmet Beg, with whom the Wortley Montagus lodged at Belgrade. He was eminently qualified to introduce Lady Mary to the culture of her new home, having "been educated in the most polite Eastern Learning being perfectly skilled in the Arabic and Persian Languages, and is an extraordinary Scribe, which they call Effendi." Mindful of the nearby "Chamber of Janizarys," Lady Mary concluded that the Effendi, in settling for a life of luxurious study, had, like her namesake, chosen the better part. Never one to underestimate her attractions (especially not in a letter to Pope) Lady Mary claimed Achmet Beg as an admirer. "You cannot imagine how much he is delighted with the Liberty of conversing with me. . . . I pass for a great Scholar with him by relateing to him some of the Persian Tales." Even these blandishments did not hinder Lady Mary from fretting at the ritualistic delay: "these amusements do not hinder my wishing heartily to be out of this place, tho the weather is colder than I believ'd it ever was any where but in Greenland."

All in his own good time, Achmet nodded. The Ambassador's party made its way to Sophia and thence to Adrianople, to which the court had removed from Constantinople. Lady Mary, fortified by Achmet Beg's instructions in Islamic culture, continued to muse upon religion, morals and the confinement of women. Upon arrival at the imperial destination she dispatched (or appears to have dispatched) letters to nearly twenty persons, all endorsed Adrianople, April 1, 1717.

At this point the *Embassy Letters* proclaim themselves to be formal travel essays rather than spontaneous communications to distant friends. Lady Mary, having cut her teeth on the suppressed critique of *Cato,* the anonymous *Spectator Paper* and *Town Eclogues,* destined the annals of her voyage to the East for posthumous publication. To that end she kept copies and "heads," or summaries of her letters, intending to self-edit them at her leisure. Mary Astell, a feminist whose views on female education were in a degree shared by Lady Mary, was in the latter's confidence, and wrote in 1724 an on-the-defensive preface to introduce the Embassy Letters to posterity. When, some twenty years after Mr. Wortley's unsuccessful mission, he and his wife separated, Lady Mary's copybooks accompanied her to the Continent. A further span of twenty-three years ensued as she wandered about France and Italy. She returned home in 1762, mortally ill of cancer. To avoid the opposition of her family to publication, she left in Holland the finished letters, to be brought out after her imminent death. Thus the most famous of her literary projects was launched from Holland where it had been begun forty-six years earlier.

Lady Mary, on that fruitful April 1st, described to an anonymous and possibly suppositious correspondent the baths of Sophia in a letter that was destined to furnish Ingres with material for "Le Bain Turc." Here were to be seen many undraped beauties "in different postures, some in conversation, some working, others drinking Coffee or sherbet, and many negligently lying on their Cushions while their slaves (generally pritty girls of 17 or 18) were employ'd in braiding their hair in several pritty manners." Lady Mary, always interested in social convention, compared the "bagnio" to the Coffee Houses of London, from which forums ladies were barred. She concluded, as was increasingly her wont, that the veiled daughters of the Prophet enjoyed some privileges denied their Christian sisters. "In short," she assured Lady Nameless, " 'tis the Women's Coffee house, where all the news of the Town is told, Scandal invented etc."

The fair bathers tried to persuade their occidental guest to be of their number. Upon Lady Mary's showing them her cumbersome European clothing, complete with what commercial euphemism calls a foundation garment, her hostesses sprang to a conclusion reminiscent of certain precautions taken by the Crusaders. The girdle of chastity had been retained in torso form! "Come hither, and see how cruelly the poor English ladies are used by their husbands:—You need boast indeed of the superior liberties allowed you, when they lock you thus up in a box!"

It was inevitable, granted Ottoman segregation by sex, that Lady Mary's social life be led entirely among women. Her tête-à-tête with Effendi Achmet during the diplomatic quarantine at Belgrade remained her only experience of the conversation of a Turkish gentleman. Her description of naked beauties at the baths of Sophia is the first of many scenes of the domestic lives of Turkish ladies among whom she made friends. The wife of the Grand Vizier invited her to dinner; the Kahya's lady was dazzling in beauty and grace, while Hafise Sultan, widow of the deposed and purportedly poisoned Mustafa II, explained the routines of the seraglio—of which Lady Mary, like most Westerners, entertained popular misconceptions.

The spectacle of physical perfection in princess and slave played its part in inspiring Lady Mary to promote the science of inoculation against smallpox. She doubtless contrasted her pockmarked cheeks and lashless eyes with "That surprizing Harmony of features! that charming result of the whole! that exact proportion of Body! that lovely bloom of Complexion unsully'd by art" possessed by the Kahya's "beauteous Fatima." "To say all in a Word," Lady Mary wrote on breathlessly, "Our most celebrated English Beautys would vanish near her."

Several weeks before Lady Mary beheld this glamor girl, she had proposed that the three-year-old Edward be immunized against the disease that had deprived him of an uncle and disfigured his mother. The letter in which she describes the oriental methods of inoculation is justly famous as a medical document. The refinements of Jenner were still in the future. Lacking them, the procedure was as follows. "There is a set of old Women who make it their business to perform the Operation. Every Autumn in the month of September, when the great Heat has abated, people send to one another to know if any of their family has a mind to have the small pox. They make partys for this purpose, and when they are met (commonly 15 or 16 together) the old Woman comes with a nutshell full of the matter of the best sort of small pox and asks what veins you please to have open'd. She immediately rips open that you offer to her with a large needle (which gives you no more pain than a common scratch) and puts into the vein as much venom as can lye upon the head of her needle, and after she binds up the little wound with a hollow bit of shell, and in this manner opens 4 or 5 veins. . . . The children or young patients play together all the rest of the day and are in perfect health till the 8th. Then the fever begins to seize 'em and they keep their beds 2 days, very seldom 3. They have very rarely above 20 or 30 in their faces, which never mark, and in 8 days time they are as well as before their illness. . . . There is no example of any one that has dy'd in it, and you may believe I am very well satisfy'd of the safety of the Experiment since I intend to try it on my dear little Son. I am Patriot enough to take pains to bring this usefull invention into fashion in England, and I should not fail to write to some of our Doctors very particularly about it if I knew any one of 'em that I thought had Virtue enough to destroy such a considerable branch of their Revenue for the good of Mankind, but that Distemper is too beneficial to them not to expose to all their Resentment the hardy wight that should undertake to put an end to it. Perhaps if I live to return I may, however, have courrage to war with 'em. Upon this Occasion, admire the Heroism in the Heart of your Freind, etc."

Inoculation, as Lady Mary here describes it, was far more dangerous than vaccination, to which it gave rise. Her confident assertions notwithstanding, patients occasionally died and, during the "take," they could communicate smallpox to the nonimmune, a consideration that prevented Lady Mary from inoculating her infant daughter at the same time Edward Junior was "engrafted." "I cannot," she wrote to her husband in March of 1717, "engraft the Girl; her Nurse has not had the small Pox."

The passage of nearly a year between the time Lady Mary determined to inoculate her son and the date of the operation is puzzling. Little Mary was born in January of 1718. Her brother constituted a threat to the nursery, despite the spacious dwellings and numerous servants of the past. Presumably, Edward Senior had to be brought to his wife's way of thinking. Dr. Charles Maitland must have consulted with Dr. Emanuel Timoni * who had, in 1714, described inoculation to the Royal Society. The former, notwithstanding Lady Mary's cynical opinion of doctors' integrity, agreed to the plan and assisted in its execution. He engaged an old Greek Sairey Gamp who undertook with her "blunt and rusty needle" to inoculate one of Junior's arms. Such an outcry ensued that Dr. Maitland "inoculated the other arm with my own instrument, and with so little pain that he did not in the least complain of it."

Without the twin evils of concubinage and slavery, inoculation would have had a different history. The Prophet had forbidden the enslavement of Islamic women, therefore "pritty" girls seen at the baths were either Christian children captured in war, or bred for slavery in southern Russia. Beautiful children of both sexes were in demand and inoculation was the best method of safeguarding the merchandise. Circassian and Georgian families engrafted a handsome boy or pretty girl just as a Georgian farmer of the New World might spray the peach crop.

Despite many oppressive practices, Islam, as Lady Mary increasingly noticed, boasted as well many enlightened attitudes not found elsewhere. The treatment of slaves is a case in point. No limitation was placed upon their schooling or consequent rise. Many boy slaves attended the Imperial School for Pages, where they received an education equivalent to the western universities. Upon reaching manhood they were expected to serve in government, the professions and, of course, the dangerous janissaries. Ibrahim, favorite and eventually Grand Vizier to Suleyman the Magnificent, had been purchased at the age of sixteen. Sinan, the most prolific of all architects, had been trained as an engineer in the janissaries.

---

* Timoni was a European physician living in Constantinople who cooperated with Maitland in the care of the Wortley Montagus.

The girls, of course, shared in the seclusion imposed upon their Islamic sisters. Lady Mary described these children in June of 1717. "The fine slaves that wait upon the great Ladys, or serve the Pleasures of the great Men, are all bought at the age of 8 or 9 year old and educated with great care to accomplish 'em in singing, danceing, Embroidery, etc. They are commonly Circassians, and their Patron never sells them except it is as a Punishment for some very great fault. If ever they grow weary of 'em, they either present them to a freind or give them their freedoms." This was surely a better fate than that suffered by the child who falls from her drunken mother's arms in Hogarth's *Gin Lane,* or that of the chimney sweeps who frequently suffocated in the flues of Paris and London.

Lady Mary's campaign for immunization against smallpox is the most dramatic example of her instinct for things to come. She lacked medical knowledge—although, in western Europe of her day, such knowledge did not necessarily include the principle of antibodies. She acted, with Dr. Maitland's blessing, on the cause and effect level. Inoculated Turks retained their complexions; she had lost hers. Therefore: Let there be Inoculation. It is one of the numerous ironies of her ironic life that she was to prove herself most progressive where she was most ignorant. She may be said to have stumbled into medical history. Unlike another prophet, she does not remain without honor in her own country. Her campaign to bring inoculation to the Christian world is recorded in the Encyclopedia Britannica's pages on vaccination.

This applause was long postponed. In the Sappho years ahead, Lady Mary's stand on inoculation contributed to the sum of her supposed eccentricities. She was guilty of child abuse. She was an unnatural mother. She flouted the laws of God and nature, thundered pulpit and press.

A more bizarre thrill was furnished by Lady Mary's familiarity with harem life. Europeans chose, like Alexander Pope, to think of the harem as an erotic free-for-all, rather than, simply, the women's apartments of any Turkish dwelling, large or small. Lady Mary, it will be recalled, was limited to the company of women. It therefore followed that whatever social life she led transpired in harems.

Eyebrows were further raised by Edward Junior. During the long years of estrangement from his parents, he perfected himself in Oriental languages, bigamy and deceit. One of his virtuoso performances in the latter field was palming himself off on the gullible as the son of Sultan Achmet who, he elaborated, had "flung the handkerchief" at his mother while she visited the seraglio, disguised as a eunuch! It was an excellent story and many believed it; so many, in fact, that a century and a half later, when Lady Louisa Stuart wrote her "IntroductoryAnecdotes," she found it necessary to deny that her grandmother had ever entered the seraglio.

Lady Mary's correspondents were probably disappointed to learn that, not only was the harem an area of decorum, but also that many Ottoman marriages were monogamous. Islam, prior to the reforms of this century, permitted four wives, but only if the first wife consented; as Lady Mary wrote to her sister, "there is no Instance of a Man of Quality that would make use of this Liberty, or of a Woman of Rank that would suffer it." Nor did the presence of costly young damsels necessarily assure debauchery. Their manless lives were spent in waiting upon the lady of the harem, singing, dancing and kneeling to serve sherbet. The Defterdar, or Treasurer, purchased she-slaves for his own recreation, but Lady Mary wrote home: "he is spoke of as a Libertine, or what we should call a Rake."

Another myth that Lady Mary exploded was the belief that Ottoman women were confined to the harem. It is true that the concubines of the seraglio ("the name Seraglio," Lady Mary explained, "is peculiar to the Grand Signor's") never left their quarters unless the court moved. But the royal Princesses, the wives of officials and Lady Mary's other hostesses made their veiled and cloaked way through the streets of Adrianople and Constantinople. If this had not been the case, Lady Mary would not have adopted Turkish dress in order to go sightseeing. Western clothing would have attracted attention; no one spared a glance for another anonymous female form.

Lady Mary was just as interested in the connubial loopholes of Adrianople as she had been in those of Vienna. Amoralist that she was, she delighted in suspecting that principles publicly proclaimed were privately flouted. Referring to the "asmak" and "ferigee" * that camouflaged her new friends, she concluded that "This perpetual Masquerade gives them entire Liberty of following their Inclinations without danger of Discovery. . . . You may easily imagine

---

* The *yasmak* was the traditional veil and the *feridji* the cloak worn as concealment by Turkish women.

the number of faithfull Wives very small in a country where they have nothing to fear from their Lovers' Indiscretion. . . . Upon the Whole, I look upon the Turkish Women as the only free people in the Empire."

A freedom more edifying than freedom to commit adultery, was freedom to survive. An erring wife or straying concubine could, it is true, be sewed in a weighted sack and flung into the Bosporus. Allowing for such inconveniences, Turkish women led safer lives than their husbands, especially the wives of government officials. Lady Mary noted this discrepancy in continuing her letter. "The very Divan pays a respect to 'em and the Grand Signor himselfe, when a Bassa is executed, never violates the priveleges of the Haram . . . which remains unsearch'd entire to the Widow."

No mutes awaited the Sultan's daughters. They were married, sometimes in childhood, not to foreign princes but to their father's friends. When they reached adolescence they were established in magnificent palaces of their own where they, too, were served sherbet by kneeling beauties.

Just such a marriage had been solemnized prior to the Wortley Montagus' arrival. Achmet's daughter, Fatma, was already at 13 "Widow of the late Vizier who was kill'd at Peterwaradin, tho' that ought rather to be call'd a contract than a marriage, not ever having liv'd with him. . . . When she saw this 2nd Husband, who is at least 50, she could not forbear bursting into Tears."

This "damat," or Imperial son-in-law, was Nevsehirli Ibrahim Pasha, a man of culture and talent, whose luxurious tastes were to prove his undoing. Sultan Achmet, in consideration of the fact that Fatma had been a widow only since the previous August, again forbade the consummation of her marriage, reminding Ibrahim that he had been chosen, not for love, but to make himself useful. The thwarted bridegroom sublimated his frustrations in a poem that Lady Mary sent to Pope, also on that hypothetical April Fool's Day. One wonders if he thought she was taunting him. Her letter opens with comments on Turkish poetry: "they have what they call the Sublime, that is a stile proper for Poetry and which is the exact scripture stile. . . . I am very glad to have it in my power to satisfy your Curiosity by sending you a faithfull copy of the Verses that Ibrahim Bassa, the reigning favorite has made for the young Princesse, his contracted Wife, whom he is not yet permitted to visit without wittnesses, tho she is gone home to his House." This unnatural state of affairs drew candid complaints from Ibrahim:

> The wish'd possession is delaid from day to day,
> The cruel Sultan Achmet will not permit me to see those cheeks
>   more vermillion than roses.
> I dare not snatch one of your kisses,
> The sweetness of your charms has ravish'd my Soul.
> Your eyes are black and lovely
> But wild and disdainfull as those of a Stag.

Lady Mary could never resist the temptation to exploit her own literary charms. She accompanied the Damat's outpourings with an English transliteration of her own devising.

Fatma became, a few years later, again a widow. The glittering Ibrahim incurred, by his extravagance, the displeasure of the mob. They demanded that Achmet imprison his son-in-law and Grand Vizier in the dungeons of Topkapi. Here, like many another statesman of the Ottoman Empire, he was murdered, and his Padishah (a synonym for Sultan or Shah) soon deposed.

Far from having the mythical handkerchief thrown to her, Lady Mary was limited to watching Sultan Achmet from afar. Her description of his procession to a Friday mosque is her opulent style at its best. "I went yesterday with the French Ambassadresse to see the Grand Signor in his passage to the Mosque. He was preceded by a Numerous Guard of Janizarys with vast white Feathers on their Heads, Spahys and Bostangées; these are the foot and Horse Guard and the Royal Gardiners, which are a very considerable body of men, dress'd in different habits of fine, lively Colours that at a distance they appear'd like a parterre of Tulips; after them, the Aga of the Janizarys in a Robe of Purple velvet lin'd with silver Tissue, his Horse led by 2 slaves richly dress'd; next to him the Kuzlir Aga (your Ladyship knows this is the cheife Guardian of the seraglio Ladys) in a deep yellow Cloth (which suited very well to his black face) lin'd with Sables; and last his Sublimity him selfe in Green lin'd with the Fur of a black Muscovite fox, which is suppos'd worth £1,000 Sterling, mounted on a fine Horse with Furniture embroider'd with Jewells. 6 more Horses furnish'd were led after him, and 2 of his

Principal Courtiers bore, one his Gold and the other his Silver Coffée Pot, on a staff. Another carry'd a Silver stool on his head for him to sit on. It would be too tedious to tell your Ladyship the various dresses and Turbants (by which their Rank is distinguish'd) but they were all extreme rich and gay to the number of some thousands, that perhaps there cannot be seen a more beautiful Procession. The Sultan appear'd to us a Handsome Man of about 40, with a very gracefull air but something severe in his Countenance, his Eyes very full and black. He happen'd to stop under the Window where we stood and (I suppose being told who we were) look'd upon us very attentively that we had full Leisure to consider him, and the French Ambassadresse agreed with me as to his good Mien."

Lady Mary's likening the Sultan's bodyguard to a tulip garden suggests that she knew that the time of the Wortley Montagu Embassy coincided with the so-called Tulip Age. As in Holland of another date, there occurred in early eighteenth century Turkey a bulb boom. Speculators bought the costly onions as if they had been diamonds. Gardens were given over entirely to tulips; tulips blossomed in Iznik tiles, in brocades, and in the fabulously illuminated volumes with which Achmet was to fill his new library. He did not deprive the seraglio lovelies of their share in the fad. Of a pleasant spring evening he would have the palace gardens cleared of "male" males and allow his concubines and slaves to run wild among the flowers. It must have been a charming sight! No pains were spared to have the tulips advantageously lighted, .turtles with candles fixed upon their shells being set to plodding up and down the flower beds.

The Tulip Age was marked by splendor rather than strength. The Ottoman Empire was, in 1717, well into its slow decline. Had the unimaginative Edward sensed, as did his wife, that he was witnessing absolute power corrupting absolutely, it might have been he, rather than another, who negotiated the Treaty of Passarowitz. Ottoman ostentation, however, had its desired way with him. He consistently presented Emperor Charles VI with terms so favorable to Achmet III that the former refused to cease hostilities.

Achmet decided in May of 1717 to command his army in person. This was a step he would hardly have taken had he been satisfied with the conduct of his campaign. It was customary, when their Padishah turned warrior, for his subjects to organize an *aláy*, or pageant, in his honor. Skeptical Lady Mary refused to be taken in by such bombast. Not for her was Islam's doctrine of the glory of dying in battle. She demonstrated again her modern mind in writing to her deistic friend, Abbé Conti, that " 'tis easy to observe that the Soldeirs do not begin the Campaign with any great cheerfulness. The War is a general Greivance upon the people but particularly hard upon the Tradesmen."

Ironically, it was the discontented merchants who stage-managed the *aláy*. It seems to have resembled an ambulatory trade fair. Lady Mary continued: "The Grand Signor was at the Seraglio Window to see the procession, which pass'd through all the principal Streets. It was preceded by an Effendi mounted on a Camel richly furnish'd, reading aloud the Alcoran, finely bound, laid upon a Cushion. He was surrounded by a parcel of Boys in white, singing some verses of it, follow'd by a Man dress'd in Green Boughs representing a Clean Husband Man sowing Seed. After him several reapers with Garlands of Ears of Corn, as Ceres is pictur'd, with Scythes in their hands seeming to Mow; Then a little Machine drawn by Oxen, in which was a Windmill and boys employ'd in grinding corn, follow'd by another Machine drawn by Buffolos carrying an Oven and 2 more Boys, one employ'd in kneading the bread, and another in drawing it out of the Oven. These boys threw little Cakes on both sides amongst the Croud, and were follow'd by the whole company of Bakers marching on foot, 2 and 2, in their best Cloaths, with Cakes, Loaves, pastys, and pies of all sorts on their heads; and after them 2 Buffons or Jack puddings with their faces and Cloaths smear'd with Meal, who diverted the Mob with their Antick Gestures. In the same Manner follow'd all the Companys of Trade in their Empire, the nobler sort, such as Jewellers, Mercers, etc., finely Mounted and many of the Pageants that represented their Trades perfectly Magnificent; amongst which the Furriers made one of the best Figures, being a large Machine set round with the Skins of Ermins, Foxes, etc., so well stuff'd the Animals seem'd to be alive, follow'd by Music and dancers. I believe they were, upon the whole, at least 20,000 Men, all ready to follow his highness if he commanded them.

"The rear was clos'd by the Volunteers, who came to beg the Honour of dying in his Service. This part of the shew seem'd to me so barbarous I remov'd from the Window upon the first appearance of it. They were all naked to the Middle, their Arms peirc'd throû with Arrows left sticking in 'em, others had 'em sticking in their heads, the blood trickling down their faces, and some slash'd their arms with sharp knives, makeing the blood spout out upon those that stood near; and this is look'd upon as an Expression of their Zeal for Glory."

Two days after these patriotic extravagances, Lady Mary rounded out her Adrianople sightseeing by visiting Sinan's masterpiece, the mosque of Selim II. Characteristically, she omits the architect's name; she probably did not know it. She described to Abbé Conti the marble pillars without, and the great dome that forms the body of the mosque, concluding candidly that she knew too little of architecture to "pretend to speak of the proportions." She was struck by the sense of interior spaciousness and the vast reaches of rich carpeting. Stating that she "thought it the noblest building I ever saw," she detailed the tiled walls that she mistook for "Japan China," the myriad low hanging lamps and the nearby "fountain to wash" which was then, and remains now, an "Essential part of their devotion."

Lady Mary's letters to Pope and Conti retain a best-foot-forward tone that has survived subsequent rewriting. In the future revisions she preserved a distinction between feminine concerns suitable for a sister, and the loftier reaches of literature and religion worthy of a poet and a theologian. She wrote to Pope that the out-of-doors diversions of the Turks, the dancing and singing in gardens and on river banks, could have been drawn from the pages of Theocritus. In rereading Pope's Homer, she found that Ottoman ladies at their "Looms under the shades of their Trees" were but following the occupations of Helen and Andromache.

Antonio Conti, to whom the principal part of Lady Mary's comments on Islam were addressed, was an Abbé as irregular in doctrine as was Abbé Lizst in celibacy. Conti was an anomaly; he was a Catholic deist. Originally a member of a religious order, he had, not long after ordination, abandoned an ecclesiastical career for that of author and mathematician. This choice would have seemed to one of Lady Mary's secular bent an indication of enlightenment. The pages on Islam, written at Conti's request, are slanted to give the Prophet a delicate superiority to Christ, at least to the Christ of Rome.

Lady Mary's chief informant on the Koran and its precepts was

Effendi Achmet Beg of the chilly stopover in Belgrade. She and her host both exemplified a double standard in matters of religion. As typical products of a material age, they equated irreligion with sophistication. The Effendi, Lady Mary wrote Conti, "was pleas'd to hear that there were Christians that did not worship images or adore the Virgin Mary" and that "The ridicule of Transubstantiation appear'd very strong to him." The Mohammedan intellectual, Lady Mary smugly concluded, had left revealed religion to the common people, who must be everywhere pacified with piety. As she put it to the Abbé, "the most prevailing Opinion, if you search into the Secret of the Effendis, is plain Deism, but this is kept from the people who are amus'd with a thousand Different notions according to the different interests of their Preachers."

Pursuant to these arrogant counsels, Turkish persons of quality also left the Prophet's strictures against alcohol to the lower orders. Lady Mary, upon expressing surprise that Achmet Beg drank wine with his guests, learned "that all the Creatures of God were good and design'd for the use of man; however, that the prohibition of Wine was a very wise maxim and meant for the common people, being the Source of all disorders among them but that the Prophet never design'd to confine those that knew how to use it with moderation."

Upon the Sultan's departure for the front, the Wortley Montagus moved on to Constantinople, crossing with their thirty-five coaches and wagons Sinan's bridge at Büyükchekmejé. They arrived in late spring, establishing themselves in a palace at Pera. Pera was, in 1717, a separate community from Constantinople—as Mayfair and Westminster, at the same period, were not yet parts of London. Pera was then, and still is, the district most frequented by foreigners. "All the Ambassadors are lodged very near each other" Lady Mary wrote Conti, continuing, "One part of our House shews us the Port, the City, and the Seraglio, and the distant hills of Assia, perhaps all together the most beautifull Prospect in the World."

The Wortley Montagus' first stay in Constantinople was short. Lady Mary was now pregnant, and summer comes early to Turkey, two considerations that favored a removal to the country. They took a house in the Belgrade Forest, a magnificent region that streches from present-day Istanbul to the shores of the Black Sea. Pregnancy seems to have made inroads upon Lady Mary's energy. To Pope, she likened her beautiful surroundings to the Elysian Fields and herself to a departed spirit, saying that "what perswades me more fully of my Decease is the Situation of my own Mind, the Ignorance I am in of what passes amongst the Living, which only comes to me by chance, and the great Calmness with which I receive it."

She was suffering, in addition to the lethargy of early pregnancy, from homesickness. She was tired of eastern luxuries and heartily longed for London's bustling controversies. She endeavored, not successfully, one suspects, to convince herself that her uneventful life in Belgrade Forest was better spent than it would have been at home. She seems to have planned her days on monothematic lines. "Monday Seting of Partridges, Tuesday reading English, Wednesday Studying the Turkish Language (in which, by the way, I am already very learned) Thursday Classical Authors, Friday spent in writing, Saturday at my needle, and Sunday admitting of Visits and hearing Musick." This was surely better, she wrote Pope, than London's perpetual round of scandal and intrigue in the dissemination of which, she was wistfully aware, both he and she excelled.

There is a hiatus from June of 1717 to January of 1718 in the *Embassy Letters*. This period saw the failure of Ambassador Wortley's mission. It is to be imagined that Lady Mary bombarded her unfortunate husband with advice on his affairs as vigorously as she had during the Hanoverian accession. She did not, to posterity's loss, do it in writing. We do not learn of her disappointment until April of 1718, when she wrote to Wortley, "You need not apprehend my expressing any great Joy for our return. I hope tis less shocking to you than to me, who have really suffer'd in my health by the uneasyness it has given me, thô I take care to conceal it here as much as I can."

Poor Lady Mary! She had doubtless envisaged a difficult task triumphantly achieved. Ambassador Wortley, having terminated an unpopular war, would advance from title to title, as had the Duke of Kingston. Lady Mary, in addition to her burgeoning prestige as a wit and an informed traveller, would become Lady Hypothetical, rather than remain, as Lady Mary, her husband's social superior.

She whiled away the last days of pregnancy by writing a nostalgic poem. It is in complete contrast to the tart *Town Eclogues* of an earlier date, reminding us that satire and sentiment were both present in her ambivalent character. Laying aside the deism of her letters to Conti, she reverently implores God to grant her a little farm in a climate just like that of Turkey where, by some unprecedented phenomenon, "The streams still murmur undefiled with rain." She also forsook her former preferential consideration of Islam by lamenting the transition of Christian churches to mosques. "Soph'a alone," she wrote with poetic license, "her ancient name retains / Though th'unbeliever now her shrine profanes."

A spirited stanza toward the poem's end gives us one of the best of Lady Mary's street scenes. She again described a procession. Instead of the Sultan's Friday progress to the mosque, she wrote of the "proud Vizier" attended by slaves and moving in silent splendor to the "dread divan." From this fateful spectacle, she went on to admire Constantinople's "rising city in confusion fair" where "Gardens on gardens, domes on domes arise / and endless beauties tire the wandering eyes." Lady Mary, like a greater poet, knew Allegro and Penseroso moods. Exemplifying the latter, she turned from her consideration of history's vicissitudes and what she had earlier called "the dangerous Honours of the Port" to the "retreat secure from humankind" afforded by the Embassy kiosk.

Some three weeks after composing these contemplative lines Lady Mary gave birth to the future Lady Bute who, as "My Dear Child," was to become the recipient of innumerable letters written during the long exile of later years.

Islam provided an exuberant environment for childbearing. The Prophet held maternity in high esteem, going so far as to value the Virgin Mary above her son. Turkey of the Sultans was, like some other supposedly male-dominated nations, a furtive matriarchy. This was especially true of the Sultan's household. It was the dearest dream of every seraglio girl to be singled out for the Sultan's pleasure and to bear him a son. If, and when, this son survived the mutes and ascended the gem-encrusted throne, she, as Valide Sultan (the title given the Sultan's mother) would enjoy more power than that exercised by the consorts of Western monarchs. It was a glittering prospect for a girl who might have been acquired in the slave market. The retired life of the seraglio, by denying its women any direct participation in public affairs, promoted a powerful petticoat underground. Sons were trump cards to be exploited and, in the case of a rival's offspring, eliminated.

The seraglio was forbidden to all but the complicated hierarchy of women and eunuchs that ministered to the Sultan's needs. Even court musicians, summoned for harem duty, played blindfolded. We have, however, two authentic accounts by English travellers of Seraglio life. The first was written by Thomas Dallam, who came to Topkapi in 1599 to install an organ presented by Queen Elizabeth to Mehmet III; the second by Lady Mary. Although the latter's comments were written more than a century after Dallam's, they were published earlier. For this reason, she may be said to have "scooped" her predecessor. Needless to say, neither the installer of the organ nor the Ambassador's lady was free to investigate the complexities of the imperial harem. Dallam was smuggled into the Sultan's bedroom and from this exalted post he saw "through the grait . . . thirtie of the Grand Sinyor's Concobines." Such escapades are not for an aristocrat of either sex, Edward Junior notwithstanding. Lady Mary relied on the evidence furnished by an unimpeachable source.

Her informant was Hafise Sultan. She was bereaved Kadin or *maîtresse-en-titre* of Achmet's older brother, Mustafa II, and, during the latter's reign, had been a prestigious resident of the seraglio. She was therefore qualified to give an authentic and frank account of its customs.

Hafise, upon her Padishah's death, was forced by her brother-in-law into a loveless marriage. She made sure it would be a Platonic union by selecting an elderly statesman "as a mark of her gratitude since it was he that had presented her at the Age of 10 to her lost Lord." She was now mistress of a gorgeously appointed harem from which her husband had, for fifteen years, been rigorously excluded.

Free from seraglio restraints, she was suitably placed for exercising the opulence that formed so important a part of Osmanli foreign policy. Sultan Achmet desired the peace terms, favorable to Turkey, for which Ambassador Wortley continued to press. It was perhaps at his behest that Hafise received Lady Mary in a style before which Versailles would have paled. Her hostess, Lady Mary wrote her sister, wore "3 chains which reach'd her knees, one of large Pearl at the bottom of which hung a fine colour'd Emerald as big as a Turkey

Egg. . . . But her Earrings eclips'd all the rest; they were 2 Diamonds shap'd exactly like pears as large as a big hazle nut." Further gems adorned her head. Five diamond rings appeared on her hands with bracelets completing the picture. The dazzled guest, in a flurry of mental arithmetic, came to the conclusion planned by Hafise Sultan: "according to the common Estimate of Jewels in our part of the world, her whole dress must be worth above £100 thousand sterling. This I am very sure of, that no European Queen has half the Quantity, and the Empresse's jewels (thô very fine) would look very mean near hers."

Patriotism takes many forms. In appearing before her guest adorned in jewels that may now form part of the treasury at Topkapi, Hafise was doing no more than her duty.

The entertainment proffered to the stunned Ambassadress was on a similar scale of magnificence. Dinner required the eating of fifty dishes of meat, served one at a time. The cutlery was of diamond-studded gold, but "the piece of Luxury" most distressing to Lady Mary "was the Table cloth and napkins . . . embroidier'd with silks and Gold. . . . You may be sure they were entirely spoilt before Dinner was over." The Osmanlis, like their enemies, the Hapsburgs, answered adversity with extravagance.

Lady Mary suspected that something more than hospitality was at work and that her hostess's costly costumes "were purposely plac'd in sight but they seemed negligently thrown on the sofa." A more appealing indication of wealth was furnished by the bevy of slaves, some forty in number, all beautiful and richly dressed, who were cared for as if they had been children of the family. Lady Mary "observ'd that the Sultana took a vast deal of pleasure in these lovely Children, which is a vast Expence, for there is not a handsome Girl of that age to be bought under £100 sterling."

Lady Mary had now a rare opportunity to learn about the seraglio from one of its ladies. The first myth to be discarded was that of the handkerchief. The Sultan, Lady Mary was told, sent the Kuslir Aga, or Black Eunuch, to tell the concubine of the hour that she had found favor in his eyes. Competing girls, after expressing their compliments, played bridesmaid and prepared the fortunate one with perfumes and finery. A detail that the prurient of the West found particularly intriguing was the manner in which the woman entered her master's bed. Many seraglio watchers of then and now have insisted that she kissed the coverlet and then crawled up under it from the foot of the bed. Hafise, with every reason to know, scoffed at the idea.

To Lady Mary, born in the hardly monogamous world of post-Restoration London, there was nothing shocking in Hafise's account of these stately matings. Was there any difference, she may have wondered, between the careers of rapacious Lady Castlemaine and Hafise? The answer would appear to be all in favor of the honest and loyal Sultana.

Permitted promiscuity did not rule out love on the part of either Sultan or Kadin. Lady Mary's portrait of the grieving widow is written with more feeling that usually characterizes her worldly pen. She seldom dealt with sorrow; in the following sympathetic passage she exhibits the novelist manquée. "She never mention'd the Sultan without tears in her Eyes, yet she seem'd very fond of the discourse. My past happyness (said she) appears a dream to me, yet I cannot forget that I was belov'd by the greatest and most Lovely of Mankind. I was chose from all the rest to make all his campaigns with him. I would not survive him if I was not passionately fond of the Princesse, my Daughter, yet all my tenderness for her was hardly enough to make me preserve my Life when I lost him. I pass'd a whole twelvemonth without seeing the light. Time has soften'd my Dispair, yet I now pass some days every week in tears devoted to the Memory of my Sultan."

The time for Ambassador Wortley's recall was, in the spring of 1718, drawing near. Lady Mary, from behind her "Turkish Vail," hurried to complete her sightseeing. She saw and described a number of mosques and monuments frequented by the bus-borne tourists of today. A stellar attraction for the present-day traveller—Topkapi— was, of course, inaccessible. From afar she stared at the seraglio and at the cypresses and "Gilded turrets and Spires" visible above its walls. She remained vulnerable to the Osmanli strategy of pride by concluding erroneously that "there is no Christian King's Palace half so large."

Nearby stands Justinian's Hagia Sophia. It is now, as Aya Sophia, a museum. During the reigns of thirty Ottoman Sultans it served as a mosque. It could be visited only by permission, a privilege that—

fortunately for Lady Mary and her companion, the Princess of Tran-
sylvania—was reserved for distinguished foreign visitors. Her description of this noble basilica does not do justice to the breathtaking
splendor the interior now reveals. In recent years the Byzantine
mosaics, which are among Aya Sofia's principal glories, have been
uncovered and restored. The modern traveller cannot gather, as did
Lady Mary, fallen and crumbled tessellata.

Perhaps it was because of the dilapidated condition of Aya Sofia,
or perhaps because she was engrossed by Islam, that Lady Mary preferred the Süleymaniyé, the Imperial Friday Mosque, built by Sinan
for Suleyman the Magnificent. With more accuracy than usual, she
defined the basic formula of every mosque as that of a circle, or dome,
set upon an "Exact Square." Another eye might have seen that Sinan
had derived his plan for the Süleymaniyé from that of Hagia Sofia
of a thousand years earlier, and that the Byzantine and Islamic temples on their neighboring hills represent continuity of architectural
tradition. Lady Mary had not such an eye.

Her description of the "Hyppodrome," like that of Aya Sofia,
points to the gains and losses experienced by travellers of three centuries. In 1718, tourists in Constantinople saw more and knew less.
The Delphic column had not yet been mutilated; Lady Mary noted
and was puzzled by "three serpents twisted together with their
mouths gapeing." These reptiles lost their heads later in the eighteenth century; today's visitor to Istanbul sees only a truncated pillar.
He has, however, access to the studies of modern archeologists, who
tell him that here is the oldest object in the city, and that the serpents
formed part of a tripod bearing a sacrificial basin. Lady Mary and
her contemporaries were obliged to content themselves with "fabu-
lous legends."

The Rosetta stone was also in the future. Close by the headless
column stands an obelisk that was, to the traveller of earlier days, as
mysterious as the entwined snakes. Lady Mary, with her characteristic rejection of the unknown, dismissed "the Hieroglyphics all very
entire" as "meer Ancient Puns."

Lady Mary's sightseeing included Constantinople's raffish waterfront. She thought herself very Bohemian to wander among the
seamen who were "worse monsters than our Watermen." She wore,
of course, her "Turkish Vail" which, she wrote, "is become not only

very easy but agreeable to me, and if it was not, I would be content to endure some inconveniency to content a passion so powerful with me as Curiosity. . . ."

The port of eighteenth-century Constantinople was far more beautiful than that of the present-day Istanbul. Modernization of Turkey, despite its undoubted social and economic gains, has played havoc with aesthetic values, indoors and out. The shores of the Bosporus and the Golden Horn now include smoke stacks, gas tanks and cranes. The caïques of a more sightly age have been replaced by an army of beetlelike ferries. Freighters from the Black Sea and the Aegean burn soft coal, and the resultant billows of black smoke obscure the view so charmingly described by Lady Mary, who stated, "the pleasure of going in a Barge to Chelsea is not comparable to that of rowing upon the Canal of the Sea here, where for 20 miles together down the Bosphorus the most Beautiful Variety of prospects present themselves. The Asian Side is cover'd with fruit trees, villages and the most delightful Landscape in nature. On the European stands Constantinople situate on Seven Hills. The unequal heights make it seem as Large again as it is. . . . Shewing an agreeable mixture of gardens, Pine and Cypress trees, Palaces, Mosques and publick buildings rais'd one above another with as much Beauty and appearance of Symetry as your Ladyship ever saw in a Cabinet adorn'd by the most skillful hands. . . ."

Lady Mary's exotic adventures were drawing to a close. Even as she was writing these lines, the warship *Preston* was cruising along the Barbary Coast bound for Constantinople. This ship was to carry back to England the variously frustrated Wortley Montagus and their enlarged family. Lady Mary had no heart for their return. She wrote to a nameless Ladyship that "I am now preparing to leave Constantinople and perhaps you will accuse me of Hipocricy when I tell you 'tis with regret, but I am us'd to the air, and have learnt the Language, and as much as I love travelling, I tremble at the inconveniencys attending so great a Journey with a numerous family and a little Infant hanging at the breast. However, I endeavor upon the Occasion to do as I have hitherto done in all the odd turns of my Life, turn 'em, if I can to my Diversion."

The *Preston*'s return voyage led, of necessity, through the heart waters of Western civilization. Lady Mary, child of a classical age, was once more in well-documented territory and proposed to make the most of it. She again selected Abbé Conti as recipient of an exuberant and, it must be confessed, somewhat innocently informative essay. In page after page she chronicled her impressions of the wine-dark sea and of those who had once peopled its shores. Her surroundings inspired her to adorn her letter with rhymed couplets because, as she told Conti, poetry was in the Aegean air:

> Warmed with Poetic Transport I survey
> Th'Immortal Islands and the well known sea,
> For here so oft the muse her harp has strung
> That not a mountain rears his head unsung.

The Dardanelles, of later and bloody memory, brought to mind the agreeably "Tragick" story of:

> The swimming lover and the nightly bride,
> How Hero lov'd and how Leander dy'd

while Mount Ida in the distance recalled that it was here that:

> Juno once caress'd her Amorous Jove
> And the World's Master lay subdu'd by Love.

Lady Mary's enraptured description of the Greek Islands was founded upon purely literary sources. We are again reminded, as in her account of the Hippodrome at Constantinople, that archeology is a newcomer to scholarship. Her lifetime was to span the transformation of antiquary into archeologist. Among her later friends was the Comte de Caylus who, with Johann Winckelmann, must be accounted in Walter Pater's word to have "laid open a new organ," the organ being a systematic study of classical remains.

Lacking such tutors, the Wortley Montagus were puzzled by the marbles to be found near the site of Schliemann's later Trojan exploits. Lady Mary describes a grave stele as being of "very fine white marble, the side of it beautifully carv'd in bas Relief. It represents a woman who seems to be design'd for some Deity sitting on a Chair with a footstool, and before her another woman weeping and presenting to her a Young Child that she has in her Arms, follow'd by a procession of women with Children in the same manner. This," Lady Mary accurately concludes, "is certainly a very ancient tomb but I dare not pretend to give the true Explanation of it."

The attempted protection of ancient artifacts is a recent ethic. The Wortley Montagus, like any other eighteenth-century travellers, would gladly have carried off the grave stele and were only prevented from doing so by the *Preston's* captain, who assured them "that without having machines made on purpose twas impossible to bear it to the Sea Side, and when it was there his long Boat would not be large enough to hold it."

Lady Mary avoided the July sun by rising at two in the morning to view "cooly" the site of Troy. The controversial excavations of Schliemann were a century and a half in the future. "All that is now left of Troy is the ground on which it stood," she continued, "for I am firmly persuaded whatever pieces of Antiquity may be found round it are much more modern." Like the fanatical Schliemann, Lady Mary accepted Homer's landscapes as factual descriptions, writing "While I view'd these celebrated Fields and Rivers, I admired the exact Geography of Homer, whom I had in my hand. Allmost every Epithet he gives to a Mountain or plain is still just for it. . . ."

The *Preston,* like today's cruise ships, sailed on from the shores of Ilium to those of Lesbos where Lady Mary, never dreaming that she would soon hate the name, mused on Sappho. The temple of Poseidon at Sounion soon came into view, reminding Lady Mary of the tragic explosion that, forty years earlier, had badly damaged the Parthenon. Crete's mountains were seen from afar and "Gnossus the scene of monstrous Passions" duly noted. Lady Mary's concluding comments about the Isles of Greece remind today's traveller that he is fortunate to live in a post- rather than a prearcheological world. After sailing past the still-to-be-enjoyed marvels of Greece, Lady Mary took leave of them thus: "I will pass by all the other Islands with this general refflection, that 'tis impossible to imagine anything more agreeable than this Journey would have been between 2 and 3,000 years since, when, after drinking a dish of tea with Sapho, I might have gone the same evening to visit the temple of Homer in Chios, and have pass'd this voyage in taking plans of magnificent Temples, delineating the miracles of Statuarys and converseing with the most polite and most gay of mankind. Alas! Art is extinct here."

To shorten their journey, the Ambassador and his wife disembarked at Genoa in August, leaving their children aboard the *Preston* for a lengthy voyage home of several months. Quarantine regulations made necessary a stay in a nearby Palladian villa "in the company of a noble Genoese Commission'd to see we did not touch one Another." When freed from these restrictions Lady Mary, of course, went sightseeing. Italian aristocracy, like that of Austria, rejoiced in the *cavaliere servente* convention so enthusiastically recommended to Lady Mary during her Vienna stay. She characteristically applauded all modifications of the Judeo-Christian mores and *cicisbeismo,* as this gallantry-*pour-la-forme* was called, received her commendation. She would one day be fluent in Italian. The time was not yet. To Lady Mar she gave these "animals" the engaging name of "Tetis beys."

At Genoa Lady Mary for the first time accorded to a painting the kind of respect she almost always reserved for literature. She wrote of a "Lucretia" of Guido Reni that "The expressive Beauty of that Face and Bosome gives all the passion of Pity and admiration that could be rais'd in the Soul by the finest poem on that Subject."

From Genoa the Wortley Montagus drove north to Turin and then to the pass over the Alps that Edward had, two years earlier, compared to the cliffs of the Elbe. It was a dreaded chapter in the annals of eighteenth-century travel, when mountains, per se, were considered hideous. Upon their arrival in Lyons, Lady Mary was confined by sore throat to a "Chamber cram'd with the mortifying objects of Apothecarys' viols and bottles." From this uncongenial retreat she wrote the following description of crossing the Alps: "The next day we begun to ascend Mount Cenis, being carri'd in little seats of twisted Osiers fix'd upon Poles, on men's shoulders, our chaises taken to pieces and laid upon Mules. The prodigious Prospect of Mountains cover'd with Eternal Snow, Clouds hanging far below our feet, and the vast cascades tumbling down the Rocks with a confus'd roaring, would have been solemnly entertaining to me if I had suffer'd less from the extreme cold that reigns here, but the misty rain, which falls perpetually, penetrated even the thick fur I was wrap'd in, and I was halfe dead with cold before we got to the foot of the Mountain, which was not till 2 hours after twas dark. This Hill has a spacious plain on the top of it, and a fine lake there, but the Descent is so steep and slippery, 'tis surprizing to see these chairmen go so steadily as they do, yet I was not halfe so much afraid of breaking my Neck as I was of falling sick, and the Event has show'd that I plac'd my fears in the right place."

Illness did nothing to brighten the unwelcome prospect of returning to England. Perversely, or perhaps teasingly, it was to Pope, who had recently written "Come for God's sake, come Lady Mary, come quickly!" that she confided her expatriate sentiments. After some doubtfully sincere fears of finding herself the star of London teatables, she continued to her lover "on paper," "I am a creature that cannot serve any body but with insignificant good wishes . . . my presence is not a necessary good to any one member of my Native Country, I think I might much better have stay'd where ease and Quiet made up the happiness of my Indolent Life. —I should certainly be melancholy if I persu'd this theam one line farther."

Lady Mary's first impressions of France were formed at a low point in the morale and morals of a country in which she was later to live. Louis XV was a child of eight and the Regent, Philippe d'Orléans, ruled (as his dissipations permitted) in his place. The poverty resulting from the war of a decade earlier had by no means been overcome. Lady Mary, still suffering from her Lyons infection, was horrified to find that, "While the post horses are chang'd, the whole town comes out to beg, with such miserable starv'd faces and thin, tatter'd Cloaths, they need no other Eloquence to perswade one of the wretchedness of their Condition."

Like many other travellers, Lady Mary had caught the fault of odious comparisons. The music of Italy, which she failed to note from Genoa or Turin, had spoiled her for that of France. By contrast to palazzi recently admired, Fontainebleau was mean and Versailles irregular. And—shades of "Le Bain Turc"—French ladies were so heavily made up that they reminded her of "fair sheep newly raddled."

Only French tragedy escaped her censure. She saw Racine's *Bajazet* and, doubtless influenced by its Turkish theme, pronounced French tragedians superior to those of England, writing in her most to-the-point style that "'tis certainly more moving to see a man unhappy than to hear him say that he is so."

The satiric flair Lady Mary had so successfully demonstrated in

Town Eclogues reasserted itself as she found herself once more in her own world. Her letters from France were written in the scornful spirit that was to remain a touchstone of her contradictory character. She found that the remote in time, place and customs is more congenial than the nearer view. The contemporary platitude "escape mechanism" was unknown to Lady Mary; its symptoms were not. Chilled by Edward's reserve, disappointed in his diplomatic career and obsessed by the conviction that her superior intellect cut her off from acceptance by her own class (which in the London of 1718 it doubtless did), she now addressed herself to satirizing the passing scene. It was to prove a more ominous subject than she had bargained for.

The first situation to be tested by proximity was Pope's infatuation-in-fantasy. As his absent lady-love approached Dover, the poet wrote letters that exhibit ardor, sentiment and caution, contrary attitudes from which he was suffering. He euphemistically longed to see her "Soul stark naked." To balance this dashing suggestion, he sent her a romantic tale of rustic lovers who were struck by lightning as they took shelter under a haycock. Lady Mary's reply to this effusion was tart. Had John and Sarah survived the thunderstorm of nature, they might not have been spared that of matrimony.

> Who knows if 'twere not kindly done?
> For had they seen the next Year's sun
> A Beaten Wife and Cuckold Swain
> Had jointly curs'd the marriage chain.
> Now they are happy in their Doom
> For Pope has wrote upon their Tomb.

These cynical lines furnish an appropriate curtain-raiser to the bitter years ahead.

In 1720, England was rocked by the "bursting of the South Sea Bubble," an economic disaster as complex and politically significant as the stock market crash of 1929. The tragedy was increased, as in 1929, by the speculations of amateurs who lacked adequate understanding of finance. Among their number was Lady Mary; she speculated, not only with her own funds, but also with those of a treacherous acquaintance, thus inflicting serious damage on her reputation.

Lady Mary had received, shortly before leaving Constantinople, a letter in an unfamiliar hand. "If you like unusual things this letter won't displease you. I have never had the honour of seeing you and probably never shall, nevertheless I cannot stop myself from writing to you. The Abbé Conti, who is one of my particular friends, has entrusted me with a letter which you wrote to him. . . . I have read it; I have re-read it a hundred times; I have copied it and I never lay it aside day or night. Consider my vanity: from that letter alone I believe I understand the singularity of your character and the infinite charms of your mind."

Thus did Nicolas-François Rémond inaugurate an ill-fated correspondence with Lady Mary, whose flattery threshold was notably low. His letters to her survive; her replies have disappeared. He was a minor author and *esprit* who trafficked in intrigue and was not above advancing his fortunes by dubious means. Letters from the sharp pen of the poetess who had written *Town Eclogues* (Rémond took pains to let Lady Mary know he had read them and had identified one of her characters) might prove interesting not only to receive but to possess.

They met during the Wortley's stay in Paris. All France at this time was engrossed in John Law's Mississippi Company that, in many ways, provided impetus for the South Sea Company. Lady Mary described Law's influence. "I must say I saw nothing in France that delighted me so much as to see an Englishman (at least a Briton) absolute at Paris. I mean Mr. Law who treats their Dukes and Peers extremely *de haut en bas* and is treated by them with the utmost Submission and respect. Poor Souls!"

Among the poor souls was Rémond. Encouraged by temporary success, he came to England with two motives; he desired to speculate in the hysterical South Sea Bubble and, more important, he proposed to further his courtship of Lady Mary, who by now had settled at "Thuydenham and Kinsington." * When she proved unencouraging, he resorted to blackmail. He returned to Paris and, shortly before the successive bankruptcy of both companies, wrote, "If I were as indiscreet as the Abbé Conti I should make as much money by having your letters printed as I have from the Mississippi stock, and nothing would flatter my pedantry as much as so delightful a connection with a person as distinguished as you."

This threat carried a real sting because the very letter showed by

* Lady Mary's spelling of Twickenham and Kensington.

Conti to Rémond had, shortly after the Wortley Montagus returned to London, been bootlegged into print and given a title that identified its author as "an English Lady, who was lately in Turkey and who is no less distinguish'd by her Wit than by her Quality." Remembering that Rémond had copied Lady Mary's letter, it becomes tempting to suspect that it was he who had it published. What could be done, he may have reasoned, with innocent observations of Moslem ways, sent as the title continues "To a Venetian Nobleman, one of the Prime Virtuosi of the Age," might be even more successful with Lady Mary's barbed comments about her London acquaintances, some of which he by now may have received.

This disagreeable letter was written in March of 1720. He wrote again in July, not on trumped-up grounds of affection spurned, but for urgent need to recoup losses he suffered in the "French Mississippi." To Lady Mary, who was now dispensing financial advice with her usual self-confidence, he wrote, in unmistakable sincerity, "Will you always stubbornly refuse me your advice because (as everyone says in Paris) you hate France and all the French? Must a poor devil . . . be unable to benefit by your knowledge—you who are the adviser of all the most enlightened people? . . . I have been given subscriptions for two thousand pounds" (in the South Sea Company) "What shall I do? Should I accept an immediate profit, or run risks in the hope of a larger one?"

Lady Mary, to her credit, urged the former course of action, but was soon persuaded by Rémond to risk his remaining capital in the South Sea Company. This calamitous step was taken in August. The Bubble burst in September, sweeping away countless fortunes, including that of Lady Mary's supposed admirer.

He took a despicable revenge. He accused Lady Mary of having cheated him. The money entrusted to her, he maintained, had never been used for further speculation in the Bubble. Instead of carrying out his instructions, she had pocketed his nest egg. He threatened that, unless she could restore his vanished two thousand pounds, he would denounce her to her husband and publish her replies to his gallant letters.

Lady Mary was terrified. Lady Mar was in her confidence during subsequent months of potential scandal and to her, in Paris with her husband, went distraught letters that are almost exclusively concerned with that "monster," as she not unreasonably called Rémond. She insisted upon the return of her letters which, she admitted to her sister, "thô, God knows very innocent in the main yet may admit of ill constructions." She evidently considered fighting fire with fire. As her letter draws to a close we read "I beg your pardon, Dear Sister, for this tedious account, but you see how necessary 'tis for me to get my Letters from this mad man. Perhaps the best way is by fair means; at least they ought to be the first try'd."

This was in March of 1721. By July the "fair means" had become a capitulation to blackmail. Lady Mary would give "£500 stock" for the return of her letters and, the offer made, she retired to her Villa at "Twict'nam," "in hopes of benefit from the Air." We do not know exactly when or how this sordid situation was settled. The disappearance of this series of Lady Mary's letters suggests that they were returned and destroyed.

Pope and Horace Walpole, all in due time, made gleeful use of Lady Mary's scrape. Walpole assured his readers that "Ruremonde" was not only her victim but her lover, thus proving it is likely that those who write indiscretions will be suspected of committing them. And yet, Rémond made his own contribution to the analysis of Lady Mary's character. He could not have known how perceptive he was when he wrote, "Tell Milady Marie, I pray you, that she loves none but the absent."

Injustice is seldom therapeutic. Lady Mary was guilty of nothing worse than bad judgment, and of that during a period when bad judgment was ruining thousands on both sides of the English Channel. For her misguided participation in Rémond's gamble she was suspected of being a dishonest adulteress. Her customary attitude of amoral detachment failed before a double libel.

So humiliating a sequence of accusations stimulated the destructive elements in her temperament. Increasingly, she considered humanity as "a certain mixture of Fool and Knave." As befitted the product of a quarrelsome age, she shared with Pope, Swift and other Augustan satirists the ability to take creative impulse from hatred. Her acid descriptions of patrician society under the first two Georges doubtless gain from the fact that they were written in anger and disillusionment.

Lady Mary probably would not have asked Lady Mar to serve as go-between in so delicate a contretemps, had she been aware of the latter's psychotic tendencies. Lady Mary's failure to realize that she was entrusting a complex, not to say distasteful, negotiation to a sick woman is strange because, at the time of the Hanoverian succession, she had noted her sister's failure to face facts as they affected Lord Mar's disgrace and impending exile. Long before Frances, Countess of Mar, was certified a lunatic (this step was taken in 1728), Lady Mary's complaints about letters unanswered or uncomprehended indicate melancholia's approach.

Lady Mary's confidence in the healing powers of spite was characteristic of a wit of her times and talents. Early Georgians took a positive view of satire and avenged themselves in the spilling of ink, rather than blood. For them, ridicule, like the quality of mercy, bestowed a double benediction; it blessed those who wrote and those who read. In accordance with the prevailing acceptance of mockery as a salutary influence, Lady Mary, during most of the 1720s, attempted to raise her sister's flagging spirits by a brilliant series of merciless letters. The paradox of malevolent content and benevolent intent gives these vignettes a bitter poignancy.

Here we have, among her several styles, the mistress of the wisecrack. Even those who carried her letters to Paris were not spared her censure. In October of 1723, Lady Lansdowne (of the next chapter) acted as courier, inspiring Lady Mary to write, "I send this by my Lady Lansdowne, who I hope will have no curiosity to open my letter, since she will find in it that I never saw anything so miserably alter'd in my life. I really did not know her." Her obliging Ladyship was soon followed by a relative of whom Lady Mary thus disposed: "The bearer of this Epistle is our Cousin, and a consumate puppy as you'l perceive at first sight. His shoulder-knot, last birthday made many a pritty Gentleman's Heart ake with envy. . . ." She contrived to give an ironic twist to her introduction of a scholar whom she sincerely admired. "Adieu, Dear Sister, I send you along with this Letter the Count of Caylus, who if you do not know allready, you will thank me for introducing to you. He is a Frenchman and no Fop which besides the Curiosity of it is one of the prittyest things in the world."

Since gossip was supposed to cheer her despondent sister, Lady Mary, of course, was especially attentive to that concerning the former's friends. In the letter delivered by Lady Lansdowne, she takes credit for relaying "some other pieces of Scandal not unentertaining, particularly the Earl of Stair and Lady M. Howard, who being your Acquaintance I thought would be some comfort to you."

It is to be wondered if among Lady Mar's acquaintance was "Mrs. West . . . who is a great Prude, having but 2 lovers at a Time . . . the one for use, the other for show." Or the lady who was "tenderly attach'd to the polite Mr. Mildmay, and sunk in all the Joys of happy Love notwithstanding she wants the use of her 2 hands by a Rheumatism, and he has an arm that he cant move." Of these limited lovers Lady Mary concluded, "I wish I could send you the particulars of this Amour which seems to me as curious as that between 2 Oysters, and as well worth the serious Enquiry of the Naturalists."

Lady Mary turned from these indelicate surmises to one of the uproars that characterized Georgian London's reigning *cause célèbre,* Italian opera. We recall that the Embassy Letters contain a delightful description of a performance in Vienna of Fux's *Alcina.* Lady Mary, in applauding on the Continent a work she would have dismissed as frippery in London, was following the insular lead of Mr. Spectator. The fluctuating fortunes of Händel and his rivals, the political implications involved and the articulate hostility to Italian opera expressed by writers from Samuel Pepys to Alexander Pope have made the foreign domination of music under the latter Stuarts and the early Hanoverians one of the most amply documented pages in all of music history. For an informed account of Händelian opera and oratorio we await Mrs. Delany, whose lesser claims to intellect permitted her to use her own judgment, rather than to heed the prejudices of men of letters.

Lady Mary, on the other hand, treasured literary ambitions that made obligatory the sort of contempt for opera and its stars that today's intellectuals reserve for television. Her interest in music was limited to anecdote and, of that, there was in the 1720s a rich selection.

In 1724, London was rocked by an operatic scandal of more than usual proportions. The great castrato, Senesino, insulted the English prima donna, Anastasia Robinson. Her long-time "protector," the elderly and gouty Lord Peterborough, rushed onto the stage and beat Senesino in full view of a delighted audience. Lady Mary's sharp pen was instantly busy. "Would any believe . . . that Mrs. Robinson is at the same time a prude and a kept woman. . . . The . . . heroine has engaged half the town in arms from the nicety of her virtue in which she could not bear the too near approach of Senesino in the opera; and her condescension in her accepting of Lord Peterborough for a champion who has signalized both his love and courage on this occasion in as many instances as ever Don Quixote did for Dulcinea. Poor Senesino, like a vanquished giant, was forced to confess upon his knees that Anastasia was a nonpareil of virtue and beauty. . . . By the providence of Heaven and the wise care of his Majesty no bloodshed ensued. However, things are now tolerably accomodated; and the fair lady rides through the town in triumph in the shining berlin of her hero, not to reckon the more solid advantage of 100 pounds a month which 'tis said he allows her."

Lady Mary's affectionate concern for Lady Mar's depression was accompanied by other anxieties of which one, at least, was of her own making. Hard on the heels of the Rémond incident occurred a scandal of truly lurid character. Griselda Murray, one of Lady Mary's acquaintances (subsequent events discourage the term "friend"), narrowly escaped being raped by her father's footman. Lady Mary's first reaction to this misfortune was entirely correct. "I am," she wrote to her sister, "too well acquainted with the world (of which poor Mrs. Murray's affair is a fatal instance) not to know that the most groundless Accusation is all-ways of ill Consequence to a Woman. . . ."

Unfortunately, Lady Mary's satiric bent got the upper hand. Mrs. Murray's humiliating experience was viewed by The School for Scandal as a priceless joke. A coarse ballad called *Virtue in Danger* was eagerly conned and Lady Mary was suspected of being its perpetrator. As she wrote her sister, "a very odd whim is enter'd the little Head of Mrs. Murray. . . . I, according to the usual Integrity of my Heart and Simplicity of my manners, with great Naiveté desir'd to explain with her upon the Subject, and she answer'd that she was convince'd that I had made the Ballad upon her, and was resolv'd never to speak to me again. I answer'd (which was true) that I utterly defy'd her to have any one single proofe of my making it, without being able to get any thing from her but repetitions that she knew it."

To be accused of having written a lampoon that gave evidence of being the work of a Grub Street hack was too much for Lady Mary's pride of craft. Let London discover what she could do with such a famous incident! She wrote, and acknowledged as her own, skillful verses entitled *Epistle from Arthur Grey, the Footman to Mrs. Murray, after his Condemnation for attempting to commit Violence.* Mrs. Murray's fury could hardly have been abated by the fact that it is the frustrated servant, of lowly origins, who is the object of the poetess's compassion rather than his intended victim. Lady Mary underlined these levelling sentiments by Arthur Grey's imagined contempt for the nocturnal habits of "my great rivals in embroid'ry gay" who

> Too dull to feel what forms like yours inspire,
> After long talking of their painted fire,
> To some lewd brothel they at night retire,
> There, pleas'd with fancy'd quality and charms,
> Enjoy your beauties in a strumpet's arms.

Such lines were not calculated to secure Griselda Murray's confidence in Lady Mary's integrity or simplicity, to say nothing of her naïveté. Others, among them Horace Walpole, raised eyebrows at a woman's realistic condemnation of the patrician vices Hogarth was even then illustrating.

An outbreak of smallpox in 1721 gave Lady Mary an opportunity to urge inoculation. She met all the resistance she had foreseen. The clergy objected to the defying of God's will. The physicians, not entirely unreasonably, asked for evidence more informed than that possessed by an enthusiastic traveller. To satisfy their inquiries, Lady Mary summoned Dr. Maitland to repeat with little Miss Wortley, now a child of three, the operation he had performed upon her brother in Constantinople. A committee of doctors was appointed to watch Dr. Maitland inoculate the child and to observe the "take." Lady Mary, characteristically, relished the conviction that her instinctive grasp of immunization was in advance of that of European medicine (as indeed it was). The mantle of martyr-to-science was not lightly to be cast aside. Lady Mary's granddaughter, Lady Louisa Stuart, more than a century later, still deemed it desirable to recall the persecutions the former had undergone at the hands of the medical profession. "We now read in grave medical biography that

the discovery was instantly hailed . . . whenever an invention or
project . . . has made its way so well by itself as to establish a certain
reputation most people are sure to find out that they always patronized it from the beginning. . . . But what says Lady Mary . . . ? Why,
that the four great physicians deputed by government to watch the
progress of her daughter's inoculation, betrayed not only incredulity
as to its success, but such unwillingness to have it succeed, such an
evident spirit of rancour and malignity, that she never cared to leave
the child alone with them one second, lest it should in some secret
way suffer from their interference."

Allowing for the fact that Lady Louisa was taken in by the familiar phenomenon of preferring persecution to recognition, it remains the case that inoculation (like Händelian opera) gained its
first acceptance by the world of fashion, rather than that of intellect.
Lady Mary's most significant ally was Caroline, Princess of Wales.
Her Highness, after arranging that condemned criminals be allowed
to volunteer for inoculation in exchange for their freedom, had two
of her daughters immunized. Other ladies of quality followed the
court's example, causing Lady Mary to write with unwonted high
spirits in June, 1723, "Lady Biny has inoculated both her children
. . . the Operation is not yet over, but I beleive they will do very well.
Since that Experiment has not yet had any ill effect, the whole Town
are doing the same thing and I am so much pull'd about and solicited
to visit people, that I am forc'd to run into the Country to hide my-
selfe."

From the country (which was, of course, "Twict'nam") Lady
Mary wrote to Lady Mar, still in Paris, of her failure to persuade their
half-sister to submit her son to inoculation. "I am sorry," she wrote
in July of 1723, "To inform you of the Death of our nephew my sister Gower's Son of the small Pox. I think she has a great deal of reason to regret it, in consideration of the offer I made her 2 year
together of taking the child home to my House where I would have
inoculated him with the same Care and safety I did my own. I know
nobody that has hitherto repented the Operation thô it has been very
troublesome to some fools who had rather be sick by the Doctor's
Prescriptions than in Health in Rebellion to the College."

Three months after this mettlesome letter, Lady Mary brought
to a close her correspondence with Pope. Her brief lines written in

October, 1723, sound an ominous note. "If you are not well enough to come hither, I will be with you to morrow morning, having something in particular to say to You."

The mystery of the bitter enmity between the lady and the poet has been a matter of endless conjecture. Sheets returned unlaundered, and a broken agreement in regard to lending a harpsichord are tangible causes often cited. Both Pope and Lady Mary, it must be objected, were historically and temperamentally far more prone to quarrel over ideas than things, even so aesthetic a thing as a harpsichord. It seems more plausible that the story of their estrangement is summed up in Lady Mary's most famous verses, written years earlier:

> Let this great maxim be my virtue's guide;
> In part she is to blame that has been try'd—
> He comes too near, that comes to be deny'd.

The "too near" that destroyed their friendship can be viewed in the light of emotion, or geography, or both. Pope had allowed himself considerable freedom in addressing a distant beloved. Upon Lady Mary's return he discovered, rather belatedly it must be admitted, that he had written himself to a point of no return. He may have tried to declare his love in the "too near" significance of Lady Mary's poem. Or the proximity to rejection and humiliation may have forced him to end an ambiguous relationship that could neither be accepted nor prolonged. His paranoid temperament made it inevitable that he should escape by his habitual avenue of hatred.

We do not know when, or how, or by whom the final rupture was effected. *The Dunciad* appeared in 1728. Pope stated in his preface that he would not refer to his numerous victims allegorically because he "judged it better to preserve them as they are, than to change them to fictitious names; by which the satire would only be multiplied, and applied to many instead of one." Pursuant to this candid scheme, Lady Mary made the first of her distasteful appearances in the guise of Lady Marie, a "sage dame, experienced in her trade" who had cheated a "hapless monsieur." The period between the undated quarrel and the publication of *The Dunciad* saw an increase in Lady Mary's family tragedies, misfortunes that Pope, in subsequent poems, did not hesitate to exploit.

Lady Mary, frustrated by lifelong impulses and endowments that could not be fulfilled in her time or class, suffered in the mid-1720s a modern affliction; Edward Junior, upon reaching adolescence, embarked upon a career of varied irregularities. He repudiated his traditions and his education to experiment with life-styles that prefigure the hippies. Like many of today's young vagabonds, he was precocious, original and independent. He possessed, as an incentive to restlessness, a talent approaching genius for languages.

This ability, which was one of his few acceptable attributes, had received powerful impetus during the Embassy months. His mother, in 1718, thus described Constantinople's polyglot population: "I live in a place that very well represents the Tower of Babel; in Pera they speak Turkish, Greek, Hebrew, Armenian, Arabic, Persian, Russian, Sclavonian, Walachian, German, Dutch, French, English, Italian, Hungarian; and, what is worse, there is ten of these languages spoke in my own family. My Grooms are Arab; my footmen French, English and Germans; my nurse an Armenian; my Housemaids Russians; halfe a dozen other servants Greeks; my steward an Italian; my Janizarys Turks, that I live in the perpetual hearing of this medley of sounds, which produces a very extrordinary Effect upon the people that are born here. They learn all these languages at the same time and without knowing any of 'em well enough to write or read in it. There is very few men, women or children here that have not the same compass of words in 5 or 6 of 'em. I know my selfe infants of 3 or 4 year old that speak Italian, French, Greek, Turkish, and Russian, which last they learn of their Nurses, who are generally of that Country. This seems allmost incredible to you, and is (in my Mind) one of the most curious things in this Country, and takes off very much from the Merit of our Ladys who set up for such extrodinary Geniuses upon the credit of some superficial knowledge of French and Italian."

His exotic childhood was a determining factor in young Edward's future. The tutors engaged upon the Wortley Montagus' return to England could not meet the boy's unusual needs. Westminster School, where he was enrolled to be groomed for an English gentleman, was viewed by the young Orientalist as "irrelevant." On two occasions he ran away, home to Twickenham where, he told later sympathizers, he was beaten, starved and locked into a cupboard. In July of 1726, Lady Mary wrote the increasingly melancholy Lady Mar that "my blessed offspring has allready made a great noise in the world. That young Rake my Son took to his Heels 'tother day and transported his person to Oxford, being in his own opinion thoroughly qualfy'd for the university. After a good deal of search we found and reduc'd him much against his Will to the humble condition of a School boy."

Young Edward's next truancies were more sophisticated. In 1727 he inaugurated a lifetime of impostures by binding himself apprentice to a fish monger. He was soon detected as he cried his wares in the London streets. He then went to sea, jumped ship in Portugal and, mastering a new language at lightning speed, disappeared in the semblance of a grape picker.

His parents advertised for him, referring to the inoculation scars on his arms. With rather more flexibility than was usual in fathers and mothers of two hundred and fifty years ago, the "Boy" was promised a kind reception and a seafaring career "if he desires it." This was the first of many solutions attempted, dropped or exchanged. Young Edward was not to be contented with gentlemanly wild oats but, long before he reached his majority, had set up for a black sheep of the inkiest persuasion.

Lady Mary's emotions during the six months of his absence comprised anger, fear and sorrow. She suggested that Lady Mar consider her anxiety in the light of "what your own would be if Dear Lady Fanny was lost." Although she did not admit it in so many words, she must have recognized in her son heredity at its most cruel. Edward Junior, with his penchant for extracurricular studies and for escapes to foreign lands, might well have seemed a caricature of the lonely bookworm of twenty years earlier, to say nothing of the runaway bride. "Don't you remember," she wrote her sister in September of 1727, "How miserable we were in the little parlor at Thorsby? We thought marrying would put us at once into possession of all we wanted. Then came being with Child etc. and you see what comes of being with Child."

In these dreary circumstances Lady Mary gave thought to the step she took twelve years later. She considered removing to the Continent, perhaps to trace her son, perhaps to escape the increasing disappointment of her marriage, or perhaps to succor her sister, who sharing her husband's exile, was fast declining into melancholia.

All three motives are suggested in the following lines: "Nothing that ever happen'd to me has touch'd me so much. I can hardly speak or write of it with tolerable temper, and I own it has chang'd mine to that degree I have a mind to cross the Water to try what Effect a new Heaven and a new Earth will have upon my Spirit. If I take this Resolution you shall hear in a few posts. There can be no situation in Life in which the conversation of my dear only Sister will not administer some comfort to me."

All rational conversation on the part of distracted Lady Mar was soon at an end. Lady Mary penned, for her sister's diversion, a sarcastic description of the coronation of George II that took place on October 11, 1727. She wrote in closing, "I have never received the long Letter you talk of, and am afraid you have only fancy'd that you writ it." Thus ended this series of letters, which exhibit the climax of Lady Mary's icily brilliant wit. It was to prove an increasingly costly talent.

A contest for the custody of Lady Mar occurred as a result of her husband's failure to obtain a pardon permitting him to return to Scotland in charge of his distraught wife. This left the way open for a prolonged quarrel between Lord Mar's brother and Lady Mar's sister, neither of whom was indifferent to the financial advantage of caring for a certified lunatic. So bitter did the accusations become that Lady Mary found herself suspected of retarding Lady Mar's recovery so that she might, in Pope's unpleasant line, profit by starving a sister.

During the years between 1728 and 1739 there occurred a deterioration in Lady Mary's fortunes that does not stop far short of Lady Mar's tragedy. The temperamental differences between impetuous wife and reserved husband had increased. Although the Wortley Montagus acted in agreement in matters pertaining to their outrageous son, they did not draw closer through so doing. Pope's including the entirely correct member for Huntingdon in his attacks on "Sappho" must have contributed to the separation of a decade hence. Their declining marriage could hardly have been sweetened by Pope's description of a quiet evening at home:

> Avidien, or his Wife (no matter which,
> For him you'll call a dog, and her a bitch)
> Sell their presented partridges, and fruits,

And humbly live on rabbits and on roots:
One half-pint bottle serves them both to dine,
And is at once their vinegar and wine.
But on some lucky day (as when they found
A lost Bank bill, or heard their Son was drowned)
At such a feast, old vinegar to spare,
Is what two souls so generous cannot bear:
Oil, though it stink, they drop by drop impart,
But souse the cabbage with a bounteous heart.

The only effective defense against such calumny would have been a silence, of which Lady Mary was temperamentally incapable. The gift of learning from experience requires a humility denied to the proud. In consequence of this lack, the most tragic of her several blind spots, Lady Mary ignored the price paid for past blunders. Pope had shrewdly studied his prey, and had counted on her worsening her dilemma. He was not disappointed. With incredible folly, she identified herself as "furious Sappho" whose suppositious lovers were "P-xed by her love or libelled by her hate." To make matters, if at all possible, worse, she asked Lord Peterborough, of the Anastasia Robinson-Senesino row, to take her part in this unseemly controversy. His Lordship was thus enabled to write the following if-the-shoe-fits reply. "Madame, I was very unwilling to have my name made use of in an affair in which I had noe concern, and therefore would not engage myself to speak to Mr. Pope, but he coming to my house the moment you went away, I gave him as exact an account as I could, of our conversation. He said to me what I had taken the Liberty to say to you, that he wondered how the Town could apply those Lines to any but some noted common woeman, that he should yett be more surprised if you should take them to your self."

Peterborough's snub predictably speeded Lady Mary on the collision course of beating Pope at his specialty of rhymed abuse. She chose as her accomplice the Vice Chamberlain to the household of George II and Queen Caroline. This was the ambiguously gendered Lord Hervey, with whom Lady Mary maintained a lifelong friendship, sturdy enough to survive her quip about humanity consisting of Men, Women and Herveys. Their attack upon Pope, entitled *Verses to the Imitator of Horace,* makes such unpleasant reading that Lady Mary's descendant-editors disagreed about including it in her collected works. The conspirators gloated over the poet's physical defects and proclaimed, quite inaccurately, that his respectable origins were "obscure." They so far forgot themselves and the standards of literary judgment as to accuse a master of satire of not knowing his craft:

> Satire should like a polish'd razor keen,
> Wound with a touch that's scarcely felt or seen:
> Thine is an oyster-knife, that hacks and hews;
> The rage, but not the talent to abuse;
> And is in *hate,* what *love* is in the stews.
> Tis the gross lust of hate, that still annoys
> Without distinction, as gross love enjoys:
> Neither to folly, nor to vice confined,
> The object of thy spleen is humankind.

Lady Louisa Stuart in her "Introductory Anecdotes" hopes that the nasty heroic couplets were chiefly of Lord Hervey's brewing and assures the reader that they will be omitted from the collected works. Her nephew, Lord Wharncliffe, seems to have possessed the realism of modern biography. He did not feel himself justified in suppressing distasteful material. Consequently, the verses remain to represent Lady Mary's shrill response to Pope's lampoons.

We do not know which of these coarse lines were written by Lord Hervey and which by Lady Mary. The object of their abuse, of course, had the last word. Pope increased his vilification of Lady Mary but reserved his most lethal couplets for her accomplice. The reading part of posterity has reason to view with regretful acceptance a quarrel that wrung from the poet the most masterful of his many rhymed revenges. It is contained in the portrait of "Sporus" from the *Epistle to Dr. Arbuthnot.* Under this intriguing sobriquet (those who chose to do so could discover that Sporus was a favorite of Nero's), the bisexual Hervey is presented as "a well-bred spaniel who contents himself with mumbling of the game he dare not bite."

Lady Mary's friendship with Lord Hervey had consequences that her family succeeded in suppressing for nearly two centuries. Through him she met, when he visited London in 1736, Francesco Algarotti. This glamorous Venetian savant belonged to the Voltaire circle and was, like him, a conspicuous guest at the court of Frederick the Great. He was handsome, brilliant and self-indulgent, with eclectic amatory tastes. He was only a year older than the increasingly disappointing young Edward. Notwithstanding the barriers of generation and temperament, Lady Mary fell wildly in love.

Although hers was a complex infatuation, it suggests a familiar pattern. She was in her upper forties, those years that have been called the now-or-never age. Her husband had proved uncongenial, her son disloyal, and young Mary was about to embark upon a marriage of which Lady Mary disapproved. She had, during the Embassy travels, noted with a not unsympathetic interest the *cicisbeo* as he trotted at his mistress's side in Vienna and Genoa. Algarotti, familiar with this convention, would be her *cavaliere servente,* the youthful lover of a disillusioned wife. Poor woman! More than years impeded her dreams of a middle-aged idyll.

Lady Mary's preference for the distant scene and the unattainable goal has already been noted, most tellingly by Rémond in his accusation that she loved none but *"les absents."* Algarotti was to prove absent in every sense of the word. Devious, elusive and versatilely sensual, he luxuriated in being pursued by Lord Hervey and by Lady Mary, both of whom he had captivated.

From the outset of their association (again the word friendship does not recommend itself), Lady Mary was the suppliant. Her first letter to Algarotti established a precedent for lamenting appointments broken and messages unanswered. In April, 1736, she set down lines that anticipate others more passionate and, it must be confessed, less dignified. "My Lady Stafford and my selfe waited for you three Hours. Three Hours of expectation is no small Tryal of Patience, and I believe some of your martyrs have been canoniz'd for suffering less. If you have repented enough to be enclin'd to ask pardon you may obtain it by comeing here tomorrow at 7 o'clock.

"Let me have a line of answer."

Algarotti was a past master at the art of playing what modern slang calls hard-to-get. He characteristically maneuvered to increase his hold over his suitors of either sex by returning to Italy during the summer of 1736. Such capricious comings and goings were to torment Lady Mary's future years. Having been long married to a man who can seldom have surprised her, she was now ripe for the fascinations of uncertainty.

During this, the first of Algarotti's many flights, Lady Mary faced squarely the fact that she was making a fool of herself. She went a long step further. She admitted to herself, and to Algarotti, that he would have preferred a male lover. She had often lamented the limitations placed upon women in terms of intellect. To be separated from her beloved by her being "made to wear skirts" was a dilemma for which her feminist instincts suggested no solution. She concluded an impassioned letter thus:

> Why was my haughty soul to woman joyn'd?
> Why this soft sex impos'd upon my mind?
> Even this extravagance which now I send
> Were meritorious in the name of Freind.
> Thee I might follow, thee my Lovely Guide
> Charm'd with thy voice, and ever by thy side,
> Nor Land, nor sea, our Common way divide.

Neither Lady Mary's past elopement nor her present frustrated passion lent her wisdom in the case of her daughter's marriage. Young Mary married in 1736 John Stuart, Earl of Bute. Her parents, little dreaming that this impecunious peer and avid gardener would one day be the most powerful man in the kingdom, grudgingly consented and dismissed their child to live on short rations in Scotland. Thus did "My Dear Child," by virtue of her absence, and that of her mother, become the central figure of Lady Mary's last letters.

Another important correspondent emerged in the late 1730s. This was Lady Pomfret. To her Lady Mary wrote the same kind of satirical vignettes of London that she had formerly devised for the amusement of Lady Mar. The most diverting (and the most bigoted) of these is her account of the marriage of Lady Harriet Herbert to the famous tenor, John Beard. Contrary to Lady Mary's gossip, posterity does not associate Beard with "farces at Drury Lane" but rather with the oratorios of Händel. Of this supposed misalliance Lady Mary was at her most disagreeable: "—since the lady was capable of such amours I did not doubt if this was broke off she would bestow her person and fortune on some hackney coachman or chairman; and that I really saw no method of saving *her* from ruin, and her *family* from dishonour but by poisoning her; and offered to be at the expense of the arsenic and even to administer it with my hands. . . ." Still smarting from Lady Bute's unforeseeably brilliant marriage, she continued, "They carried Lady Harriet to Twickenham though I told them it was a bad air for girls."

Lord Wharncliffe, in the 1837 edition of Lady Mary's *Letters and Works,* added a shuddering footnote to the effect that John Beard was of "indifferent character," an erroneous opinion he retracted in the edition of 1861. It remains only to be said that this great tenor was to excel in a world of superlative singers, a consideration that would not have found favor with Lady Mary, nor any other Georgian or Victorian aristocrat.

A major part of Lady Mary's printed poems and essays were written during the London years when she lived within speaking (or not speaking) distance of friends and enemies. A handful of these works appeared, usually anonymously, during her lifetime. These included, of course, the attempted retaliation upon Pope. A far happier example of her talents is the lovely poem written at Pera, discussed earlier in this chapter. Shortly after the return from Constantinople, the kinsman to whom she had sent these verses permitted them to be included in Hammond's *A New Miscellany of Original Poems,* published in 1720. She was to lament many years later that her lines had been "miserably printed." Her longing for literary recognition must, however, have been assuaged by Hammond's use of her name, in company with Prior and Pope. She had advanced from the *Town Eclogues* period of four years earlier when Curll had called her a mere "lady of quality."

Lady Mary's poetry won a prestigious admirer. Voltaire, in a letter written in 1733, asked for "les vers de mylady Mary Montaigu." This request has puzzled Theodore Besterman, the distinguished Voltaire scholar. Clearly not knowing of Hammond's Miscellany, he supplies a footnote to his edition of Voltaire's *Correspondance* in which he states that "it is a little surprising that Voltaire knew the verses of Lady Mary Wortley Montagu; a single volume had appeared and this occurred in 1716 entitled Court Poems; the work was rebaptized Town Eclogues."

Voltaire's philosophy did not preclude the concocting of unabashed flattery. He found it appropriate to quote from Lady Mary's Pera verses in a letter written in 1736 to Falkener, the then British Ambassador to the Porte. He chose as his vehicle for extravagant compliment the lines quoted earlier in this chapter that describe the Vizier's procession to the "dread divan." Voltaire's use of these lines raises doubts as to his ability to comprehend English poetry, doubts that are notoriously confirmed by his abuse of Shakespeare.

To Falkener, whom he had with ineffable condescension honored as "the honest, the good and simple Philosopher of Wandsworth," he continued thus to misread Lady Mary: "I would not admire, as sais mylady Mary Wortley"

> The visier proud distinguish'd from the rest.
> Six slaves in gay attire his bridle hold,
> His bridles rich with gemms, his stirrup gold?

"For how the devil should i admire a slave upon a horse? My friend Fawkener i should admire."

Others found Lady Mary's verses of use in their own concerns. Among them was Lord William Hamilton, who had received amatory verses from the Countess of Hertford, a woman many years his senior. Little dreaming that she would soon find herself enslaved by a man young enough to be her son, Lady Mary, in 1733, armed Lord William with the lines that in three years' time were to be painfully pertinent to her own dilemma. Lady Hertford was Lady Mary's warm admirer. This explains the extreme candor of the last stanza:

> That you're in a terrible taking
> By all these sweet oglings I see:
> But the fruit that can fall without shaking,
> Indeed is too mellow for me.

A year after Algarotti made his fateful inroads upon her emotions, the Wortley Montagu marriage had dwindled to such an extent that Lady Mary did not hesitate to differ in print, although in anonymous print, with her husband in matters political. Mr. Wortley was all his life a Whig but, in that he was never a Walpole supporter, an Opposition Whig. His refusal to fall in line with the Prime Minister placed severe limitations on his career.

Lady Mary's resentment of these limitations becomes evident by her joining, in 1737, the freelance journalists who played so contentious a part in Georgian life. Because the Opposition organ was called *Common Sense* she named her one-woman newspaper *The Nonsense of Common Sense,* thus suggesting endorsement of Walpole. This paper, she assured her readers, would continue as long as they felt like reading it and she like writing it, a state of affairs that came to an end in a year.

The most important of these papers in included in both the 1837 and 1861 editions of the *Collected Letters and Works.* It contains an eloquent and dignified statement of Lady Mary's feminist creed. A companion piece, also in the *Collected Letters and Works,* is an essay in French written a decade earlier. Here Lady Mary took issue with La Rochefoucault's maxim that some marriages are convenient but none delicious. These two essays, taken with her girlhood letter to Bishop Burnet, set aside the worldly wit in favor of the disappointed idealist. They do more. They place Lady Mary squarely in the Judeo-Christian ethic, a position thoroughly inconsistent with her stylish skepticism. In her contrary character, orthodoxy, skepticism and amorality may be said not so much to combine, as to collide.

The Age of Reason, like today's "Age of Aquarius," cultivated, though for different motives, a contempt for fidelity in marriage. Lady Mary, in her refutation of La Rochefoucault's cynical maxim, revealed herself capable of what can only be called spiritual values. She viewed, as indeed she should have, husband and wife as married lovers, a theory not widely held or admired in the world of "marriage à la mode." Her summation of the duties and privileges of the married state are variations on the vows she and Edward had repeated so many years ago. Viewed in the light of their bankrupt union, these lines are as wistful as they are idealistic. "The smallest details of economy become noble and delicate when they are lighted by sentiments of tenderness. To furnish a room is not to furnish a room—it is rather to adorn a place where I await my Lover; to order supper is not simply to give orders to my cook—it is to amuse myself with delighting him I love: these necessary occupations as seen by one who loves are pleasures a thousand times more lively and touching than the shows and the gambling that constitute the happiness of those incapable of real love."

The article from *The Nonsense of Common Sense* that is contained in her *Collected Letters and Works* gives us, as in her long-ago letter to Bishop Burnet, Lady Mary as an idealist despite herself. She resented all her life the low esteem in which woman's character and intelligence were held. She returned to the theory set forth in her youth that we respond to what is expected of us. A pretty girl programmed to win admiration by physical, rather than intellectual, charms is well on her way to becoming a vapid woman. She was far too much in earnest for her usual raillery in stating that "Among the most universal errors, I reckon that of treating the weaker sex with a contempt which has a very bad influence on their conduct. How many of them think it excuse enough to say they are women, to indulge any folly that comes into their heads."

Middle-aged Lady Mary took occasion in this spirited paper to modify her earlier, and questionably sincere, statement that women are a lower order of creation. "As much greatness of mind may be shown in submission as in command; and some women have suffered a life of hardship with as much philosophy as Cato traversed the deserts of Africa. . . ."

It says a great deal for Lady Mary's generosity that she did not, as have some of today's feminists, decry family obligations in which she had failed, and been failed. She is to be admired for her loyalty to a code it would have been very easy to mock. "A lady who has performed her duty as a daughter, a wife, and a mother, raises in me as much veneration as Socrates or Xenophon; and much more than I would pay either to Julius Caesar or Cardinal Mazarine, though the first was the most famous enslaver of his country; and the last the most successful plunderer of his master."

It is one thing to formulate principles; it is another to put them into lifelong practice. By the time Lady Mary wrote her correct, not to say noble, tribute to woman's domestic dedications, she was doing so in a spirit of renunciation. She had tried and she had failed. Ten years earlier, in the agony caused by her son's flight, she had given thought to going abroad in search of a new heaven and a new earth. She now returned to this plan without recognizing in it all the hints of a new hell. She proposed to follow Algarotti to Italy.

Lady Mary's infatuation with Algarotti is recorded in a series of love letters written from the summer of 1736 to that of 1739. From the pen of a woman who believed herself to be the acme of worldly wisdom, they make exasperating reading; a schoolgirl should have known better. She confessed herself reduced to timidity in the face of her passion for the elusive stranger. She apologized lest her letters annoy him and she was ready to faint when her tormentor replied. Even in the fire of these extravagances, she did not forget the literary allusions suitable in wooing a savant. These took the form of likening herself to sad Dido (only, she assures her wandering Aeneas, a thousand times more to be pitied). She reinforced this symbolism with a quotation from Virgil and added, beside the date (10 Sept. 1736), "minuit passé."

Most of these outpourings succeed in being simultaneously beautiful and embarrassing. Their tone of grovelling ardor explains why her descendants, like those of Boswell (again for different reasons) delayed their publication for a century after the appearance of her *Collected Letters and Works.* The letters are in large part written in French. Her distracted frame of mind is indicated by the fact that the errors in grammar and syntax that occasionally marked her excursions into that language are multiplied. She apologized for the bad French "que j'écrive" and feared, with good reason, that Algarotti would laugh over her letters with some "belle Parisienne." (Here she was being optimistic.) She was finally reduced to asking Lord Hervey if he had heard from him they both loved. It must have been small comfort to be answered in the affirmative.

Lady Mary first suggested joining Algarotti abroad some six months after he left London. In December of 1736 she sent him her picture and wrote, "If you seriously wish to see me, it will certainly happen; if your affairs do not permit your return to England, mine shall be arrang'd in such a manner as I may come to Italy."

Thus did Lady Mary commit herself to twenty-three years of futile wanderings from city to city. Her reckless suggestion was followed by months of apparent silence. No letters to or from Algarotti exist for the period, during which she diverted herself with *The Nonsense of Common Sense.*

Her correspondence with her "little Aeneas" begins again in February of 1738. She had now arrived at the point of rationalizing her removal to the Continent. London exemplified everything she hated: "Noise, crowd, Division . . . Infection." As if these external nuisances were not enough, she threw in "a cursed tooth ach." It was not, perhaps, the most skillful note to sound while she implored the "Lovely Youth" to "tune my soul to Love."

Lady Mary included in her letters to Lady Pomfret who, like Algarotti, was on the Continent, many of the same complaints. English weather, politics and society were equally deplorable. What with young Mary's marriage to Lord Bute and her own erotic frustrations, she was in no mood to consider tolerantly the matches occurring among the younger members of her acquaintance; her bitter account of Lady Harriet Herbert's union with John Beard was only one, if the most brutal, of such condemnations.

By May of 1739 Lady Mary was projecting her flight. In setting out to pursue Algarotti, she planned to make use of dear Lady Pomfret's being abroad. She fabricated a not entirely insincere camouflage by writing to her distant friend to thank her for a recent letter. She found it timely to state that "you have given me so great an inclination to see Italy once more, that I have serious thoughts of setting out the latter end of this summer. And what the remembrance of all the charms of music, sculpture, painting, architecture & even the sun itself could not do, the knowledge that Lady Pomfret is there has effected."

Although she had knowledge of Lady Pomfret's whereabouts, she often did not know those of Algarotti. She wrote him in July to tell him that she had resolved to join her life to his. Her choice of French for this fateful letter betrayed her into a prophetic blunder that she would not have committed in English. She commenced her letter with, "Je pars pour vous chercher" (I leave to seek you). She did not write—and the difference is noteworthy—"pour vous trouver" (to find you). Lady Mary was to learn, to her cost, that between seeking Algarotti and finding him stretched a dreary wasteland of duplicity and evasion. She wrote him again on the eve of her departure from Dover, likening her decision to a profession of faith. "I leave tomorrow with the Resolution of a man well persuaded of his Religion, clear of conscience and filled with faith and hope. I leave my friends weeping my loss and I bravely dare the step to another world. If I find you to be such as you have vowed, I find the Elysian Fields of Felicity beyond imagining; if. . . . But I wish no more doubts and at least I prefer to enjoy my hopes. If you desire to recompense me for all I sacrifice hurry to find me in Venice where I shall arrive as soon as I can."

This letter is also in French. Again Lady Mary's subconscious led her into a significant interchange of "chercher" and "trouver." She is to be found and he to be sought.

Pursuant to this pattern, Lady Mary proceeded obediently to Venice. Algarotti, who had returned (with her financial help) to London in the early spring of 1739, had, according to her letters, encouraged her flight and had settled upon Venice for their irregular honeymoon. She was inured to the idea of his "other attachments" and declared she would turn a blind eye upon them. While he was in England, he agreed with Lord Baltimore, who, like himself and Hervey, found men and women equally alluring, to travel by yacht to St. Petersburg for a state function. The two young men were in no hurry to end their luxurious trip. Thus, as Lady Mary made her way through France, over the Alps and across Italy to Venice, Algarotti and Lord Baltimore, the Russian visit over, went to Potsdam to pay their respects to the future Frederick the Great. The Crown Prince and Algarotti were immediately entranced with one another, the latter being ear-marked for the "Academy" that the former planned to found in imitation of the French salon—along, of course, stag party lines. Algarotti, characteristically, postponed his obligations to "sad Dido" while he cultivated a glittering future at the Prussian court. His next move was worse than frivolous or opportunistic; it was cruel. He returned to London just as Lady Mary arrived in Venice.

It is evident that Lady Mary's passion for Algarotti sprang in large part from escape mechanism. Having dared a marriage that failed, why not, she may have daydreamed, risk a reckless liaison? Doing violence to her self-respect may have seemed preferable to the chill of Wortley's reserve or the scandals fabricated by Pope. Had she left her family solely to pursue an undignified escapade, she would probably have returned to England at its conclusion. The fact that she never saw Wortley again, and that their letters to one another discuss in sober detail family matters having often to do with expense and their son's eccentricities, suggest that their separation had been planned and accepted with no evidence of rancor.

Lady Mary went to great pains to conceal from Wortley and Lady Pomfret the existence of Algarotti. In writing to her husband she frequently cited health as the motive for her travels. This minor deception may well have been intended to throw posterity off her track, an objective in which she and her descendants succeeded. The eighteenth century took "air" very seriously, Lady Mary finding that of Burgundy especially salubrious. She was cheered in spirit by noting that the French peasantry, whom she had seen during the famine years following the War of the Spanish Succession, were now plump and well clothed.

Lady Mary not only stressed improvement to health of body and mind, she went out of her way to convince Wortley that Venice was a spontaneous destination. While staying in Turin she had learned, apparently just by chance, that "next to Rome the best place to stay in Italy is, without contradiction, Venice." Fortunately for the wife of a Whig M.P., the presence in Rome of the Old Pretender and his entourage could be made to rule out the Eternal City. She made it clear to Wortley that her arrival at her Mecca of Love was impromptu by writing very plausibly, "I am at length happily arrived here, I thank God. I wish it had been my original Plan, which would have saved me some money and fatigue, thô I have not much reason to regret the last, since I am convinc'd it has greatly contributed to the Restoration of my Health."

Venetian society had none of the prejudice against female intellect that so deeply marked the England of Lady Mary's day. She was accorded the sort of reception proper for a woman of her rank and ability. That this was the case was owing initially to her old friend, Abbé Conti, whose visits were followed by those of the "French, Imperial, Neapolitan and Spanish Ambassador and his Lady." Hostilities between England and Spain broke out in October of 1739. The conflict in due time grew into the War of the Austrian Succession, with France again assuming the role of England's traditional opponent. These considerations did not deter Lady Mary from basking in the hospitality of enemy embassies. During the eighteenth century alliances formed and reformed as rapidly as they have in the twentieth. Persons of quality kept cosmopolitan communications intact, knowing that yesterday's foe might be encountered at tomorrow's assembly. Lady Mary, exemplifying this useful detachment, wrote Wortley that she "desir'd to be thought quite neutral in all national Quarrels." The war would bring, as wars do, inconveniences. Her household goods must be shipped before French privateers became a threat. She feared that because she had so often been the object of scandal she might be taken for one of the "innumerable little dirty spies about all English." And then, at her most inconsistent, she suggested to Wortley that she send him "what she can hear amongst the Foreign Ministers" who were, of course, her hosts. Wortley thought well enough of this suggestion to urge that she send pertinent news not "in your own hand but your maid's, or some merchantlike hand. —If I could have any good intelligence from abroad it might be of use to me in many respects."

Lady Mary's first of several visits to Venice lasted from September of 1739 to August of 1740. During these months she awoke to the fact that her proposed liaison with Algarotti was a mirage. His conquest of Crown Prince Frederick ended the extremely remote likelihood of his keeping faith with self-styled Dido. A summons from Potsdam, Algarotti doubtless reasoned, would be more promptly sent if he associated with Lord Hervey rather than Lady Mary. She pressed her case by sending to her London rival tempting descriptions of the delights of Venice and of her popularity there, hoping to win back her triply wandering Aeneas. Hervey did honor to her letters by writing that "Your Descriptions of Venice are delightfull. Cagnioletti (sic) never drew any Views of it half so amusing; I prefer your mezzotintos to all the Arts of his colouring." Then, lest she think he had permitted Algarotti to read her blandishments, Hervey continued innocently, "Our Friend is in London; he dined with me to day. I did not say I had hear'd from you, because you gave me no Directions to do so—."

Lady Mary wrote an admirably tart letter to Algarotti on Christmas Eve, 1739. She declared herself quite unable to believe that he had received none of her letters and asked if he imagined she ran about Europe simply to assist at carnivals. It is to be regretted that three months later she retreated from this spirited attitude. In March of 1740 she was once more the suppliant. She reminded the treacherous charmer that Venice was his suggestion, adding that she preferred it to London and that she had made a place for herself among its dominoed aristocrats. All this the deluded woman offered to sacrifice for his pleasure and his company by following him to any city his caprice dictated. Having placed herself at his disposal, she remained in Venice to await instructions which never came.

Being thus courted by was the wine of Algarotti's caddish life. Predictably, Frederick carried the day. Hervey chose to inform Lady Mary of Algarotti's departure in a letter that carried a double snub. He refused, on Walpole's behalf, Lady Mary's offer to supply foreign intelligence. After expressing what she later called "cold thanks," Hervey concluded, in a possessive vein, "I am at present in great Affliction for the Loss of my Friend Algarotti, who left England last Friday for the Court of Berlin on a Sumons he received from the new King of Prussia, and a very kind one, under his own Hand, before he had been five Days on the throne."

The blow had fallen. That she knew it as such can be inferred from the deterioration of Lady Mary's French, emotion having an unsettling effect upon her command of that language. Hervey's unwelcome announcement of Algarotti's exalted prospects arrived in July of 1740. A month later Lady Mary wrote the savant-become-courtier a reproachful but ungrammatical letter. French syntax again laid a Freudian trap. "J'ai peur," she wrote, "que vostre grande visite est destinée à une grande sotte." ("I fear that your visit is destined for a great folly.") That she mistook the word for fool (and a female fool to boot) for the word for folly was a revealing error.

Algarotti's promotion to Frederick's inner circle at Sans Souci had an immediate effect upon Lady Mary's plans. Freed from the necessity of awaiting him or his commands, she was now able to join Lady Pomfret, the project which originally served as an alibi for her illusory tryst in Venice.

It had not been difficult to conceal from Wortley in England the Algarotti fiasco. Lady Pomfret, who was supposedly her *but de promenade,* posed a problem. Lady Mary's first strategy was to attempt to persuade her friend to exchange Siena for Venice. She dwelt eloquently upon the brilliance and cheapness of public life, commenting as well upon the prevailing absence of gossip. Could it be that the writer of those deliciously wicked letters to Lady Mar penned the following improving sentiments? "And it is so much the established fashion for everybody to live in their own way, that nothing is more ridiculous than censuring the actions of another. This would be terrible in London where we have little other diversion; but for me, who have never found any pleasure in malice, I bless my destiny that has conducted me to a part where people are better employed than in talking of the affairs of their acquaintance."

The splendors that characterized the Queen of the Adriatic were increased by a state visit from the Electoral Prince of Saxony. Here was a circumstance perfectly suited to Lady Mary's procrastinations. To Lady Pomfret, who was beginning to doubt the sincerity of her friend, Lady Mary thus rationalized: "The Prince of Saxony is expected here in a few days and has taken a palace exactly over against my house. As I had the honour to be particularly well acquainted (if one may use that phrase) with his mother when I was at Vienna I believe I cannot be dispensed with from appearing at some of the conversations which I hear he intends to hold."

His Electoral Highness obligingly remained in Venice all winter. It is interesting to compare Lady Mary's accounts of this brilliant season with the Embassy Letters of so many years ago. Her present humiliation proved as effective a literary stimulus as had the happy curiosity of her months in Adrianople and Constantinople. Faced with the necessity of saving face with husband and friend, she created a series of charming scenes that merited Hervey's commendation.

The great families of Italy were well known to the travelled English. Lady Mary, doubtless for this reason, wrote of ceremonies and social life rather than personalities. She continued indifferent to the history of art, architecture and music, going so far as to supply the Gothic cathedral at Milan with a dome. She went occasionally to the opera but, to posterity's loss, failed to report the work performed. She did little better by the famous girls of the *Incurabili,* whose musical needs were supplied by the greatest of Venetian composers. She wrote in March of 1740, "Last night there was a Consort of voices and Instruments at the Hospital of the Incurabili, where there are 2 Girls that in the Opinion of all people excel either Faustina or Cuzoni." For a detailed account of these mysterious invalids, musicology turns to Dr. Burney's travels of thirty years later.

Lady Mary sent to Wortley a splendid account of the Regatta of May 4, 1740. It is in a class with her procession scenes written from Turkey twenty-three years earlier. "You seem to mention the Regata in a manner as if you would be pleas'd with a Description of it. It is a race of Boats; they are accompany'd by vessells which they call Piotes and Bichones, that are built at the Expence of the nobles and strangers that have a mind to display their magnificence. They are a sort of Machines, adorn'd with all that sculpture and gilding can do to make a shineing appearance. Several of them cost £1,000 sterling and I believe none less than 500. They are row'd by Gondoliers dress'd in rich Habits suitable to what they represent. There was enough of them to look like a little Fleet, and I own I never saw a finer sight. It would be too long to describe every one in particular; I shall only name the principal. The Signora Pisani Mocenigo's represented the chariot of the night, drawn by 4 sea Horses, and showing the rising of the moon accompany'd with stars, the statues on each side representing the hours to the number of 24, row'd by Gondoliers in rich Liveries, which were chang'd 3 times, all of equal richness; and the decorations chang'd also to the dawn of Aurora and the midday Sun, the statues being new dress'd every time, the first in green, the 2nd time red, and the last blue, all equally lac'd with silver, there being 3 Races. Signor Soranzo represented the Kingdom of Poland with all the provinces and Rivers in that Dominions, with a consort of the best instrumental music in rich Polish Habits; the painting and gilding were exquisite in their kinds. Signor (Simoni) Contarini's Piote shew'd the Liberal Arts; Apollo was seated on the stern upon Mount Parnasso, Pegasus behind, and the muses seated round him. Opposite was a figure representing painting, with Fame blowing her Trumpet, and on each side Sculpture and music in their proper dresses. The Procurator Foscarini's was the chariot of Flora, guided by Cupids and adorn'd with all sorts of Flowers, rose trees, etc.

"Signor Julio Contarini represented the Triumphs of Valour; Victory was in the Stern, and all the Ornaments warlike Trophys of every kind. Signor Correri's was the Adriatic Sea receiving into her Arms the Hope of Saxony. Signor Alviso Mocenigo's was the Garden of Hesperides. The whole Fable was represented by different Statues. Signor Querini had the chariot of Venus drawn by Doves, so well done they seem'd realy to fly upon the water; the Loves and Graces attended her.

"Signor Paul Dona had the chariot of Diana, who appear'd Hunting in a large wood, the trees, hounds, Stag, and Nymphs all done naturally, the Gondoliers dress'd like peasants attending the chase, and Endimion lying under a large Tree gazing on the Goddess.

"Signor Angelo Labbia represented Poland crowning of Saxony, waited on by the Virtues and subject provinces. Signor Vicenzo Morosini's Piote shew'd the Triumphs of Peace, discord being chain'd at her Feet, and she surrounded with the Pleasures, etc.

"I beleive you are allready weary of this description, which can give you but a very imperfect Idea of the show. . . . I can get no better Ink here, thô I have try'd several times, and it is a great vexation to me to want it."

The letters in which Lady Mary regaled Mr. Wortley with Venetian ceremonies contain many references to their children. They do not, by today's standards, reveal her as a talented mother. In her defense it must be remembered that idealism in educating and protecting children is a very recent goal. English society has always taken its cue in morals, or the lack of them, from the royal family. The first four Georges provided an appalling example of family hostilities; the generation gap of their time consisted of the parents' rejection of the child, rather than the reverse exhibited by today's counterculture. In accordance with these destructive customs, Lady Mary allowed herself six years to forgive her daughter for a love match that was in every way a suitable marriage. Three years after the union of Miss Wortley and Lord Bute, the affronted mother was capable of the following combination of pique and self-deception: "she has been the passion of my Life and in a great measure the cause of all my ill Health." Lady Mary's next mention of their supposedly erring daughter is still more severe. Writing her husband in January of 1740, she regretted that "your Daughter continues troubling you concerning me. She cannot believe . . . that it is possible to persuade me of any real Affection and all beside it is an affectation that is better left off now. Decency no longer exacts it." After a few more strictures having, for reasons of history, more to do with "the regard due to a Parent" than with the loyalty owed to a child, Lady Mary moderated her anger. She relented to the extent of proposing to write Lady Bute because Mr. Wortley desired it. A month later a reconciliation was suggested by "whatever reason I have to complain of my Daughter's behaviour, I shall allways wish her well and if it was in my power to give her any solid mark of it I would do it, and shall ever be of that Opinion."

Distance worked its familiar magic with Lady Mary. Lady Bute, now enshrined among *les absentes,* was increasingly an epistolary confidante. The letters sent by mother to daughter suggest, probably by design, Mme. de Sévigné's correspondence with the absent Mme. de Grignan, Lady Mary having for years cultivated a posthumous rivalry with her great French predecessor. She possessed the knack of timely forgetfulness and, making use of it, she penned in 1742 a masterpiece of fence-mending. Mr. Wortley must have been startled to read that "You give Lord Bute the character I allways believ'd belonged to him from the first of our Acquaintance, and the opinion I had of his Honesty (which is the most Essential Quality) made me *so easily* [italics added] consent to the match. The faults I observ'd in his temper I told my Daughter at that time. She made answer . . .

that she did not dislike them. I have nothing to desire of her; I never wish'd anything but her affection. . . . I have allways answer'd her Letters very regularly, and if she shews them to you, you will see in them nothing but kindness. . . ."

It is to be regretted that Lady Mary's early letters to "My Dear Child" do not exist. The reason for their disappearance is not hard to surmise. She had blundered in her estimation of her son-in-law's potential. Lady Bute may have preferred to destroy the evidence of a mother's opposition to a husband. Later editors who, like Lord Wharncliffe and Lady Louisa Stuart, were not only Lady Mary's descendants, but also those of Lord Bute, must have experienced conflicting loyalties to both sides of the family. These considerations may, or may not, account for a silence that lasts until 1746.

Lady Mary's letters to her husband about their erratic son make disagreeable reading. When she set out on her wanderings, young Edward was skulking in Holland under the attempted supervision of one Gibson. His debts had made him liable to imprisonment elsewhere. He chafed at being confined at the provincial town of Ysselstein because, as Lady Mary reported to Mr. Wortley, "he says that there is no Temptation to Riot and he would shew how able he is to resist it." In addition to mountainous debts, he was encumbered by a wife of low origins who was years older than he, a circumstance that did not deter him from offering to marry a second wife of his parents' choice.

Freudian speculation suggests that it was not by chance that the mother of a licentious son should fall in love with a youth of equally bad character. There are resemblances between Algarotti and Edward Junior; there are also discrepancies. The former may be said to have misbehaved to a purpose; the latter to none. Algarotti was capable of laying a devious course and of advancing himself by shady steps. He lacked morals but not rationality. On the other hand, Edward scrambled from scrape to scrape with no thought of consequences to himself or others. The eighteenth-century standard for wild oats was a spacious one. Living beyond one's means, risking ancestral acres on the throw of dice, living abroad (as were the Pomfrets) to escape one's creditors—all this was part of patrician privilege. To these permissible irregularities Edward added a fault that his mother could less easily forgive. He was a fool. "His offering to marry while his wife is alive," wrote Lady Mary, "is a proofe of his way of thinking."

For her son's lack of principle and commonsense, his mother felt contempt rather than guilt. He was, as far as she was concerned, without a redeeming quality, a state of affairs for which she was not prepared to assume responsibility. She went so far as to disown him. She learned, shortly before her postponed reunion with Lady Pomfret, "that my Son has several considerable Debts in Italy, particularly at this Place, but as he kept himselfe altogether in low Company he did not pass for my Son. The Procurator Grimani ask'd me once if a young man that was here was of your Family, bearing the same name. I said slightly I knew nothing of him, and he reply'd that he had allways suppos'd from his behaviour that he was some sharper that had assum'd that name to get credit. I was glad to have it pass over in this manner to avoid being daily dunn'd by his creditors. . . . If he should come where I am, I know no remedy but running away myself."

We remember that Lady Mary often found occasion to reproach her son with his inability to tell the truth. In her letters to her husband she sometimes deceived him by failing to tell the whole story, but she was never guilty of a deliberate falsehood. Her lying to Grimani indicates an inferior parental code.

The esteem in which Lady Mary's letters are rightly held has blinded her admirers to her shortcomings as a mother. A case in point is furnished by a communication from her son received on the eve of her departure from Venice. The letter has been called absurd. An absurd person may write a sensible letter. On August 1, 1740, Edward Junior did so.

He proposed joining Lady Mary during her travels. By acting as companion and escort, he would be constantly under her eye and, by making himself useful, he would make reparation for past misconduct. His suggestion was, of course, not disinterested, but a man must be taken for what he is, rather than what he is not. Lady Mary is to be pardoned for reading into the following lines promise of exotic expenditures: "I should have no occasion for any allowance att all since everything would be att Your Ladyship's disposal." His reference to the "Happiness of being continually near so tender a Mother" was the sort of insincere flourish to which letter writers of

the Age of Reason were addicted. Allowing for these slips—if slips
they were—Edward's half-hearted attempts at reconciliation with his
mother merited being taken seriously by her, and by posterity. His
career as Prodigal Son had been impressive. Whether or not his
belated offer of reform was only a prelude to further escapades must
remain unknown. Lady Mary chose to think so. The next move was
hers and she made it in the negative. From now on his meager sense
of filial loyalty was reduced, and not without his mother's doing.

Dismissing the proposed reconciliation from her thoughts, Lady
Mary pressed for departure to Florence. Crossing the Apennines was
complicated by the fact that she had a swollen face and was accompanied by married servants who had become parents only two weeks
previously. Upon arriving at the Pomfret's *palazzo,* she forwarded
Edward's letter to his father with condemnatory comments. "I send
you the enclos'd from your Son to show what simple projects he is
capable of, but as he appears in the Intention of being submissive, I
hope the Letter I shall write to him this post will prevent his coming near me."

Lady Mary's removal from Venice to Florence opened a new
chapter in her wanderings. She was, in place of the tryst Algarotti
continued to deny her, faced with a solitary future. During the
twenty-two years of her remaining life span, she was to write masterly
letters, to read voraciously, to make a few friends and to try her
hand at housekeeping in numerous residences. However, the rootless
years had begun, as she exchanged one city for another, remaining
always an exile in a cosmopolitan wilderness.

Lady Mary spent the late summer and early fall with the Pom-
frets in Florence. Her visit to them gave rise to her being more writ-
ten against than writing. A new adversary was at hand to take up
Alexander Pope's cudgels. For all her supposed shrewdness, Lady
Mary failed to recognize in him an eloquent enemy; this was Horace
Walpole.

The Prime Minister's son, recently come of age, was making the
Grand Tour with his protegé and recent schoolmate at Eton,
Thomas Gray. The two young men had allocated the summer of
1740 to be spent under the wing of Horace Mann, Walpole's cousin,
who was for many years English Resident at Florence. A reason often
cited for Walpole's vilification of Lady Mary was the friendship be-

tween her and Maria Skerret, his father's former mistress and later his second wife. Lady Mary, during her Twickenham days, was widely supposed to be forwarding the liaison of "Moll" Skerret and Sir Robert. That Horace Walpole believed this to be the case may be inferred from his dubbing his victim "Moll Worthless." Whatever his motives, his reports of Lady Mary's appearance and conduct are both savage and scandalous. Walpole, like Pope and Lady Mary herself, relished condemnation. He drew his characters, as did they, to divert rather than depict. In keeping with this habit, he cast Lady Mary in the role of sluttish pedant before she arrived from Venice. She was pronounced a "she-meteor" who, pretending to knowledge of philosophy and classical authors, was an expert only in debauchery. He drew heavily on Pope for subsequent material by emphasizing personal slovenliness and morals as soiled as her clothes. Her swollen face, which she herself mentioned, he put down to a "social disease" and he threw in, for good measure, "The half she yet retains of nose." The portrait is completed by accusing her of cheating at cards. These libels would not be worth repeating had they not played their part in fixing the frustrated expatriate in the unspecified character of a dirty demimondaine.

Little suspecting that she had been done unto as she had done unto others, Lady Mary, her two-month stay in Florence over, moved on to Rome. She took the precaution of letting Algarotti know where he could send those elusive commands by which she remained willing to regulate her travels.

She arrived in Rome at a significant period. In August of 1740 Cardinal Lambertini of Bologna had become Pope Benedict XIV. It is to Lady Mary's credit that her mistrust of Christianity, and of Catholicism in particular, did not blind her to the merits of this great Pope whose ideas about female intellect and preventive medicine satisfied even her progressive standards. Rome, at the time of his election, was in the grip of an inflation that recalled the "French Mississippi" of dreadful (and varied) memory. His Holiness, like so many of today's statesmen, viewed the runaway cost of living as the first item on his agenda. As Lady Mary put it in a letter to Wortley dated November, 1740, "there is literally no money in the whole Town, where they follow Mr. Law's System and live wholly upon Paper. . . . They go to market with paper, pay the Lodgings with paper and, in short, there is no Specie to be seen, which raises the prices of every thing to the utmost extravagance. . . . It is said that the Present Pope (who has a very good character) has declared he will endeavor a remedy thô it is very difficult to find one. He was bred a Lawyer and has Pass'd the greatest part of his Life in that proffession and is so sensible of the misery of the State that he is reported to have said that he never thought himselfe in want till his Elevation." Lady Mary's next comment about the new Pope can be understood only in the light of that sometime Vatican virus, family interest. In writing her husband that "He has no Relations that he takes any notice of" she was distinguishing him from sundry nephew- and in-law-exploited predecessors.

Lady Mary's continental sojourn was to outlast the reign of Benedict XIV by some five years. Although her letters give no indication that they ever met, she proved herself extremely perceptive to his merits, writing to Wortley in February of 1741 that "The present Pope is very much belov'd, and seems desirous to ease the people and deliver them out of the miserable poverty they are reduc'd to. I will send you the history of his Elevation as I had it from a very good hand, if it will be any amusement to you." Considering Lady Mary's flair for pageantry, it is to be regretted that this is the last we hear of the Elevation or the good hand.

Lady Mary, having by the late fall of 1740 sampled Venice, Florence and Rome, now considered Naples. She arrived there at a dramatic time. Herculaneum had recently been discovered. In the absence of as yet unknown techniques of archeology, the first diggings were disastrous. To Wortley, who had encouraged her trip to Naples, Lady Mary described the confusion. "I have taken all possible pains to get information of this Subterranean Building and am told 'tis the remains of the ancient City of Hercolana, and by what I can collect there was A Theatre entire with all the Scenes and ancient Decorations. They have broke it to pieces by digging irregularly." And again, a few days later from Rome, "I return'd hither last night after six weeks stay at Naples; great part of that time was vainly taken up in endeavoring to satisfy your Curiosity and my own in Relation to the late discover'd Town of Hercolana." Naples was at this time under Spanish domination. Lady Mary, having earlier written favorably of "Spanish honour," considered them rapacious custodians of the past. "The Court in General is more barbarous than any of the ancient Goths; one proofe of it, amongst many others was melting down a Beautifull Copper Statue of a vestal found in this new Ruin, to make Medalions for the late Solemn Christening."

During her second Roman stay, Lady Mary once more sat for her portrait and was again unconscious that her likeness was being taken. She encountered, as she had in Florence, two Englishmen making the Grand Tour. One was a distant cousin, young Lord Lincoln; the other was his tutor, the Reverend Joseph Spence.

Spence anticipates, without equalling, Boswell in the art of celebrity watching. Like the great biographer, he cultivated acquaintance with persons of rank and attainment for the express purpose of writing about them. He was, as were so many Georgian writers, essentially a journalist. His book, *Spence's Anecdotes,* prefigures the interviews that are so familiar a feature of today's periodicals and television programs. Conversations predominate, and they are presented, as in Boswell's *Life of Johnson,* in the form of theatrical dialogue. The *Anecdotes* have been thoroughly combed by Augustan and Georgian scholars, especially for material concerning Alexander Pope.

Spence, as befitted a Pope expert, was eager to meet the lady who had played fast and loose with the poet's emotions. She arrived in Rome in January of 1741; he wrote soon thereafter to his mother: "I always desired to be acquainted with Lady Mary, and could never bring it about, though we were so often together in London; soon after we came to this place her ladyship came here, and in five days I was well acquainted with her."

There follows a portrait of Lady Mary that admirably puts into perspective the unsubstantiated slanders fabricated by Pope and Walpole. Spence was fascinated by the woman whose minor fame calumny had transformed into major notoriety. Avoiding tattle about cleanliness and propriety, he caught her most salient characteristic, which was her inconsistency and, fortified by a misquotation from Dryden, set her down as ambivalent. "She is one of the most shining characters in the world, but shines like a comet; she is all irregularity, and always wandering; the most wise, most imprudent; loveliest, most disagreeable; best-natured, cruellest woman in the world, 'all things by turns and nothing long.' "

It is to our loss that Lady Mary's letters ignore Spence in favor of fashionable Lord Lincoln. Her emphasizing the latter's "Spirit and sense" and her finding him to possess understanding suggests that he took part in her talks with Spence and proved also a sympathetic listener. The pages of the *Anecdotes* devoted to Lady Mary complement her letters. They contain stories of her harem visits of the Embassy period. (The corset-mistaken-for-girdle-of-chastity reminiscence occurred during one of these conversations.) There are also expressions of her literary opinions, her theories about dowries, marriage and separation and, doubtless for Spence's special benefit, her side of the quarrel with Pope.

The flattering audience furnished by tutor and pupil softened Lady Mary's former contempt for Grandtouring Milords. She had written from Venice in 1740 that "Their whole business abroad (as far as I can perceive) being to buy new cloaths, in which they shine in some obscure coffee-house, where they are sure of meeting only one another; and after the important conquest of some waiting gentlewoman of an opera Queen . . . they return to England excellent judges of men and manners. I find the spirit of patriotism so strong in me every time I see them that I look upon them as the greatest blockheads in nature."

A year of lonely wandering, of spasmodic visits to persons and places, and of frustrated waiting for Algarotti's summons contributed to Lady Mary's more lenient view of her young countrymen. In any event, they were, she must have realized with a pang, a distinct improvement on Edward Junior. With Spence and Lincoln doubtless at their head, droves of Grand Tourists came to call during her stay in Rome. Both pathos and irony are present in her account of herself in an *in loco parentis* role. Writing to Wortley from Leghorn in February of 1741, she narrated the cordial reception accorded her in the novel character of a good example: "The English Travellers in Rome behave in general very discreetly. I have reason to speak well of them since they were all exceedingly obliging to me as if I had been their Queen and their Governors told me that the desire of my aprobation had a very great Influence on their conduct. While I staid, there was neither Gameing or any sort of extravagance; I us'd to preach to them very freely, and they all thank'd me for it."

Here again was the principle of absence. Lady Mary, like many another parent of every age, was discovering that it is easier to be heeded, or to seem to be heeded, by other people's children than by one's own. There is also the possibility that the court paid to her by the Milords was a tongue-in-cheek sham. She was often obtuse, especially where men were concerned. Horace Walpole's picking up where Pope left off went completely over her head; she remembered him only as having been "particularly civil to me." Since Horry was a glittering member of the touring "ton," the unpleasant suspicion remains that some of her young visitors found it a priceless joke to hear improving precepts pronounced by a purportedly disreputable slattern.

Lady Mary's cultivation of son substitutes was, in prepsychiatric times, unlikely to be diagnosed as such, least of all by herself. The leading candidate to fill the vacancy left by egregious Edward was James Stuart Mackenzie. In that he was Lord Bute's younger brother, he could quite suitably be viewed in a familial light. That Lady Mary did so view him can be inferred in a letter that she wrote to Wortley from Venice in June of 1740, the letter in which she wrote of having deceived Procurator Grimani about young Edward's identity. Immediately after telling Wortley of this uncdifying incident, she introduced the subject of Mackenzie. The transition from rejected son to preferable kinsman is revealing. The following lines are the first of many tributes she paid the chivalrous young Scot. "Mr. Mackenzie, younger Brother to Lord Bute, is here at present. He is a very well behav'd Youth; he makes great court to me, and I have shew'd him as many Civillitys as are in my power."

One of these attentions was to make the amiable Mackenzie known to a Venetian friend, Mme. Chiara Michiel. Lady Mary's letter of introduction inaugurates a new series of letters, all in French, to the wife of the Venetian Ambassador to the court of Spain. "Ma Belle Ambassadrice," whose maiden name was Bragadin, was of the family of one of the most venerated figures in Venetian history. Lady Mary, who was, we remember, adept at adjusting her topics to her correspondents' tastes, selected this patrician daughter of the Venetian republic for discussions concerning the superiority of republics over monarchies. Lady Mary wrote her first letter to Mme. Michiel as she prepared to return to Rome from Spanish-dominated Naples. It would have raised Bourbon eyebrows. To Mme. Michiel, whose husband was soon to be posted to Madrid, Lady Mary unburdened herself of the following sentiments: "it is impossible for me to find fulfillment in a monarchy so much do I find occasion to murmur against the Power that suffers it on earth. I do not doubt, Madame, that you have often thanked God for your birth, but when you are established in a Court I am sure you will be so conscious of the happiness of freedom that you will daily offer Acts of Thanksgiving."

Lady Mary's approval of republics played its part in influencing future travels. It is noteworthy that the communities she selected for her various sojourns were almost without exception those governed by right of suffrage rather than heredity. It was a pattern that did not escape the notice of her contemporaries.

In her second letter to Mme. Michiel, Lady Mary sounded a note even more in tune with modern thought than her republican sympathies. She gives no indication in her voluminous correspondence of having any knowledge of Jean-Jacques Rousseau nor of his veneration for youth. Still in a glow from her success among the travelling lordlings she had met in Rome, and solaced by the attentions proffered by Mackenzie, she set down lines that anticipate the principle so widely held today that

> The Youth, who daily farther from the east
> Must travel, still is nature's priest,

Speaking of young people in general, and of "Mons Mackinsie" in particular, she confessed herself to have been prejudiced against youth. "I had Preconceptions that they were all giddy creatures and that I would do well to avoid them. This was my habit until my travels forced me to become acquainted with them, and I assure you that I have found among them good Faith and honor, qualities that are rare elsewhere, and naturally it should be thus. There are few People gifted with virtue so strong that it can be preserved in the commerce of the world; Young people still have what remains of sincerity and this, combined with the maxims of a noble Education make them more to be esteemed than their elders who are usually corrupted by bad Example."

The arrival of Lady Mary's household goods, shipped by Wortley to Leghorn, made it imperative that she determine upon a place to settle. Her republican principles favored Venice, Genoa or Switzerland. The widening of hostilities between England and Spain complicated her plans. As the War of the Austrian Succession expanded, so did the network of foes and allies of the opposing kingdoms. It was not only necessary for Lady Mary to avoid regions to which Spain laid claim but also those in which she might be thought a spy. Her offer to supply Wortley with military intelligence still obtained. Then, as now, the distinction between spy and patriot was, like beauty, in the eye of the beholder.

These practical considerations were, in March of 1741, obscured by the dazzling discovery that Algarotti had been sent by Frederick the Great on a diplomatic mission to Turin. This time, Lady Mary determined, he should not slip through her fingers. Republics could wait. Her rendezvous with Algarotti could not. Although Lady Mary had barely arrived after a stormy voyage from Leghorn to Genoa, she set out immediately for the capital of Savoy.

It must be supposed that Lady Mary learned of Algarotti's mission to Turin from Lord Hervey. He alone knew of her infatuation for the young man he also loved. It was a confidence, it must be added, that, despite his propensity to malice, he loyally maintained. His awareness that the reunion for which Lady Mary had so long waited was *fait accompli* was marked by a flurry of letters from Grosvenor Street containing references to, or messages for, our *Friend* (the capital and italics are Hervey's).

The period that Lady Mary and Algarotti passed in Turin remains a tantalizing vacuum. All that is certain is that it was a double failure. Lady Mary, predictably, could not get the better of the indifference of her illusory lover. Algarotti could not persuade Charles Emanuel of Savoy into an alliance with Prussia. Lady Mary repaid the discreet Hervey with letters that do not survive. That she made a clean breast of her humiliating defeat in a humiliating relationship is evident from Hervey's replies. She not only paid her onetime rival the compliment of frankness, she also asked his advice. His answer refers to the Turin debacle "as a very disagreeable Epoque of your Life" and his advice, quoted in Latin from Ovid, suggests that she forget Algarotti in favor of a more propitious affair, a counsel that could hardly have been original when Ovid first set it down.

Lady Mary finished her wooing of Algarotti in a letter of bitter rebuke. Because it is undated, Robert Halsband conjectures that it may have been written during an earlier period of clear-sightedness. This surmise would indicate a degree of commonsense belied by Lady Mary's subsequent actions. Allowing even for her propensity for shifting course, it seems unlikely that she would propose to follow where his fancy should dictate one whom she had previously sent packing in these furious lines: "Yes, I will pass the morning writing to you even though I risk enraging you. I have decided to despise your contempt and on that point I no longer wish to restrain myself. In the time (of stupid memory) when I was frenetically attracted to you, the desire to please you (even though I knew this to be impossible), and the fear of annoying you stifled my voice when I talked with you, and, even more significantly arrested my hand five hundred times a day when I took up my pen to write to you."

Considering the ardor and number of Lady Mary's outpourings to her slippery idol, it is to be wondered of what flights of passion she would have been capable had she not felt herself to be inhibited.

Algarotti, in common with many philosopher-scientists of his time, had studied Newton's principles. Soon after meeting Lady Mary he had popularized Newton in a treatise called, in male-oriented style, *Il Newtonismo per le dame*. It was a title of which she now made acid use. "I have studied you, and so well studied, that Chevalier Newton has not dissected the rays of the Sun with more exactitude than I have deciphered the sentiments of your soul. Your eyes served me as a Prism for unravelling the ideas you harbor. I watched with such a great Aplication that I almost blinded myself (because those prisms are very dazzling)." Of his taste and intelligence she had never been in doubt, but love needs heartier nourishment than "manuscripts, statues, Pictures, verses, wine" and "conversation." Lacking sturdier and, by implication, more manly qualities, Lady Mary could find only vulgarity and indifference in him who was incapable of progressing from the graces to the passions. She rattled back to Genoa to resume her solitary course.

Twenty years of expatriate life remained to Lady Mary. The detachment she had so assiduously cultivated soon hardened into isolation. Of her family, only one member, her dishonest son, had sought her out, and him she had repudiated. Her activities were henceforth to be concerned with having a palace in this city, planting a garden in that village, awaiting news and books from England and writing brilliant descriptions to distant friends and relatives concerning the various communities in which she alighted.

She had, in her long-ago letters to Lady Mar, expressed her fear of insensibly dwindling into a spectatress. At the time of writing those discontented lines, she did not recognize that her gifts were for observation rather than participation. Her unhappy marriage and her still unhappier search for compensatory romance forced her into what was, in one sense, a life of frustrated idleness. It was, in another, a life perfectly suited for the exercise of her most significant talents. Lady Mary's career as a spectatress was not a dwindling; it was a growth.

In the fall of 1741 she exchanged the republic of Genoa for that of Switzerland, being "frighted out of Italy" by fears of a Spanish invasion. She found, as do modern travellers, that the cost of living in the Calvinist region of plain living and high thinking was "as dear as it is in London." She continued to proffer intelligence that might be of use to Mr. Wortley and his political colleagues. Never one to doubt her competence (especially in areas usually reserved to men), she felt sure she could improve on the performance of those charged with English foreign policy. From Geneva she wrote her husband, "If you have any Curiosity for the present state of any of the States of Italy, I believe I can give you a truer account than perhaps any other Traveller can do, having allways had the good fortune of a sort of Intimacy with the first persons in the Governments where I resided, and they not guarding themselves against the Observations of a Woman as they would have done from those of a Man."

It will be recalled that, at a time earlier in her wanderings, Lady Mary had proposed "opening a further Correspondence" with Sir Robert Walpole for purposes of just such genteel espionage. The "cold thanks" with which her offer was met continued to rankle. From Chambéry, where she had removed from Geneva, she wrote lines that anticipate today's columnists. "I suppose you know before this" ran her letter of November 30, 1741, to Mr. Wortley, "the Spaniards are landed at Different Ports in Italy etc. When I receiv'd early information of the Design I had the charity to mention it to the English Consul (without nameing my Informer). He laugh'd, and answer'd it was impossible. This may serve for a small specimen of the general good Inteligence our wise Ministry has of all Foreign affairs. If you were acquainted with the people they employ, you would not be surpriz'd at it. . . . There is not one of them who know any thing more of the Country they inhabit than that they eat and sleep in it."

Rumors that French troops would soon occupy Chambéry caused Lady Mary again to seek a neutral residence. Although war between England and France had not yet been declared, she had no desire to find herself in enemy territory when that foreseeable rupture should become official. She decided upon Avignon, which was still a papal possession. Her sincere admiration for His Holiness was a factor in making this choice; as she wrote her "belle Ambassadrice," Mme. Michiel, "Here I am established for some time at Avignon. It was with great regret that I quitted amiable Italy which will (they say) become a Theatre of War, and I did not dare to stay. I have at least the Consolation to be under the domination of an Italian Prince and, let us admit it, the only Prince that I esteem because he seems to consider his people as under his protection and he studies means to care for them, while other sovreigns consider them as being created to serve their passions." To her compatriot, Lady Pomfret, she sent a less flowery account of her removal. "I have changed my situation, fearing to find myself blocked up in a besieged town; and not knowing where else to avoid the terrors of war, I have put myself under the protection of the Holy See."

Young Edward's affairs were, during the years Lady Mary passed in Avignon, still in disarray. His parents' comments on their son's conduct and prospects (or rather lack of them) give the impression that it is a boy who is being censured, rather than a man of twenty-nine. Even in an age when aristocrats did nothing in particular and did it very well, Edward's situation resembled that of a perpetual undergraduate, striking, as undergraduates do, a series of colorful poses.

The widening of the War of the Austrian Succession suggested to his parents that a commission in the army might be a way out of his and, more tellingly, their dilemmas. Since it was by no means certain that he would fall in with this plan, Wortley proposed that Lady Mary meet with their son to sound him out. The resultant scheme reads like the libretto of a Verdi opera.

While both his mother and father desired, in a disillusioned way, to salvage the fortunes of Edward Junior, they were, above all, bent upon not paying the gambling debts which might, according to their computations, amount to any sum between one thousand and ten thousand pounds. Lady Mary had no objection to conferring with her son providing that he could not be identified as such. She had often bitterly reproached him with assuming false identities that suited his purposes; she proposed, in June of 1742, a deception that suited hers. Pursuant to this devious scheme, she exchanged, for a few days, Avignon for Orange. At Orange she passed two days in conversation with a Dutch army officer unaccountably called Monsieur du Durand.

Lady Mary's letter to her husband, in which she tells of the strained reunion between mother and son, anticipates a rejection expressed nearly a year later. She wrote in 1743, "As to what regards my Son, I have long since fix'd my Opinion concerning him. I am not insensible of the misfortune, but I look upon it as on the loss of a Limb which ceases to give Solicitude by being irretreivable." The fixed opinion dated back to Edward's schoolboy truancies and the subsequent years of feckless extravagances. Her meeting with "Monsieur du Durand" served to confirm her condemnation of her son: "he will allways be led by the person he converses with, either right or wrong, not being capable of forming any fix'd Judgment of his own. As to his Enthusiasm, if he had it I suppose he has allready lost it, since I could perceive no turn of it in all his Conversation, but with his Head I beleive it is possible to make him a Monk one day and a Turk three days after." Here Lady Mary's hostility to her unstable son took a prophetic turn. The Orientalist and teller of tall tales did, in due time, make his way back to Constantinople, where he embraced Islam and allowed himself to be supposed the son of Achmet III. Ironically, he followed his mother's precedent in wearing Turkish dress, thus convincing her many ill wishers of the baleful effects of heredity.

Although their meeting at Orange served to widen the breach between mother and son, it achieved the purpose for which it was intended. Edward was delighted with the prospect of a military career. A commission was purchased in Sir John Cope's Dragoons. It was to be Cornet Wortley Montagu's perilous privilege to ride into battle carrying his regiment's colors. With England's military situation worsening, it was a duty that gave every indication of becoming a swashbuckler's nightmare. Lady Mary, learning, in July of 1743, of her son's commission, set down one of her very few constructive opinions about his potential. "Perhaps the same rashness which has ruin'd him in other affairs may be Lucky to him there." This unwonted optimism proved not entirely illusory. Edward's military career was to include service at Fontenoy, one of England's bloodiest defeats. He survived the carnage, suffering nothing worse than contusions occasioned by being blown from his horse by the wind from a passing cannon ball, a deliverance his mother chose to believe fictitious.

Lady Mary never saw her son again and wrote to him only as her husband required it. When she did so she could not bring herself to forgive his past or to trust his future. Here are her chilling comments upon Cornet Wortley Montagu's participation in the battle of Fontenoy: "I am very well pleas'd with the accounts I have had of your behaviour this Campaign. I wish nothing more than that your future conduct may redeem your past. . . . I hope experience will correct the Idle way of talking that has done you so much injury." Was Lady Mary, we wonder, thinking of the, to her, imaginary cannon ball? Edward must have permitted himself a retaliatory grain of salt as he read that, "Your welfare is allways wish'd by your affectionate etc." (This letter to their son was copied into one of Lady Mary's letters to her husband; presumably she signed the original "your affectionate mother.")

Avignon, because it was a papal state, was a rallying point for supporters of the Stuart interest, a circumstance that placed Lady Mary at a significant listening post. In February of 1744, she had occasion to test her theory that a man is less guarded in conversation in female company than in male. Obscured by a mask, she assisted at an elaborate entertainment offered the Duc de Richelieu by the Society of Free Masons at Nîmes. She took this suitable moment to intercede with the Duke on behalf of Protestants condemned to the galleys. Her interview with the guest of honor proved unexpectedly fruitful. The Duke not only agreed to free the Huguenots but, perhaps disarmed by his own benevolence, went on to let slip a secret of great importance that Lady Mary preferred not to entrust to the public carriers. Her English servants, who were still given to enriching her household with inconvenient babies, were returning home. Their departure furnished her with the means of warning the English Whigs of Bonnie Prince Charlie's plans for a Jacobite uprising in Scotland. The Duc de Richelieu, she wrote Wortley, "ask'd me what party the Pretender had in England. I answer'd as I thought, a very small one. We are told otherwaies at Paris (said he); however, a Bustle at this time may serve to facilitate our other projects, and we intend to attempt a descent. At least it will cause the Troops to be recall'd. . . ." In other words, the opening of a second front would weaken the English campaign in Flanders. Lady Mary's surmise that the Pretender lacked the support necessary to replace Hanoverians with Stuarts was to prove true in the brutal crushing of the Jacobite uprising of 1745. Her subsequent letters give no indication of the use to which Mr. Wortley may, or may not, have put her timely warning.

Lady Mary's isolation was increased, even in neutral Avignon, by her being viewed as an enemy alien. She was suspected, not without reason, of being an informer. Always able to play contradictory roles, she was at her most characteristic in writing Wortley, less than four months after her tête-à-tête with the Duc de Richelieu, that her acquaintances were "afraid to converse with me and others drop Speeches on purpose to hear my Reply in which they are allways disapointed by my being invincibly silent."

One of Lady Mary's dropped speeches provided an unexpected windfall. She had discovered, in her solitary ramblings, an old ruin which had once been used as a fort and again as a mill. She made an "accidental speech" to one of Avignon's town fathers, saying that if it were hers she would make of it a "very agreeable belvidere." The upshot of this conversation should have caused her to repent of having earlier accused the French of being incapable of friendship. The Hôtel de Ville presented her with the ancient tower which, into the bargain, commanded a magnificent view. Lady Mary, fired by the example of that zealous amateur of architecture, Lord Burlington, amused herself by converting the ruin into a summerhouse where she could read, as well as write her increasingly delightful letters.

Among the friends to whom she wrote during the expatriate years was Lady Oxford, who will reappear in the next chapter as the mother of Margaret, Duchess of Portland. Lady Louisa Stuart's "Introductory Anecdotes" to her grandmother's *Letters and Works* have fixed Lady Oxford in the character of a stupid woman. Subsequent biographers have not questioned this verdict.

Lady Mary's existing letters to Lady Oxford, like those to Lady Bute, date from the mid-1740s. It is to be regretted that we have so slight a history of an association that progressed from hostility to devoted friendship. Lady Mary, in the distraught days of her engagement and runaway marriage, described the then Lady Henrietta Cavendish Holles in a wholly condemnatory fashion. Her future friend had been a childhood playmate whom she did not hesitate to write off as "peevish," "ill-tempered," "stupid," "the most insipid thing breathing" and cursed, in addition, with red hair. Presumably marriage to Robert, Lord Harley (later Lord Oxford), opponent of Marlborough and himself a man of letters, threw the mantle of intellect over his dull bride. Lord Oxford's patronage of Pope during the years following the Wortley Montagus' return from Turkey promoted an intimacy between the formerly uncongenial children. Strangely enough, Lady Oxford in her new character of confidante and friend does not appear in the letters Lady Mary wrote to Lady Mar in Paris. We turn for an account of this changed relationship to Samuel Johnson's *Lives of the Poets,* where we learn, in his essay on Pope, that the Oxford "table was indeed infested by Lady Mary Wortley who was the friend of Lady Oxford. . . ." (This fetching phrase was not inappropriate from the pen of him who, even while writing it, was making such lavish use of the Thrales' hospitality.)

Lady Mary's lonely wanderings brought about a dramatic change of heart toward both friend and daughter. She had learned, by snub, to be reserved in writing to her husband; no such inhibitions existed with Lady Oxford or Lady Bute. Her need to be loved had been successively thwarted by her partings from Pope, Wortley, Algarotti and young Edward. The concomitant need to love could now be safely projected upon a pedestrian friend and a conventional daughter. The fact that her letters to these two women begin during the same period suggests that they were written for emotional rather than literary motives. Although her informative letters to Wortley retained their cool and friendly tone, it was to Lady Oxford that she wrote the following outpouring: "Your Ladyship need not mention your command of continuing our Correspondance; it is the only Comfort of my Life," and a few weeks later, "if I am so unfortunate to survive you, I have no more prospect of any pleasure upon Earth.

It is a very great Truth, that as your Freindship has been the greatest Blessing and Honor of my Life, it is only that which gives me any pleasing view for those years that remain. . . ." Despite the eighteenth century's skill in concocting of flattering flourishes, today's reader finds in these lines not only sincerity but also a nostalgia that must often have approached desperation.

Lady Bute's reinstatement in her parents' favor was accomplished by several factors. Over and above the passage of time, there were the excesses of her only and older brother. Mackenzie had (probably with Bute encouragement) charmed the expatriate mother and mother-in-law and, upon the public stage, there occurred the last of the Stuart crises, the " '45."

At the time of this melodrama, Mary, Countess of Bute, was twenty-eight. She was already the mother of several children; the Bute offspring, even by the generous standards of the past, were to achieve notable numbers, Lady Louisa Stuart, one of Lady Mary's granddaughters and her biographer being the youngest and thirteenth. Until the campaign of questionably Bonny Prince Charlie, the Butes, for reasons of economy, had lived upon their own estates in the west of Scotland. When, encouraged by Fontenoy, the Young Pretender, during the summer of 1745, unfurled his banner in the adjacent highlands, the Butes, who were supporters of the Hanoverian line, removed to England. They determined upon Twickenham, which had been Lady Bute's girlhood home. It was a step vigorously disputed by budget-minded Wortley. It is at this point that the existing letters of Lady Mary to Lady Bute commence.

Lady Mary was far too proud to omit from her first letter a sigh for the "unsuitable" marriage. "My Dear Child," she wrote in March of 1746, "I will not trouble you with repetitions of my concern for your uneasy Situation, which does not touch me the less from having foreseen it many years ago; you may remember my thoughts on that subject before your marriage.—God's will be done. You have the blessing of happiness in your own Family, and I hope time will put your affairs in a better condition. . . . I am flatter'd here with the hopes of Peace. I pray heartily for it, as what can only put an end to your troubles, which are felt in the tenderest manner by your most affectionate Mother." Never were modest wishes more stunningly fulfilled.

Her son-in-law, on a rainy afternoon a year later, progressed at a single bound from the inexpensive ruralities of the Isle of Bute to a fruitful intimacy with Frederick, Prince of Wales. His Highness and companions were caught in a downpour as they prepared to return from the Egham races. To pass the time until the rain should stop, a party of whist was organized and Lord Bute commandeered to take a hand. Prince Frederick was charmed with the handsome Scottish peer who, unlike so many of his deplorable compatriots, had not rallied to the Pretender's cause. Under these haphazard circumstances was inaugurated a political career which was to be marked by controversy, contention and scandal.

The Jacobite uprising and its resultant slaughters proved crucial not only to the Butes' future but also to that of Lady Mary. After the decisive Hanoverian victory at Culloden, the Pretender sped "over the sea to Skye," leaving his supporters to go to the block or into exile. Those who survived fled in great numbers to the American colonies or to the Continent where, in search of armed revenge, they enriched the forces of England's enemies.

Avignon was, in the summer of 1746, thronged with Scotch and Irish rebels who, as Lady Mary wrote Wortley, made it "impossible to go into any Company without hearing a Conversation that is improper to be listen'd to and dangerous to contradict." To escape these treasonable companions, she determined to return to the Venetian republic. Two centuries ago it was unthinkable for a lady to travel without a male escort. In the absence of her English servants, who had, we remember, departed bearing with them military intelligence of significance, Lady Mary and her French maid were delayed until they could join others making the hazardous trip through potential battlefields lying between Avignon and Venice.

A platonic protector materialized in the person of an impecunious Venetian nobleman, Count Ugolino Palazzi. He was returning home and proposed himself as travelling companion to Lady Mary, who agreed "to pass under the notion of A Venetian Lady." The party sailed from Marseilles to Genoa, then continued overland through the Apennines. They met, in a mountain pass, Spanish troops in headlong retreat and closely pursued by England's allies, the Austrians. It was a situation made to order for Lady Mary, who had not had, one suspects, such a thrilling adventure in many months. Palazzi paid his respects to the commanding officers, revealing his fair charge's identity. Her letter to Wortley describes the encounter with characteristic self-assurance: "there was no sort of Honor or Civility they did not pay me. They immediately order'd me a Guard of Hussars (which was very necessary in the present disorder) and sent me refreshments of all kinds. Next day I was visited by . . . all the principal officers with whom I pass'd for a Heroine, shewing no uncasyness thô the Cannon of the Citadelle (where was a Spanish garrison) play'd very briskly." These emergencies were doubtless a refreshing reminder of the journey of nearly thirty years earlier from Vienna to Adrianople.

Lady Mary prided herself, not without reason, upon being made of sturdier stuff than other women. A telltale gap of more than two months occurs between this spirited martial scene and her next letter to her husband. The hardships of her journey did not leave her unscathed; she contracted a dangerous infection, involving so high a fever that her recovery was in doubt. A lengthy convalescence followed, during the course of which she believed herself to be in a general decline.

The Palazzis lived in Brescia, which was at that time part of the Venetian republic. Upon Lady Mary's falling ill, they received her into their own home, where she was cared for by Palazzi's mother. The Countess shared her son's by no means disinterested concern for their guest's recovery. To place under obligation to themselves the wife of a man with a seven-figure fortune promised all sorts of tempting opportunities. Lady Mary's association with this shady pair complicated the ensuing decade of her sojourn in the Veneto. She took good care that the financial hazards to which they exposed her should not come to the attention of thrifty Wortley. Her letters, therefore, contain no record of the sordid traffickings of mother and son. The history of her victimization by yet another plausible rogue is contained in an unpublished essay written in Italian and preserved among the Wharncliffe papers.

Palazzi, or sometimes Palazzo, who was younger than young Edward, played his part in the myth of Lady Mary's gallantries. He was a perfect candidate, in terms of the times and the place, for the role of *cicisbeo*. To this fictitious scandal were added tangible injuries. Financial chicanery was attempted and frequently succeeded. Real estate transactions of not even a dubious kind transpired. Jewelry disappeared. Hard-luck stories and hysterics proliferated. In fact, Count Palazzi was not only Rémond revisited, but also the culmination of Lady Mary's inability, in relationships with men, to distinguish gems from paste.

The Palazzis owned a white elephant of a palace in nearby Gottolengo. The fact that extensive repairs were needed and that it was unfurnished suggested that the tumbledown residence was just the spot for Lady Mary's convalescence. Thither she was borne upon a litter during the winter of 1746–47. Her own furniture had, of necessity, been left in Avignon, so she was persuaded to buy at high prices a few odds and ends supplied by her ever-resourceful hosts. By the following November she had bought the house and, into the bargain, made it once more habitable. She described to Lady Oxford her second venture in architecture: "I have bought the house I live in. . . . It is not much more than the shell of a Palace, which was built not above 40 years ago, but the master of it dying before it was quite finish'd, and falling into Hands that had many others, it has been wholly neglected; but being well built the walls are perfectly sound and I amuse my selfe in fitting it up. I will take the Liberty of sending your Ladyship a plan of it, which is far from magnificent but I believe you will be of my Opinion that it is one of the most convenient you ever saw."

Predictably, Palazzi, who parted with his ruin for a mere "Trifle," was acting in bad faith. Nine years later, when his persecutions forced Lady Mary to leave Gottolengo, she discovered that the palace upon which she had lavished money was entailed. It was not hers to sell but, restored and renovated, reverted to its perfidious owner. As one of her acquaintance shrewdly surmised, it was harder for a woman of her temperament to have been made a fool of than to be thought to be maintaining a youthful lover.

Lady Bute became the central figure of her mother's old age. The letters to My Dear Child have, like the Embassy Letters and those bitter satires sent to psychotic Lady Mar, a character all their own. Benevolence replaces sarcasm. Landscapes and descriptions of the theatres, the carnivals and the amusements of her neighbors abound. There are homely details of housekeeping and gardening in an Italian village. The Bute's enormous family prompted improving precepts having frequently to do with the still-nagging subject of female intellect. Lady Mary's comments upon the novels sent from England constitute a sort of informal bibliography of mid-Georgian best-sellers. These cozy letters, in sum, achieved two widely disparate purposes. They successfully screened out the scandalous Palazzi and his unceasing efforts to fleece her. More significantly, they enshrined her daughter as the generous recipient of affection previously rejected by others and, in consequence, repressed by herself.

During the years when Lady Mary was writing these agreeable letters, she was making considerable progress in her respect for the arts, especially the performing arts. She overcame the English preference for language read or spoken, as opposed to the Italian genius for language sung. By the middle of the eighteenth century, opera had attained its abiding domination over all Italian music. Lady Mary discovered, as have many other English-speaking travellers, that opera, which was fathered by Mediterranean mythology, is more readily at home under the skies of Venus and Mars than those of Beowulf.

To her new-found enjoyment of the lyric theatre, Lady Mary added esteem for the comedies of Carlo Goldoni. She found herself, during the carnival season of 1748, requested by the local clergy to lend her house for amateur theatricals. She was so delighted with the "neatness" of the scenery and with the untutored skills of the Gottolengo artisans and tradespeople (especially with those of the "Taylor of the Village," who played Arlecchino) that she treated her diverting guests to a "Baril of Wine," reflecting, as befitted the wife of Mr. Wortley, that it cost less than London's small beer.

Palazzi, having in appearance "sold" an erstwhile ruin to unsuspecting Lady Mary, now persuaded her to buy a large garden "a long mile from the Castle." It must have been an enchanting spot. Lady Mary's luxuriant description of her vineyards, her woods carpeted in violets and strawberries, the path that led down to the river, Oglio, and her al fresco "dineing room of Verdure capable of holding a Table of 20 covers" is, like her letters from the gorgeous East, rich not only in pictorial values but also in social history.

The conclusion of a charming letter to Lady Bute, written in July of 1748, is Lady Mary at her most English. She reverted in

her faraway surroundings to the husbandry practiced by her ancestors on the broad acres of Thoresby; she determined to cultivate
her acres for profit. Her time was divided, like that of a Yorkshire
gentleman-farmer, between her plantations, her poultry, her books
and the diversions of cards and outdoor exercise.

My Dear Child, who was the wife of a skillful gardener and
botanist must have felt thoroughly at home with this chronicle:
"Perhaps I shall succeed better in describing my manner of life,
which is as regular as that of any Monastery. I generally rise at six,
and as soon as I have breakfasted put my selfe at the head of my
Weeder Women, and work with them till nine. I then inspect my
Dairy and take a Turn amongst my Poultry, which is a very large
enquiry. I have a present 200 chicken, besides Turkys, Geese,
Ducks, and Peacocks. All things have hitherto prosper'd under my
Care. My Bees and silk worms are double'd, and I am told that,
without accidents, my Capital will be so in two years time. At 11
o'clock I retire to my Books. I dare not indulge my selfe in that
pleasure above an hour. At 12 I constantly dine, and sleep after
dinner till about 3. I then send for some of my old Priests and either play at picquet or Whist till tis cool enough to go out. One
evening I walk in my Wood where I often Sup, take the air on
Horseback the next, and go on the Water the third. The Fishery
of this part of the River belongs to me, and my Fisherman's little
boat (where I have a green Lutestring Awning) serves me for a
Barge. He and his Son are my Rowers, without any expence, he
being very well paid by the profit of the Fish, which I give him on
condition of having every day one dish for my Table. Here is plenty
of every sort of Fresh Water Fish, excepting Salmon, but we have a
large Trout so like it that I, that have allmost forgot the taste, do not
distinguish it.

"We are both plac'd properly in regard to our Different times of
Life: you amidst the Fair, the Galant and the Gay, I in a retreat
where I enjoy every amusement that Solitude can afford. I confess I
sometimes wish for a little conversation, but I refflect that the commerce of the World gives more uneasyness than pleasure, and Quiet
is all the Hope that can reasonably be indulg'd at my Age."

Lord and Lady Bute's progress "amidst the Fair, the Galant and
the Gay" was soon to play an ominous role in the history of the

English commonwealth. Lady Mary's response to her son-in-law's advance to powers which he had not been educated to exercise was opportunistic. A letter dated July 26, 1748, suggests place-seeking and prosperous alliances. "I am very glad you are admitted into the Conversation of the Prince and Princess. It is a favor that you ought to cultivate for the good of your Family, which is now numerous and it may be one day of great advantage." The "advantage," if it can be so called, is envisioned by Lady Mary in a letter to Wortley written during this same summer.

Frederick, Prince of Wales, died in 1751. His demise advanced, with resultant scandal, Bute's influence in the fatherless royal household. The young widow, Princess Augusta, having turned to her deceased husband's friend for counsel, especially in the educating of her pathetic son, the future George III, was delightedly supposed to be Bute's mistress. That the future Prime Minister's career was to depend upon the favor of Princess rather than Prince was foreseen by Lady Mary long before it became the case. Her prophetic letter reads, "What I think extrodinary is my Daughter's continuing so many years agreable to Lord Bute, Mr Mackensie telling me the last time I saw him that his Brother frequently said amongst his companions that he was still as much in Love with his Wife as before he marry'd her. If the Princesse's favor lasts, it may be of use to her family." It is to be hoped that when, fourteen years later, Lady Mary returned to London to die, she was spared seeing Bute and Princess Augusta, symbolized by a boot and a petticoat, hung in effigy in the neighboring streets.

Lady Mary's dual establishment at Gottolengo fascinated the neighboring gentry and peasantry. It was a holiday custom in eighteenth-century Italy for groups of the well-to-do to organize itinerant house parties. The Palladian palazzi that dot the Veneto, with their vast rooms and unlimited servants, were thought to obviate being invited, expected or, as Lady Mary was to learn, even acquainted with the hosts-designate. She found herself thus honored at Epiphany of 1748 by a party of some thirty merrymakers who, although she knew none of them, proposed to stay a fortnight. A woman with far more ample notions of social life than those permitted to the wife of Mr. Wortley might well have blanched at the prospect of such lavish hospitality. Lady Mary confined her entertainment to a "plentifull

Table" and sent out for fiddles. Because her guests danced until the next day she was spared the need to find beds for them. The following Christmas a still more impressive invasion was headed by the Duchess of Guastalla. Her Highness dropped in unexpectedly "with the greatest part of her Court, her Grand Master . . . the first Lady of her Bedroom 4 pages and a long etc of inferiour Servants, beside her Guards." The Duchess, like the local peasants, was intrigued by a Milady whose profitable hobby was the cultivation of silkworms and garden produce. To Wortley, who would be sure to approve of her use of time and land, Lady Mary wrote that one of the purposes of this visitation was for the Duchess to "eat a salad of my raising haveing heard much Fame of my Gardening."

Gottolengo was delighted to find itself the seat of a Stately Home presided over by a generous chatelaine. Lady Mary's housewifery came to comprise not only the skills of the garden, but also those of the kitchen. She busied herself during her years in the Brescia with teaching her humble neighbors how to make the kinds of pudding Italians still call *zuppa inglese*. The fattening delights of fools and trifles were varied by those of "custards, minc'd Pies and Plumb pudding." French rolls were introduced. The line must be drawn somewhere; Gottolengo drew it at sillabub, being unable to watch their instructress refreshing herself with a mixture of cream, wine and gelatin. Lady Mary, who had so frequently come to blows with the sophisticated, was thoroughly gratified by her domestic triumphs, considering that the star in her culinary crown was "Butter makeing" pedagogy. In a letter written in 1751 to Lady Bute, homesickness may be inferred from her "bragging" (her word) that under her tutelage the butter of Gottolengo had become worthy of any English dairy.

These benevolent occupations were interrupted in the spring of 1749 by malaria. Lady Mary was urged to try the waters at Lovere, a resort situated on the Lago d'Iseo. She remained there all summer and returned every year during the remainder of her Brescia sojourn. Her letters written from this lovely spot describe the Italian lakes very much as they appear today, with mountains ringing the horizon and adorned with villas, gardens and cascades. Lovere, like Bath, emulated Epidaurus in supplying lavish entertainment for those taking the cure. Opera, Lady Mary told her daughter, was to

be heard three times a week. The mother had so far forgot the musical xenophobia exemplified by Mr. Spectator as to write, "I . . .
should have been surpriz'd at the neatness of the Scenes, goodness of
the voices and justness of the actors if I had not remember'd I was in
Italy." Her letter predictably fails to report the name of the opera
or the composer.

The ending of the War of the Austrian Succession facilitated
communications between Italy and England. At last Lady Mary was
able to regale her aging eyes with the novels of Richardson and
Fielding. She requested her son-in-law to select for her a book on
practical gardening, without, it appears, reflecting that instructions
intended for the British Isles might be of little use in northern Italy.
Encouraged by the reception accorded to English cookery, she asked
Wortley to ship casks of ale, a project that was abandoned out of fear
that it would not arrive in a condition to compete with the native
Lambrusco. By dwelling upon such innocent activities, Lady Mary
successfully concealed from both husband and daughter her victimization at the hands of Ugolino Palazzi.

The 18th Century marks a giant step in adult attitudes toward
youth. Writers as diverse as Mme. de Maintenon, Lord Chesterfield,
Hester Chapone, Hannah More and, most significantly, Rousseau,
had an immense amount to say about the education of children and
the conduct of young people. The Bute's large family prompted
Lady Mary to write letters of precept that deserve a place in this
literature. She had sound ideas about the upbringing of daughters.
On the subject of sons she was, for the best of reasons, reserved. Her
lively imagination played about the vision of her granddaughters
making their way through the mazes of the "ton" or, alternatively,
being prepared to live in retirement on the Isle of Bute.

Her letters to Lady Bute on the theme of child rearing exhibit a
philosophy that Lady Mary could have applied to advantage in
many of her own life's stormy passages. Perhaps aware of this, she
was at pains to observe that " 'Tis much easier to give Rules than to
practise them." The idea that childhood is a crucial period was one
of the more reasonable aspects of the Age of Reason. With this theory Lady Mary was in agreement; she wrote that first impressions are
important and that prejudices contracted in the nursery can adversely
affect the future. Years earlier she had defined to Bishop Burnet her

feminist creed. To these beliefs she now added strictures aimed at the world of fashion in which the Butes were established. Girls should be encouraged to read because "Ignorance is as much the Fountain of Vice as Idleness and in deed generally produces it. People that do not read or work for a Livelihood have many hours that they know not how to imploy, especially Women, who commonly fall into Vapours or something worse." At a time when aristocrats derived their wealth from their tenantry, and acres were worked by peasants in the Old World and slaves in the New, Lady Mary's tribute to self-support sounds a modern note. This sturdy attitude doubtless reflects her gratification in working side by side with her "weeder women" and going fishing on the Oglio. Her constructive years at Gottolengo taught her that "the short and simple annals of the poor" might, Gray's *Elegy* notwithstanding, make for happier lives than those frittered away at Versailles and Bath.

Lady Mary, in the spring of 1750, suffered an illness from which it was not expected that she would recover. It was an oral infection that, according to the barbarous medical practice then obtaining, was treated by the application of red-hot irons to the gums. To recover from this ordeal, she returned to the waters of Lovere.

She exchanged, as fall drew on, the Lago d'Iseo for the "vast Lake of Gardia." This magnificent region prompted her to send to Lady Bute one of the most delicious of all her landscape descriptions. She detailed in her letter of October 17th the palace of Salò, whose bankrupt owner, Count Martinenghi, had, like Palazzi, lost a fortune by gambling and was now encumbered with property he could not maintain. He rented to Lady Mary an apartment that gave on a magnificent garden where man, rather than nature, was "the measure of all things." She strolled under the "Shade of Orange Trees," admired sculptured divinities and fed carp that were housed in a pool "supply'd by water from a cascade that proceeds from the mouth of a Whale, on which Neptune is mounted, surrounded with Reeds." Martinenghi did his best to convert his guest from Gottolengo to Salò, but Lady Mary, who was seldom motivated by aesthetic considerations, successfully resisted not only the "Paradise" of Salò but also the allurements of neighboring palaces pressed upon her by her eager host.

Her glamorous sojourn at Salò, despite her prudent resolve to return to Gottolengo, proved unsettling. The winter of 1751 was severe. As Lady Mary stared out at snow and ice she was tempted to imagine that Salò, not more than a few miles distant, would have been free of the drifts that kept her housebound. It was natural under these circumstances that her thoughts turned toward old age and death.

Lady Mary, with advancing years, retreated from the anticlericalism that marked much of Enlightenment philosophy. She laid aside the witty worldliness of her London letters and defended to Lady Bute the virtues of "Sincerity, Friendship, Piety, Disinterestedness, and Generosity." Of these five attributes the first and last pairs can be conformed to deist thought. Piety cannot. In adopting the language of prayer Lady Mary was again revealing herself to be an instinctive Christian.

In writing to Wortley during the summer of 1751, Lady Mary took occasion to define her attitude toward religion. Her letter was prompted by meeting Horace Walpole's sister-in-law, Lady Orford, whom she had known during the "she-meteor" visit to Florence ten years earlier. Lady Orford presided over a deist salon clearly modelled on those of prerevolutionary Paris. Upon being asked to make one of the party Lady Mary refused, writing in an unprecedented strain that Lady Orford "had a collection of Free thinkers that met weekly at her House to the Scandal of all good Christians." Had these orthodox sentiments been expressed to Lady Bute, they could have been construed as motherly moralizing. She would hardly have been inspired to waste improving reflections upon Wortley; it can therefore be inferred that old age made inroads upon her erstwhile skepticism. Lady Mary's letter continues, "She invited me to one of those Honorable Assemblys, which I civilly refus'd, not desiring to be thought of her Opinion, not thinking it right to make a Jest of Ordinances that are (at least) so far Sacred as they are absolutely necessary in all Civiliz'd Governments and it is being in every sense an Enemy to mankind to endeavor to over throw them."

Lady Mary's correspondence contains a casual letter from Montesquieu and several references to Voltaire, who admired her writing more than she did his. There is no evidence that she followed the theories of Rousseau, nor those of Diderot and d'Alembert. The first volume of the *Encyclopédie* to which most of the radical French authors contributed, and which was to have so significant an impact upon the future, appeared in 1751, the year that Lady Mary took up her pen on behalf of religion. It is the more remarkable that, not having read the materialistic philosophers who were her contemporaries, she should have diagnosed their influence as fostering revolution. As in the case of her championing immunization against smallpox, here is an impressive instance of prescience.

Lady Mary's esteem for Benedict XIV played its part in her eleventh-hour acceptance of religion. His was one of the most resourceful of all papal reigns. He was called upon to defend the church from the mockery of salon, theatre and press. It was a contest to which he brought humor and erudition. His command of law elicited from Montesquieu, author of *L'Esprit des Lois,* a colleague's tribute. His Holiness was, declared the philosopher, a scholar's Pope. Voltaire, who led his century in mockery of the church, found Benedict XIV "rempli de la lumière" and dedicated to him the drama *Mahomet.* By the use of wit, rather than outrage, Benedict thus kept pace with the enemies of the church. It was an accomplishment by no means lost on Lady Mary.

She was still more impressed by the encouragement proffered by the Pope not only to female studies, but to female scholarship as well. The Italian women intellectuals were not mocked as were the *Précieuses Ridicules* of the seventeenth century, nor the English Blue Stockings of the eighteenth. Such women as Vittoria Colonna, Saint Catherine of Siena and various noblewomen of the Sforza, d'Este and Visconti families had for centuries exerted an acknowledged influence upon the histories of their times. Benedict XIV was an enthusiastic forwarder of this tradition. In 1732, when he was still Archbishop of Bologna, he appointed to the Faculty of Science at the Archiginnasio the prodigy, Laura Bassi, who combined marriage and rearing twelve children with writing on abstruse subjects. Her paper entitled "On the Compression and Elasticity of the Air" was published under the aegis of the university. Maria Gaetana Agnesi, another scientist and mathematician, was also appointed by His Holiness to the University of Bologna in 1753. Lady Mary's account of this event is contained in one of the saddest of her letters.

She formulated during her Brescia sojourn a disheartened scheme for the education of her numerous granddaughters. In letter after letter she projected her literary frustrations upon the Bute sisters who must, she cautions, leave shining to their brothers. If the girls, especially young Lady Mary, find learning diverting, by all means let them be so indulged. Books are cheap and, since a woman's time is not so valuable as that of a man, reading will serve very well to fill idle hours. There are among these pessimistic reflections a few thoughts that remain constructive today. "There are two cautions to be given on this subject; first, not to think herselfe Learned when she can read Latin or even Greek. Languages are more properly to be called Vehicles of Learning than Learning it selfe. . . . True knowledge consists in knowing things, not words." Equally admirable is the following: "You should encourage your Daughter to talk over with you what she reads, and, as you are very capable of distinguishing, take care she does not mistake pert Folly for Wit and humour, or *Rhyme for Poetry* . . ." (italics added).

After setting down these precepts, Lady Mary reverted to the obsession that had since childhood damaged her capacity for happiness, in particular the happiness of friendship. A tragic combination of arrogance and loneliness is here present. "The second caution to be given her (and which is most absolutely necessary) is to conceal whatever Learning she attains, with as much solicitude as she would hide crookedness or lameness. The parade of it can only serve to draw on her the envy, and consequently the most inveterate Hatred, of all he and she Fools, which will certainly be at least three parts in four of all her Acquaintance. The use of knowledge in our Sex (beside the amusement of Solitude) is to moderate the passions and learn to be contented with a small expence, which are the certain effects of a studious Life and, it may be, preferable even to that Fame which Men have engross'd to themselves and will not suffer us to share. You will tell me I have not observed this rule my selfe, but you are mistaken; it is only inevitable Accident that has given me any Reputation that way. I have allwaies carefully avoided it, and ever thought it a misfortune."

Lady Mary's keen sensitivity to the injustice done to Englishwomen of intellect received, a few months after writing this disillusioned letter, rude confirmation. Cardinal Querini, with whom Voltaire corresponded, was, at the time, Bishop of Brescia. His Eminence had previously served as Librarian to the Vatican. He was an author whose vast output marked him, by some, a pedant. In October of 1753, Lady Mary found herself visited by one of his chief chaplains, who requested her complete works for inclusion in Querini's library. She stammered her apologies and replied (untruthfully) that she had never printed "a single line in my Life." The Cardinal's emissary refused to believe that a lady of her prestige remained in manuscript and, rubbing salt into the wound, "answered in a cold tone, his Eminence could send for them to England but they would be a long time coming and with some hazard and that he flattered him selfe I would not refuse him such a favor and I need not be asham'd of seeing my Name in a collection where he admitted none but the most Eminent Authors." Lady Mary understandably was ready to "cry for vexation."

Cardinal Querini's flattering blunder created for Lady Mary ironic dilemmas. It was, in the first place, quite out of her secularistic code, modified though it was, that the church should grant the acceptance of her gifts which the world had denied. Upon learning that the clergy supposed her to enjoy the reputation from which social usages of her time, place and class had excluded her, she was prompted to compare her lot with that of Italian ladies. She chose as her example Maria Gaetana Agnesi, whose precocious studies furnished a painful contrast with her own neglected childhood.

Lady Mary's account of the honors heaped upon this scientist, whose career suggests that of Madame Curie, is brief. Her letter continues, "the character of a learned Woman is far from being ridiculous in this Country, the greatest Familys being proud of having produc'd female Writers, and a Milanese Lady being now proffessor of Mathematics in the University of Bologna, invited thither by a most obliging Letter wrote by the present Pope. . . ."

It is unlikely that Lady Mary knew anything more of His Holiness's letter to Maria Gaetana Agnesi than that it was said to be obliging. Could she have seen it she would doubtless have experienced the ambivalent emotions of justification and envy aroused by the intellectual privileges accorded the ladies of France and Italy. The Pope's letter goes a great deal further than Lady Mary's protest of fifty years earlier to Bishop Burnet or her present suggestions for her granddaughters' education. It reads in part, "The Soul becomes frivolous when it occupies itself only with frills and trinkets, but it is sublime when it knows how to reflect. I promise you that in browsing through libraries I should be really delighted to find there beside our learned doctors sensible women who enshrine their knowledge in modesty." The Pope was clearly thinking of the Vatican library; he continued with the dry wit he used to such good effect in his dealings with the reigning spirit of secularism. "This would be the way for women to inhabit the Palace of the Popes. . . ." Although His Holiness's recommending womanly modesty to his protegée was a concession to a male-dominated society, it is in every way an advance from Lady Mary's bitter theory that her granddaughters' studies should be concealed like deformities.

The novel was slow to gain acceptance in Lady Mary's day. Even at so late a date as the early nineteenth century Jane Austen felt compelled to devote some pages of *Northanger Abbey* to its defense. Like the movies and television of this century, fiction's wide appeal aroused contempt. Lady Mary's world did not think better of a book for being the "Joy of Chambermaids of all Nations." Such a novel was *Pamela,* one of Samuel Richardson's grandiloquent tear-jerkers. This best-seller was followed by *Clarissa Harlow* and *Sir Charles Grandison,* whose spotless maidens, treacherous men-about-town, brutal brothers, mercenary parents, duels and deaths from remorse occupied many of Lady Mary's hours. She suspected, not without reason, that her delight in these melodramatic stories did not keep pace with her lofty literary standards. Far from pleased to discover that she and the chambermaids shared a debased taste, she complained to Lady Bute that "This Richardson is a strange Fellow. I heartily despise him and eagerly read, nay, sob over his works in a most scandalous manner."

Lady Mary undervalued the genius of Henry Fielding. Her attitude toward him was complicated by the fact that he was her second cousin and therefore, as Richardson was not, a gentleman. The most destructive of her many ambivalences remained the supposed conflict between aristocratic birth and the writer's trade. Hardly had she done grieving that she was not in print, than she was regretting that Fielding was. Of her cousin, whose limited means forced him to combine writing with the practice of law, she wrote that the self-styled "Hackney Writer" was obliged "by necessity to publish without correction and throw many productions into the World he would have thrown into the Fire if meat could have been got without money, or money without Scribbling." Still more Olympian is the next sentence, "The Greatest Virtue, Justice, and the most distinguishing prerogative of Mankind, writeing, when duly executed do Honor to Human nature, but when degenerated into Trades are the most contemptible ways of getting Bread." Evidently, Cardinal Querini's request for her complete works continued to rankle.

Lady Mary found in nearby Verona a very idealistic application of the leisure principle. Here lived the public-spirited Marchese Maffei, dramatist and archeologist, who passed his last years in bringing to his city amenities and culture. Having made a study of Verona's antiquities, he inaugurated city planning to assure harmonious views of the ruins. He opened to his fellow Veronese his private collections of curios, medals and cameos. Close at hand was his library, his palazzo having also apartments devoted to dancing, cards and chamber music. The heart of this benevolent establishment was the salon. Maffei presided from an easy chair over social seminars that "turned upon some point of Learning, either Historical, or Poetical . . ." (Maffei's salon, unlike those of Paris, did not challenge government or church) "Controversie and Politics being utterly prohibited." His palace boasted formal gardens and a theatre. The young people who preferred these diversions were expected to describe the plants noted or the play presented. Following this tradition, the Veronese nobility every autumn in a "Band of about thirty join their hunting Equipages and carrying with them a Portable Theatre . . . every Sunday perform an Opera and other plays the rest of the Week, to the Entertainment of all the Neighborhood." Dazzled by such a display of "Polite Pleasure," Lady Mary fell back upon a phrase she had used in the *Embassy Letters*. The Veronese, she declared, were, like the Turks, a "Set of rational philosophers"

> Who sing and dance and laugh away their Time
> Fresh as their Groves, and happy as their Clime.

"My paper is out."

Lady Oxford died in December of 1755, leaving her expatriate friend a legacy of two hundred pounds. In compliance with the laws of the time, Lady Mary wrote to Wortley to ask his permission to receive her inheritance; women then, and for years later, had no right even to money they earned! Lady Oxford's bequest had lurid results which were to hasten Lady Mary's leaving Gottolengo.

Learning of the windfall (two hundred pounds was in 1755 a handsome sum) whetted Palazzi's insatiable demands upon the victim of a decade of cheating. He employed extravagances, not unworthy of Gianni Schicchi, to divert Lady Mary's inheritance to himself, suggesting that a merchant acquaintance in London be empowered to collect the sum and forward it to Gottolengo. To keep the transaction in her own hands, Lady Mary, after a series of sordid scenes and threats of blackmail, left the entailed property in Gottolengo, never to return.

She settled in the autumn of 1756 at Padua. Here she learned of Lord Bute's appointment as Groom of the Stole to the Prince of Wales, now only four years away from being crowned George III. Lady Mary's congratulations to her daughter are a tribute not only to her uncertain generosity but also to her democratic view of the interdependence of king and subject. On November 23, 1756, she wrote that Lord Bute's career had followed "a very uncommon road; I mean an acknowleg'd Honor and Probity." She then went on to discuss government's deriving its just powers from the consent of the governed. "I have but one short Instruction (pardon that word) to give on his account, that he will never forget the real interest of Prince and People cannot be divided and are almost as closely united as that of Soul and Body." Had more statesmen (including Bute) been of her mind, George III might have kept his thirteen American colonies, and Louis XVI his head.

A disarming example of Lady Mary's maternal pride was her suggestion that a set of furniture made entirely, it would seem, of Venetian glass deserved being placed in a royal residence. "They would be," she hinted, "a very proper Decoration for the Apartment of a Prince so young and beautifull as ours." Not only, she must have conjectured, would so lavish a gift contribute to her son-in-law's favor at court but, were she entrusted with its purchase, would mark her a participant in his career and its resultant intrigues. Lady Mary, who so frequently was in advance of her time, could not entirely free herself from the combination of servility and arrogance that prevailed in royal circles. Setting aside the idealism she so frequently manifested, she pronounced in the same letter the terrible slogan:

"Carress the favorites, avoid the unfortunate and trust no body."

Fifteen years had passed since Lady Mary had broken with Algarotti. Had her relationship with him not been, on her part, what contemporary psychology calls hostile dependency, the rupture would have been permanent. However, in such patterns of alternating quarrels and reconciliations, it was to be expected that sooner or later the paths of the elderly lady and the middle-aged courtier would cross. They did so in 1756, the year of Bute's court appointment and, far more significantly, the year that saw the inauguration of the three-continent struggle known as the Seven Years' War, or the French and Indian War.

Three years earlier Algarotti had withdrawn from the "Academy" at San Souci, the palace that was the reply of Frederick the Great to Versailles. The renewed correspondence between the scientist-philosopher-courtier and Lady Mary gave rise to the latter's spirited attacks upon the cult of military glory. Although she had personal reasons for reproaching Algarotti's "Roial Patron," Lady Mary's detestation of warfare marks her as instinctive a pacifist as she was a Christian. It was not in the eighteenth-century order of things that aristocrats should think of battles, won or lost, in terms of human suffering rather than personal prestige and territorial gain. In her letter to Algarotti in December of 1756, Lady Mary, writing in English, Italian and French, defines true heroism as the cultivation of peaceful arts rather than those of "diabolical destruction." The widening theatres of war prompted her, in letters both to Algarotti and to Lady Bute, to inveigh against slaughter in the name of empire. Since these two correspondents were "roial" favorites, Lady Mary hoped that her words would carry weight at the Prussian and English courts. Her letter of July, 1757, was clearly intended to come to the attention of the Groom of the Stole. Life on the Continent had resulted in disillusionment with dynastic warfare. Of the recently concluded struggle to keep Maria Theresa on her throne Lady Mary was thoroughly critical. She wrote, clearly for Bute's benefit, "I have often been complimented on the English Heroism who have thrown away so many millions without any prospect of advantage to them selves purely to succour a Distress'd Princesse." The idea that economic advantage is to be preferred to military glory did not prevail in Lady Mary's time or class. A distinctly mercantile reasoning appears in the following counsels. Doubtless referring to the War of the Austrian Succession, she wrote, "Some late events will, I hope, open our eyes. We shall see we are an Island and endeavor to extend our Commerce rather than the Quixote Reputation of redressing wrongs and placing Diadems on Heads that should be equally indifferent to us." Having thus disposed of the strategy known as the balance of power, Lady Mary turned her attention to the pressing problem of European possessions in the New World. "When Time has ripen'd Mankind into common Sense, the name Conqueror will be an odious Title. I could easily prove that had the Spainyards establish'd a Trade with the Americans, they would have enrich'd their Country more than by the addition of 22 Kingdoms and all the mines they now work. . . ." For these astute comments, Lady Mary was indebted not only to the businessman husband from whom she was separated but also to her years spent in the Venetian republic, whose wealth was derived from trade, not empire.

Lady Mary divided the last four years of her Italian sojourn between two residences, one in Padua and one in Venice. With England again at war, she found herself exposed to the suspicious surveillance that had plagued her at Avignon. The Queen of the Adriatic was, as she remains, a focal point on Grand Tour itineraries. Thither flocked numbers of English tourists who were, of course, of varying political persuasions.

The reverses suffered by England in the early months of the Seven Years' War had brought to the fore one of the greatest of her statesmen, the elder William Pitt. In June of 1757, he formed a coalition ministry that Bute, at its inception, supported. Lady Mary, mother-in-law to a powerful and unpopular figure, found herself in a sensitive position. She and the English Resident at Venice, John Murray, entertained for one another a lively hatred based upon their contrary positions in regard to the new ministry, against which the Resident did not hesitate to propagandize among English travellers. His disloyal conduct contributed greatly to Lady Mary's isolation; she wrote that "Our great minister, the Resident, affects to treat me as one in the Opposition. I am inclined to laugh rather than be displeas'd at his political Airs, yet as I am amongst stangers they are disagreeable, and could I have foreseen them, would have settled in some other part of the World." In these circumstances Lady Mary's favorite posture of detachment was difficult, if not impossible.

Old age did not erode Lady Mary's penchant for imprudent

friendships. There came to Venice in the spring of 1758 Sir James Steuart who, with his wife and son, was living in exile as a result of his support, thirteen years earlier, of the Young Pretender. Starved for English-speaking companionship, attracted by a Scottish name and probably reminded of her tragic sister, Lady Mar, Lady Mary flung herself into an enthusiastic intimacy with the newcomers. She was not long in discovering that her championship of a recent enemy of England's reigning house afforded the Resident useful incriminatory evidence. She had not been in such a compromising situation since the Rémond scandal. In a thorough panic she wrote Lady Bute that her hospitality to the Steuarts exposed her to guilt by association and to Murray's "new Persecution which may be productive of ill Consequences."

Sir James and Lady Frances provided congeniality that Lady Mary, now approaching her seventieth year, was unwilling to sacrifice to the forces of faction. She must have reasoned that, between them, Bute and Pitt could counter the intrigues of the English Resident at Venice. Taking the precaution of retreating to Padua, she was once more her independent self when she wrote her daughter that "I am now restor'd to my usual calmness of mind . . . being assur'd (from I think good Hands) that my Civility to a Distress'd Lady and Gentleman can no way be an Injury to you or give any Suspicion of my being engag'd in an Interest that was allways foreign both to my Principles and Inclination." It is pleasant to report that Lady Mary's last gamble in friendship was successful. She had at the eleventh hour singled out persons who not only merited but reciprocated her affection. In their company she found the stimulus she had lacked during the rural years at Gottolengo, and in their absence (their continental home was at Tübingen) she sent them letters as polished as those she had written years ago to Abbé Conti.

Sir James, who conformed to Lady Mary's preference for brilliant men of the age of her son, had eclectic tastes. In common with most of eighteenth-century intelligentsia, he was an exponent of Newton. He also wrote on German numismatics. His crowning work is entitled *Inquiry into the Principles of Political Economy*. Upon its completion he sent Lady Mary a fair copy bound and gilt with a "dedication to her Ladyship."

Lady Frances Steuart, whose companionship Lady Mary enjoyed

as much as that of Sir James, was, like the now-demented Lady Mar, given to melancholy. This tendency gave her a special claim upon Lady Mary's sympathy. It also supplied her with an opportunity, of which she made enthusiastic use, to prescribe from her own experience of "hysteric complaints." Always on the lookout for double standards in male-female situations, she recommended the works of a physician who stated that the so-called vapors of weak women resembled the so-called spleen of romantic men. Here was a truth upon which Lady Mary could not resist elaborating. Masking her earnestness in banter, she wrote Sir James in the early fall of 1758 that "you vile usurpers do not only engross learning, power and authority to yourselves, but will be our superiors even in constitution of mind and fancy you are incapable of the woman's weakness of fear and tenderness. Ignorance!" It is to be regretted that Lady Mary confined the expression of these pertinent theories to Sir James Steuart. They might have proved useful to John Stuart, Earl of Bute, who was shortly to be confronted with the first derangement of George III.

Sir James, as befitted a Celt, respected not only the supernatural, but also superstition. Lady Mary, some two months after her advice on Lady Fanny's depression, wrote him about witchcraft, and again in a bantering style. Until late into the eighteenth century, solitary or eccentric old women risked being supposed to be agents of the devil. The Duke's daughter possessed the qualifications that had committed her humbler sisters to imprisonment and worse. John Murray's hostility, which Lady Mary considered persecution, brought her to the edge of paranoia. Her indifference to notoriety forsook her and she was made increasingly uneasy at the thought of finding herself a potentially suspicious character. The fact that she camouflaged fear with mockery should not blind us, as it blinded Lady Louisa Stuart, to the sincerity of the letter she wrote to Sir James on November 14, 1758. If she had been really amused at being thought a witch, she would hardly have written thus: "This letter will be solely to you, and I desire you would not communicate it to Lady Fanny. She is the best woman in the world and I would by no means make her uneasy." Lady Mary continued in a tone of simulated amusement that served to increase, rather than conceal, anxiety for her own good name and, because she was widely supposed to be a figure of scandal, that of Sir James. Horace Walpole and Alexander Pope had not found it inconsistent to accuse her of simultaneous promiscuity and physical repulsiveness. Whether or not she was the slattern they proclaimed her, we shall never know. However, many years before she confided to Sir James her fears of being suspected of witchcraft she had become so disgusted with her appearance that she resolved never again to look into a mirror. To be an acknowledged eccentric who, into the bargain, was ugly must have augmented her apprehension. There is surely something beyond facetiousness in the following: "every period of life has its pleasures . . . even the most despicable creatures alive may find some pleasures. Now observe this comment: who are the most despicable creatures? Certainly Old Women. What pleasure can an old woman take?—Only witchcraft. . . . I own all the facts, as many witches have done before me and go every night in a public manner astride a black cat to a meeting where you are suspected to appear." Lady Mary then varied sarcasm with, it must be confessed, a tasteless coquetry, "This last article is not sworn to, it being doubtfull in what manner our clandestine midnight correspondence is carried on. Some think it treasonable, others lewd (don't tell Lady Fanny), but all agree there was something very odd and unaccountable in such sudden likings. I confess, as I said before, it is witchcraft."

Lady Louisa Stuart desired to deny the implications of this letter in much the same way as she had denied Pope's erotic fantasizing about her grandmother. She assures us in a breathless aside that "It seems almost needless to observe that this letter is written in a spirit of jesting or to use a lower word of *fun*." Again, it will not do.

Lady Mary supposed that her being shunned by an increasing number of English travellers was owing to Murray's enmity. Lady Bute, to whom such complaints were addressed, may have read into them evidence of popular opposition to her husband. Bute, as his domination over Princess Augusta and the Prince of Wales hardened, dared not go about unless escorted by a bodyguard of prize fighters. Mobs frequently rioted outside their house and My Dear Child became inured to rocks being flung through the windows.

Bute's bad press continues. J. C. Long's biography of George III, published in 1960, summarized Bute's ascendancy at court with the deadly phrase, "The snake had entered the garden." Fortunately for what remained to Lady Mary of family feeling, she saw her son-in-law's career in the rosiest terms and put down the negligence of her touring countrymen to the malice of the Resident who, according to her letters to Lady Bute, frustrated her holding court at Venice as she had formerly done at Rome. As loneliness increased and health and spirits declined, Lady Mary treasured every English association, finding a reminder of home even in the straw used in packing the books and china sent by Lady Bute. She yearned for the "little colony" of thirteen grandchildren, sending the girls trinkets for which she exacted, in disciplinary style, letters of thanks. She diverted herself with planning her granddaughters' marriages. This harmless amusement was also marred by the paucity of lordlings in her drawing room, among whom, she fumed to Lady Bute, were it not for the quarantine contrived by the Resident, she could have supplied any number of qualified suitors.

Lady Mary's last months in Italy were solaced not only by the Steuarts but also by a renewed correspondence with James Stuart Mackenzie. Lord Bute's brother was now with his wife, Lady Betty, established at Turin in the position of British minister. His presence on the other side of Italy and that of the Steuarts at Tübingen prompted Lady Mary to plan visits which her failing health prohibited. She put the most flattering construction possible upon her being unable to see the Mackenzies; over and above the fatigues of travel she desired to avoid Turin where her numerous "Acquaintance . . . would draw me into a Croud, as displeasing to me at present as it would have been Delightful at fiveteen." The interposing Alps simplified admitting herself unable to travel to Tübingen. She must limit her daydreams to "a stove in winter and a garden in summer" and, in future, learn to live within the confines of her armchair and her gondola.

Another Bute relative who made himself attentive to Lady Mary was General William Graeme, a mercenary who, at one time, commanded the Venetian troops. He, like Mackenzie, acted as go-between for the elderly expatriate and her family in England. He also attempted to reconcile John Murray and Lady Mary, having it doubtless in mind that an aging lady living among strangers might find herself in need of the services of her country's representative. Such an eventuality is suggested by a leave-taking letter she wrote Lady

Bute early in 1760. There were, in addition to Murray's hostility, other troubles that disposed her to welcome death as the "end of all vexations." Her depression was increased, rather than lightened, by receiving from an unknown sender a copy of young Edward's *Reflections on the Rise and Fall of the Antient Republics*. Having long ago determined to despise her unstable son, she found only nonsense in the lessons to be learned from the respective disappearances of Sparta, Athens, Thebes, Carthage and Rome. Other readers were more generous. Edward's *Reflections* went into several English editions and was translated into French. One of his successive "governors" paid the work the sincerest of all tributes; he claimed to have written it himself. Without knowing of this accusation of plagiarism, the doting mother dismissed Edward's debut as historian as a "very sorry Book printed in his name."

Lady Mary's letters to My Dear Child had for many years contained appeals for sympathy and even for pity. She clearly longed to go home. We must assume that her separation from Wortley forbade her to do so during his lifetime. This bargain became increasingly painful upon her learning, at the time of the appearance of Edward's book, that her husband was threatened with blindness, a disability which Lady Mary feared would be exploited not only by dishonest servants but also by their shady son. It was in these circumstances that she permitted herself the liberty of confiding to his sibling that she had "long wept the misfortune of being mother to such an Animal." This comment was hardly calculated to reassure Lady Bute as to her mother's being court material.

That the Butes harbored grave doubts on this subject is made clear by a letter from Mackenzie to his brother written a year earlier. Employing the vocabulary of conspiracy, he reassured Lord Bute, "I am glad You have acquainted me with Your Sentiments as to that Person's return home. . . . I fancy You need not be under great apprehension of such an Event taking place for I am assured that the Person is much failed within these two or three last years and that at times the visible signs of dotage appear. . . ."

The Butes are to be pardoned for encouraging the Person to remain in Venice. What with Mr. Wortley, stingy to the point of eccentricity, the frequently criminal Edward, and Lord Bute's purportedly scandalous relationship with Princess Augusta, they can have had little heart for such commotions as Lady Mary tended to foment. That this was the case the Person seems to have sensed, in writing My Dear Child that "My Life is so near a Conclusion that where or how I pass it . . . is almost indifferent to me. I have outliv'd the greatest part of my Acqaintance; and to say truth, a return to Croud and Bustle after my long Retirement would be disagreeable to me yet if I could be of use either to your Father or your Family I would venture shortening the insignificant days of your most affectionate Mother. . . ." It is to be hoped that Lady Bute told Wortley that his reckless wife, always the more generous of the spouses, offered a terminal reconciliation which had as a principal objective the solacing of his sightless old age. It was a handsome gesture. It was also futile. Wortley, having managed alone for over twenty years, preferred to keep to the terms upon which he and Lady Mary had separated.

Bute's power was tremendously increased by his royal patron's ascendance to the throne in 1760. Lady Mary's first concern, upon the accession of George III, was Sir James Steuart's pardon. After urging this act of amnesty in a letter to My Dear Child, she wrote her friend "that as soon as my daughter informed me of the late great event I immediately put her in mind of your affairs in the warmest manner. I do not doubt it will have the effect I wish."

It was to the same friend that Lady Mary wrote her most eloquent reflections upon the "end of all vexations." Almost twenty years earlier Lord Hervey had written of his approaching death thus: "The last stages of an infirm life are filthy roads and like all other roads, I find the farther one goes from the capital the more tedious the miles grow, and the more rough and disagreeable the ways." Hervey's metaphor, modified by Lady Mary's confidence in Bute's prospects, reappears in a letter written to Sir James in 1761. "Tho' I am preparing for my last and longest journey and stand on the threshold of this dirty world, my several infirmities like post-horses ready to hurry me away, I cannot be insensible to the happiness of my native country, and am glad to see the prospect of a prosperity and harmony that I was never witness to." The American Revolution! The French Revolution! The Industrial Revolution! The Napoleonic Wars! All these convulsions were to transpire while Farmer George's pendulum swung between benevolent mediocrity and derangement.

Lady Mary's pathetic references to her impending death suggest that she knew she had cancer. While she was preparing for life's last journey Wortley, whom she had believed to be in sound health, unexpectedly predeceased her. He had made a will in 1755 that stressed the reward and punishment potentialities of his vast holdings. Lady Bute and her second son, who was required to adopt the Wortley name, came into millions. Lady Mary received a modest legacy. To Edward was left an annuity that, in relation to his extravagant habits and crippling debts, could be considered only a token.

Edward, who had never been restrained by the laws of cause and effect, took leave of his remaining stock of principle. Furious at finding himself passed over in favor of his sister, he attempted to challenge his father's will, "in his mother's name." Lady Mary, appalled at "those infamous libels," enclosed the following in a letter sent to Lady Bute: "Son, I know not how to write to you and scarcely what to say. Your present conduct is far more Infamous than the past. It is a small sign of reformation of manners when you durst disturb an Indulgent (too indulgent) Father's dying pangs on mercenary Considerations, and are now defaming a too fond mother by the most impudent Forgery. . . . You have shorten'd you Father's day and will perhaps have the Glory to break your mother's heart—I will not curse you—God give you a real not affected Repentance."

Where one kind of misrepresentation failed, mused the resourceful Edward, another might succeed. Many would be delighted to believe that he had been slighted by Wortley's will because his father was Sultan Achmet III. Had he known of Lady Mary's intended publication of the *Embassy Letters,* in which he appears as a child of three, let alone the part he had played in her campaign for inoculation, even so reckless a rogue might have hesitated to make use of this preposterous story. It was his engaging suggestion that the Butes, beleaguered by troubles of their own, buy off the suppositious Osmanli.

Lady Mary, without knowing of what they consisted, feared Edward's threats. She urged the Butes not to "compound" with him and promised that she would never see him again. He sent her a letter that "frighted" her as to what chicanery he might employ to obtain a portion of his sister's fortune.

Whether or not Lady Mary sensed that the Butes dreaded her

return we do not know. Far gone with cancer, harassed by the Resident's malice, and released by his death from whatever pact she may have had with Wortley, the widow decided to flee to My Dear Child. Misgivings abounded. Would her health permit a long overland passage through war-torn Europe? Would she be equal to the necessarily emotional meeting with her family? Would she be a source of embarrassment? All these considerations kept her in an agony of indecision. Mackenzie, in these difficult circumstances, was charged with acting as go-between. To the Butes he wrote of Lady Mary's vacillations: "She is so undetermined about everything, she makes fifty resolutions every day and changes them before night." By spring of 1761 her plans began to take shape. She wrote her daughter that if she survived the summer she would return to England, via Germany, in September.

Preparations for the journey were complex. Old age and terminal illness made her "timorous and suspicious." What if the Resident should succeed, in the event of her death, in diverting to himself possessions intended for others? To forestall this, she made a will containing many special bequests and wrote to Lady Bute where it was hidden. She asked that a house in London be engaged for her and requested assistance in getting her goods through customs, lest she or her servants be suspected of smuggling. After a delay caused by an eye infection, she was on her way.

Her forebodings about the journey were justified. Upon arriving in Rotterdam, many weeks after leaving Venice, she wrote the Steuarts that, had she foreseen the dangers to which she and her retinue would be exposed, she would never have undertaken to return to England. She was delayed for over two months in Holland by both the illness of her maid and winter storms so severe that channel crossings were impossible. It is to this delay that the 1763 publication of the *Embassy Letters* is owed.

At Rotterdam Lady Mary met an obscure English clergyman, Benjamin Sowden, who, of course, does not appear in her last letters. Knowing that a dignified and acknowledged publication of the *Embassy Letters* would be forbidden by considerations of family, class and her own dubious reputation, she proposed them as a nest-egg for Sowden. His poverty, she hoped, would prompt him to publish them for his own profit. The history of this transaction was to become fully as tangled as that of the Boswell papers. The annals of attempts to regain the letters, of nocturnal copies being taken by persons unknown and of Lady Bute's fears for her mother's revelations belong to the months following Lady Mary's death in August of 1762. When at length a January thaw made a channel crossing possible, she left the Continent solaced by the conviction that she had secured her long-denied literary fame. She had.

Lady Mary's return home has a Rip Van Winkle ring. Husband, sister, friends and enemies were gone, and her son was lost through a cleavage more painful than death. For her mother's last residence Lady Bute had leased a small house on Great George Street that compared unfavorably with Italian palazzi. There flocked not only the Butes and their "Satellites" but also callers who desired to look over the colorful traveller. Among these was Horace Walpole, who wrote a venomous description of the dying woman, replete with his habitual accusations of physical filth. Lady Mary's cousin-by-marriage, Elizabeth Robinson Montagu, was, if without affection, also without malice. Her description of the invalid's household, into which a "Tower of Babel" staff was packed in polyglot confusion, is humorous, but not unkind.

Lady Mary's last letter was written to the melancholy Lady Fanny Steuart. It is again tempting to read into her attempts to help these Jacobite exiles a reminder of her efforts on behalf of Lady Mar, the beloved sister of so long ago. Lady Mary had never ceased to urge that Bute obtain a pardon for Sir James. Confident that her request would be granted, she wrote in July, 1762, "Dear Madam, I have been ill a long time and am now so bad I am little capable of writing, but I would not pass in your opinion as either stupid or ungrateful. My heart is always warm in your service and I am always told your affairs shall be taken care of." On this benevolent note she laid down her pen.

Only a few weeks of life remained. They were passed in the merciful haze of hemlock. To those who asked how she was, she replied that she had lived long enough. As she lay dying, she came close to wrecking her plans to publish the *Embassy Letters*. She admitted that they had been confided to the Rev. Mr. Sowden of Rotterdam for this purpose, thus innocently inaugurating Lady Bute's efforts at suppression. This blunder may have been prompted by sedation, suffering or the lifetime habit of plain speaking. Perhaps she scrupled to deceive Lady Bute, from whom she was at any moment to part. Or, as her biographer, Robert Halsband, has surmised, were such words as she may have spoken a "fitting conclusion to her whole life?"

She believed, perhaps in competitive emulation of Mme. de Sévigné, that My Dear Child had been her ruling passion. She was wrong. Lady Mary belonged, heart and soul, to literature. This was, in terms of time and class, her tragedy. The reading part of posterity is grateful for excellence that survived hostility, loneliness and neglect. Time, once her enemy, has become her champion.

3

THE ARTIST

Mary Granville Delany

1700-1788

MARY GRANVILLE DELANY was born a decade after Lady Mary Wortley Montagu. The younger woman was to be as much admired for propriety as the elder had been censured for eccentricity. Both were born into the upper reaches of Augustan society. Lady Mary found the patrician world a prison and fled it. Mrs. Delany accepted the stately routines of the Great House, the Deanery and eventually Windsor itself with almost unswerving serenity.

That this was to be the case is a tribute to a nature both poised and resourceful. Her youth was filled with national and familial crises. Her father, Bernard, was the younger brother of George Granville, whose courteous encouragement of Pope has been recorded in one of the latter's heroic couplets. An even more significant well-wisher was Queen Anne, who bestowed upon George Granville the Lansdowne title. His Lordship further improved his prospects by marrying the widow of Thomas Thynne, a step that made him master of Longleat, today still one of the most imposing of English houses.

Then in 1714 the predictable blow fell. Queen Anne died and, pursuant to the Act of Succession, George I started on his laggardly journey from Herrenhausen. Here was a decline in the Granville expectations! When in 1740 Mary began to write her autobiography, she recounted candidly that "The Death of Queen Anne made a considerable alteration in our affairs. We were of the discontented party, and not without reason; not only my father but all my relations that were in public employments suffered greatly by this change. My father being a younger brother, his chief dependence was on the court and his brother's friendship."

A period of fear and disorder ensued. Lord Lansdowne, suspected of disloyalty to the new regime, was imprisoned in the Tower while the Bernard Granvilles retired to prudent exile in Gloucestershire, a reversal that caused Mary's mother to fall "into hysterics fits one after another."

Such excesses suggest that Mrs. Delany's firmness of character was inherited from the Granvilles, rather than the Westcombs, her maternal grandparents. This supposition gains credibility in her accounts of the powerful influence exerted upon her concerns not only by Lord Lansdowne, but by his sister Lady Stanley, a state of affairs that even in a male-dominated society suggests an overpliant wife and sister-in-law.

Lady Stanley, who appears in her niece's autobiography as *Valeria,* had been Maid of Honor to Queen Mary. She undertook to prepare Mary Granville for the same exalted future, a destiny that was frustrated by the fact that the consort of George I was suffering life imprisonment for adultery, and her spouse was openly consoling himself with two mistresses, known as the Maypole and the Elephant. Lady Stanley's schooling had to be denied fulfillment for the more than seventy years that elapsed before the aged Mrs. Delany became a mother substitute to George III and Queen Charlotte.

Lord Lansdowne remained in the Tower for two years. When he emerged he needed desperately to regain the ground he had lost both financially and politically. He required friends with money and influence and was to prove cruel in the steps he took to secure them; according to his niece he was "magnificent in his nature and valued no expense that would gratify it, which in the end hurt him and his family extremely." In particular it hurt Mary.

Shortly after his release from prison "Alcander," as Lord Lansdowne appears in her autobiography, invited the seventeen-year-old Mary to pay a prolonged visit to Longleat. This opportunity was viewed by the impoverished Granvilles as advantageous and by their spirited daughter as enchanting, there "Being a very good band of music in the house" with dancing every evening. Soon after her

arrival an elderly Cornish squire, Alexander Pendarves, joined the
house party. "Gromio" was sixty years of age and under the best of
circumstances unappealing. A journey in the rain on horseback had
done nothing to increase his meager charms. Mary had expected that
an intimate of her extravagant uncle would have "the appearance of
a gentleman when the poor, old, dripping almost drowned Gromio
was brought into the room, like Hob out of the well, his wig, his
coat, his dirty boots, his large unwieldy person, and his crimson
countenance were all subjects of great mirth and observation to me."

Laugh as she would, it was borne in upon the unfortunate girl
that she was to be the means of recouping her uncle's fortunes.
Gromio was the well-heeled friend with political pull. She was
forced into marriage with a man old enough to be her grandfather
who, in addition to being a sot, was suspected by his bride of "maintaining some very close relations," in other words, illegitimate children.

The wedding was hurried on. Her parents urged their pitiful
child to accept a fate she viewed as less desirable than the immolation
of Iphigenia, pointing out that she owed it not only to herself, but
to her family, to marry the distasteful Gromio for purely pecuniary reasons. She was removed by her unsuitable husband to his castle
at Roscrow, where she found "an old hall that had scarce any light
belonging to it; on the left hand of which there was a parlour, the
floor of which was rotten in places, and part of the ceiling broken
down; and the windows were placed so high that my head did not
come to the bottom of them."

"Here my courage forsook me at once and I fell into a violent
passion of crying. . . ."

This grisly *mariage de convenance* was destined to be of mercifully short duration. It was to prove as unpleasant in its termination
as in its commencement. Gromio died in his sleep and Mary Pendarves awoke to find herself lying beside a corpse that had turned
black. There was nothing inconsistent about Alexander Pendarves.
At twenty-four Mary was liberated into widowhood. A long and
uncommonly varied life awaited.

The annals of her many years have been preserved by Lady Llanover, a great-great niece, in the six volumes entitled *The Autobiography and Correspondence of Mary Granville Delany*. Her Ladyship,

Mary Granville Delany with, inset, one
of her series of paper mosaics to which she
gave the name *Flora Delanica*

a great-granddaughter of Ann Granville Dewes, Mrs. Delany's younger sister, had access to the hundreds of letters addressed not only to a sister, but to a sister's daughter and, eventually, a sister's granddaughter. The reader is carried from the period just before the Hanoverians replaced and displaced the Stuarts, to the years following the loss of the American colonies.

Lady Llanover's editorial methods were eclectic. She included not only letters from Mrs. Pendarves (later and more happily Mrs. Delany) to friends and family, but their letters to her, and occasionally to one another. In middle life Mrs. Delany, using the stately sobriquet, "Aspasia," wrote autobiographical chapters that tell of her childhood, her tragic first marriage and of any other matters she judged too delicate to discuss openly in her correspondence at the time of their occurrence. These fragments and the letters she wrote and received tell Mrs. Delany's story of eighty-eight years.

Among the myriad characters of the *Autobiography and Correspondence,* Lady Llanover herself must be included. Not content to leave Mrs. Delany and her friends to their own devices, she bestowed praise or blame according to Victorian standards. She was, even by these, a snob and prejudiced to a degree that borders on bigotry. Burke's *Peerage* must have lain open before her; from it the ancestry, births, marriages and deaths of Mrs. Delany's distinguished friends are enthusiastically quoted. Nor, to be fair to the editoress, is she remiss in supplying similar statistics for singers heard and actors seen.

Lady Llanover had little respect for her contemporaries. She viewed the years when the American Civil War broke out and the Prince Consort died as a frivolous period. It was her intention to set forth Mrs. Delany's virtues in so emphatic a manner that her readers, especially her female readers, would mend their giddy ways. The dear Queen herself and the Victorian novelists had exploited the good woman. To the company of Thackeray's Amelia Sedley and Dickens's Esther Summerson and Agnes Wickfield, Lady Llanover longed to add Mary Granville Delany.

The Georgian world, particularly that of the first two Georges, was brilliant, hard and cynical. Mary, with her orthodox piety, her effusive friendships and her domestic virtues, could be adjusted to Victorian rather than Georgian ideals, such as they were.

As a result of Lady Llanover's editorializing, the reader is sub-jected to distortions. She would have us believe that standards of behavior during the eighteenth century were loftier than was the case, that Fanny Burney was a deceitful minx and that no well-born mother can successfully nurse her babies. Of the six volumes devoted to her charming great-great aunt, fully one could be filled with the editor's facts and fancies.

A more modest presentation is that of Emily Morse Symonds. Using the pen name, "George Paston," she published in 1900 *Mrs. Delany: A Memoir*. She was assisted in this task by Mrs. Herbert, Lady Llanover's daughter, who made available material omitted or suppressed by her infatuated mother. From these we learn, to our relief, that Mrs. Delany could be, on occasion, spiteful, inconsistent and envious. "George Paston" gives us a delightful, fallible woman, while Lady Llanover presents "A perfect woman nobly planned, to warn, to comfort and command."

The two versions of Mrs. Delany's life and correspondence fulfill in a lesser way the function of Pepys's *Diary*. In the latter we have nine years of middle-class life in Restoration London. In the former we experience the patrician world of Georgian England and Ireland as it was relished by a great lady of exuberance, compassion and versatility.

Mrs. Delany was a creative conformist. She participated in the social routines of her class and times without sacrifice of her many talents. It would be unfair to accuse her, as a person or an artist, of superficiality. Her attainments, however, were in breadth rather than depth. She excelled in music and in the applied arts. She loved sea shells, from which she made "lustres." Moralist that she was, she admired the didactic painting of Hogarth, writing in 1731 that "there is more sense in it than any I have seen." Her own drawing interested him sufficiently to proffer "some instructions about draw-ing that will be of great use . . . some rules of his own that he says will improve me more in a day than a year's learning in the common way." Armed with these precepts, she made numerous copies from the old masters and, during her years of residing in Ireland, sketched the landscape of County Down, an Irish harper playing at her side to heighten local color. Her embroideries, of which only photographs remain, were detailed by Lady Llanover as examples of the superior feminine skills of the eighteenth century.

Posterity chiefly remembers Mrs. Delany as the friend of Händel, Swift and Fanny Burney, and as the inventor, when she was already an old lady, of a new method for illustrating flowers. Using such commonplace materials as paper, scissors and paste, she depicted a thousand botanical specimens. These charming productions, which she called *Flora Delanica,* have won for Mrs. Delany a place in the Print Room of the British Museum and at Windsor Castle.

In so long a life many changes of mood, companions and environment are inevitable. The appalled little Mrs. Pendarves gave way to the young widow who, making her home with Sir John and Lady Stanley, savored the gaieties of London, which had been denied to her in girlhood. Her earliest letters are those written to her younger sister, Ann Granville, who remained with their mother in Gloucestershire. From town she detailed gossip of *la cour,* who will marry whom, who is wearing what and how it is made and, most significantly, the operatic ups and downs of the 1720s.

Händel, who was the central figure in these varying fortunes, was an intimate friend of the Granville family. Bernard Granville, Junior, was one of Händel's most loyal patrons, an example his sister, Mary Pendarves, emulated with affection and delight. She went constantly to hear music; her accounts of opera and oratorio are staples of Händelian studies.

Mary Granville met Händel during his earliest years in London. She was an impertinent child of ten. Years later in her autobiography she described Händel, whose career as one of the most prolific of all composers did not impinge upon his virtuosity at the keyboard. The great man had kindly played for the child upon her spinct. "My Uncle archly asked me whether I would play as well as Mr. Handel. 'If I did not think I should' cried I, 'I would burn my instrument,' such was the innocent presumption of childish ignorance."

Opera is essentially a turbulent medium. In early Georgian London its very existence was controversial. Political rivalries encumbered composers and singers, as the court of George II championed Händel, and that of Frederick Prince of Wales supported Bononcini. The financial depression that followed the South Sea Bubble panic deprived opera of patronage. During Händel's career the literary source for opera libretti was the mythology and history of the ancient world. Gods and goddesses, the heroes and heroines of antiquity and, for variety, "gentle shepherds" from Arcady were impersonated by exotic virtuosi who sang in Italian. They had for the London public only limited appeal. Addison in the *Spectator Papers* mounted a jeering campaign against Italian opera and his country-men who suffered themselves to listen to "harmonies" sung in a language they did not understand. In 1728 the operatic situation rapidly worsened. That ancestor of topical musical comedy, *The Beggar's Opera,* was produced. The public was enchanted to ex-change the residents of Mt. Olympus and Parnassus for those of Gin Lane. Loyal Mrs. Pendarves wrote to her sister that "yesterday I was at the rehearsal of the new opera composed by Handel. I like it extremely but the taste of the town is so depraved that nothing will be approved of but the burlesque. *The Beggars' Opera* entirely triumphs over the Italian one."

In a letter written a month later, Mrs. Pendarves continued her sarcastic appraisal of the new hit. "I desire you will introduce *The Beggars' Opera* at Gloucester, you must sing it everywhere *but at church if you have a mind to be like the polite world.*"

She gave up opera in December of 1729 as a lost cause. "The opera is too good for the vile taste of the town; it is condemned never more to appear on the stage after this night. I long to hear its dying song, poor dear swan. We are to have some old opera revived, which I am sorry for, it will put people upon making comparisons between these singers and those that performed before, which will be a disad-vantage among the ill-judging multitude."

Mrs. Pendarves proved in her next comment to be a shrewd judge of taste—more shrewd, certainly, than she knew. *The Beggar's Opera* succeeded because it was earthy, cheerful and embellished with bal-lads John Bull either knew already or could easily remember; the Händel operas were lofty, grave and, in music and text, highly for-malized. "The present opera," Mrs. Pendarves quite accurately con-cluded, "Is disliked because it is too much studied."

During these years of attendance at court, at the opera and other haunts of fashion, Mrs. Pendarves did not lack for suitors. Sir John and Lady Stanley were quite prepared to look out a second husband for their niece, but she had had enough of avuncular matchmaking. Marriage was a subject on which she could be waspish. "Matrimony! I marry! Yes, there's a blessed scene before my eyes of the comforts of that state. A sick husband, squalling brats, a cross mother-in-law, and a thousand unavoidable impertinences."

Among the admirers of Mrs. Pendarves were swains she camouflaged as "Clario," "HaHa," "Germanicus," "Tom Tit," and "Henricus." Their intentions toward the vivacious widow were not uniformly honorable. She was indifferent to becoming wife or mistress to any of them.

She had met, before Mr. Pendarves made his welcome exit from this world, "Herminius." In later years she described him as "a young man in great esteem and fashion at that time, very handsome, genteel, polite and unaffected. He was born to a very considerable fortune, and was possest of it as soon as he came of age, but was as little presuming on the advantages he had from fortune as on those he had from nature."

This charmer was Lord Baltimore. His family held the patent for Maryland, for which they paid "yearly as a acknowledgment to the crown two Indian arrows at Windsor Castle on Easter Tuesday and the fifth part of the gold and silver ore."

Mrs. Pendarves would have been less than human in terms of her class-obsessed times if she had been indifferent to becoming the First Lady of one of the American colonies. It is perhaps an indication of her involvement in a love affair marked by procrastination and evasions that she devised not one but four fictitious names for his eligible but elusive Lordship. She called him Bas, Guyamore, The American Prince and Herminius.

Her letters are guarded on the subject of the young man with whom she seems to have been sincerely in love. She wrote in 1729 that "poor Bas" absent in Italy "was then dangerously ill of a fever that had reduced him so much that should he recover the fever it was not possible for him to live long." A month later she was erroneously informed that Bas was lost at sea. She was at the opera when the blow fell. "The news of Bas was confirmed. I had not so much hardness in my nature as to hear of his deplorable end without being shocked, and whether it was owing to that, or that the opera is not so meritorious as Mr. Händel's generally are but I never was so little pleased with one in my life."

Two weeks later Herminius, hale and hearty, reappeared in London. Again the opera was to be interrupted by extramusical emotions. He told Mrs. Pendarves that he had been in love with her for five years. In an account of her disappointment, written many years later, she wrote, "I was in such confusion I knew not what I saw or heard for some time, but finding he was going on with the same subject, I softly begged he would not interrupt my attention to the opera, as if he had anything to say to me, that was *not* the proper place."

Lord Baltimore asked if he might call the next day. Mrs. Pendarves awaited his visit, hoping to be freed from "the anxiety of uncertainty." Marriage was soon the topic of conversation, with Herminius saying, not too promisingly that "he was determined never to marry, unless he was well assured of the affection of the person he married." Mrs. Pendarves framed an adroit reply. " 'Can you,' " she asked, " 'have stronger proof if the person is at her own disposal than her consenting to marry you.' He replied that was not sufficient. I said he was *unreasonable* upon which he started up and said, 'I find, Madam, this is a point in which we shall never agree,' looked piqued and angry, made a low bow and went away immediately," leaving Mrs. Pendarves to face the unflattering fact that she had been virtually jilted.

She made as light of her disappointment as she could. In writing to Ann Granville she dismissed her fickle lover as a "deserter," adding that "he can be of no use, he was a pretty plaything enough— could sing and dance, but as he has listed under another banner, I strike him out of my list."

Lord Baltimore soon married a woman who brought him a far more ample dowry than the modest inheritance left by Gromio. It has been suggested by the indefatigable Lady Llanover that the expensive habits of the "American Prince" required marriage with an heiress and that he deliberately provoked a quarrel with Mrs. Pendarves to rid himself of her. A period of depression and illness followed which, in good time, prompted the long visit to Ireland that was to make so important a contribution to her happiness.

Among the companions of Mrs. Pendarves's widowhood were daughters of the Chief Justice of Ireland, Miss Donnellan and Mrs. Clayton. Under their aegis she journeyed to Ireland. Hospitality in this period of slow travel was, of necessity, a prolonged matter. Mrs. Pendarves had planned to stay a mere six months, but was so pleased with Ireland and the friends she made there that she remained for a year and a half.

Mrs. Clayton's husband was bishop of Killala and, at the time of

Mrs. Pendarves's visit, was maneuvering in a manner prophetic of Trollope for preferment to a more prosperous see. The Claytons moved in the first circles and entertained lavishly. They were in a position to introduce their interesting guest to everyone of significance in the narrow world of Anglo-Ireland. Mrs. Pendarves was delighted with her reception, which she described to her sister, Ann. "The Bishop of Killala and his Lady, as you know, are agreeable, and never so much so as in their own house, which is indeed magnifique, and they have a heart answerable to their fortune—Sunday we went to church, and saw all company that came, which was numerous, for Mrs. Clayton is extremely liked, and visited by everybody. Yesterday we were at the same sport, and this morning we are to go to the Duchess of Dorset's to pay our court. So much for our company, now for our habitation. Stephen's Green is the name of the square where this house stands; the front of it is like Devonshire House. The apartments are handsome, and furnished with gold-coloured damask, virtues, busts and pictures that the bishop brought with him from Italy. A universal cheerfulness reigns in the house. They keep a very handsome table, six dishes of meat at dinner, and six plates at supper."

It was in the Fall of 1731 that Mrs. Pendarves travelled to Dublin. The Battle of the Boyne, at which William of Orange defeated his father-in-law, James II, was some forty years in the past. This overthrow spelled disaster to James's Irish-Catholic supporters. What the Celtic Irish still call "The Bad Century" was inaugurated by the Williamite Settlement and the Penal Laws. By the first of these measures, the lands of the Irish gentry were bestowed on the Orange faction. The Penal Laws forbade the practice of their religion and inhibited the means of education and even the commercial transactions of Catholics.

To their recently acquired acres flocked the newcomers from England, building the city squares and country mansions that are still among the glories of the Irish republic, excluding such Big Houses as were destroyed during the "troubles." Dublin was intended as a great Georgian city. As such, it remains a tribute to its builders.

While the Age of Reason saw the advance of many peoples toward more humane and egalitarian practices, the Gaelic world declined.

Ireland during the eighteenth century became as English in culture and politics as the mother country could make it. For the Gael, the Bad Century spelled silence, persecution and degradation. For the Ascendancy, as the Anglo-Irish are tellingly known, it was a time of expansion, luxury and literary flowering. Posterity owes to this heritage Swift, Goldsmith, Burke, Sheridan, Wilde and Shaw. Ironically, we owe to the same heritage poets associated with the Irish renaissance and the founding of the Abbey Theatre, with Yeats, the grandson of an Anglo-Irish pastor, at their head.

Ireland was to provide Mrs. Pendarves with a powerful stimulus to her chief literary gift. She possessed to a high degree the ability to describe her environment, whether it was that of the countryside, the theatre or the drawing room. With personalities she was less expert. The general social scene she captured because she had a flair for occasion and ceremony. The complexities of human motivation were either beyond her or a matter of indifference. She was not, where individual persons were concerned, analytical. Like her mentor, Hogarth, she possessed a photographic sense and, like him, her concern was with society "in the round."

The Duke and Duchess of Dorset * held court at Dublin Castle, headquarters of English domination. Mrs. Pendarves, as befitted the guest of a fashionable clergyman, went there frequently, reporting to her family in England that "the apartments consist of three rooms, not altogether so large as those at St. James's, but of a very tolerable size. In the farthest room there is placed a basset table at which the Duchess of Dorset sits down after she has received and made her compliments to the company. It is very seldom any ladies sit down to basset but quadrille parties are made up in the other rooms just the same as at St. James's."

Royal birthdays were a Hanoverian obsession. The celebrating of them supplied a focal point for court life, requiring that the guests wear new clothes or, as Fanny Burney was some fifty years later to observe, clothes that seemed to be new. On November 4, 1731, Mrs. Pendarves participated in such an occasion. She "never saw more company in one place; abundance of finery, and indeed many pretty women—. The whole apartment of the Castle was open, which consists of several good rooms; in one there was a supper ordered after

* The Duke of Dorset was Lord Lieutenant of Ireland during the 1730s.

the manner of that at the masquerade, where everybody went at what hour they liked best and vast profusion of meat and drink, which you may be sure has *guined the hearts* of all guzzlers."

In March the Duke and Duchess gave a ball that must have been influenced by Irish conviviality, repressed as it was. Mrs. Pendarves wrote to her brother that at eleven o'clock minuets were finished and the Duchess went to the basset table.

"After an hour's playing the Duke, Duchess and nobility marched into the supper room which was the council chamber. In the midst of the room was placed a holly tree, illuminated by a hundred wax tapers; round it was placed all sorts of meat, fruit, and sweetmeats; servants waited next, and were encompassed round by a table to which the company came by turns to take what they wanted. When the doors were *first* opened, the hurly burly was not to be described; squawling, shrieking, all sort of noises; some ladies lost their lappets, others were trod upon. Poor Lady Santry almost lost her breath in the scuffle and fanned herself two hours before she could recover herself enough to know if she was dead or alive. . . . The famous tree," Mrs. Pendarves concluded, "occasion'd more rout than it was worth."

Some two months after these disorderly gaieties, Bishop Clayton bestowed a summer's worth of attention upon his remote diocese. Killala lies on the northern Atlantic. The trip from Dublin involved a coast-to-coast crossing of Ireland. It was done in the usual leisurely style of Georgian travel, with luxurious visits to relieve the fatigue of days spent on roads which Mrs. Pendarves found better than those in England "mostly causeways, a little jumbling, but *very safe.*"

The Bishop's party made its first stop at Dangan, the seat of Richard Colley Wesley, or Wellesly, grandfather of the Duke of Wellington. Mrs. Pendarves was delighted with their entertainment, finding that "we live magnificently, and at the same time without ceremony. There is a charming large hall with an organ and harpsichord, where all the company meet when they have a mind to be together and where music, draughts, dancing, shuttlecock and prayers take their turn. Our hours for eating are ten, three and ten again."

During this, her first experience of rural Ireland, Mrs. Pendarves, unlike many of her conquering compatriots, deplored the contrast between the rich and the poor. It was not the custom for great ladies of the 18th century to concern themselves with the practical relieving of misery. Mrs. Pendarves found that her hosts were guilty, even in those days of gargantuan meals, of downright gluttony. She tells us that "I have not seen less than fourteen dishes of meat for dinner, and seven for supper during my peregrinations; and they not only treat us at their houses magnificently but, if we are to go to an inn, they provide us with a basket crammed with good things. . . . The poverty of the people as I have passed through the country," Mrs. Pendarves continued on a strangely modern note, "has made *my heart ache*. I never saw greater appearance of *misery;* they live in great extremes, either profusely or wretchedly."

Several months before writing these perspicacious observations, Mrs. Pendarves had met the man she was, a decade later, to marry. He was the Reverend Patrick Delany. In addition to his ecclesiastical office, he was a Fellow of Trinity College, Dublin, and lived just outside the city in a villa called Delville. Mrs. Pendarves was often among his guests; she wrote very favorably of him in her letters to her family and, in later years, included in her autobiography her first impressions of him. He "lived in a very agreeable manner, and reserved one day in the week for his particular friends among whom were those of the best learning and genius in the kingdom. I thought myself honoured by being admitted to such a set. . . . By this means I grew intimate with 'Dessario' and had an opportunity of observing his many excellent qualities. His wit and learning were to me his meanest praise; the excellence of his heart, his humanity, benevolence, charity, and generosity, his tenderness, affection, and friendly zeal gave me a higher opinion of him than any other man I had ever conversed with, and made me take every opportunity of conversing and corresponding with one from whom I expected so much improvement."

Dr. Delany seems to have been partial to widows; he married two. The first was an immensely rich Mrs. Tennison, whose fortune added luxury to Delville's life and hospitality. Little dreaming that she would one day be mistress of Delville, Mrs. Pendarves went, during her Dublin visit, to observe her future husband in his pastoral role. In a letter omitted by Lady Llanover, she wrote on January 13, 1733, "Last Sunday I went to hear Doctor Delany preach and was extremely pleased with him. His sermon was on the duties of wives to husbands, a subject of no great use to me at present. He has an easy, pathetical manner of preaching that pleases me mightily."

At Delville Mrs. Pendarves met Jonathan Swift, the Dean of St. Patrick's Cathedral. He was at this time far gone in the love-hate conflicts that were later to madden him. Reversal of political fortunes had pursued his family, who were of the Royalist party during the Civil War of the previous century. His was an unhappy childhood of poverty and neglect. He harbored countless grudges caused by slights to his voracious pride. He was afflicted by dizziness that modern medicine has diagnosed as Ménière's disease. Frustration, disappointment, deafness and pain lashed Swift into a chronic rage that would now be called paranoia. He exemplified the negative idealism which is so widely practiced by the revolutionaries of today. Because society is not perfectible it should be loathed. Humanity's failures in justice, sincerity, intelligence and cleanliness were equally objects of his fury.

St. Patrick's was, in terms of the so-called Church of Ireland, as potent a symbol of English power as Dublin Castle. It was part of the apparatus of oppression. Swift, knowing it as such, hated himself for representing the oppressors. In a characteristic ambivalence, he also despised the Celtic Irish for cringing before the sadistic Penal Laws.

It was in 1732 that Mrs. Pendarves had described the starving Irish peasantry. At about the same time Swift expressed himself on the same subject. He had written one of the most savage of all satires. This was *A Modest Proposal,* in which he gravely recommended cannibalism as a means of solving Ireland's economic problems. Since the Ascendancy was bent, he reasoned, on the slow starvation of the Gael, why not practice race suicide? Irish children, bred for butchering, would be a luxurious variation in the ample fare of the Big House, as well as a source of income for their parents. Roasted, fried or boiled, the flesh of a well-nursed baby would be deliciously delicate while that of twelve-year-old boys and girls might be mistaken for venison. In this way, by implication, Irish acres could be cleared for English occupation and Celtic youth spared the degradation of their parents.

A Modest Proposal set forth this monstrous suggestion so coolly and with such an appearance of sweet reason that certain readers (unlike the Bishop, who refused to believe a word of *Gulliver's Travels*) did not know the satire for what it was—a raging attack upon the conquerors who enriched themselves with the lands of their starving tenants.

If *A Modest Proposal* was totally inconsistent with the office of a prelate of the Church of Ireland, *The Tale of a Tub,* written years earlier, was hardly a suitable work for the authorship of any clergyman of any faith. Although the second Mrs. Delany refers with the greatest reverence to Swift's intellectual gifts, she gives no indication of having read any of his treasonable books. With her orthodox piety and her rather bland view of mankind, she would have been incapable of condoning such radical opinions or pitying the twisted anger that inspired them. In place of a maddened giant she found that "Swift is a very *odd companion* (if that expression is not too familiar for so extraordinary a genius); he talks a great deal and does not require many answers, he has infinite spirits, and says abundance of good things in his common way of discourse."

There are certain resemblances between Swift of this chapter and Dr. Johnson of the next. Both men were prisoners of their own eccentricities. Johnson feared, all his life, insanity. Swift became its victim. Both sought shelter with friends who were skilled in soothing their complexes. Something of what the jaunty Mrs. Thrale was to the Great Cham, Patrick Delany was to the Dean of St. Patrick's. Mr. Thrale appointed Johnson an executor of his estate. Swift conferred the same honor upon the kindly, if stuffy, Delany, who was called upon to preside over his friend's affairs during the period of "idiotism" that intervened before, in Swift's own words, he was laid "where furious rage can rend his heart no more."

Swift's insatiable lust for power was the touchstone of his character and the source of his unhappiness. Twenty years earlier his voracious need to direct others had almost been satisfied. He had played for high stakes and lost.

After a succession of military triumphs had made the Duke of Marlborough the commanding figure of Queen Anne's Court, Swift was sought out as pamphleteer by Robert Harley, the future Lord Oxford. The great warrior was the hero of the Whigs. Harley, of the Tories, desired to topple him and his Duchess who, styled as Mrs. Freeman,* was the emotional center of Queen Anne's declining years.

* In this sentimental tête-à-tête the Queen was Mrs. Morley.

The plot succeeded. The general and his consort were sent packing. With Harley in power and the Marlboroughs in exile, Swift hoped to have his satiric skills rewarded by impressive ecclesiastical preferment. He had probably dreamed of St. Paul's or Canterbury. Instead he found himself Dean of St. Patrick's in Dublin among the Irish whom, as was his wont, he simultaneously despised and compassionated.

Swift's compulsive pride was a determining factor not only in his professional careers of churchman and author but in his relationships with women. It gratified him to preside over the minds, morals and even hygiene of numerous ladies who were flattered to be taken in hand by so truculent a tutor. Lord Orrery, in his *Remarks on the Life and Writings of Dr. Jonathan Swift,* tells us in a passage to be later refuted by Dr. Delany that the Dean's coterie constituted a "constant seraglio of very virtuous women who attended him from morning to night."

Mrs. Pendarves was shortly to return to London and was thus removed from the scene of these admiring excesses. The awe in which she held Swift deprives her letters to him of the charm found in her spontaneous outpourings to her family. The tone of this exalted correspondence was set forth in April of 1733, just a month before she went home. In a letter written from Dangan she reports that "The day before we came out of town we dined at Dr. Delany's, and met the usual company. The Dean of St. Patrick's was there in *very good humour;* he calls himself 'my master,' and corrects me when I speak bad English, or do not pronounce my words distinctly. I wish he lived in England; I should not only have a great deal of entertainment from him, but improvement."

The letters that were exchanged between the young widow and the elderly clergyman came to an end in 1736, only three years after they had begun. Swift suffered an increase in the dizziness and deafness that heralded brain disease. The bitter pen was laid aside and its enraged wielder passed into the peace of oblivion, becoming, according to the now Mrs. Delany, "a very venerable figure with long silver hair and a comely countenance; for being grown fat, the hard lines which gave him a harsh look were filled up."

Exactly ten years passed before Mary Granville returned to Ireland as the second wife of the improving Dr. Delany. The most important event of this decade was the enduring friendship she formed with the Duchess of Portland. This patrician and talented woman, like Swift, harked back to the days of the Tory conspiracy to dislodge the Duke and Duchess of Marlborough. She was a child at the time and, as was proper for Harley's granddaughter, a suitable subject for the muse of Matthew Prior who was poet to the Harley circle. She is ensconced in the *Oxford Book of English Verse* in "A Letter to Lady Margaret Cavendish Holles-Harley when a child":

> My noble, lovely, little Peggy
> Let this my first epistle beg ye,
> At dawn of morn and close of even
> To lift your heart and hands to Heaven.
>
> . . .
>
> If to these precepts you attend,
> No second letter need I send,
> And so I rest your constant friend.

Until Mrs. Pendarves became the close friend of the "Duchess of Duchesses," her principal interests had been in music, in graceful correspondence, and in the applied arts. To this last aptitude the Duchess of Portland gave new direction. She was, above all, a naturalist. She had expert knowledge of botany and is an important figure in the annals of conchology. Under her tutelage Mrs. Pendarves commenced "running wild after shells." Not only did she collect shells, but she transformed them into cornices and moldings, and used them for the encrusting of that reigning Georgian toy, the Grotto.

Bulstrode, the country home of the Portlands, was frequently visited by Mary Granville, in both her Pendarves and Delany years. Here she lived much the same kind of leisured life she had described at Dangan. They had a routine "of reading, working and drawing in the morning; in the afternoon the scene changes, there are billiards, looking over prints, coffee, tea, and by way of interlude pretty Lady Betty" (the Portland's daughter) "comes upon the stage, and I can play as well at bo-peep as if I had a nursery of my own."

During her sojourns in London, Mrs. Pendarves returned to the life of the Great World, particularly that of opera and court. More than most, she was aware that opera, upon which depended the careers of Händel, Bononcini and Porpora, was threatened by Whig and Tory factionalism which had nothing to do with music. In a later letter to Swift, written in 1735, she wrote nostalgically, "I believe you have had a quiet winter in Dublin; not so has it been with us in London; hurry, wrangling, extravagance and matrimony have reigned with great impetuosity. Our operas have given much cause of dissension, men and women have been deeply engaged, and no debate in the House of Commons has been urged with more warmth. The dispute of the merits of the composers and singers is carried to so great a height that it is much feared by all true lovers of music that operas will be quite overturned. I own I think we make a very silly figure about it."

Her interest in handicrafts of all kinds prompted Mrs. Pendarves to write detailed descriptions of the clothing of our forebears of both sexes. Dress in the eighteenth century was by turns pictorial and architectural. At a court ball given in January of 1739 to celebrate the Prince of Wales's birthday, she encountered Selina, Countess of Huntington, who in a few years' time would become one of Methodism's most useful converts. One wonders what John Wesley would have said of a "petticoat—of black velvet embroidered with chenille, the pattern *a large stone vase* filled with *ramping flowers*." Mrs. Pendarves concluded that "it was a most labored piece of finery, the pattern much properer for a stucco staircase than the apparel of a lady."

She was pleased to the point of envy with the toilette of John Gay's patroness, the Duchess of Queensberry. For inspiration, Her Grace had had recourse to forestry and was apparelled in an embroidery of *"brown hills* covered with all sorts of weeds, and every breadth had an *old stump of a tree,* than ran up almost to the top of the petticoat—round which turned nasturtiums, ivy, honeysuckles, periwinkles and all sorts of twining flowers."

Such finery was not to be resisted. Wistfully Mrs. Pendarves confessed that "I never saw a piece of work so prettily fancied, and am quite angry with myself for not having the same thought, for it is infinitely handsomer than mine, and could not have cost *much more.*"

Pangs of a more painful kind were endured when Mrs. Pendarves found herself in company with "Herminius" and the usurping Lady Baltimore. This incident has provided Lady Llanover and Emily Morse Symonds with an opportunity to differ in their presentation of their heroine. Mrs. Pendarves so far forgot her customary benevolence as to describe her successful rival as looking like "a frightened owl, her locks strutted out and most furiously greased, or rather gummed." Lady Llanover, in a more than usually breathless aside, assures her readers that this lapse is "one of the very few instances when Mrs. Pendarves permitted herself to joke on the absence of personal charms."

Emily Morse Symonds, free of ancestor worship, is more realistic. She puts down Mrs. Pendarves's cattiness "to a touch of malice which . . . shows that though the writer's heart may have recovered from Lord Baltimore's defection, there was a little wound left in her vanity."

Ann Granville, warned perhaps by Mrs. Pendarves's connubial misfortunes, did not marry until she was well past thirty years of age. In accordance with the businesslike views of matrimony which prevailed in 1740, Mr. John Dewes had been recommended as a suitor to the aging spinster. Remembering Mrs. Pendarves's sour strictures upon marriage, Miss Granville did not confide in her sister, but in another member of the Portland circle, Lady Throckmorton. She camouflaged her interest in Mr. Dewes by the time-honored method of referring to herself as "my friend."

Her reasons for marrying were hardly romantic. "A cheznous with a man of sense" would do away once and for all with deciding which friend to visit next. Yet, for the materialistic times in which she lived, Anne Granville, like her sister, was an idealist; she preferred character to fortune and acted accordingly. She inquired of Sir Robert and Lady Throckmorton if "my friend" was likely to find in Mr. Dewes a man of "agreeable conversation, generous principles" and one who, in her engaging phrase, was "not a lawyer in his manners." The replies must have been all that she required. The marriage took place and the bride and groom removed to "a cot between two aged oaks."

Ann Granville's marriage to John Dewes was destined to play an important part in her sister's epistolary career. The succeeding generations of Deweses, and later Ports, were to furnish their Aunt Delany with almost another half-century of correspondents. It may also be suspected that Ann's preference for a congenial comrade rather than a patrician fortune prompted Mary to marry her elderly admirer, Dr. Delany of Delville.

It will be recalled that the child, Mary Granville, had been

raised in expectation of a post at court. In 1742 these aspirations revived. Mrs. Pendarves, like her sister, desired a mode of life more
settled than a series of visits to "dear" Bulstrode and to the stately
homes of other friends and relatives. Having, she thought, no desire
to remarry, she looked to the court to supply a home and an occupation that could be savored in single blessedness.

At this time, familial influence was the acknowledged avenue to
advancement in affairs of the state, the court and the church. The
Granvilles were a powerful clan, the most able being Mrs. Pendarves's cousin, Lord Carteret, later Lord Granville. He was a statesman of great ability who had served as Secretary of State in 1721.
Falling out with Walpole, he had been placed in the cold storage of
the Lord Lieutenancy of Ireland. It was to Carteret that Mrs. Pendarves made application for a position at court.

She could not have made a worse choice of patron; nor was her
sense of timing fortunate. That top-heavy structure of treaties, alliances and invasions known as the War of the Austrian Succession
was dragging out its dreary course. In this conflict Carteret, who was
strongly of the King's party, played a vital role. He had an almost
modern dislike of influence peddling, particularly, one suspects, of
nepotism. He has been quoted as saying, "What is it to me who is
judge or who a bishop? It is my business to make kings and em-
perors and to maintain the balance of Europe."

Apparently oblivious of these higher claims upon Carteret's
attention, the Duchess of Portland offered to approach his mother,
Countess Granville. It was not for nothing that this fierce relative
was known as the Dragon. Upon asking "whether the report of our
friend's promotion was to be depended on," her Grace of Graces
learned that Carteret "was never interested in anybody's business,
his whole mind was taken up in *doing good to the nation,* and till
the French was drove out of Germany and Prague was taken, he
could not think of such *a bagatelle as that.*"

Several months after this chilling interview, Mrs. Pendarves wrote
a disheartened letter to Mrs. Dewes. Lord Carteret was to travel with
the King to Hanover, leaving nothing settled about the longed-for
appointment. As she dispatched her letter to Mrs. Dewes she was the
recipient of an important communication. It was a proposal from
Patrick Delany, now a widower.

This letter, which is dated April 23, 1742, supplied Lady Llanover with inspiration for her most ineffable footnotes. It contains, she points out, "no unmeaning phrases," meaning perhaps that, in accordance with eighteenth-century mores, the practical arrangements of marriage take precedence over affection. Best of all, the bourgeois clergyman entertained "more fear than hope," a sentiment which was, of course, eminently suitable when addressing the great-granddaughter of Sir Bevil Granville, from whom the editoress had also the honor to be descended.

"You, madam," wrote Dr. Delany to the doubtless startled Mrs. Pendarves, "are not a stranger to my present unhappy situation, and that it pleased God to desolate my dwelling; I flatter myself that I have still a heart turned to social delights, and not estranged either from the tenderness of true affection or the refinement of friendships."

To the Austen buff, Dr. Delany's next sentence is somewhat prophetic of the infelicitous cry of "In vain have I struggled" with which, to return to *Pride and Prejudice,* Mr. Darcy secured Elizabeth Bennet's refusal when he first asked her to marry him. "I feel a sad void in my breast," continued the suitor, "and am reduced to the necessity of wishing to fill it . . . as I have been long persuaded that perfect friendship is nowhere to be found but in marriage. I know it is late in life to think of engaging anew in that state, in the beginning of my 59th year. I am old and I appear older than I am. . . .

"I have a good clear income for my life; a trifle to settle, which I am only ashamed to offer; a good house (as houses go in our part of the world), moderately furnished, a good many books, a pleasant garden (better I believe than when you saw it), etc. Would to God I might have leave to lay them all at your feet."

A period of stress and indecision followed. In Georgian England middle-aged widows did not marry without the consent of their relatives. Mrs. Pendarves's brother, Bernard Granville, was opposed to the union because, as Lady Llanover complacently explains, "Dr. Delany had no claim of ancestry to bring forward."

On May 6th the matter was still unsettled. Dr. Delany, although "scarcely able to hold a pen," pointed out to his beloved that at her time of life she had a right to marry whom she chose. This excellent advice she followed, becoming his wife a month later.

It was, Lady Llanover's footnotes pronounce "an exception to the general order of things" that a person born out of the exalted sphere of the Granvilles should have made her great-great aunt happy "setting, aside," of course, "all feelings of family pride."

The bride and groom remained in England for a year after their marriage. It was a time largely devoted to securing ecclesiastical preferment for the Granvilles' new in-law. In accordance with the policies of the Ascendancy, the clergy of the Church of Ireland looked to English patronage for promotion. This being the case, the Delanys did their lobbying from Bulstrode and their house in London. The approach to Lord Carteret was, in this instance, made more circuitously than in the matter of a court position. Dr. Delany not only preached before noble persons including the King, but wrote a volume entitled "Twenty Sermons upon Social Duties and their Opposite Vices" which he took the precaution of dedicating to the Dragon. One of these productions he voiced at Bulstrode, selecting for the Portland's large family "The Duty of Children to Parents." It seems probable that the sermon heard by Mrs. Pendarves a decade earlier upon "The Duties of Wives to Husbands" formed part of this edifying collection.

Lord Carteret, in this second application, was at last alive to the duties of a highly placed statesman to a kinswoman who had married shockingly below her social station. The best way, Carteret must have reasoned, to remedy the discrepancy in status between Patrick Delany, the son of a servant, and a Granville was to seek church preferment in Ireland, the former's native land. Carteret was willing to act as mediator for his relatives and to request promotion from the Duke of Devonshire, who had succeeded Dorset as Lord Lieutenant. Carteret, during his term of office at Dublin Castle twenty years earlier, had known both Swift and Delany. Lady Llanover includes in Mrs. Delany's correspondence a charming letter written by Carteret to the Dean of St. Patrick's in which His Lordship sent sincere respects to Dr. Delany, who had supplied "potted woodcocks in perfection." His letter closes on a note of interest as regards both Swift and the Irish Bad Century: "When people ask me how I governed Ireland, I say that I pleased Dr. Swift."

His eagerly awaited Grace returned to England in the spring of 1744. On May 8th Mrs. Delany wrote to Mrs. Dewes that Carteret "desired we would send the servants away and when they were gone he told D.D." (her pet name for her husband) "he was come from the Duke of Devonshire to offer him the Deanery and that the first bishoprick that fell in he might have if he cared afterwards to leave Down."

In matters ecclesiastical (as different from matters religious), our Georgian forebears were as practical as they were about marriage. Mrs. Delany wrote on in this vein, "the deanery is a much better thing than any small bishopric and we are well pleased with the possession of it."

The new Dean of Down and his lady set forth promptly for Ireland. They crossed in a yacht reserved to the use of government officials, including, in terms of the established faith, the clergy. They were at Delville by June 14th. A month later Mrs. Delany was joyfully redecorating her new home.

In accordance with the easygoing methods of the Church of Ireland at this time, the Delanys were not obliged to fix themselves permanently among their Down parishioners. They could live at Delville, well remembered by Mrs. Delany from her visit of the previous decade. "Dear" Delville was to promote an abiding frustration in the mind of its new mistress. If only D.D. had been appointed to neighboring Kildare, Delville could have served as deanery or, perhaps all in the fullness of time, episcopal palace! As it was, Down was nearly a hundred miles to the north, a formidable distance in 1744. Mrs. Delany was to remain torn between frequent trips in fulfillment of D.D.'s deanly duties and a very housekeeperly longing to remain at Delville, rejoicing in the flowering of a favorite shrub, completing a shell lustre or "dead coloring" the Madonna and Child she was copying.

The letters written during her residence in Ireland indicate an involvement not present in the letters of her earlier visit. She was an enthusiastic deanery wife, and relished describing a life unknown to her family in England. Although her resourcefulness and sense of adventure lend warmth to these accounts, she was to remain at her best in setting forth the outer scene, the Irish landscape, its houses and social customs. Her impressions were both vivid and mixed.

On the positive side there was Delville itself, which boasted rooms of generous proportions, "cool in summer and warm in winter." Here were to be found tapestry, japan work, marble tables, crimson mohair and damask and, in the library, the "modern poets nicely bound." Out of doors the prospect was, if possible, even more pleasing. The garden sloped down to a brook. There was a bowling green and hayrick, a terrace walk, the remains of an old castle, a portico, shrubs, elms and roses and, in the distance, a view of Dublin.

Ecclesiastically the situation was less promising. Church posts during the Bad Century were all too often sinecures, with right reverends and wrong reverends drawing handsome salaries to serve as absentee shepherds to parishes which they abandoned for life in England or on the Continent. Dr. Delany soon found that "although the church of Down is very large, the Curate has been so negligent as *never to visit any of the poor* of the parish." This neglect on the part of the established church had opened the door to proseletyzing: "a very diligent and watchful dissenting preacher has visited them on all occasions of sickness and distress and by that means gained great numbers to the meeting."

Dr. Delany, in a spirit of ecumenism considerably in advance of his times, visited not only his own parishioners, but designed to go to the Presbyterians and, all in good time, to the Papists. His wife concludes in a passage often quoted by historians of the Penal times, "they bless him and pray for him wherever he goes, and say he has done more good already than all his predecessors; the last Dean was here but *two days* in *six years!*"

As a step toward remedying these deplorable conditions, the Delanys provided Sunday dinner at an inn in Down, receiving all the citizenry, "by turns." Even ecclesiastical hospitality in Georgian times was of impressive proportions, as evidenced by the following menu offered by the Delanys:

FIRST COURSE	SECOND COURSE
Turkeys endove	Partridge
Boyled Neck of Mutton	Sweet Breads
Greens, etc.	Collared pig
Soup	Creamed apple tart
Plum-pudding	Crabs
Roast loin of veal	Fricasse of eggs
Vension pasty	Pigeons
	no dessert to be had

In 1745 Lord Chesterfield became Lord Lieutenant of Ireland. His term of office was brief, lasting only eight months. This is to be regretted because that cynical writer on worldly demeanor proved an administrator of compassion, imagination and, most important when dealing with the Celt, humor.

On August 24th, the state yachts were dispatched for His Lordship and his entourage. Mrs. Delany proposed to visit them upon their arrival "in an *Irish Stuff manteau and petticoat* and a *head* * the Dean has given me of Irish work, the prettiest I ever saw of the kind."

This encouragement of native trades is a telling instance of the Delany's concern for their people. It was destined to success, for, on a royal birthday in November of 1745, "there appeared at court a great number of Irish stuffs. Lady Chesterfield was dressed in one, and I had the *secret satisfaction* of knowing myself to have been the cause, but *dare not say so here;* but I say, 'I am glad to find my Lady Chesterfield's example has had so good an influence.' The poor weavers are starving, all trade has met with a great check this year."

A check upon trade and all other manifestations of Irish well-being was assured by the Penal Laws which, for a century after the Battle of the Boyne, hounded the descendants of King James's supporters. The Hanoverian interest did not foresee that an imaginative people of vigor and resource would leave Ireland to make the history of other lands. Men who were denied education, professional advancement, the practice of their religion and the possession of their lands, flocked to the colors of England's enemies. This mass emigration was known at the time of its occurrence as "The Flight of the Wild Geese."

During the War of Jenkin's Ear, as the War of the Austrian Succession was also known, Irish defection had far-reaching results. The Duke of Cumberland, son of George II, had, as the result of conspicuous bravery at the earlier Battle of Dettingen, received military promotion. At the succeeding Battle of Fontenoy, he was thoroughly out-soldiered by the commander of the French troops, Marshal Saxe, whose crack regiments were composed of Irish exiles, thirsting for revenge. His Royal Highness, in a spirit of chivalry that was to prove conspicuous by its absence in his military future, cried out as the

* A "head" meant a headdress.

Wild Geese charged, "God's curse on the laws that have made these men our enemies."

Fontenoy was eloquently described to Mrs. Delany in a letter written to Mrs. Dewes and forwarded by her to Ireland. The writer, Lady Sarah Cowper, was the daughter of a former Lord Chancellor and possessed, for a woman of her day, an unusually clear grasp of public affairs. Mrs. Delany's comments on Lady Sarah's letter again prove her a perspicacious critic. "How extremely well written Lady Sarah Cowper's letter is! she has an uncommon strength and clearness in her manner of expressing herself."

Lady Sarah Cowper credited the Duke of Cumberland with a compassion he was not to evidence when, a year later, his ruthless extinction of the Stuart supporters secured him the name of Billy, The Butcher. Lady Sarah wrote that His Highness, upon hearing of "particular persons killed or wounded . . . lost all command over his passions and burst into a violent fit of crying! I own these tears of generousity and humanity make him appear *much greater* to me even than all the instances of his courage."

Even Louis XV, in accordance with the sporting code that prevailed in the wars of other times, paid tribute to the English dead. *"Ma foy, ces gens meritoient de vivre."* (Upon my soul, these people deserved to live.) Marshal Saxe added *"Cette poignée de gens m'a fait plus de peine que tout le reste"* (This handful of men caused me more sorrow than all the rest).

The defeat of the English at Fontenoy had tragic consequences. Charles Edward, the Young Pretender, was heartened by the triumph of the French and Irish forces. He sailed, with a few henchmen, from Nantes to Scotland in an irresponsible attempt to reclaim the English throne for the Stuarts. Without money, arms or a coherent plan, he relied upon personal charm and the pathetic loyalty of Highland chiefs, who were all too soon to be lamented as "The Flowers of The Forest."

It had been the intention of the Delanys to pay an annual visit to England. In September of 1745 Mrs. Delany wrote to Mrs. Dewes that "the insurrection in Scotland has made it at this time *unsafe to cross the seas."* Lady Sarah Cowper again served as war correspondent, opining in words closely parallelled two centuries later by Sir Winston Churchill, that "without any foreign force at hand to assist him" the Pretender's attempt was "wild and rash." She continued in her clear-sighted way to foresee general distress and the victimizing of humane people.

Ireland had, only fifty years earlier, ridden the whirlwind in support of James II. Would she stagger to her feet in favor of his handsome grandson? Mrs. Delany, who lacked Lady Sarah Cowper's acumen in matters of state, wrote in a splendidly myopic passage that the Irish "in general are very well affected towards the present Government, and even the papists who are not in number what they were, seem to know their happiness in a quiet possession of what they have, so that had England been so unhappy as to have struggled under a civil war, we should have been the quietest part of his majesty's dominions."

During this troubled autumn, the Delanys were in daily expectation of a visit from Lord and Lady Chesterfield. This was a privilege that entailed frustration. Mrs. Delany's ores, mosses and shells had to be put aside and her brushes and colors removed from the parlor. After three weeks of living in a tidy vacuum, the Dean and Mrs. Delany received the Lord Lieutenant and his lady. Delville boasted a portico; it was dedicated to the Duchess of Portland and, in recognition of Her Grace's attainments, was called The Minerva. Here were "two tables covered with all sorts of breakfast." Mrs. Delany entertained at the harpsichord, the garden was praised and, for a sunny morning, the uprising overseas was forgotten.

Also forgotten was the fact that thirty years earlier, upon the accession of George I, the Granvilles were of the discontented party. As befitted a fervent Händelian, Mrs. Delany's loyalties lay wholly with the King. The doomed troops of Bonnie Prince Charlie, who had made impossible her annual visit to her sister, consisted of "ugly rebels." When she learned in the spring of 1746 that the slaughter of Culloden had brought the Stuart dream to a bloody end, she rejoiced at the "glorious news from Scotland," continuing, "I hope in God, the affair of the rebellion is now at an end, and that we shall meet in peace."

Mrs. Delany's desire for a reunion was much increased by Mrs. Dewes having "been brought to bed" in February of 1746 of a girl. The child, named Mary, was christened in honor of her aunt. She remained the only daughter and was to play an important role in Aunt Delany's future.

Mrs. Delany, early in the babyhood of her niece, Mary, assigned to her an extrafamilial role which I have not seen commented upon by editors or biographers. Shortly after the birth of the little girl, she wrote very significantly, "You remember Mme. de Sévigné; Mary must be my *Pauline.*"

Less than a decade before Mrs. Delany wrote these words, the letters of Mme. de Sévigné had been, in part, published. Her style, spontaneity, charm and wisdom were immediately admired. She became what she to a degree still is, the epitome of the patrician authoress. Even Lady Mary, at odds, as Mme. de Sévigné was not, with most of humankind, desired that her letters should compare favorably with those of the chatelaine of the Hôtel Carnavalet.

It was under the aegis of Mme. de Sévigné's granddaughter, Pauline de La Simiane, that letters to the beloved daughter, Mme. de Grignan and to other friends and relatives became available to the reading public. In this way Mme. de Sévigné might be said to have had two incarnations. During her decorous lifetime she exemplified the amateur status preferred by a great lady. After her death her granddaughter released her into the world of print she still inhabits.

Mrs. Delany clearly desired to become also a posthumous professional. Lacking a direct descendant, she commandeered a collateral Pauline. Lady Llanover's lack of comment on this would seem to lend credence to the theory. Her Ladyship was just the person to prefer a kinswoman who was above the traffickings of commercial publication. Mary Dewes Port did not assume the mantle of Pauline. Neither did Georgina Mary Ann Port Waddington. It remained for Augusta Waddington Llanover to do so.

Mrs. Delany, like many another childless woman, compensated for her deprivation by devoting herself to the children of her relatives and friends. She was particularly assiduous in the epistolary cherishing of her "Pauline." Her health, education and morals were all objects of Aunt Delany's concern. Two hundred years ago, living to grow up was by no means a certainty. It was to be expected that Mrs. Dewes should be bombarded with medical advice, most of it, viewed from today, alarming. Sanitation and the sciences of nutrition and immunization did not play a striking role in the life of our ancestors. Lacking these preventive measures, they suffered diseases now extinct.

When, in March of 1744 one of the Dewes's sons had ague (which we today call malaria), Mrs. Delany provided "two *infallible re-ceipts*": "1st Pounded ginger, made into a paste with brandy, spread on sheep's leather, and a plaister of it, laid over the navel. 2ndey A spider put into a goose-quill, well sealed and secured, and hung about the child's neck as low as the pit of his stomach. Either of these, I am assured, will ease. *Probatum est.*"

Lady Llanover employs heroic measures to defend the spider remedy by supplying a short history of its use. A modern author, Elizabeth Burton, in her *Pageant of Georgian England* goes Her Ladyship one better. She tells us that Mrs. Delany's encapsulated spider "goes straight back to Dioscorides, a doctor in Nero's army, and was still being used as late as 1837."

The simple diseases of childhood were often fatal. We read in Mrs. Delany's Irish letters of poor Biddy Barber, who mourned a fine boy who died of measles. One of the common scourges was, until recently, "hooping" cough. For this or "any nervous cough," the Duchess of Portland recommended "rubbing the palms of the hands, soles of the feet, and pit of the stomach with oil of amber and harts-horn, an equal quantity night and morning and the back-bone with rum." Worms in children could be vanquished, Mrs. Delany advised, by "A pound of quicksilver boiled in a gallon of water till half the water is consumed away to be constantly drank at his meals or whenever he is dry." Whether the sufferer, who was little Bunny Dewes, was cured by this metallic remedy, his mother has not recorded.

These ignorant nostrums are matters of laughing that we may not weep over the prevalence of needless death and suffering. Antiseptic surgery awaited Pasteur and Lister. Lacking it, childbirth was often effected by dirty forceps which guaranteed a steady supply of orphans. Famine was a common spectre, particularly in a one-crop agriculture like that of Ireland.

The practice of inoculation, which has already made its appearance in this book, was still attended by risks; it was a step Mrs. Delany did not care "to advise either for or against." Without its protection smallpox ravaged the homes of rich and poor, including Bulstrode, being paid in the coin of life or looks.

Mrs. Delany was even more solicitous for her young friends' spiritual progress than for their bodily well-being. Marriage to a man of the cloth lent an exalted tone to her sound but predictable views on religion, morals and education, views which Lady Llanovei never tired of applauding from the footnotes.

Submission to the will of That Great Disposer of all things is very suitably recommended. First impressions of childhood will secure against later temptations. Sparing the rod will spoil the child (birch twigs to be preferred). Children must be raised in accordance with the principles of love and awe; if little Mary injures her brother in a nursery fracas, Mother must not withhold her hand.

A deplorable exception to these precepts was exemplified in little Sir John Meade. When brought to call at Delville, the six-year-old heir to a great estate proved himself to be most *"unreasonably indulged*—a fine sensible boy but under *no sort of command*. I had twenty frights for my china, shells and books; his little fingers seized everything with such impetuosity that I was ready to box him; had I been his mamma I should have been *most heartily ashamed of him*. With pleasure," continued Aunt Delany, "I recollected that my little nephews would have been much scandalised at his behavior and wished them here to set him a good example."

Among the young people of Mrs. Delany's correspondence, the most interesting is Garret Wesley of Dangan, later to be Lord Mornington. At thirteen he was a very good scholar and a proficient violinist. Mrs. Delany wrote to her sister that "he understands fortification, building of ships, and has more knowledge than I ever met with in one so young." Unlike the impertinent Sir John, the future father of the Duke of Wellington was a "child among children and as tractable and complying to his sisters . . . as the little children can be to you."

Some of these musings on child development strike a surprisingly modern note. The infant "Pauline" had three older brothers, of whom Court was the best scholar. Their mother consulted the Delanys about sending the boys to separate schools to avoid what contemporary psychology calls sibling rivalry, a problem from which an only daughter of two centuries ago would be automatically excluded. She would, according to the mores of her time, be made over to the care of her female relatives, with Mrs. Delany playing the stellar role so often occupied by the childless aunt. From distant Delville, Aunt Delany wrote nostalgically of her "dear little Mary playing on the

grass" under her mother's eye. Mindful of the gender gap then existing in the fondest of families, Mrs. Delany pointed out that Mary "is
too much of a jewel to be trusted out of sight, and though the boys
are as valuable, you must be a little weaned from them as their different education must call them from you."

Such discrepancies in the education granted to brothers and sisters had far-reaching sociological results. As we have noted earlier, a
talented woman of the lower orders could sing, act or connive her
way into fame or, at least, notoriety. Ladies had no such luck. This
being the case, Mrs. Delany, thinking doubtless of her brother-in-
law's will, warns her sister of the "one *error* which most fathers run
into, and that is providing *too little* for daughters; young men have a
thousand ways of improving a little fortune, by professions and employments, if they have good friends, but young gentlewomen have
no way, the fortune settled on them is all they are to expect—they
are incapable of making an addition."

Lady Llanover supplements this pessimistic picture with further
detail. "Mrs. Delany" she tells us, "was a strong advocate for all
young gentlewomen who had not any fortune assisting in their own
maintenance by practical usefulness in the families of richer persons."

This cruel expedient was not without its literary uses. To it Jane
Austen owes Fanny Price and Jane Fairfax; Dickens, Rosa Dartle
and Kate Nickleby; and, to climax them all, Charlotte Brontë her
melodramatic governess, Jane Eyre.

Mrs. Delany did not confine her moralizing to the Dewes children, but commented on virtue and vice as it was to be experienced
in the world of the "ton." The fountainhead of inspiration remained
the oratorios so frequently supplied by Mr. Händel. These works,
with their marriage of scripture and *bel canto,* answered for the Delanys, as they have for countless others, the needs of soul and ear.
Messiah was often performed to benefit imprisoned debtors in Dublin and Captain Coram's foundlings in London, D.D. and his spouse
being present in both capitals. It is, in fact, the Dean of Down who
is credited with having cried out, when Mrs. Cibber sang "He was
Despised," "Woman, for this be all thy sins forgiven." *

Where edification was concerned, the legitimate theatre was less
reliable. Mrs. Delany was shocked when David Garrick parodied seven

---

* Mrs. Cibber had recently been involved in a notorious case of adultery.

identifiable men of fashion in *Miss in her Teens,* the takeoff being considered, in Georgian times, malicious and cowardly. Smollett's *Peregrine Pickle* was not read; Richardsons's *Clarissa* was read and reread when swimming eyes permitted. The design of following in Mme. de Sévigné's epistolary path was nearly shaken by the latter's referring to her son's mistress as *ma belle fille* (my daughter-in-law). It was a temptation to exchange the writer of such bad principles for Mme. de Maintenon who, as the wife of the Sun King's old age, penned letters which exhibited "such a strain of piety, good sense and fine sentiments . . . no boasting of favors, no pride . . . no presuming."

Mrs. Delany reserved her severest censure for gambling, the deadliest vice of her time and class. Two centuries ago it was widely believed that natural disasters were expressions of divine displeasure. In accordance with this theory, she saw, in the earthquake which destroyed Lisbon in 1755, God's warning to "those wretches at Whyte's," * who risked patrimony and sanity upon the toss of a card. Among the most tragic victims of the fashionable compulsion was Lord Chesterfield. Mrs. Delany had, it will be remembered, known him during the months when he had proved himself one of the most capable and compassionate statesmen who have presided over *John Bull's Other Island.* Having observed the former Lord Lieutenant when he was at his best, she regretted his servitude to chance in lines which are more perceptive than was usually the case with so objective a chronicler.

"Lord Chesterfield," Mrs. Delany wrote late in January of 1756, "has had a stroke of apoplexy. It is generally thought the anxious life he has had among gamesters has occasioned this stroke. Whatever effect it may have had on his constitution, it is a severe reproach and blemish to his character as a man possessed of superior talents to most of his sex, so good an understanding, such brilliancy of wit, so much discernment in seeing the foibles of others, and when he thought his example of consequence (as when Lord Lieutenant of Ireland) so *great a command* of himself for nearly a whole year! Is it not strange he should at last fall a sacrifice to that desperate vice, gaming? It can be accounted for but in one way—the want of religion: without which there is no ballast to keep the vessel steady—it is tossed by

* Whyte's was a fashionable London gambling club.

every blast, and liable to be overset whenever the storm arises and must at last perish."

Harking back to the Lisbon earthquake of the previous year, she related earth faults to character faults. "Gaming is indeed an earthquake to the mind, keeps it under continued tremblings, breaks out into horrid eruptions of oaths and eventually destroys the superstructures though ever so beautiful and well-formed."

Mrs. Delany's favorite novelist was that celebrator of virtue, Samuel Richardson. Her remarks on *Sir Charles Grandison* indicate that, conformist as she was, she sensed the emergence of the woman novelist and approved it. The only blot on Sir Charles's character was "permitting his daughters to be brought up Papists." In a society that in all matters held Canterbury to be right and Rome wrong, such prejudice was not only typical, it was historical. However, Mrs. Delany's remedy for Sir Charles's want of religious principles marks her as a modern in the world of fiction: "had" she opined "a woman written the story she would have thought the *daughters of as much consequence as the sons.*"

This casual passage speaks volumes. Some forty years earlier Lady Mary, with doubtful sincerity, had consigned her sex to a lower part of the creation. By the middle of the same century the gentle Mrs. Delany not only insists on equality between sons and daughters, but puts forth the idea that a woman might have more insight into women's problems than a man. That so conventional a person foresaw the role of the woman novelist is a telling indication of the inevitability of *Evelina,* which was still twenty years away.

The pleasant occupations of shell work, embroidery, music heard, books read and morals inferred were varied by incidents, private and public. The first was the appearance in 1751 of *Remarks on the Life and Writings of Dr. Jonathan Swift* by John Boyle, Earl of Cork and Orrery. Lord Orrery, as he is known, had been an intimate of the Delville coterie during Swift's lifetime; he is the first of Swift's many biographers. Any truthful account of this tormented character would teem with the pride, inconsistency and anger that made the man as he was. The Delanys disapproved; a letter from Delville to Mrs. Dewes states that "every failing is exposed, every fault is magnified, every virtue almost either tarnished or concealed." Mrs. Delany feared that the book would prove entertaining to those who had "no regard for memory of the Dean of St. Patrick." Even more significantly, she feared that "there are too many truths in the book."

Three years later the curiosity of the reading public was titillated by the appearance of an anonymous reply, entitled *Observations on Lord Orrery's Life of Swift*. Patrick Delany, friend and host of both men, was the unsuspected author—so thoroughly unsuspected that his opinion of the second biography was widely sought; "this" wrote his delighted spouse, "has given us some sport."

Shortly before the publication of Dr. Delany's *Observations*, he became trapped in litigation of Dickensian proportions. The Tennisons, relatives of the first Mrs. Delany, contended that D.D. had burned a paper necessary to the settlement of her will. Her fortune had been large and well worth attempting to remove from the enjoyment of the second mistress of Delville.

The suit opened with near blackmail on the part of the prosecution. Miss Tennison apparently believed that a man of the cloth would settle out of court rather than submit to having his word questioned. This compromise D.D. stoutly refused, and in so doing committed himself and his wife to six years of harassment and contumely.

Mrs. Delany's letters to Mrs. Dewes during this time of stress are of special interest. She was denied her annual visit to England because it was necessary to remain in Ireland until the Lord Chancellor should pronounce sentence. Attempts to persuade the Deweses to visit Delville were unsuccessful. Travel with four children in 1752 was a formidable undertaking. Absence and anxiety gave to Mrs. Delany's letters a fervor not always present in her description of everyday activities. In addition to the need to unburden herself to her sister, there were professional reasons for confiding in "our friends," as the Georgians called their relatives. Mr. Dewes was a lawyer, although, we remember, "not in his manners." To him, Mrs. Delany sent documents to give "a more perfect account of our affairs," adding pathetically that it was impossible that "calumny and falsehood should long reign . . . we must consult our friends about an appeal in case sentence is given against us and shall be greatly obliged to Mr. Dewes if he will read over our case and give us his opinion."

A year later the law was still delaying. It was decided to "*appeal to the House of Lords in England directly.*" The Delanys went to

England in the summer of 1753 and there spent five years awaiting the settlement of their case. On March 7, 1758, a letter went to Mrs. Dewes announcing that the verdict had been given in the favor of D.D. *"The Dean's character is cleared* and set in the fair light it deserves. . . . A cause was never so well attended, nor a more universal joy seen than when Lord Mansfield,* after an hour and half's speaking with angelic oratory, pronounced the decree in our favour . . . on the very arguments my good brother Dewes always insisted on!"

About two years before D.D.'s exoneration, the "First World War" (as Sir Winston Churchill has called the Seven Years' War) was declared. Mrs. Delany, perhaps because of her anxiety about her husband's lawsuit, does not bestow as much attention to Clive in India and Wolfe in Quebec as she had devoted to the defeat of the Stuart cause ten years earlier. Scant as her comments are, they serve to exhibit to posterity Georgian public opinion of the military gains and reverses that cost France her Canadian provinces and that taught tactics to a young officer from Virginia.

This global conflict opened upon one of the most discreditable pages in the illustrious annals of English justice, the court martial and execution of Admiral John Byng.

In the spring of 1756 the French found it advantageous to lead the English to believe that an invasion was imminent. Clues to this effect were planted; they were heeded. The Delanys were in London at the time, acting *in loco parentis* to ten-year-old Mary Dewes, who had come up to town for instruction in drawing, penmanship and the clavichord. Her aunt, amid reports of these studies, evidenced the prevalent fear that England was in jeopardy. A certain "Mr. Smith was to have sailed in a few days' time, when to the great distress of the merchants the press-gang has *seized all their sailors,* which looks ill for us. Pray God defend us, but I fear we really are in danger of an invasion."

By these deceptions the French concealed their objective, which was the British naval base at Minorca. A sizable fleet was reported to be massing at Toulon. Would it sail down through the Mediterranean and out through the Straits of Gibraltar, or was it bound for

* Lord Mansfield, formerly "silver tongued Murray," was Lord Chief Justice of the Court of the King's Bench.

Minorca? To prepare for the latter eventuality, Admiral Byng was ordered to the Balearic Islands. It was a tragic example of too little and too late.

The ships supplied to Byng were in wretched condition. He was obliged to hoist sails upon condemned masts; his speed was reduced by fouled bottoms and leaking hulls. Rations were short. Worst of all was the lack of manpower. The square-riggers of former times required huge crews, often "recruited," as in the case of Mr. Smith, by kidnappers hired by the navy to raid the docks and taverns of waterfront towns in search of able-bodied, if reluctant, young men. Byng was forbidden by his superior, Lord Anson, to interfere with the crews allocated to other ships; he departed to the defense of Minorca lacking several hundred hands.

Nor was Byng fortunate in the adversaries who awaited him. The Georgians were resigned to the superior performance of such land-based commanders as Marshal Saxe and Frederick the Great. Sea power was another matter. The Englishman in the street and, for our purpose, lady in the parlor, looked upon naval victory as a perquisite. It was not to be imagined that the effeminate world of Versailles could put forward admirals as capable as the Marquis de la Gallissonnière and the Duc de Richelieu.

Even that most capricious of elements, the wind, favored the French. The Toulon fleet sailed south in a spanking north wind while Byng and his fleet, lying off Gibraltar, struggled with the light airs typical of the Mediterranean. The outcome was, or should have been, predictable. Complacency had failed to arm Admiral Byng against a worthy foe. Cynicism demanded his life to protect the popular image of an invincible navy.

Dissent not being the engine that it is today, Mrs. Delany loyally supported government. "Public news," she wrote in the early summer of 1756, "is very bad indeed; Admiral Byng, with 16 ships of the line and two frigates, sailed from Gibraltar to Minorca where they found the French ready to receive them, and after three hours fight, made a running fight back to Gibraltar."

Her next letter repeats these facts with the patriotic exclamation "so shameful and painful to all true English hearts." She concludes on a note far more shameful and painful than honorable defeat.

Gallissonnière's murderous broadsides had made further resistance on Byng's part suicidal. The French fleet returned promptly to Toulon while the English limped back to Gibraltar and from thence to England. For this reason, news of a French victory reached London from Paris long before Byng had arrived to tell his own story. To save face, the Admiralty determined upon a charge of cowardice to be derived from Gallissonnière's account rather than that of Byng. As Mrs. Delany innocently put it, "no other account is come—this one is from France."

Having determined upon sacrificing Byng to the folklore of patriotism, the Admiralty took the precaution of censoring his despatches, tampering with his logbook, and intercepting a letter written in his defense by his recent enemy, Richelieu, who had the decency to urge that Byng's own testimony be heard rather than that of Gallissonnière. The much-touted English virtue of fair play had, in this instance, crossed the channel. Voltaire devoted the twenty-third chapter of *Candide* to the execution of Byng. Here is to be found the famous comment that the English find it good "from time to time to kill an Admiral to encourage the others."

By September, the Seven Years' War was official, with a reversal of the alliances that existed during the War of the Austrian Succession. Byng, whose luckless voyage had served as curtain raiser to the Black Hole of Calcutta and the Plains of Abraham, was jailed. Further to inflame public prejudice, the Admiralty encouraged burning "Mr." Byng in effigy. The effigies were supplied by government, a measure some viewed as a needless expense. Mrs. Delany's usual concern for moral values was unequal to these simplistic appeals. She wrote to Mrs. Dewes, "As to the wretched admiral, he remains as he was, and no time yet named for his trial; he seems in good spirits and has been entertained out of his window with seeing himself burnt in effigy. . . ."

Six months later John Byng was shot, like a common traitor, on the deck of the *Monarque*. Mrs. Delany does not refer to this jingoistic travesty of justice; we can only suppose that she heard Dr. Arne's recent hit, "Rule Britannia," with a lighter heart.

The period from 1759 to 1768 was for Mrs. Delany a time of trouble and transition and, for her correspondence, one of decline. Händel died in 1759. Mrs. Delany's musical activities had been almost totally centered upon his mammoth output. His death put an end to her comments on opera and oratorio until she was regaled in her old age by the royal band at Windsor, whose repertoire consisted largely of his music.

Ann Granville Dewes, to whom the major part of her sister's letters were written, died in 1761. This loss caused Mrs. Delany to lay aside her pen for nearly two years, and when her letters to friends recommenced, they lacked the spontaneity characteristic of her earlier accounts of life in London and Ireland.

Another deterrent to letter writing was the failing health of Patrick Delany. He was, as he had been at pains to point out in his proposal, already elderly at the time of his second marriage. The years of anxiety over his legal difficulties had taken their toll. His death occurred in Bath in 1768, a death undoubtedly hastened by the renewal of these harassments.

The widows of two centuries ago were, like those of today, often faced with a reordering of their lives. As relict of the Dean of Down, Mrs. Delany no longer had an Irish part to play. After a brief trip to bury her husband she left Ireland, never to return. A period of indecision followed. Should she settle in Bath or London? The matter was decided by her old friend, the Duchess of Portland, who proposed that Mrs. Delany should make her home at Bulstrode for a major part of each year while maintaining a pied-à-terre in the wider world of London.

Prior's "noble lovely little Peggy" was at this time the Dowager Duchess. As companions, the ladies were perfectly suited to one another. In fact, Mrs. Delany's widowhood is the most important period of her lengthy career. She did not yield to the lethargy of old age, but advanced in her talent for the applied arts and for the writing of letters which depict her life at Bulstrode and later at Windsor.

Lady Llanover did not pass over these instances of her widowed kinswoman's resourcefulness and fortitude without favorable comment. Just prior to the publication of the *Autobiography and Correspondence,* the Prince Consort had died, a public bereavement that called from the editoress a paragraph of condolence to close her last volume. Was she perhaps thinking of the theatrical immurement of Queen Victoria when she scolded from the footnotes that "In this age of selfishness and absurdity when even the outward signs of mourning are so often rendered ridiculous by the outrageous exaggeration of the types of woe—when sorrow is to be computed by the apparent absence of all clean linen,—and the unhappiness of a widow is often estimated by the number of months she has been totally invisible or her sensibility extolled in proportion to the tears shed in company; it is refreshing to the mind to read the simple journal of Mrs. Delany's life written by herself four months after the death of the Dean."

This journal, composed of letters written and received, gives an enthusiastic account of life at Bulstrode. The ducal offspring with whom she had sported in earlier years had, by the 1760s, married and dispersed to homes of their own. She returned to a household that revolved around the Duchess's many hobbies. Like her guest, her "Grace of Graces" loved the applied arts. Bulstrode boasted a turning shop from which issued objects "turned in wood, jet, ivory and amber." She made a study of spinning, in which she was assisted by Mary Dewes, and she amassed an important collection of *objets d'art* and porcelains, her most famous acquisition being the Barberini vase (more usually known as the Portland vase), now in the British museum.

The Duchess reserved, however, her greatest enthusiasm for the natural sciences. To assist her in forming and cataloguing her cabinets of plants, minerals and shells, she employed in the dual capacities of chaplain and librarian a distinguished conchologist and botanist, the Reverend John Lightfoot. Through him, Sir Joseph Banks, naturalist to the explorations of Captain Cook, became part of the Bulstrode circle.

An even more notable colleague was that philosopher of back-to-nature, Jean Jacques Rousseau. Like his enemy, Voltaire, he found it expedient to live outside France. He settled at Calwich, becoming neighbor to Mrs. Delany's cantankerous brother, Bernard Granville. Despite his patronage of the noble savage, Rousseau cultivated his intimacy at Bulstrode. He styled himself *l'herboriste de la Duchesse* (the herbalist of the Duchess), whom he attended during botanical expeditions into Derbyshire. Mrs. Delany was unmoved by these blandishments; as widow of a "Xtian" clergyman, she was unable to accept Rousseau's tenets. She warned the motherless Mary Dewes against the colorful exile, whose "writings are ingenious no doubt and were they weeded from the false and erroneous sentiments that are blended throughout his works . . . would be as valuable as they are entertaining."

The Duchess did not confine herself to "the varieties of stalac-
tites, selenites, ludus helmontii, etc. etc," but equipped Bulstrode
with a menagerie including "beautiful deer, oxen, cows, sheep of all
countrys, buffalos, mouflons, horses, asses; all in their proper places.
Then *hares* and *squirrels at every step you take,* so confident of their
security that they hardly run away! The great lawn before the house
is the nursery of all sorts of pheasants, pea fowl and guinea fowl, besides interlopers of Bantam pidgeons; and notwithstanding these
numerous *familys* the lawn is kept with as much neatness as the drawing room; such is the diligence of their attendants and the diligent
eye of their sovereign lady, who delights in having everything in the
best order, and is herself not only valuable to all that have the happiness of knowing her, but a blessing to *every creature* within her
possessions."

Never one to lose an opportunity for moralizing, Mrs. Delany
asks her niece "But what makes her so, my dearest child? *Not* her
great fortune—*not* her high station: but the *goodness of her heart,*
the excellence of her principles, the sweetness of her manners, an understanding improved by reading, and observation of her many *ingenious pursuits* which are a constant source of entertainm't to
herself and those she honors with her conversation. How happy,"
Mrs. Delany concluded triumphantly, "must I be with such a friend!"

All in all, it was an Indian summer, and Mrs. Delany has described it in letters as winning as those she had written to Mrs. Dewes
from Ireland.

The latter's death required that Mrs. Delany form new epistolary
companions. Granted the strong family ties characteristic of her and
her times, it was to be expected that "Pauline" should follow her
mother as Mrs. Delany's chief correspondent. Mary Dewes was now
in her early twenties. Aunt Delany had long showered her sister and
her niece with strictures, medical and moral. With one important
exception, our forefathers left women to their own devices in such
matters. The important exception, as Mary Pendarves had learned
to her sorrow, was the commerce of marriage à la mode.

There appears in the *Autobiography and Correspondence* a demure letter from Mary Dewes to Mr. John Port of Ilam. It is dated
"half an hour after 7, June 9th, 1770." The mere fact of a letter written, at this time, by a spinster to a bachelor presupposed an engage-

ment. It was destined to be a frustrated courtship because Uncle Granville, thirty years after the Pendarves-Delany romance, was still celibate and still resolved upon opposing the connubial prospects of the ladies of his family. Some six months before her marriage, Miss Dewes expressed a not unreasonable wonder that her uncle should object to a match approved by her father. She urged her fiancé to contend with the difficult bachelor; "say to him" she insisted, "how disappointed and mortified you were upon coming up to London and finding so different a reception from what you had reason to expect, especially *after* your *circumstances* and *estates* had undergone all the examination Mr. Dewes thought proper to make, and that you could not help wishing Mr. G. would stand your friend."

Mrs. Delany boldly championed the young lovers by means both spiritual and diplomatic. Her habitual references to the Great-Disposer-of-all-Things multiplied. Setting aside the respect exacted by brothers of sisters, she wrote frankly to the lovelorn Mary that she "can never cease wondering at the unaccountable behaviour of ——." Even allowing for the eloquent dash, such a comment was, two hundred years ago, near-liberalism. Mrs. Delany continued in a critical strain, still without naming the obstructive kinsman. "I must write to him but with painful reluctance as I never expect that cordiality which I feel I have a claim to and cannot guess why it is withdrawn."

In November of the same year, the Duchess of Portland intervened. A month later Mary Dewes became Mrs. Port and chatelaine of Ilam Hall in Staffordshire, whose beautiful gardens are still in existence.

John Port, as he appears in the correspondence, is a shadowy figure. Even the zealous editoress is somewhat vague about her enigmatic grandfather. We learn that he changed his name from Sparrow to Port of Ilam upon becoming heir to his uncle's estate. Some years after his marriage he was obliged to let Ilam because of pecuniary misfortunes. We receive a hint of insecurity, either legal or financial, in a letter from Mrs. Delany to Mrs. Port written in 1771. Thinking doubtless of the vanished document that sparked the Tennison lawsuit, she wrote to congratulate "my dearest M. on your dear Mr. Port's finding his lost papers etc; it might have been an affair of bad consequence, and for the time the *distress* lasted a very *great one, . . .*"

More objective correspondents were found among the Learned

Ladies who, as Blues and Hostesses, appear elsewhere in these pages. They constituted an imitation of the Paris salons and their aims were literary and feminist, aims which Mrs. Delany did not entirely share. She was of an older generation; she had found her way to excellence within patrician conventions. She admired the literary exertions of "Fidget" Montagu without finding herself at home in the latter's feathered parlor. Mrs. Thrale she preferred not to meet.* Mrs. Carter, the translator of Epictetus, appears in the correspondence, as does the Sylph, Mrs. Vesey. Where Hester Chapone's *Letters on the Improvement of the Mind* were concerned, the older lady was on sure ground. She drew up at Mrs. Port's request a set of rules to govern the conduct of Mr. Port's niece, Frances Mabel Sparrow, in which she urged the child to copy from the exalted work no more than six lines "at a time," going on to opine that she knows "no book for a young person (next to the Bible) more entertaining and edifying if read with due attention. I must again repeat *not* to write more than six lines at a time."

With the approach of the American Revolution, the letters of one of the Blue Stockings are of special interest, those of Frances Boscawen. Admiral Boscawen had, during the Seven Years' War, wrested Louisbourg from the French, a feat that gave to his widow decided views on transatlantic problems.

While the fortunes of the English in America declined, so did the health of Bernard Granville. Mrs. Delany, forgetting the trauma of suitors despised and hopes deferred, wrote constantly during his long ordeal in the submissive vein he preferred. She wrote only a few months before Paul Revere sprang into the saddle that "The American affairs are perplexing and require great adroitness in the Ministery. Incendiaries are busy to raise discontent, but these are matters too high for me."

Two months later she continued to soothe her moribund brother with, "The world is in a bustle about the American affairs but I am no politician and don't enter into these matters. Women lose all their dignity when they meddle with subjects that don't belong to

---

* Mrs. Delany, to say nothing of Lady Llanover, would not have found acceptable either Henry Thrale, the brewer, or his guest, Samuel Johnson, the tea-table polemicist.

them: their own sphere affords them *opportunities eno'* to show their *real consequence."*

Mrs. Boscawen was under no such necessity for deference. Not only was she the widow of a naval hero, but the mother of a "poor little soldier" who had sailed for Boston almost a year before the outbreak of hostilities. During the summer following the battles of Lexington, Concord and Bunker Hill, she reproached herself for tardiness in replying to Mrs. Delany, saying, "I shou'd certainly have wrote if my thoughts had not been at Boston, and alas! My cares also; I do not mean that I give credit to all these stories of the insurgents (and as yet we have no other), but the sword is unsheathed! And it cannot be but its *glare* must be painful in eyes so *sore* as mine."

This Georgian Cornelia had nothing but contempt for "Orator" Burke's noble address to Parliament in favor of conciliation with the colonies. She would have liked to export his rhetorical skills to America, where they might be employed in persuading *"that turbulent* people to be quiet and enjoy their own happiness and plenty."

Mrs. Delany, in the late fall of 1777, set aside her fashionable aversion to feminine interest in public affairs; she wrote to Mrs. Port of Ilam of the defeat of General Washington and the capture of Philadelphia, events which presaged the ghastly winter at Valley Forge. As the victories of the insurgents multiplied, Mrs. Boscawen and Mrs. Delany turned to pleasanter topics. There is a noncommittal mention of the taking of Ticonderoga but we read nothing of Saratoga, the crossing of the Delaware, nor of the surrender of Cornwallis at Yorktown. By the time the colonies had passed from the jurisdiction of George III, Mrs. Delany had become an intimate friend of the "Royals." A tactful silence seemed indicated.

Mrs. Boscawen also had decided views on obstetrics. The natural phenomenon of childbirth she called, with chilling candor, the "lit de misère." The first Port child, the resoundingly named Georgina Mary Ann, was born as promptly after her parents' marriage as decorum permits. To the childless aunt, all in a flutter about her attendance at Ilam, Mrs. Boscawen furnished realistic comfort; she wrote in the fall of 1771, "Your dear niece being *pure* well is indeed an earnest of pure good news shortly. . . . The first time I experienced the pains of child bearing, I concluded that no woman had ever endured the like upon the like occasion, and that I could not possibly recover it, whereas I danced a minuet about my room in ten days to insult my nursekeeper." In conclusion, Aunt Delany is urged to heed what the midwife says rather than "what Mrs. Port *screams* for scream she will and must."

Fortified by these counsels, Mrs. Delany absented herself from the accouchement, an act of self-indulgence soundly approved by Mrs. Boscawen. Four days after the child was born, she expressed herself "extremely pleased to find you did *not* attend the 'lit de misère' for indeed, my dear madam, it is an office so painful that I dreaded it for you, however, I shall be quite satisfied if you own to me a few days hence (as, I flatter myself strongly that you will) that notwithstanding all her sufferings she is as well as ever she was in her life. Amen. Ainsi Soit-il."

Although Georgina Mary Ann (usually shortened to her initials) was only seventeen when her adored Aunt Delany died, she is the key figure of the *Autobiography and Correspondence*. Without her it could not have been compiled. As Mrs. Waddington, she was Lady Llanover's mother; it was from her that the long-deferred "Pauline" derived the materials and inspiration for her publication.

Because of the triumphant nature of Mrs. Delany's old age, "the sweet bird," as her infatuated great-aunt called her, came upon the scene at a time of climax, rather than decline.

The close companionship of a child of seven with an elderly relative of seventy-eight was brought about by Mr. Port's failing fortunes. It was found practical to send the little girl for the winter months to London, where Mrs. Delany passed her non-Bulstrode time in St. James's Place. Writing, dancing, drawing and French masters were engaged and the "little jewel" went through much the same routines that her mother had traversed a generation earlier. Reading the letters that tell Mrs. Port of G.M.A.'s precocity in the minuet, and later her letters of precept to the young lady herself, produces a sensation of dejà vu.

G.M.A. was just one year old when Mrs. Delany began her most impressive achievement, the *Flora Delanica*. We first read of this experiment in collage in a letter written to Mrs. Port from Bulstrode in October of 1772. "I have," Aunt Delany wrote, "invented a new way of imitating flowers. I'll send you next time I write a sample."

Five years later another letter to Mrs. Port concludes, "This morning I have finished my 400th plant."

The Duchess of Portland had not only contributed to her guest's store of botanical knowledge; she had introduced her to Lady Andover, who was a skilled practitioner in the fashionable medium of "cutting" in paper. The eighteenth century was the heyday of the silhouette portrait which, cut in black paper mounted on white, anticipated the snapshot. Years before the "hortus siccus" or *Flora Delanica* was begun, a letter written from Delville described Lady Andover's adapting this skill to the depiction of "a landscape in an oval and a wreath round it of oak branches." It was, in Mrs. Delany's opinion, the finest thing of its kind she had ever seen.

In making her floral illustrations, Mrs. Delany reversed the black on white method used in the silhouette portraits of our ancestors. According to Lady Llanover the inspiration for her "hortus siccus," as Mrs. Delany often called her new craft, was caused by "a piece of Chinese paper on the table of bright scarlet." Because the paper was of the same color as a nearby geranium, Mrs. Delany, "taking her scissors—amused herself with cutting out each flower, by her eye, in the paper which resembled its hue; she laid the paper petals on a black ground and was so pleased with the effect that she proceeded to cut out the calyx, stalks and leaves in shades of green, and pasted them down; and after she had completed a sprig of geranium in this way, the Duchess of Portland came in and exclaimed, 'What are you doing with the geranium?', having taken the paper imitation for the real flower." Fired by such praise, Mrs. Delany embarked on the craft that has earned her a place in the annals of botanical illustration.

Mrs. Delany's hobby was destined to enlarge her already wide horizons and to bring her new admirers. Botanists were eager to supply rare specimens. Papers of unusual and streaked colors were solicited from captains in the China trade and from manufacturers of wallpaper. Horace Walpole pronounced the paper mosaics extremely beautiful and Sir Joseph Banks stated that they were "the *only* imitations of nature that he had ever seen from which he could *venture* to describe botanically any plant without the least fear of committing an error."

By far the most glamorous, not to say most providential, admirers of the *Flora Delanica* were the King and Queen.

Pretty Lady Betty of Bulstrode's nursery years was now Lady Weymouth and a member of the ponderous court at Windsor. To celebrate the birthday of their worthless eldest son, the royal family breakfasted with the Dowager Duchess of Portland on August 12, 1778. Even in those days of lavish hospitality, it was an impressive pageant, comprising phaetons, post chaises, coaches and persons on horseback, numbering in all thirty-three servants and fifty-six guests. The cavalcade arrived at noon and Mrs. Delany was soon summoned to show her book of flowers; she kept her distance until the Queen called her to "answer some question about a flower." The King, who wore his crown with a gravity worthy of Charles I, "brought a chair and set it at the table opposite to the Queen." Not all Lady Stanley's precepts were adequate to such sudden proximity to royalty. It was, confessed Mrs. Delany, "an hon'r I could not receive without some confusion and hesitation: 'sit down, sit down,' said her majesty, 'it is *not* everybody has a Chair brought to them by a King.' "

The Royal family was eventually to comprise fifteen children. In addition to the fifty-six guests who honored Bulstrode, there were infant Princesses left behind in the Windsor nursery. Mrs. Delany, emboldened by the Queen's praise of her "paper mosaick," confessed that she longed to see *"all* the royal family." It was promptly settled that the Duchess and her guest should come the next day to be entertained by their Majesties, the King promising " '*no stairs* to go up and a cool room.' "

It is, of course, Mrs. Delany's protégée, Fanny Burney, who remains chronicler-in-chief of the court of George III. Her time was not yet. When Mrs. Delany first met the royals, Fannikins was the self-conscious young lady who had recently stumbled into publishing the best-seller, *Evelina*. Five years were to elapse before Hester Chapone presented her to Mrs. Delany, and many more months before the latter was inspired to propose her as a royal lady's maid.

Mrs. Delany's letters concerning Windsor anticipate, but do not equal, Fanny Burney's journal. As I have already observed, she saw life from the outside. At seventy-eight, she retained her sense of occasion and her relish for a landscape or an interior. The Windsor she gives us is externally that of Fanny, with its undeviating routines of terracing, Händelian concerts and daily prayers in a chilly chapel. Where Fanny saw tedium and a deadening formality, Mrs. Delany was edified by the practice of every domestic virtue on the part of Queen Victoria's grandparents.

The older woman arrived on the royal scene in a calm before storm. The thirteen American colonies were still English and derangement had not yet claimed the King. To Mrs. Delany's uncritical eye, "Farmer" George appeared what he believed himself to be, the benevolent father of peoples and persons. When Miss Burney, some years later, entered into waiting, the King's paternal mechanism was equally outraged by his rebellious transatlantic subjects and his undutiful heir. Madness, or, according to modern research, the appearance of madness, was his destiny. In August of 1778 these misfortunes were ten years away.

Mrs. Delany, perhaps in acknowledgment of the part played by the *Flora Delanica* in her promotion to royal circles, wrote her first letter thereafter to Lady Andover. A second, more detailed account went to "Pauline" a week later. As the Queen had promised, all the royal family was on hand. There was the King and his seven sons and, among the royal babies, three-year-old Princess Mary, who called "the Duchess of Portland 'Lady Weymouth's Mama.' " Was Mrs. Delany " 'another mamma of Lady Weymouth's?' "

The King and Queen, according to their unvarying habit, showed themselves to their subjects in the early evening, returning to minuets, country dances and cotillions. These diversions took place in a setting of "beautiful Indian paper, chairs covered with embroideries of ye liveliest colors, glasses, tables, sconces, in the best taste, the whole calculated to give the greatest cheerfulness to the place and it had its effect."

Among the royals assembled to greet the ladies from Bulstrode was Prince Frederick, the future Duke of York. He was to serve during the Napoleonic wars as Commander in Chief of the Army, a position he relinquished when it was discovered that his mistress, Mary Anne Clarke, was doing a thriving trade in the selling of commissions to personable young officers. When Mrs. Delany went to court he bore, in deference to German origins, the singularly unsuitable title of Bishop of Osnaburg.

"The Prince of Wales and Bishop of Osnaburg" began the ball, Mrs. Delany happily reported to her niece, "and danced a minuet better than I ever saw danced. Then the Prince of Wales danced with the Princess Royal who has a very graceful agreable *air* but *not a good ear*. . . . At a little after nine it broke up. The *delightful* little Princess Mary who had been spectator all this time then danced with Prince Adolphus a dance of their *own composing* and soon all were dispersed." Stodgy Windsor kept early hours. Mrs. Delany brought her letter to a purring conclusion. "We got into the chaise about ten and got home very well by moonlight and chaise lamps, much pleased wth our entertainment and less fatigued than I could have imagined."

Year by year the intimacy ripened. The comings and goings between Bulstrode and Windsor increased. Mrs. Delany was honored with gifts, including a lock of the Queen's hair sent by "her own royal fingers." Her Majesty's dignity, condescension, religious principles and propriety came to rival the perfections of Georgina Mary Ann Port in Aunt Delany's enraptured pages.

Because of failing eyesight, she sometimes dictated accounts of those exalted activities to a servant, whose spelling adds an earthy tone to the King's stag hunt: "(wee) went to Garard Cross. . . . Where His Majesty met the (Duchess of Portland Carage)—the queen was (thear)—as were a (grate many carages)."

Better was to follow. Only a few weeks after the hunt the Queen, during a visit to Bulstrode, surprised Mrs. Delany at her spinning wheel. The latter was suddenly promoted to tutorial status; "the Queen," Mrs. Delany wrote again to G.M.A., "was so gracious as to take a lesson from me, and has desired the DSS to get her just such a wheel; I am to set it in order and have the honor of giving Her Majesty another lesson."

To make doubly certain Charlotte's progress in the homely craft, Mrs. Delany furnished supplementary instruction to "my dear Miss Hamilton," a lady-in-waiting. The wheel was presented early in 1782, accompanied by the following sentiments:

> Go, happy wheel! Amuse her leisure hour,
> Whose Grace and affability refin'd
> Add lustre to her dignity and power
> And fill with love and awe the grateful mind.

During the same year failing sight forced Mrs. Delany to bring to an end the *Flora Delanica*. Her letters and her many crafts had made heavy inroads on her elderly vision. It must have been a sorrowful moment when she entered these lines in a volume of her paper flowers:

> *The time is come!* I can no more
> The vegetable world explore;
> No more with rapture cull each flower
> That paints the mead or turnes the bower
>
> Come Holy Spirit, on thy wing
> Thy sacred consolation bring
>
> O sanctify the pointed dart
> That at this moment rends my heart;
> Teach me, *submissive to resign*
> When summoned by thy Will Divine

Hester Chapone, of the *Letters on the Improvement of the Mind,* wrote promptly to sympathize with Mrs. Delany's deprivation. Her letter closed on a prophetic postscript: "Have you read *Cecilia*? I hope it finds favour at Bulstrode for I am fond of the book and its writer."

Its writer was, of course, Fanny Burney. She met Mrs. Delany in January 1783 and became the close companion of her elderly mentor's remaining years. Some of the most attractive pages of her exhaustive journal are concerned with the talented old lady, whose presence was one of the few—very few—bright spots in the monotonous years of service to Queen Charlotte.

Lady Llanover, as we have had occasion to observe, was far from impartial. Her opinions, especially her opinions of her relatives, were what we today would call slanted. As regards the late Frances Burney d'Arblay, she was more than prejudiced; she was vicious! She harbored, in the 1860s, a posthumous hatred for the badgered Second Mistress of the Queen's Wardrobe. Both Emily Hahn, in her biography of Fanny entitled *A Degree of Prudery,* and Emily Morse Symonds, in her life of Mrs. Delany, advance a Granville theory: Miss Burney had, while at court, meddled in an affair of the heart concerning Georgina Mary Ann, or Miss P. as Fanny calls her in her journal.

This explanation, in terms of our generation-gapped times, seems far-fetched. Fanny was in her middle thirties when she went to

Windsor and Miss P. only fifteen. This seems a wide span of years for jealousy until we remember that women, among them Mrs. Delany, often married (or were forced to marry) men many years older than themselves. We will read in the chapter called "The Pioneer" of Fanny's setting her cap for Colonel Digby, the middle-aged widower who was Vice Chamberlain to the Queen. Was the "Sweet Bird" also smitten by the bereaved courtier? Then too, Lady Llanover was hardly the person to quarrel, by implication, with the marriage of which she was the result. If Miss P. had married the unknown charmer, supposedly spirited away by Fanny, instead of Mr. Waddington, would Augusta Waddington Llanover ever have existed?

The first editorial tantrum occurs just prior to the date in Mrs. Delany's correspondence when Mrs. Chapone took Fanny to call at St. James's Place. It suggests that Lady Llanover's fury had its source in possessiveness, pride and envy rather than a futile reproach for her mother's being crossed in love.

Mme. d'Arblay had, in a word, scooped Lady Llanover. Her *Diary* and *Memoirs of Dr. Burney,* with the delightful renditions of Mrs. Delany, had reached the press before Lady Llanover's stately work. This was sheer impertinence on the part of a music master's daughter, a commercial scribbler of fiction, and the widow of a penniless French refugee. The editoress spared no effort to discredit her rival. Because Fanny had succeeded with novels, it must be that her accounts of happenings and conversations were also works of the imagination. Her low antecedents caused her translation to court to turn her head. She was so clumsy that she often gave pain to her royal mistress by catching the back hair in a ribbon. She fancied all the courtiers in love with her. In a word, "Fanny Burney has taken possession of the ear of those who found their amusement in reading her twaddle," here a pause is made for a genuflection to Georgina Mary Ann "(that piece of old-fashioned *slang.* I should not have dared to write, or utter, within hearing of my dear mother . . .) and there appears to be little help against the *spell* by which she (Fanny Burney) contrived to drag down the person and position of Mrs. Delany to her own level."

Two years after Fanny met Mrs. Delany, the Duchess of Portland died after a short illness caused by "a bilious complaint which terminated (it is apprehended) in a mortification." Thereafter things moved rapidly. Her Grace of Graces died in July of 1785. Less than a month later the King and Queen invited Mrs. Delany to exchange Bulstrode for Windsor. We read of this benevolence in a letter dated August 14, 1785; its writer "could not read the account, without a sort of shivering, and tears coming into my eyes. . . . Such instances of friendship are rare in their Majesties exalted rank, and I congratulate *them* on having felt a pleasure so few of the royal race has ever known."

A house, adjacent to the castle, was made over to the bereaved Mrs. Delany. The King himself oversaw the workmen and the Queen provisioned the pantry, with special attention to pickles. While preparations were in progress, Mrs. Delany lived in her house in St. James's Place. She had, to Lady Llanover's subsequent displeasure, Fanny as her guest. "Miss Burney," the editoress wrote, "appears to have been for the first time admitted to the house, and to have so conducted and comported herself as to have made a most favourable impression."

Mrs. Delany wrote that "I have had in the house with me, ever since my nephews *were obliged* to leave me, Miss Burney (the author of Evelina and Cecilia), which, excellent as they are, are her meanest praise. Her admirable understanding, tender affection, and sweetness of manners, make her valuable to all those who have the happiness to know her."

This affectionate tribute was more than Lady Llanover could bear. Until now every opinion of Mrs. Delany had been sacred writ; she took the unprecedented step of flatly differing with her heroine. From the footnotes she contradicted that "For 'admirable understanding' *talent* might be substituted for '*tender affection*' a gentle sympathizing voice; and for '*sweetness of manners*' (*apparently*) timid and undividing attention and respect to Mrs. Delany."

In September, just two months after the death of her Grace of Graces, Mrs. Delany, accompanied by G.M.A., moved to her new home. A letter to greet her awaited Windsor's new resident; it read, "My Dearest Mrs. Delany, if coming to me will not fatigue your spirits *too* much, I shall receive you with open arms, and am, Your affectionate friend, Charlotte."

Mrs. Delany's account of Windsor exists in two forms; there are detailed letters written, for the most part, to Miss Hamilton, a friend of the Irish years, and there is—equally eloquent in its own way—a laconic diary.

To Miss Hamilton, Mrs. Delany narrated that, upon arriving at the house prepared for her, she flung herself at the King's feet "indeed unable to utter a word." She learned that she was to receive an allowance from the King's privy purse of three hundred pounds per annum. In view of her recent sorrow, she was not expected to wait upon their Majesties; they and the royal youngsters condescended to take tea with *her*.

Mrs. Delany was, by November, sufficiently restored to pass her evenings at the Queen's Lodge. She wrote a charming description to Miss Hamilton of the innocent domestic scene. The royal children were gathered about a large table covered with books and pencils and paper. The Queen chatted with her elderly guest; the Princesses drew; the infant Princess Amelia played on the floor with Papa—all of this to Händelian strains coming from the next room. Probably with a view to a glittering future for G.M.A., Aunt Delany concluded with "Miss Port is *very well* and *very happy*. I am much flattered with the approbation she meets with."

By July of the following year, Mrs. Delany had become a staple of the routine-ridden court. She went daily to prayers in the King's chapel, an event which, like the evening terracing, provided their Majesties with an opportunity to speak to "everybody of consequence as they pass." After a nine o'clock breakfast she spent two hours outdoors. Her afternoons were consecrated to the likelihood of a royal visit. "They *always* drink tea here," she wrote, "and my niece has the honor of giving it about to all the Royal family, as they will not suffer me to do it."

This letter ends upon a significant note: Fanny Burney's appointment to Queen Charlotte's entourage. Mrs. Delany informed the friend in Ireland that "An event has taken place lately which gives me great satisfaction. I am sure you are acquainted with the novel entitled Cecilia. . . . There is nothing good, amiable and agreeable mentioned in the book that is not possessed by the author of it, Miss Burney. I have now been acquainted with her three years: her *extreme diffidence of herself,* notwithstanding her great genius and the applause she has met with, adds lustre to all her excellences and all improve on acquaintance."

The upshot of this tribute was Fanny's entrance, during the summer of 1786, into royal servitude. Some of the disadvantages of her new honor were inadvertently suggested in the same letter. The place was open, Mrs. Delany continued innocently, because "One of the principal ladies that attends the Queen's person as dresser is going into her own country, being in too bad a state of health to continue her honourable and delightful employment (for such it must be near such a Queen). Miss Burney is to be the happy successor. . . ."

Mrs. Delany has been scolded by some of Fanny's biographers for her part in securing for the latter what was to prove a laborious post. Like Lady Llanover's anti-Burney footnoting, this is prejudice. Mrs. Delany knew nothing of the backstairs life at Windsor. She had a simple, straightforward mind; it remains one of her charms. She was disposed to believe that persons and situations were just as they appeared to be. An ancestor had died in defense of the Divine Right of Kings; it therefore followed that to live in the service of this exalted error was part of the same mystique. She wished the young novelist nothing but good, never dreaming that lacing the Queen's stays, sorting her ribbons and mixing her snuff was not an improvement upon a successful literary career.

Then too, in her upper eighties, she was of an age when childhood impressions take precedence over the present. "Valeria" had prepared her for a career at court. It remained in her elderly opinion a universally desirable destiny. She did not live to discover her mistake.

Mrs. Delany died a month before her eighty-eighth birthday. In her long life, the bright days outnumber the dark. She was, with the dramatic exception of her first marriage, successful in the pursuit of happiness as recommended by His Majesty's treasonable subjects. She possessed and perfected many talents, including a gift for friends. She was even fortunate in death. In October of 1788 her beloved King suffered the "intellectual disease" of which, Lady Llanover notwithstanding, Miss Burney is the acknowledged historian. Death spared Mrs. Delany horrors she could neither have understood nor endured. Subjected to being bled white, she was drained of life in April.

Although Mrs. Delany's literary abilities did not equal her skill in the applied arts, her exhaustive correspondence supplies an invaluable picture of the day-to-day activities, concerns, convictions and even limitations of her class and times. Some of the immediacy of her letters and those of her friends is owing to the fact that they were written by amateurs. Style seldom competes with news. We are never diverted from a ballroom or a recipe by rhetoric. Like her sometime tutor, Hogarth, her interest was in the general human scene. She loved her life, her friends and her projects. In recording them, she remains witness to a vanished world.

4

THE QUEEN

Elizabeth Robinson Montagu

1720-1800

CONVERSATION as English literature came into its own during the second half of the eighteenth century. Following in the sonorous wake of Samuel Johnson, this age was to become as vocal as that of Shakespeare. Many of its masterpieces originated in spoken language. The theatre of Garrick and of Sheridan, the oratory of Burke, the insolent wit of John Wilkes and, above all, the voluminous dialogues that play so large a part in Boswell's *Life* and Fanny Burney's journal—all of this was ear-borne. It remains ironic that "talking for victory," a skill more French or Irish than it is English, should have found its chief exponent in Johnson, whose John Bullism was both insular and provincial.

In consequence of this gregarious period, there remains a heritage of "good things" heard or heard of, rather than read. Those who are not familiar with Goldsmith's works know that he wrote like an angel but talked like poor Poll. Others who have never seen the *Rivals* refer to malapropisms. Posterity remembers that Johnson said that he who is tired of London is tired of life itself, and that Chesterfield's *Letters* to his son taught the manners of a dancing master and the morals (according to Mrs. Montagu) of a prostitute.*

Given this social approach to literature, it was natural that the intellectual women of London should look to those of Paris for a precedent. They did so and, in part as a result, there came into being

_____
* Johnson was less delicate. He said the "morals of a whore."

that engaging company of ladies known as the Blue Stockings, an expression that was not then, as it is today, pejorative.

The English Blue Stockings, like the ladies of the French Enlightenment, used the avenue of entertainment to achieve intellectual goals. Denied in many cases formal schooling, and in all cases the Sorbonne, Oxford and Cambridge, they were, in the most admirable sense of the word, self-educated. Their goals were eloquently summed up by Mme. du Deffand, who complained that she had found a given evening disappointing because she had learned nothing new. One of the most earnest in this discipline was Elizabeth Robinson Montagu, whom it pleased Dr. Johnson to dub "Queen of the Blues."

Through this medium the later and lesser Montagu rejoiced in the recognition denied to her cousin-in-law, Lady Mary. Other factors of temperament, associations and time were in her favor. She was not inconvenienced, as was the elder woman, by genius nor by passionate and conflicting impulses. Her intellect was cultivated by parents and grandparents. She and her only sister, Sarah, shared equally in the education supplied to four older brothers. From her father, Matthew Robinson, she received instruction far superior to that usually proffered to fledgling "gentlewomen."

Mrs. Robinson, when she was still Elizabeth Drake, had been sent to a school maintained by Mrs. Makin, formerly governess to Princess Elizabeth, daughter of the Royal Martyr. Mrs. Makin inveighed against "The Barbarous custom to breed women low." This error, she continued, "is grown so general among us and hath prevailed so far that it is verily believed that women are not endowed with such reason as men." Not only were little girls of nine offered Latin, Greek, Hebrew, French and Italian, but "Repositories also for Visibles shall be prepared; by which from beholding the things, Gentlewomen may learn the Names, Natures, Values and use of Herbs, Shrubs, Trees, Mineral-pieces, Metals and Stones."

Chatelaines-to-be might also master "Limning, Preserving, Pastry and Cookery. . . ." Lest this might alarm the parents of gentlewomen, "those that think these Things Improbable or Impracticle" were urged to "have further account every Tuesday at Mr. Mason's Coffee-house in Cornhill near the Royal Exchange."

Thus it was that "Fidget" Robinson escaped the blight that had wrung from the older Lady Mary the words, "we are a lower order of creation."

The Robinson children who survived infancy numbered seven boys and two girls. In addition to lessons, family debates were encouraged as tending to sharpen wits. Mrs. Robinson, in her capacity of "Mrs. Speaker," presided from her mending basket to soften sarcasm and cool blushes. In these fortunate circumstances, Elizabeth early developed the balanced nature she was to retain through eighty incredibly busy years. The great hostess of the future was in her girlhood committed to her studies and, in her words, as fond of dancing "as if she had been bitten by a tarantula." This equilibrium between scholarly and social values was the secret of the unique part she played in late Georgian England.

Grandparents also contributed to bringing forward the precocious Fidget. Mrs. Robinson's mother, the former Mrs. Drake, had taken for her second husband Conyers Middleton, the freethinking philosopher of Cambridge. They delighted in having Elizabeth to stay. When Middleton's colleagues called to defend scripture against skepticism, the child was seated close by and required later to repeat what was said. If it was Middleton's plan to steer his young guest toward the deism made fashionable by the French philosophers and their English admirers, he was doomed to disappointment. Other influences were at work.

One of the earliest of these was supplied by the Duchess of Portland. "Noble lovely little Peggy" was only a few years older than Fidget. Her charms were considerably enhanced in her young friend's eyes by her progressing from Your Ladyship to Your Grace. Mrs. Delany's "Duchess of Duchesses" was, of necessity, not only a monument of propriety, but also of orthodoxy. As Elizabeth's circle widened it came to include Gilbert West, who was, declared Johnson, equally to be honored as a poet and a Christian. To his edifying company was added over the years Edward Young of "Night Thoughts," Lord Lyttleton, to whose "Dialogues of the Dead" Elizabeth contributed, James Beattie, who wrote an *Essay on Truth* in defense of revealed religion, and that exemplar of Anglicanism, Dr. Johnson himself.

We find in Mrs. Montagu's girlhood letters the common sense, love of study and of company and absence of sentimentality that were

Elizabeth Robinson Montagu

to mark her career. Her placid piety, rivalling that of Mrs. Delany, belongs to a later period. In a very early letter to the Duchess of Portland, her contribution of many years later to Lyttleton's *Dialogues* is prefigured. "Madam," wrote the future authoress and mentor, "As I always acquaint Your Grace with my motions from place to place I think it incumbent upon me to let you know I died last Thursday; having that day expected to hear of a certain dutchess and being disappointed I fell into a vexation and from thence into a chagrin and from that into a melancholy with a complicated et cetera and so expired." The Shakespearean scholar of the future was clearly inspired by Polonius's description of Hamlet's madness, Act II, Scene II. These sprightly lines, written when Elizabeth was fourteen, furnished a point of departure for the "Dialogues of the Dead" that appeared in 1760.

Smallpox, despite Lady Mary's importation of inoculation, still stalked the land, twice afflicting the Robinson neighborhood and household. In the fall of 1739, when she was nineteen, Elizabeth, whose health was never robust, was sent from her home to be quarantined among strangers. She has left us a plucky description of her rude surroundings: "the goodman and his wife snored, the little child cry'd, the maid screamed, one little boy had whooping cough, another screamed with chilblains." Equally courageous was the philosophy she brought to bear upon her privations. "I endeavor . . . to be wise when I cannot be merry, easy when I cannot be glad, content with what cannot be mended and patient when there is no redress."

She must have been immensely cheered in these uncongenial surroundings by a letter from her brother Matthew, in which he praises her social gifts and her ability to accept uncomplainingly a lonely situation. "Tho in company" he wrote, "one would swear that your parts and spirits were contrived purposely for laughter and the cheerful round of mirth, yet study and thought, contemplation of the ways of men, or works of nature and consequently enjoyment of your ease and happiness, the end of all good, never desert your leisure and retirement . . . when driven from your friends and almost alone in a manner you never were before and probably may never be again; you were fairly left to the food and entertainment of your own thoughts. . . . I don't remember that I ever saw your thoughts stamped upon a piece of paper with greater force of discernment than in the letter I received from you today." Judging from Elizabeth's frequent references to Milton, it seems reasonable to infer that an Allegro and Penseroso alternation of mood and activity was a pattern she consciously cultivated. In the following Allegro passage, we find an early instance of her rejection of love in a romantic sense, a rejection not only avowed by herself but commented on by her friends, especially Hester Chapone, who declared Mrs. Montagu to be an ignoramus in love. "Vapours and love," wrote the detached Fidget, "are two things that seek solitude, but for me, who have neither in my constitution a crowd is not disagreeable, and I always find myself prompted . . . to go where two or three are gathered together." In this preference she was entirely at home in Johnsonian London.

The shortest-lived of her youthful qualities was, as we shall learn to our regret, the ability to laugh at herself. Fidget possessed powers in this regard undreamed of and undesired by "Minerva" Montagu of Portman Square. Plagued all her life by ill-health, she wrote in her dancing days, "I am confined by a little feverishness. I thought as it was a London fever it might be polite so I carried it to the Ridotto, court and opera but it grew perverse and stubborn so I put it into a white hood and double handkerchief and kept it by the fireside these three days and it is better; indeed I hope it is worn out."

The Romantic Movement of the later Georgian years was to give Mrs. Montagu a fondness for mountain scenery, for pseudo- and neo-Bardic poetry, and a respect for the supernatural. Psychologically, it did not touch her. Lacking an emotional view of matrimony, she planned her marriage in a businesslike spirit combined with an earthiness that must have given her Victorian editor pause. Setting aside tenderness for a cheerful materialism, she pronounces that "Gold is the chief ingredient in the composition of worldly happiness. Living in a cottage on love is certainly the worst diet and the worst habitation one can find out. As for modern marriages they are great infringers of the baptismal vow; for 'tis commonly the pomps and vanities of this wicked world on one side and the simple lust of the flesh on the other." Her own marriage to Edward Montagu, which took place in 1742 when the bride was twenty-three and the groom fifty-one, was, despite the disparity in ages, by no means a "marriage à la mode." Although she was accustomed to say of herself, and others to say of her, that she knew nothing of love, the facts do not bear out this accusation. Given the parent-child span of years existing between husband and wife, theirs was the love of friendship rather than passion. Nevertheless, it gave a real glow, albeit a gentle one.

Marriage to Edward Montagu answered Elizabeth's preference for an in-the-world-and-out-of-it life. He owned, as did his first cousin, Edward Wortley Montagu, collieries in the north of England. A part of each year was to be spent at Allerthorpe in Yorkshire. There were also farmlands at Sandleford Priory in Berkshire and, successively, houses in Dover Street, Hill Street and Portman Square in London. With this varied prospect Fidget was delighted. Her father, sociable Matthew Robinson, wrote to his elderly son-in-law on the subject of his daughter's happiness. "As I think that no letters that come from your wife ought to be a secret to you I cannot help telling you I saw one from her last week to her mother and another to her brother Tom so full of the happiness of her present condition and the prospect of her future that I begin to be suspicious that they are designed as a reproof to me for the deplorable state under which she passed twenty-three years."

Mr. Montagu proved himself an excellent, if unexciting, husband. He had, at the time of his marriage, succeeded to Mr. Wortley Montagu's seat in Parliament as member for Huntingdon, an office for which his retired habits would hardly have seemed to suit him. His political career was little more than fulfilling the duties of a country gentleman whose family dominated a part of the East-Anglican electorate. His passionate and abiding interest was mathematics, a hobby which afforded shelter from his wife's Blue Stocking activities. He was indolent, amiable, kind, proud of Elizabeth and quite willing that she should take the lead in matters social and literary.

His first act upon bringing his bride to his "old and not handsome" house was charming. Elizabeth had three younger brothers at a boarding school near Allerthorpe. They had not been home in five years. To the Duchess of Portland Elizabeth writes in the late summer of 1742, "Tomorrow I believe will be one of the happiest days I ever spent. I am to go to fetch my brothers from school. How delightful will be such a meeting after so many years' separation." The same letter tells us that six days were required to make the journey from London to Yorkshire. No wonder holidays were an impractical luxury!

Of these little brothers, William, the eldest, was to play a signifi-cant role in his sister's vast correspondence. He eventually took orders and with his wife removed first to Rome, then to Naples. Elizabeth's letters to this particular sister-in-law are excellent. They are warm, easy and lack the mistaken majesty that sometimes inflects her letters to persons of eminence. They form the background for Dr. Doran's biography of Mrs. Montagu, entitled *A Lady of the Last Century*.

The problems arising from the War of the Austrian Succession required that Mr. Montagu leave his pregnant bride and devote him-self to parliamentary attendance. Elizabeth "desired him to go and half wished him to stay." A lonely period ensued, despite the presence of her sister, Sarah. Elizabeth was too much the daughter of her urban-minded father, Matthew Robinson, to view her provincial neighbors as anything but oafs. During this period she amused her-self with a caricature of a rural beau that owes a good deal to Field-ing and to Hogarth; in its simplified condemnation it anticipates Fanny Burney. "Had you seen the pains this animal has been taking to imitate the cringe of a beau, the smartness of a wit, till he was hideous to behold, and horrible to hear, you would have pitied him! He walks like a tortoise, and chatters like a magpye: by the indul-gence of a kind mother, and the advantage of a country education, he was first a clown, then he was sent to the Inns of Court, where he first fell into a red waistcoat and velvet breeches; then fell into vanity. This light companion led him to the play house, where he ostenta-tiously coquetted with the orange wenches, who cured him of the bel-air of taking snuff by abridging him of his nostrils, grown even in his own eyes no very lovely figure; he thought Bacchus, no critic in faces, would prove in the end a better friend than Cupid: accord-ingly he fell into the company of the jovial, till want of money and want of taste led this prodigal son, if not to eat, to drink with swine. He visited the prisons, not as a comforter, but as a companion to criminals; shook hands with the gold finder, and walked in the ways of the scavenger; so singular his humility, none were his contempt. At last, having lost his money, ruined his constitution, and lost all the sense nature gave him, he returned to the country where all the youths of inferior rank, admiring his experience, and emulating his qualities, and copying his manners, grew, some fit for jail, others for transportation."

Mrs. Montagu would never have forgiven herself had she omitted classical deities from this cautionary tale.

She travelled to London in the early spring of 1743 for her confinement. In charge of the convoy was Mr. Carter, steward of the Allerthorpe estate. It was, in those days of highwaymen, overturns and dirty inns, a sensitive responsibility. He was determined that his mistress should not only be spared physical danger but also, for prenatal reasons, the dread thereof. At each stop he reassured Mrs. Montagu and her sister of the excellence of meals, of accommodations, of the safety of fords and roads and of the adequacy of horses, carriage and postillions. Mr. Carter, the kindly servant for so many years of a bachelor, was to prove himself the tenderest well-wisher to a short-lived heir. "Mr. Carter in his care," wrote the mother-to-be, "often bid me be of good courage; as there was noe occasion for any I could not be disgraced for want of it; from our first setting out I have not been less entertain'd than guarded by him, he has really acted the part of Sir Roger de Coverly all the way."

Mrs. Montagu was "brought to bed of a son" on May 11, 1743. The baby was nicknamed Punch. The charming old man who had shepherded the party south from Allerthorpe was, wrote Mrs. Montagu, "half bewitched with Punch." He exclaimed in his north country speech, "Bonnie Bairn, ye are a fine one, weel worth it; . . . I warrant hee's think of me when I be.dead and gone, I'se to make all t'improvements I can for him. . . . Oh, my Lady, he's brave company. God's blessing light on him."

God's blessing was to prove prompt and final. After a few tumbles on his blanket and a few staggering steps, he died before he reached his second birthday—of, it was believed, teething convulsions. With him died Fidget. Wit she retained; happiness returned, but merriment was gone forever.

Elizabeth wrote a moving letter to the Duchess of Portland that should vindicate her from accusations of coldness. It reads, in part, "I am much obliged to my dear Friend for her tender concern for me; I would have wrote to you before but I could not command my thoughts so as to write what might be understood. I am well enough as to health of Body, but God knows the sickness of the soul is far worse. . . . Adieu, think of me as seldom as you can, and when you do, remember I am patient, and hope that the same Providence that snatched this sweetest blessing from me may give me others, if not I will endeavor to be content, if I may not be happy. Heaven preserve you and your dear precious Babes; thank God you are far removed from my misfortune and can hardly be bereft of all."

The Montagus never had another child. This was a double loss, taking its toll in sorrow and in character. Both man and wife were methodical; both were formal. A nursery and the ensuing household of young people would have considerably enlivened their pre-determined lives. Although Georgian and Victorian parents could, by means of nurses, tutors, governesses and schools, screen out their children, Elizabeth had, it will be remembered, grown up in another, more human tradition. She would have delighted in re-creating Mrs. President to her own sons and daughters.

Then, too, a child by the very fact of its existence suggests mystery and proposes questions. It was to be Mrs. Montagu's role in Blue Stocking circles to "have all the answers." She would have been greatly enriched by participating in the freemasonry of motherhood. She needed this commonplace challenge, as did her self-protective husband. Lacking children to disturb the calm of Sandleford, Aller-thorpe and Hill Street, the parents-denied pursued their increasingly separate paths.

A year after Punch's death, Bonnie Prince Charlie and a handful of followers inaugurated the ill-fated Jacobite rebellion of 1745. Lady Mary watched this drama unfold from the Continent, Mrs. Delany from Ireland, but the Montagus, by reason of their north country holdings, were right in the path of the Stuart campaign. Edward hurried to his Yorkshire and Northumberland acres to raise troops, while Elizabeth's parents, who lived in Kent, trembled for fear of a French invasion. Elizabeth offered to join her husband in what bade fair to become a dangerous situation, a gesture of wifely loyalty that inspired him to liken her to a Roman matron.

The tragic civil strife was brought to an end at Culloden by the Duke of Cumberland. Händel wrote *Judas Maccabeus* to celebrate a brutal victory, and scores of bewildered highlanders went to the block on charges of treason. London persons of quality had no more scruples about public executions than had the *tricoteuses* of the

French Revolution. On one occasion Mrs. Montagu received a letter that read, "Madame Granville desires her duty, she is sorry you are not in town, there was a charming execution yesterday, two smugglers and a Jew and a fine view from her windows." The beheading of Lord Lovatt and his brothers-in-arms promised a holiday for vicarious sadists. "I hear," wrote Lady Andover, "of great interest making for tickets to see the executions. I fear humanity is at a very low ebb."

Allowing for its finality, the headman's axe of two centuries ago was doubtless a more merciful blade than the surgeon's scalpel. Mrs. Robinson, Elizabeth's mother, contracted cancer of the breast and underwent unanesthetized surgery, after making the usual stipulation that no member of the family be in the house while the grisly operation went forward. It was to no avail. In the spring of 1746 Mrs. Speaker joined her departed little grandson.

Elizabeth was now twenty-seven. Childless, motherless and with a husband either absent on business, or absent-minded at home, she started to create the family of friends and friends of friends that gives this chapter its title. Many of Mrs. Montagu's friends we already know; others will appear in later pages. Her birth in 1720 was too late for her to have more than a secondhand acquaintance with the age of Pope and Addison. She was to become, in her rôle of "Queen of the Blues," a linchpin of London in the days of Johnson, Garrick and Reynolds. The world was infinitely smaller in the eighteenth century than it is in the twentieth. Men and, increasingly, women were certain to meet when they went to see Garrick at the Drury Lane, to hear Händel give "Messiah" to benefit Captain Coram's Foundling Hospital, to go botanizing with Mrs. Delany and the Duchess of Portland at Bulstrode, or to discourse with Mrs. Montagu at Bath or on the Pantiles * at Tunbridge Wells.

In her "Fidget" days, Elizabeth had taken the waters at Bath. These were the years when she feared boredom more than disease or death. From her nineteenth year, she has left this charmingly intolerant description of card-playing invalids. "The morning after I arrived I went to the Ladies' Coffee House, where I heard of nothing but the rheumatism in the shoulder, the sciatica in the hip, and

---

* A promenade that derived its name from its paving. It was the resort's fashionable meeting place.

the gout in the toe. After these complaints I began to fancy myself in the Hospitals or Infirmaries; I never saw such an assembly of disorders. I dare say Gay wrote his fable of the 'Court of Death' from this place. After drinking the waters I go to breakfast, and about 12 I drink another glass of water, and then dress for dinner; visits employ the afternoon, and we saunter away the evening in great stupidity. I think no place can be less agreeable. 'How d'ye do?' is all one hears in the morning, and 'What's trumps?' in the afternoon."

The next day matters were, if anything, worse. She was now obliged to play cards, a pastime she despised. "Lord Berkshire was wheeled into the rooms on Thursday night, where he saluted me with much snuff and civility, in consequence of which I sneezed and curtseyed abundantly; as a further demonstration of his loving-kindness, he made me play at commerce with him. You may easily guess at the charms of a place where the height of my happiness is a pair royal at commerce, and a peer of fourscore."

Gambling in the eighteenth century in England was the opiate of the rich. Despite the disasters it threatened to family fortunes, stately homes, inheritances and personal honor, it was responsible for a constructive backlash. To this fashionable vice we owe the equally fashionable virtue of Blue Stocking coteries. Conversation was the weapon Mrs. Montagu and her circle proposed to employ against "deep play." In doing so they wrote a page significant not only in the annals of English literature but also in those of feminism.

We have already met in the previous chapter five of the Blues and their friends. They are Mrs. Delany, the Duchess of Duchesses, Mrs. Boscawen, Mrs. Chapone and that post-Blue, Fanny Burney. Of these, in 1750, Mrs. Montagu knew only the first two. Others whom she will meet are Mrs. Carter, Mrs. Vesey and Hannah More. The salon in England, unlike that of France, was frequented by an equal number of men and women conversationalists. That this was the case meant that none of the Blues attained the glamorous isolation of a Mme. Récamier.

It is not customary to number Hester Thrale among the Blues. She had her own coterie that revolved around the majestic presence of Dr. Johnson and, for this reason, confined herself to his opinions and his needs, even in matters of her choice of clothes. She played little or no part in contributing to the literary gatherings of other "female pens."

The Blue Stockings constituted a movement, not an organization. Unlike Johnson's Literary Club—with its dues, its discussions as to who was or was not "clubable," and its regular times of meeting—it was a trend. Its purpose was to provide a spoken and written avenue for the exchange of literary opinion. Its inception coincided with the new respect accorded to intelligent women and it culminates in the establishment of acknowledged authoresses. When the Prince Regent kept all Jane Austen's novels in each royal residence, the Blue Stockings became superfluous. They had won the day.

The most prolific of their number, Hannah More, has celebrated the movement in two poems, *The Bas Bleu* and *Sensibility*. Her subtitle to the former poem, *Conversation,* pinpoints the purpose of the salon. Both poems present an admirable history of the Blues, how they originated and of whom they consisted. She confirms the theory that cultivated men and women intended to put down gambling.

> Long was society o'er-run
> By whist, that desolating Hun.

To free themselves from this incubus:

> Genius prevails, and conversation
> Emerges into *reformation.*
> The vanquished triple crown to you
> Boscawen sage, bright Montagu
> Divided fell;—your cares in haste
> Rescued the ravaged realms of taste.

Assisting in the rescue was Lord Lyttleton, whose colleague in print Mrs. Montagu was soon to be. There was William Pultney, Earl of Bath, whose gallantries might have threatened a less tranquil marriage than that of the Montagus. Horace Walpole, a strange friend to the prim Hannah More,

> showed the way,
> How wits may be both learned and gay.

When conversation faltered, Garrick obliged with readings. And chief among the Blues' well-wishers was Johnson. He commented frequently "on the amazing progress made of late years in literature by the women." Remembering the days when a young woman like Lady Mary was taught to carve but forbidden Greek and Latin, he rejoiced to see clever women "vie with the men in everything." He made no secret of the pleasure he took in well-informed feminine companions, reinforcing his point by inveighing against "wretched, unideaed girls."

It seems to have been quite impossible for any English writer of this period to eschew odious comparisons with those of France. The usual pattern was to contrast supposed French artificialities with equally supposed English spontaneity. Hannah More enthusiastically followed suit. Since the English salon was modelled on the French, it must be proclaimed an improvement upon its great predecessor. Thus, in due time:

> O! how unlike the wit that fell,
> Rambouillet! at thy quaint hotel;
> Where point, and turn, and equivoque
> Distorted every word they spoke!

Rather too much of this! We and Hannah are happier when she leaves the French to their own and excellent devices and confines her muse to her English friends. It is quite possible in the following passage to identify specific frequenters of gatherings at Mrs. Vesey's or at Mrs. Montagu's:

> Here sober duchesses are seen,
> Chaste wits, and critics void of spleen;
> Physicians, fraught with real science,
> And Whigs and Tories in alliance;
> Poets, fulfilling Christian duties,
> Just lawyers, reasonable beauties;
> Bishops who preach, and peers who pay,
> And countesses who seldom play;
> Learned antiquaries, who, from college,
> Reject the rust, and bring the knowledge.

It has ever been youth's office to challenge the status quo. Hannah More now takes cognizance of this ageless function:

> And—hear it, age, beleive it youth—
> Polemics, really seeking truth.

Travellers in this predominantly stay-at-home age were assured of listeners. They were to be found among the conversationalists having, according to Hannah, "seen the countries they describe."

Granted the Irish genius for talk, it was entirely fitting that Mrs.

Vesey of Lucan, near Dublin, play a leading part in domesticating conversation among the less loquacious English. She must be accounted a stage Irishwoman in that she exemplified everything the English think of the Irish. The "Sylph" was scatterbrained and given to writing unpunctuated letters that seem carefully careless. She was deaf and was encumbered with hearing aids shaped like vast ears. These frequently fell off; her guests were charmed with Mrs. Vesey's stooping to pick up her silver ears as she darted among her guests.

Seating conversation parties was a matter for as much consideration as giving a state dinner. Mrs. Montagu favored a semicircle that faced the fire. She placed the person of highest social position on one hand and the one of greatest intellectual distinction on the other. Her guests spoke one at a time upon scholarly subjects. At the "Sylph's," feasts of wit were served in buffet style. She confessed to a horror of the circle and arranged her visitors in small groups of two or three. Viewed in the light of the 1970s, Mrs. Vesey's method, or lack of it, seems entirely natural, but the 1770s found "a vesey" a madcap affair.

Fanny Burney's *Diary* and her *Memoirs of Dr. Burney* give detailed accounts of the Blues. In the latter ponderous work, she describes how Mrs. Vesey "pushed all the small sofas, as well as chairs, about the apartment so as not to leave even a zig-zag path of communication free from impediment." This is, for Fanny's elderly style, fairly straight sailing. She was once more her exalted self when she concluded that "there was never any distress beyond risibility."

Mrs. Montagu, despite the fact that she preferred the circle method, wrote "risibly" to the Sylph that she was "in the hope of a most delightful winter in your society and in that blue room where all people are enchanted tho' the magic figure of the circle is vanished thence. A Philosopher, a fine Lady and a Gallant Officer form a triangle in one corner; a Maccaroni, a Poet, a Divine, a Beauty and an Ottaheite Savage, a wondrous Pentagon in another. . . . Great Orators play a solo of declamation. Witts lett off epigrams like minute guns; the Sage speaks sentences, every one does his best to please the Lady of the enchanting room."

> For all contend
> to win her grace whom all commend.

Mrs. Montagu met the Sylph in 1749 and a year later she met Mrs. Boscawen, whose opinions on American affairs are already familiar. She found the admiral's lady to be a "very sensible, lively and ingenious woman" and to possess "good moral qualities." Because the admiral, of necessity, was frequently from home and Mr. Montagu was immured with his logarithms, the two Blues, as befitted their calling, often spent evenings together, partly in conversation, partly in reading. Mrs. Montagu and Mrs. Boscawen, similar in many respects, remained lifelong friends. Both women brought to the Blue Stocking movement inquiring minds, a firm grasp of public affairs, wide reading and a modern spirit of leadership.

Mrs. Montagu in the latter 1740s began to vary the waters of Bath with those of Tunbridge Wells. Recovered to a degree from recent sorrows, she was once more able to find amusement in the social scene. She wrote of her new companions, "Such hats, capuchins and short sacks as were never seen. One of the ladies looks like a state bed running upon castors." A good deal more severe was her castigation of the bigamous Miss Chudleigh, whose trial was to furnish late Georgian England with a major *frisson*. Miss Chudleigh was seen at a masquerade in classical costume. Her "dress or rather undress was remarkable. She was Iphegenia for the sacrifice but so naked the High Priest might easily inspect the entrails of his victim. The Maids of Honor, not maids of the strictest, were so offended they would not speak to her." The occasion thus enlivened was a ball on May 1, 1749, to celebrate the signing of the Treaty of Aix-la-Chappelle, which brought to an end the War of the Austrian Succession.

Sarah Robinson became engaged at this time to George Lewis Scott. Mr. Scott, who bore both Christian names of George I, remains a shadowy, or indeed, a shady character. He and Sarah apparently married on the eve of his becoming subpreceptor to Prince George. "His Royal Highness," wrote the delighted fiancée to her sister, Mrs. Montagu, "has left it to Mr. Scott's friends to name whatever [salary] they think proper and has behaved in the handsomest manner imaginable." His Royal Highness, Frederick, Prince of Wales, died suddenly a few months after making this appointment. Of Scott we know nothing more than that he was shortly to be unmasked as "a very bad man," dismissed from his preceptorship and separated from Sarah.

Commenting somewhat smugly upon Sarah's misfortune, Mrs. Montagu wrote to her husband that, "In a good marriage each has the credit of the others virtues; they have double honour, united interests and all that can make people strong in society. This, my Dearest, is my happier lot, enriched by your fortune, ennobled by your virtues, graced by your character and supported by your interest." Such a letter, though she doubtless believed herself to be paying a tribute to her spouse, comes perilously near giving thanks that one is not as the rest of men. The prominence given to being "enriched by your fortune" can hardly be called disinterested. Here is the woman of whom it was to be said *elle n'a pas le don d'aimer* (she has not the gift for loving). Far more attractive is a letter written on August 5, 1750, the Montagus' wedding anniversary, in which she thanks her "friend and companion" for "eight years' happiness in a state so often wretched."

Sarah Scott, who was not for nothing sister to "Minerva," celebrated, or sublimated, her return to celibacy with a novel called *Millenium Hall*. Anticipating Elizabeth's contribution to Lyttleton's *Dialogues of the Dead* and her *Essay on Shakespeare* by several years, the book attracted many readers. The younger sister nearly equalled the elder in literary skill. Dr. Doran has included many of her letters in *A Lady of the Last Century*.

Blue Stocking feminism thrived upon platonic friendships. When we think of Mrs. Delany, Händel and Swift come to mind. Fanny Burney was to be petted by an entire retinue of distinguished old men, including the Great Cham,. who was domesticated with, and by, Mrs. Thrale. Mrs. Carter wrote for his *Rambler* and Hannah More for Garrick's Drury Lane. Horace Walpole, who preferred criticism to affection, made a striking exception in the case of the virtuous Hannah, whom he most uncharacteristically and quite accurately called a saint. That the social worker *avant la lettre* and Horry should become fast friends is one of the period's striking examples of an admirable sympathy between men and women.

Mrs. Montagu approached the platonic convention methodically. Her male companions were chosen chiefly among the poets. She called them her choir. Two of her songsters are contained in Dr. Johnson's *Lives of the Poets,* these being Gilbert West and Lord Lyttleton. Johnson praised West's religious motives; Mrs. Montagu went further. She described West "as the miracle of the Moral World, a Christian Poet, an humble philosopher, a great genius without contempt for those who have none. . . . I am charmed with Mrs. West . . . she is neither a tenth muse nor a fourth grace but she is better than all put together. . . . Her vivacity, easiness of behaviour and good sense delight me." The Wests' religion, to have elicited such commendation from Johnson and Mrs. Montagu, must have been that of the Established Church. They held, in common with their circle, narrow views. Catholicism to the right and Methodism to the left were equally to be condemned, to say nothing of the deism of Voltaire or Rousseau's noble savage. Mrs. Montagu's description of the God-fearing life led by Sarah Scott and her friend Lady Bab Montagu, reveals a great deal of her own views on faith and works. Writing to Gilbert West from Sandleford on October 16, 1755, she says: "My sister rises early, and as soon as she has read prayers to their small family, she sits down to cut out and prepare work for 12 poor girls, whose schooling they pay for; to those whom she finds more than ordinarily capable, she teaches writing and arithmetic herself. The work these children are usually employed in is making child-bed linen and clothes for poor people in the neighbourhood, which Lady Bab Montagu and she bestow as they see occasion. Very early on Sunday morning these girls, with 12 little boys whom they also send to school, come to my sister and repeat their catechism, read some chapters, have the principal articles of their religion explained to them, and then are sent to the parish church. These good works are often performed by the Methodist ladies in the heat of enthusiasm, but thank God, my sister's is a calm and rational piety. Her conversation is lively and easy, and she enters into all the reasonable pleasures of Society; goes frequently to the plays, and sometimes to balls, etc. They have a very pretty house at Bath for the winter, and one at Bath Easton for the summer; their houses are adorned by the ingenuity of the owners, but as their income is small, they deny themselves unnecessary expenses. My sister seems very happy; it has pleased God to lead her to truth, by the road of affliction; but what draws the sting of death and triumphs over the grave, cannot fail to heal the wounds of disappointment. Lady Babs Montagu concurs with her in all these things, and their convent, for by its regularity it resembles one, is really a cheerful place." It was probably this edifying program that inspired Mrs. Montagu's later philanthropies among her miners in Yorkshire.

Mrs. Montagu's friendship with Lord Lyttleton was a fruitful association. Here customary patterns of hospitality and patronage were reversed, the lady exchanging the role of giver for that of recipient. Lord Lyttleton entertained lavishly at Hagley, his country seat; under his lordship's aegis was published her delicious *Dialogue* between Mercury and Mrs. Modish. And after Lyttleton's death, in loyalty to his memory Mrs. Montagu took issue with Dr. Johnson's disparaging essay on her friend in his *Lives of the Poets*.

Letters from Mrs. Montagu were often as indicative of the interests of her correspondents as of her own. Since it was Lord Lyttleton who brought about the publication of her three *Dialogues,* her letters to him, and even about him, are literary both in content and in style. She was probably planning her Essay on Shakespeare when she wrote a comment on Sophocles that shows her grasp of Greek tragedy to have been limited. "The *Œdipus Coloneus* affected me extreamly and would have so more if it had not been for the constant presence of the Chorus but the passions are awed and checked by a crowd." It would not have occurred to Mrs. Montagu that British reticence was not an Aegean characteristic.

Lord Lyttleton was entirely of her opinion. He replied that "the moral reflexions in Shakespeare's Plays are much more affecting by coming warm from the Heart of the interested persons than putt into the mouth of a chorus as in the Greek plays."

A member of the Montagu-Lyttleton circle was the incredible Dr. Messenger Monsey. This tedious *enfant terrible* was buffoon to the Blues who, believing with Shakespeare that there's no harm in an allowed fool, gave him every encouragement. Mrs. Montagu was thoroughly charmed with him, writing from Tunbridge Wells that "The Great Monsey came hither on Friday. . . . He is great in the Coffee House, great in the rooms and great on the Pantiles." To Dr. Stillingfleet, also of Blue circles, she described Monsey's laborious gallantry. "You must know, Sir, Dr. Monsey is fallen desperately in love with me and I most passionately in love with him, the darts on both sides have not been the porcupines but the grey goose quill. . . . the Doctor is a perfect Pastor Fido and I believe when we get to Elysium all the lovers who wander in the Myrtle Groves there will throw their garlands at our feet." Minerva Montagu must have thoroughly wished him among the absent when obliged to travel with Monsey from Warwick to Hill Street. He varied the clown with the raconteur. "Stories," she complained, "like the dropping of water on the head give a pleasant refreshment at times but continued for many hours grow a torment." It remains only to be said that the trip from Warwick to London required "12 hours every day and for 4 days together."

Chief among Mrs. Montagu's men friends was William Pultney, Earl of Bath. His Lordship had served as Secretary at War under George I and, at a later period was, like the Montagus, an opponent of Walpole. Although he did not have a political career of lasting significance, his parliamentary attendance was marked by scholarly and graceful oratory. He appears in Hannah More's *Bas Bleu* as "Witty Pultney." Reginald Blunt, one of Mrs. Montagu's editor-biographers, considers Bath to have been the "greatest attachment" of her life. That this may have been the case again gives evidence that in her cool temperament the friend dominated the lover, Lord Bath being her senior by forty years. Although the letters that passed between the middle-aged lady and the elderly statesman are fulsome, they avoid the facile familiarity that marks her correspondence with Monsey.

Lord and Lady Bath were unhappily married, a circumstance that predisposed them both to seek companionship elsewhere. Her Ladyship was, in Georgian slang, a great "screw," in other words, stingy. This failing Mrs. Montagu discovered in 1753, when she went to an overcrowded assembly given by Lady Bath consisting of "eight hundred Christian souls many of which had liked to have perished from famine." When in 1758 death separated His Lordship from his economical spouse, Mrs. Montagu's comment reads, "Lord Bath is so apparently rejoiced at his deliverance it makes people smile, he ordered a plentiful table to be kept as soon as she was dead and is very gay and jolly at the Bath like a young heir just come into his estate." It is to Mrs. Montagu's credit that she viewed her own shortcomings as ruthlessly as those of Lady Bath. Writing that keeping the Seventh Commandment had posed no problems, she said in her old age, "The sins which grow on the animal part of the human creature are more pardonable than those that spring from the mind; this is a virtuous confession for me who was never prone to any but spiritual sins; I am in body a Saint in mind a great sinner."

A friend who could lay claim to no form of sanctity was Edward Wortley Montagu, Junior. His first-cousin-once-removed, Elizabeth's husband, thought with good reason that he had been very harshly penalized by his parents for having, as Elizabeth put it, inherited the "rapidity of his mother's genius." To rectify these injustices, Mr. Montagu became patron to his peripatetic relative. Writing to his wife, he said, "My cousin gives great satisfaction. . . . I think his nature to be good as well as his parts and I hope he will be an ornament to his family." Poor Mr. Montagu! He lived to discover that good parts do not assure a good character. Because a member of Parliament could not be prosecuted for debt, it was the elder Edward's inspiration that the younger become M.P. for Bossiney, a Cornish borough. The office was obtained and shortly abandoned in favor of "rabbinical" studies, bigamy, polygamy and the begetting of blackamoors.

Edward's defection was extremely embarrassing to his cousin-patrons, to say nothing of his sensitively placed sister and brother-in-law, the Butes. To warn Lady Bute that the member for Bossiney had disappeared, Mrs. Montagu wrote thus to the Duchess of Portland: "I was misinformed the other night when I told your Grace Mr. Wortley Montagu was gone abroad, he is in England but where is a secret even to his lawyers and those who are employed on his affairs. I thought it right to let your Grace know this as it appears to me very singular as he is now under protection of privilege." Elizabeth believes Lady Bute "had better know the circumstances," an office that Edward Montagu, an escapist in his own more innocent way, was clearly reluctant to undertake.

The Seven Years' War was now at hand. The Blue Stockings, because Mrs. Boscawen was of their number, tell us more about the American theatre of this global conflict than of the battles on the Continent or the horrors being perpetrated in Calcutta.

Mrs. Montagu, whose friendships often omitted or minimized spouses was urged to include Admiral Boscawen in her association with his lady. A letter from Mr. Montagu's sister reads, "I think of Mrs. Boscawen as you do, I expect you should be fond of the Admiral, his cool courage, his firmness, good nature, diligence and regularity, with his strong sense and good head, make a great character." It was too early in 1750 when these lines were written to know that the same qualities would produce the hero of Louisburg.

Shortly after the recommencement of hostilities in 1755, Mrs. Montagu visited Hatchlands, the country seat of Admiral and Mrs. Boscawen. Her letter from there to her husband indicates that war in the eighteenth century was pursued with a professional detachment quite absent from this century's saturation bombings and concentration camps. Boscawen had sent to his wife the following account of "the taking of 2 French men of war. M. Hoquart had been taken twice by Mr. Boscawen in the last war but did not surrender himself in this engagement 'till 44 men were killed on board his ship." Boscawen continues that "he lived at great expense having 11 French officers at his table whom he entertained with magnificence and there were 8 companies of soldiers on board the Adelaide and the Lys"—a dramatic contrast tυ Dunkirk or Pearl Harbor!

Such handsome behavior was not extended to the Indians nor to the French colonists. Lord Jeffrey Amherst, brother-in-arms to Boscawen, may be said to have been a father of germ warfare. He obviated the necessity of expending ammunition by gifting Indians with blankets and handkerchiefs impregnated with live smallpox matter. The French settlers who dwelt in the "forest primeval" were driven from their Nova Scotian homes to become the Cajuns of Louisiana and to furnish Longfellow with inspiration for *Evangeline*.

The strategic French fortress, Louisburg, on Cape Breton Island, makes its first appearance in Mrs. Montagu's correspondence in July of 1755. Fom one of her innumerable friends, the Reverend John Botham, she learned that Colonel Warburton had besieged Louisburg from the land and Admiral Boscawen by sea, "so there is good reason to suppose we shall soon be masters of Louisburg." Her informant continues that "We have taken papers of the utmost consequence, which let us into the secret schemes of the French, which were nothing less than a design of taking all our Plantations from us in America and Hallifax in the first place was destined for destruction."

Two years later Louisburg was still in French hands. From another correspondent Mrs. Montagu learned that Boscawen might be following in Admiral Byng's tragic wake. On August 30, 1757, she received a letter that read, "The Mediterranean Tragedy seems to be acting over again in the American seas. A Council of War was call'd to advise whether 10,000 men brought to Louisburgh should be landed or not; it was determined in the negative upon finding the French had two more ships than we had."

Mrs. Montagu wrote to the Admiral's wife a beautiful letter bidding her to commend the sailor-warrior to God's care. Her reference to the death of Punch again must exonerate her from being supposed to know nothing of love. In the following lines dated October 25, 1757, she evidences love of a friend, of a child and of God. "Be not afraid, but commit it all to the great and wise Disposer of all events; a firm hope and cheerful reliance on Providence I do believe to be the best means to bring about what we wish, and that such confidence does it far better than all our anxious foresight, our provident schemes and measuring of security. I remember with sorrow and shame, I trusted much to a continual watching of my son, I would not have committed him to a sea voyage, or for the world in a town besieged, I forgot at Whose will the waves are still, and Who breaketh the bow and knappeth the spear asunder. What was the reward of this confidence of my own care and diffidence of His who only could protect him? Why, such as it deserved, I lost my beloved object, and with him my hopes, my joys, and my health, and I lost him too, not by those things I had feared for him, but by the pain of a tooth. Pray God keep you from my offence and the punishment of it. I do not mean that you should be void of anxiety in times of hazard, but offer them to God every night and sleep in peace, the same every morning, and rise with confidence."

Mrs. Boscawen, when in good spirits, had recourse to French. On August 1, 1758, she had every reason to rejoice. While she was *enfin* leaving London and *chemin faisant,* an officer in a post chaise hailed her postillions wth a shouted "stop." Upon herself echoing "stop," she learned that the messenger was an "express sent by the governor of Nova Scotia with news of our troops having taken the Forts of Beau Séjour Chigneato, that he attended Admiral Boscawen for his orders 23 days ago and left him in perfect health, he added that Admiral Boscawen had saved North America where all our Colonies were in utmost danger, as well as consternation 'till he came, Papers having been found which showed the French had a design to destroy Halifax where the people imagin'd the French

would let the Indians in to massacre them." A year later the mastery
of Canada had passed from the Fleur de Lys to the Union Jack,
costing, it will be remembered, the lives of the opposing generals.

Of General Wolfe, who said he would rather have written Gray's
Elegy than take Quebec, Mrs. Montagu wrote Lord Lyttleton in
1759, "The encomiums on Mr. Wolf run very high, a great action is
performed and every one can endure to give praise to a dead man. . . .
He is the subject of all people's praise and I question whether all the
Duke of Marlborough's conquests gained him greater honor."

Mrs. Montagu's reference to Sir Winston's mighty ancestor remains pertinent. Blenheim increased England's stately homes, the
Plains of Abraham her empire. History annuls many battles and time
has erased Marlborough's stunning victories. Wolfe and Montcalm
gave their lives in a brief contest that changed the face of North
America.

The ethics of acquiring military intelligence posed some of the
same problems in the 1750s that it has in the 1970s. "National security" then, as now, fostered double standards; thus, it was highly meritorious to ferret out French plans for the taking of Halifax but,
writes Mrs. Montagu, "It astonished all Europe to find the King of
Prussia had got copies of the plans of the Imperial Court and Dresden." Even though Frederick the Great was England's ally, Mrs.
Montagu by no means approved the forms of espionage he employed.
"To get false keys to cabinets," continued Mrs. Montagu in a familiar
tone of patriotic hypocrisy, "is but a poor low trick and it is very
strange to see a hero guilty of burglary, but as Mr. Pope observes 'the
story of the great is generally a tale that blends their glory with their
shame.' " It is to be wondered how Admiral Boscawen "found" the
papers revealing his enemy's strategy.

During the latter years of the Seven Years' War, Mrs. Montagu's
correspondence with Elizabeth Carter and Dr. Johnson commenced.
It is not certain whether she met first the "learned lady" and then
"the sage," or was it perhaps the other way around? Mrs. Carter, in
terms of learning, may be said to tower above her sister Blues. Her
linguistic attainments included, over and above the more accessible
classical and modern languages, Portuguese, Hebrew and Arabic.
Before she was twenty-two, she had published two philosophical
works, one a translation from French and one from Italian, the lat-

ter being Algarotti's *Il Newtonismo per le dame.* Her translation of Epictetus is, two hundred years later, available in the *Everyman* edition. She seems to have possessed that rare combination, genius and simplicity. It was doubtless in her favor as a scholar that she was, unlike Lady Mary, Mrs. Delany and Mrs. Montagu, a pastor's daughter and therefore free from the limitations of the great world. Where Lady Mary defied, Mrs. Delany conformed and Mrs. Montagu presided, Elizabeh Carter worked and overworked with a refreshing indifference to prestige.

Mrs. Montagu's correspondence with Elizabeth Carter (called by courtesy Mrs. Carter) does honor to both women. The former, although she possessed wealth and prestige, craved to find favor in the eyes of one who was her inferior in rank and her superior in learning. The latter, when invited to visit Mrs. Montagu in Hill Street, consented to come only if she might be accommodated in lodgings because, as she wrote in 1759, "my spirit of liberty is strangely untractable and wild; I must have something like a home; somewhere to rest an aching head without giving anybody any trouble; and some hours more absolutely at my own disposal than can be had in any other situation." Over and above Mrs. Carter's legendary headaches, due, one would suppose, to eye strain and lack of sleep, her preference for a boarding house as opposed to the luxury proffered by Mrs. Montagu evidences complete independence, a rare virtue in an age of personal patronage. She was equally at home with the fashionable society frequented by Lord Bath and his friends, in Dr. Johnson's testy company or with her Kentish neighbors at Deal, where she lived. In social versatility she anticipates the younger Hannah More.

Mrs. Montagu received, on June 9, 1759, her first letter from Dr. Johnson. It was to thank her for contributing to an annuity purchased for Mrs. Anna Williams, the blind poetess to whom Johnson offered asylum together with sundry other poor and homeless. When it was suggested that Mrs. Montagu's philanthropies were prompted by purse pride, Johnson was quick to reply, "I have seen no beings who do as much good from benevolence, as she does, from whatever motive."

Johnson, in emulation of the *Spectator* and the *Tatler,* began to issue his own periodical in 1750. Entitled *The Rambler,* it appeared on every Tuesday and Saturday for two years. The title is unfortunate; Samuel Johnson stalked, paraded, lumbered, shambled and, by his own confession, often dawdled. Rambling was not in his nature. It is indicative of the new respect for woman's literary potential that he included in his biweekly essays four letters to "Mr. Rambler" written by women. Two of them were the work of Elizabeth Carter.

The second, *Modish Pleasures,* is dated Saturday, March 2, 1751. It clearly influenced Mrs. Montagu in her *Dialogue between Mercury and a modern Fine Lady,* published under Lyttleton's banner and name in 1760.

Mrs. Carter, satirizing her sometime capacity of Kentish recluse, begs Mr. Rambler to lighten her ignorance by "a complete history of forms, fashions, frolics, of routs, drums, hurricanes, balls, assemblies, ridottos, masquerades, auctions, plays, operas, puppet-shows and bear-gardens." Concluding that present pleasure is humanity's sole concern, she brings her edifying reflections thus to an end: "All the soft feelings of humanity, the sympathies of friendship, all natural temptations to the care of a family and solicitude about the good or ill of others, with the whole train of domestic and social affections which create such daily anxieties and embarrassments will be happily stifled and suppressed in a round of perpetual delights; All serious thought but particularly of the *hereafter* will be banished out of the world: a most perplexing apprehension but luckily a most groundless one too as it is so clear a case that nobody ever dies. I am, etc, Chariessa."

Nine years later, Mrs. Montagu revived "Chariessa" in her *Dialogue* between Mercury and Mrs. Modish. The messenger of the Gods summons a lady of fashion to the realms of death. She cannot heed the beckoning of Charon because she can't fit it into her other commitments. "Look on my chimney piece and you will see I was engaged to the Play on Mondays, Balls on Tuesdays, the opera on Saturdays and to Card-assemblies the rest of the week for two months to come; and it would be the rudest thing in the world not to keep my appointments. If you will stay with me till the Summer season I will wait on you with all my heart. Perhaps the Elysian Fields may be less detestable than the country in our world."

In her long-ago letter to "noble lovely little Peggy," Fidget Robinson had not only supposed herself to be speaking from beyond the grave, she had experimented with definition by negatives. She could define matrimonial happiness not by what it was but what it was not. Some twenty years later the same sallies obtained. Mrs. Modish, when asked by Mercury what was meant by "le Bon Ton," replied, "It is one of the privileges of the bon ton never to define or be defined. It is the child and parent of jargon. It is—I can never tell you what it is; but I will try to tell you what it is not. In conversation it is not wit; in manners it is not politeness; in behaviour it is not address; but it is a little like them all. It can only belong to people of a certain rank, who live in a certain manner, with certain persons who have not certain virtues, and who have certain vices and who inhabit a certain part of the town." Mercury replies, "I will follow your mode of instruction. I will tell you what I would not have you do. I would not have had you sacrifice your time, your reason, and your Duties to fashion and folly. I would not have had you neglect the happiness of your husband and the education of your children." As Mrs. Montagu was herself of the "ton," the numerous Mrs. Modishes of her acquaintance were inclined to complain that stones were being thrown from a glass house on Hill Street.

Lord Lyttleton, who had stood godfather to the newborn authoress, cautioned her that she was eminently suited to arouse resentment. "There is Envy and Malice enough against Beauty alone, but Beauty, Wit, Wisdom, Learning and Virtue united (to say nothing about wealth) are sure to excite a Legion of Devils against the Possessor. It is amazing to me that with all these dangerous things about you you have not been driven out of Society a great while since." These reflections were offered for Mrs. Montagu's consideration in 1760, the year the *Dialogues* appeared.

Mrs. Montagu, knowing that patrician ladies like her old friend, the Duchess of Portland, viewed "female pens" with the contempt in which the Victorians held actresses, did not put her name to her *Dialogues*. That she was the concealed essayist might have been inferred from her outspoken disgust at ladies thronging to the trial of Lord Ferrers for murdering his steward. "I own the late instance of their going to hear Lord Ferrer's sentence particularly provoked me. The Ladies crowded to the House of Lords to see a wretch brought loaded with crime and shame to the Bar to hear sentence of a cruel and ignominious death." The Modishes to whom these condemnations applied could not have been solaced by Mercury's last words to their allegorical sister, "the neglect of Duties may bring on a sentence not much less severe than the commission of Crimes."

By 1760 it was beginning to be possible, the "ton" notwithstanding, for Mrs. Montagu to write thus to Mrs. Carter (the ladies addressed one another in the third person): "With her encouragement I do not know but at last I may become an author in form. It enlarges the sphere of action and lengthens the short period of human life. To become universal and lasting is an ambition which genius's should indulge but to be read by a few a few years may be aspired to." Nine years were to pass before her most considerable product, *The Essay on Shakespeare,* appeared.

They were years not only of innumerable letters, countless evenings of Blue conversation, visits to Bath and Tunbridge Wells, but also of constant travelling between London, Sandleford and Allerthorpe. In 1758 the Montagus inherited a fourth residence, Denton, in Northumberland. It was the bequest of a wealthy cousin whose death, by reason of his having been both insane and bedridden, occasioned only token mourning. Mrs. Montagu, in her usual down-to-earth style, wrote Mrs. Carter "that she had always designed to be rather pleased and happy when he resigned his unhappy being and his good estate."

Taking possession of the invalid's home prompted Mrs. Montagu to write one of her few housekeeping letters. To Mrs. Carter, with whom she usually discoursed of higher things, she complained that "As soon as I rise in the morning, my housekeeper with a face full of care, comes to know what must be packed up for Newcastle; to her succeeds the Butler, who wants to know what wine, etc. is be sent down; to them succeed men of business and money transactions; then the post brings twenty letters, which must be considered and some answered. In about a week we shall set out for the North, where I am to pass about three months in the delectable conversation of Stewards and managers of coal mines, and this by courtesy is called good fortune, and I am congratulated upon it by every one I meet; while in truth, like a poor Harlequin in the play, I am acting a silly part 'dans l'embarras des richesses.' "

Mrs. Montagu varied the style and content of her letters not only in accordance with the preferences of her correspondents, but also to reflect the circumstances in which she found herself. Thus the London letters abound in personalities and functions; Sandleford is the haunt of the muses; and the north country anticipates Dickens in its realistic descriptions of early industrial life. There is abundance of Bounderby and Podsnap in the following description of her new neighbors: "Every gentleman in the country from the least to the greatest is as solicitous in the pursuit of gain as a tradesman. The conversation always turns on money; the moment you name a man you are told what he is worth, the losses he has had, or the profit he has had by the coal mines."

Mrs. Montagu's attitude toward poetry was conventional. It was better to say "silver Cynthia" than moon, unspecified birds became "Philomel," and after a busy day at Sandleford, Allerthorpe or Denton, night unvaryingly "drew his sable curtain." It would not have occurred to her that squalor has its own beauty and that her description of Newcastle is as effective as those she composed in praise of rural scenes: "The town of Newcastle is horrible, like the ways of thrift it is narrow, dark and dirty, some of the streets so steep one is forced to put a dragchain on the wheels: the night I came I thought I was going to the center. The streets are some of them so narrow, that if the tallow chandler ostentatiously hangs forth his candles, you have a chance to sweep them into your lap as you drive by, and I do not know how it has happened that I have not yet caught a coach full of red herrings, for we scrape the Citty wall on which they hang in great abundance."

Sandleford was in complete contrast to the ugly materialism Mrs. Montagu found at Newcastle. There she gives us her Penseroso character. "Mr. Montagu has been studiously disposed ever since we came to Sandleford so that I pass seven or eight hours entirely alone. Five months are to pass before I return to the Land of the Living but I can amuse myself in the regions of the dead: if it rains so that I cannot walk in the garden Virgil will carry me into the Elysian fields or Milton into Paradise." Milton did so at the bidding of Lord Lyttleton, whom the Montagus visited in 1762 at Hagley. (Edward "Had been much pulled down by the fashionable cold called l'influenza.") English weather must have smiled because Lyttleton had "arranged agreeable entertainments of musick in different parts of the Park and adapted to the scenes. In some places the French horns reverberated from hill to hill. In the shady parts near the cascades the soft music was concealed and seemed to come from the 'unseen genius of the wood.' " And equally when Hill Street beckoned it was because

Towered Cities please us then
And the busy haunts of men.

Mr. and Mrs. Montagu appear to have held different views on George II. When His Majesty died in October of 1760, Mrs. Montagu wrote an account of his reign that would greatly have surprised Thackeray. Instead of the choleric roué given us in *The Four Georges,* Mrs. Montagu's letter to Lord Lyttleton reads, "With him our laws and liberties were safe; he possessed in great degree the confidence of his people and the respect of foreign governments; and a certain steadiness of character made him of great consequence in these unsettled times." Was she perhaps remembering the unfaithful husband and the father who did not scruple to hate both his heir and his daughter-in-law when she conceded that "His character would not afford a subject for Epic poetry but will look well in the sober page of history"?

Upon the accession of George III, the question arose as to whether or not Mrs. Montagu should "kiss hands." Court attendance during the reigns of the first four Georges was complicated by the hostilities nurtured by fathers (and sometimes mothers) and sons. It became customary for successive sovereigns and their heirs to hold separate courts with separate courtiers and even to support separate authors and artists. The Montagus' relationship with the influential Butes encouraged attendance at court, a situation that the member from Huntingdon had long avoided out of political conviction. Husband and wife were, as was so often the case, at some distance from one another, a circumstance that gave rise to a beautiful letter from elderly husband to middle-aged wife. It is worthy of remark that the implied nepotism of being presented by Lady Bute is to be avoided. "At present I can only say that if you mean nothing more than paying your duty to our new sovereign I think Lady Cardigan of all others the properest person to introduce you; but if you go further, before you give your attendance at a Court, I wish you would take the consequences into your most serious thoughts. The principal reason of my absenting myself ever since I was a Member of Parliament was that I did not concur in the measures that were then taking, and the Principal members in the opposition thought they had no business at St. James, and I believe neither the wifes of the Peers nor of the members of the House of Commons were found there. If I should be still so unhappy as out of dislike for the present measure not to alter my way of acting, and not to appear at Court, would it be proper for you to be attendant? Indeed, it seems to me that it would not, but if you can make out the contrary upon any sound Principles of reason I will readily submit."

Mr. Montagu then evidenced the tender admiration in which he held the wife young enough to have been a daughter. "While I flattered myself that we were in the same way of thinking and that my conduct met with your approbation I did hardly suffer anything. I then thought and still reflect with the utmost sense of gratitude on the sacrifice you made me in your early bloom, by giving up all the pleasures and gaieties of a Court, and it was the greater because you had all the advantages of beauty and sense to shine and make a figure there. I think that capacity is not so far gone as you in your modesty are pleas'd to say, and I may add in some sense perhaps improv'd, either at a Court or anywhere else I wish you every thing that is good that you may long enjoy that good will and esteem which your merit has acquired'd you, and leave the rest to your own candid and impartial consideration."

Mrs. Montagu's reply is equally admirable. She will attend "two drawing rooms a year and not those" if Mr. Montagu's political independence is threatened.

That "boiling youth," as George III described himself to his father-figure, Lord Bute, chose as his bride in 1761 Charlotte of Mecklenburgh. The princess was virtuous, diminutive, sturdy, unimaginative and was said to have a mouth that occupied most of her face. We have met her in Mrs. Delany's charming company, and she will reappear at the "Magnolia" whose stays it was Fanny Burney's unhappy privilege to lace.

The young couple were crowned on September 22, 1761. Mrs. Montagu arose at four-thirty and, as Mr. Pepys would have said, "took water" to the "Cofferer's office where I was to see the show. I had a perfect view of the procession to and from Westminster to the Abbey, and I must say it rather exceeded my expectation. The ladies made a glorious appearance; whenever there was any beauty of countenance or shape or air they were all heightened by the dress. Lady Talbot was a fine figure. The Queen, being very little, did not appear to advantage. The King had all the impressions of decent satisfaction and good-natured joy in his face; looked about him with great complacency, and tried to make himself as visible as he could to the mob, but the canopy carried over his Majesty's head and the persons who carried his train made him not so conspicuous. His behavior at the Abbey pleased much." Mrs. Montagu, in a parallel letter to her pious friend Mrs. Carter, paid a tribute to one of England's saddest kings that suggests Mrs. Delany's espistolary ejaculations. Upon receiving the sacrament, George III "pulled off his crown," a gesture that inspired Elizabeth to exclaim, "How happy in the day of the greatest worldly pomp he should remember his duty to the King of Kings."

Mrs. Montagu fulfilled a family duty and compensated for the loss of Punch by undertaking the education of one of her many nephews. This was Matthew Robinson, son of her older brother, Morris. Such an arrangement was quite usual in Georgian and Victorian times, affording relief to large families and meager fortunes. Morris Robinson, an eccentric hermit, died in middle age, leaving two sons and a spendthrift widow who was by no means sorry to see a child's fortune and future assured at no cost to herself.

Never one to do things by halves, Mrs. Montagu renamed her nephew Matthew Montagu and made him her heir. He became in due time Baron Rokeby. As custodian of her vast correspondence he brought out, in 1813, the first collection of letters to and from her. His granddaughter, Mrs. Climenson, published almost a century later a new edition with which, as well as with Dr. Doran's biography, we have until now been concerned. The letters written during the second half of Mrs. Montagu's life, Mrs. Climenson confided in her own old age to Reginald Blunt.

That Blunt intended to present his two volumes as sequels to the two volumes of "my old friend Mrs. Climenson" is made clear by his using as title *Mrs. Montagu, Queen of the Blues* to recall the earlier *Elizabeth Robinson Montagu: Queen of the Blues*. He retains Mrs. Climenson's format. Gone, however, is the tone of unquestioning family loyalty that characterized Mrs. Climenson, Fanny Burney and Lady Llanover. The second two volumes gain by Blunt's detachment and post–1914-18 matter-of-factness, as opposed to Mrs. Climenson's elderly Edwardianisms. Then, too, Blunt is aware that modern readers of Georgian letters seek social history rather than obscure *bon mots* or edifying reflections. In this regard Mrs. Montagu strikes a note quite distinctive from other Blues. She was, by force of circumstance and nature, a businesswoman. Her wool-gathering husband was only too glad to have her vigorous attention expended on the Northumberland collieries and the Berkshire farms. Thus, in her letters, we find an account of the workaday world of pre-Industrial Revolution England that is not duplicated in her friends' letters.

Until the signing of the Peace of Paris in 1762, Mrs. Montagu's travels were domestic. A progress from Newcastle to London required seven days. She rode in a coach drawn by six horses with an outrider trotting alongside in case of an overturn. She was, according to her young friend, Fanny Burney, "a great coward in a coach." In her latter years she never dined out for fear her coachman and postillions would be in no condition to return her home. Despite these precautions, overturns were frequent. From Tunbridge Wells she sent to her husband this description of a narrow escape: "I went to the ball last Friday it was the first time I had been to the public rooms and it had like to have been fatal to me for the coachman not being acquainted with the place, the night dark and having no flambeaux had like to have overturned . . . down a place where the coach would have been entirely topsy-turvy. . . . My fright was such I did not get my rest 'till six o'clock in the morning. . . . If the coach had fallen it would have gone down some feet but the standers by behaved with great humanity bearing a very heavy load on their shoulders. I believe our new coachman is too lazy to serve us." In Mrs. Montagu's housekeeping lexicon laziness and drunkenness were synonymous.

Country inns posed other threats, among them contagion. On trips to collieries it was often necessary to submit to accommodations that provoked this complaint. "I was devoured by bugs and the coal carts clattering by ye window every moment gave me such a night that I rose far more fatigued than when I went to bed. The night following I got some rest . . . but not much for I lay in a room that had so many evil odours, the collected perspiration I suppose of 10,000 travellers that I could not sleep any longer than my senses were subdued by fatigue."

Fired perhaps by reading the pirated edition of Lady Mary's *Embassy Letters* that appeared in 1763, Mrs. Montagu in the summer of the same year organized a tour to Spa. Lord Bath, Mrs. Carter and Mr. Montagu had been persuaded to be of the party. It was represented that taking the waters would restore Bath's spirits, which had been much lowered by the death of his only son. Mrs. Carter's migraines, having defied the springs of Bath and Tunbridge Wells, might respond to those of the Geronsterre and the Pouhon. Mr. Montagu, being by no means of a travelling temperament, was coaxed by such indirections as frequent references to when-we-go-to-Spa or while-we-are-at-Spa. "Altogether," reported Mrs. Montagu to her sister from Calais on July 4, 1763, "we make 27 Christian souls and horses innumerable."

Two accounts of the same trip exist, one by Mrs. Montagu, the other by Mrs. Carter. They brought to their adventures completely different attitudes, the former attracted by the unknown and the latter repelled. In new and gregarious circumstances, Mrs. Montagu's urbane father supplied sociable genes, while Pastor Carter from his distant parish in Kent diffused an inhibiting influence over his daughter's enjoyment of Popery's domains. Then too, Mrs. Carter's principal correspondent on her travels was a certain Miss Talbot, adopted daughter of Dr. Secker, Archbishop of Canterbury. This association tended to bring out the always lurking lay preacher in her friend. Knowing that her letters from the deplorable Continent would be shared with His Grace, Mrs. Carter stressed visits to Papist churches, taking care not to kneel lest she be supposed to have reverted to idolatry, and rushing out before the elevation of the "hostia." English nunneries abounded. Here the ladies observed "unmeritorious" seclusion that Mrs. Carter be the better empowered to bear loyal witness against Rome.

Mrs. Carter's learning and Mrs. Montagu's wide reading did little to illumine their provincialism. They held, with Lady Mary, that what is worth knowing is contained in books. Although they lived in the golden age of English painting and were respectively painted by Sir Thomas Lawrence and Sir Joshua Reynolds, they ignored the Van Eycks in Ghent, Rembrandt in Amsterdam and had only a word to spare for Rubens in Antwerp. Their comments about "Gothick" Cathedrals continue to reflect religious prejudice rather than an understanding of architecture or sculpture.

The party crossed the channel at night to catch the tide. Predictably, Mrs. Carter was seasick and her hostess was not. It was the custom at Calais to bring the boats into shoal water and then have the passengers carried ashore piggyback. Mrs. Montagu wrote to the Sylph that, "At Calais we were met by certain mermen crown'd with sea weeds who carried Mesdames Carter and Montagu on their backs; as the petticoats were a little discomposed in this way of walking on other mens legs it is better not to be too minute in the description of it."

The travellers' route led through St. Omer, which disappointed Mrs. Carter by being "a very pretty town; the houses handsome, and the streets wide and well paved; which, to the mortification of my English vanity is the case with every town we have seen." Some towns she discovered to be "vexatiously superior to ours in England . . . and the people look very clean and have nothing of that air of wretchedness that one should have expected in a land of slavery." At Douai the Jesuit College was visited. Mrs. Carter and Mrs. Montagu "endeavoured to talk to some of the school-boys who are chiefly Irish, but they looked stupified and had such a dejected spiritless air that it quite sunk one." It would not have occurred to the patriotic minds of our ladies to reflect that these dejected boys were being educated abroad because the Penal Laws forbade adequate education of Catholics in Ireland.

It is amusing to contrast Mrs. Carter's melancholy approach to gaieties with that of Mrs. Montagu. To Miss Talbot the former writes with laborious tongue-in-cheek, "I am sorry to confirm any part of Mrs. Montagu's scandal but it is an undeniable truth that I am going to dress for the ball."

Of this concession to worldliness Mrs. Montagu, in the same jaunty letter to the Sylph that describes the Calais arrival, tells us that the translator of Epictetus has "translated her native timidity into french airs and french modes; bought robes trimmed with blonde and souci denton, colliers, bouquets, des engageantes, and all the most labor'd ornaments of dress; and so soon as she is equip'd, wish'd for a walk into the tuilleries more than she had ever done for onc in the Portico."

The line had to be drawn somewhere; Mrs. Carter drew it at hoops. When Prince and Princess Ferdinand of Prussia came to take the Spa waters, everybody "prepared to pay their court but with this I have nothing to do; for I am told a hoop is absolutely necessary, no hoop have I and no hoop do I design to have, so I shall decline the honour and happiness of looking silly in the presence of Princess Ferdinand."

Spa, in the southeast corner of modern Belgium, was, during the reign of Maria Theresa, in Hapsburg Flanders, a region that was then as in later times the crossroads of northern Europe. Unlike Bath, it was a summer resort and commanded a cosmopolitan clientele, of whom their hoop-requiring Royal Highnesses were typical. Mrs. Montagu found at Spa a combination of mountain and social scenes, in both of which she delighted. She is at her best in the following description: "The Town of Spa is situated in a little valley surrounded every way by mountains, and is therefore ill-placed in regard to exercise in a voiture, and wd be so for walking, if a generous spirited englishman had not cut walks round the mountains, by which you are carried to the summit by an easy ascent; from thence you look down on the Town of Spa which is so rudely and irregularly built one might imagine it had been raised in the first beginnings of architecture; all the Country round is wild, and the eye in a wide circuit perceives no vestiges of society; no plows are going, no windmills turning, no Cottage chimney smoaks nor is there a church or village in sight. The imagination suggests from various appearances that the family of Noah are just settled at Spa after the flood, while the rest of the World is desolate and in ruins; by striking into other paths you are led round another mountain, and descend into the promenade de sept heures; there you will find ages have past since the deluge, for it was surely many ages e're Heralds rose and titles were invented, and you find yourself walking with son altesse Royal, son altesse Serenissime, son Excellence Mr. le Comte, and Monsieur le Marquis. Here you meet all the various orders and professions in which mankind are classed; The Friar is walking with the soldier, the nun with the Matron, the Financier with a Chanoinesse, the long robe with the staff officer. All professions and all Nations are assembled at Spa in the summer; in a few months we all disappear, and the Wolves and bears reassume their Dominions from the Mountains."

Mrs. Montagu's preoccupation with everything that concerned Lord Bath is consistent with Reginald Blunt's theory that he was the emotional focus of her blameless life. Although, she writes home, many "milords" are at Spa it is Lord Bath who is chiefly cultivated by the *Almanach de Gotha*. Princess Emilie, sister of Frederick the Great, commended his Lordship to her care, saying in fashionable French, *"Veillez sur les jours de ce digne milord qui a le respect et l'admiration de toute l'Europe"* (Watch over the days of this worthy milord who has the respect and admiration of all Europe).

After a month of taking the waters, Mrs. Montagu reported that all the party, with the exception of Mrs. Carter, had derived great benefit from the sojourn. It was proposed to vary the return journey to Calais and to visit Germany and the Lowlands. Although Mrs. Montagu lacked sensitivity to the arts she possessed, for a woman of her class and time, an unusual awareness of the human condition. Her familiarity with agriculture and mining had given her an eye for a fertile field or a poverty-stricken town. The regions through which they passed were ravaged by war, with resultant civil disorders, starving peasantry and impassable roads. After paying their respects to Charlemagne at Aix-la-Chapelle and visiting the cathedral and the electoral palace at Cologne, the party crossed the frontier into Holland. Mrs. Montagu was quick to comment on the contrast in prosperity with Hapsburg dominions: "such is the vivifying and nourishing spirit of liberty that even in this barren land no poverty or distress appear'd, the houses were tight, the people clean, whereas in the rich and fruitfull domains of the house of Austria haggard poverty appeared everywhere. If one wants to respect liberty one shd come into Holland, if to love and respect it too one must go into England."

It is surprising that Mrs. Carter did not share her hostess's enthusiasm for self-respecting Holland, bastion of the Reformed Church. Her headaches being unassuaged by the Geronsterre and the Pouhon, she complained to Miss Talbot that, "So far as I have seen of Holland it is just as wretched and unpleasant as I had always supposed it to be." On September 20th she was at last able to write from her "Vinegar Bottle" of a house in Deal, "I have now the pleasure to inform you that, thank God, we are all returned safe to England." The literature of travel owes little to Elizabeth Carter.

Mrs. Montagu, at their return, congratulated herself upon bringing home a coquette in Mrs. Carter and a young man in Lord Bath.

In the fall of 1763 London was in an uproar. During April of that year John Wilkes, M.P. for Aylesbury, published the notorious no. 45 of his scurrilous *North Briton*. This rabble-rousing periodical had as its principal objective the bringing down of the Scottish Lord Bute. No. 45 not only suggested the '45, but was also intended to rekindle the hostilities of that contest. Never one to avoid libel or obscenity,

Wilkes accused Bute of being the lover of Princess Augusta, the King's mother. This scandalous performance was defended as freedom of the press. The mobs who delighted in burning boots and petticoats in symbolic effigy had now as their rallying cry, "Wilkes and Liberty."

Wilkes, like that other rogue, Edward Wortley Montagu, Jr., enjoyed parliamentary privilege. To get around this, Secretaries of State Halifax and Egremont issued a general warrant to "search for authors, printers and publishers" suspected of sedition. Wilkes spent a week in the Tower, a punishment that won a hundred thousand pounds in a libel suit against Halifax and his other enemies.

In order to strip Wilkes of his immunity from prosecution, it was proposed to expel him from Parliament. The case against him was strengthened by the fact that he was an enthusiastic member of the Hellfire Club, whose obscene activities furnished the "ton" with delicious horror. As his contribution to these gaieties, he had printed on his private press an unspeakable parody of Pope called *Essay on Woman*. Lord Sandwich opened Parliament in November of 1763 by reading this pornographic work to the House of Lords, many of whom must have thoroughly relished the turn thus taken by patriotism.

Mrs. Montagu, who saw nothing amusing in Lord Bath's return to the House of Lords for such colorful deliberations, was at her most exalted in writing, "I had rather the Duke of Marlborough's helmet had been made a housewife's skillet the morning of the battle of Blenheim than that a certain person should stay at home in his indolent nightcap the first day of business in the H. of L. . . . to stand neuter during the important contention would be unpardonable."

Although the peers expelled Wilkes for blasphemy, libel and breach of privilege, they expressed some very pertinent scruples about the methods employed in gathering evidence. The following letter from Lord Lyttleton would not look out of place in the American press of today. "I hear Wilkes says he would not take £20000 for the Damages he shall get of all the different persons concerned in robbing his house. To say the truth tho' one is sorry that any Reformation of a Grievance should turn to his benefit I can't but approve of the check given to the illegal and dangerous Practise of violating the safety of men's Houses and seizing their Papers for Libels."

Alas for Mrs. Montagu's displaced optimism! Lord Bath, whom she believed to have been rejuvenated by his recent travels, died in July of 1764, almost a year to the day after his arrival at Spa. The loss to Mrs. Montagu was complex. Not only did she lose a dear friend and a lavish host, but she also learned the truth of her favorite poet's lines, "The evil that men do lives after them; the good is oft interred with their bones." So, because of a slovenly will, was it to be with Lord Bath. Georgian England was every bit as intrigued with bequests as with marriages. There was an outcry when it was learned that, still in "sullen despair" over the death of his son and heir, His Lordship had left his huge fortune to his brother, General Pultney, ignoring other relatives, friends, servants and philanthropies. Cynical Chesterfield commented that "the words *give* and *bequeath* were too shocking for him to repeat so he left all in one word to his brother."

Mrs. Montagu was painfully disillusioned that one whom she had venerated as the pattern of right principles should prove in death so selfish. She lamented to Lord Lyttleton that "The Will has obscured his fame; the leaving such an unwieldy mass of wealth to a weak old man, set the world in an uproar. Some of it should have been sanctified to publick uses, his relations should all have been remembered, such of his friends as were in strait or unhappy circumstances should have tasted of his bounty. Care should have been taken to have transmitted his Memoirs into honest hands. What I say to your Lordship on this subject I would not say to any other person, but I am truly hurt that the last and solemn act was not such as was worthy of him. This will compared with the Wills of other rich Men may pass without very severe censure, but one should suppose so great, so good, so benevolent a mind as my friends would have exerted itself in acts of generosity on such an occasion. It is the duty of the rich to justify the ways of God to Man, by imparting to unendow'd merit some of their abundance; in his life time he did generous things, but the objects of his bounty were all forgot in the final settling of his affairs."

Friends of impecunious Mrs. Carter were indignant that she had received no annuity from Lord Bath, whose attentions to her were so marked as to suggest that she might become his second wife. With these reproaches Mrs. Carter refused to associate herself. She is at her best in taking leave of him whom others were prepared to pronounce a fickle friend. "None of his friends will remember him longer and with equal affection. Indeed there was something in his conversation and manners more engaging than can be described. . . . For so many months as I passed continually in his company last year I do not recollect a single instance of peevishness the whole time. His temper always appeared equal, there was a perpetual flow of vivacity and good humor in his conversation and the most attentive politeness in his behaviour." Mrs. Carter's magnanimity, like that of Mrs. Delany, was handsomely, if not royally, rewarded. Upon the predictable death of ailing and aged General Pultney, his heirs not only granted her an annuity but, again recalling Mrs. Delany, made of her a mother figure, thus doubly enriching her old age.

Although Mrs. Montagu's much-acclaimed *Essay on Shakespeare* was not published until 1769, it owes a great deal to previous years of theatrical theorizing. At hand was Garrick's Drury Lane, where transpired a glorious period in the four-centuries-long history of Shakespeare in performance. Mrs. Montagu's correspondence contains many references to plays seen and actors admired. Before her marriage she went to see *As You Like It*. One of Garrick's stars, Quin, played the melancholy Jacques. Of his performance the then Miss Robinson wrote, "I never heard anything spoke with such command of voice as the seven stages of man." She was especially struck with the way Quin's voice "sunk" from the rough bass of the capon-fed Justice to the childish treble of sans eyes, sans teeth, sans everything. About *Henry the Fourth* she commented, "I am this instant from the play where I have been extremely entertained with that most comick of all personages Sir John Falstaffe; as to Hotspur he was in a very violent passion in the first act and I think it is a part not equal to the genius of Garrick." Her admiration for Falstaff was repeated at a later time. "There is one thing which I have never heard remark'd by the cricks but which I think makes Falstaffes the most pleasing of all Comick characters which is that his wit seems to arise from the mirthfulness of his disposition and therefore more readily excites the affection from whence it proceeds. Wit is generally satyrical and severe and oftener the cause of mirth than the original effect of it. To laugh with Falstaffe is only a natural sympathy and one must be illnatured as well as dull not to do so." Mrs. Montagu's conviction that she has spotted "one thing" unremarked by the critics suggests that she dreamed of joining the growing number of Shakespeare scholars.

Also at work was a negative inspiration. Like most of her contemporaries on both sides of the channel, Mrs. Montagu cultivated a futile comparison between English and French conventions. Voltaire was her *bête noir*. She pronounced him in philosophy an atheist, in literature a coxcomb, and in friendship a sycophant. Long before his attack on Shakespeare triggered her replying *Essay,* we find her writing to Mrs. Carter in apparent misunderstanding of *Candide.* "I am glad you agree with me in detestation of Voltaire's Optimism. Are you not provoked that such an animal calls itself a Philosopher? What pretence can he have to Philosophy who has not fear of God which is the beginning of Wisdom." Voltaire as a playwright was even more objectionable than as a philosopher. To Lord Bath, who had lent her *Tancred,* she took up the well-worn contrast of English naturalness with French artificiality. The following condemnation is entirely in the mood of her 1769 manifesto: "Pompous declamation season'd with moral reflections is surely far from the perfection of dramatick writing, tho' in a nation too much polish'd and refin'd it is to be prefer'd to the natural sallies of passion as fops love essences better than the flowers from where they are extracted." In his *Preface to Shakespeare* Johnson more temperately likens the "work of a correct and regular writer" to a garden, and that of Shakespeare to a forest.

Mrs. Montagu's contempt for Voltaire was increased by his servile courting of "benevolent" despots. His friendship with Frederick the Great, the self-styled *Philosophe sans souci* (carefree philosopher), being at an end, he was now engaged in the profitable flattering of Catherine the Great, whom Mrs. Montagu astutely characterized as a "monster with talents." His well-known genius for mockery is singularly absent in his assuring the "monster" that her court is more enlightened than were ever Greece or Rome. Of this performance Mrs. Montagu wrote, "a vast present to Mr. Voltaire has procured a compliment which dishonors a Man of Genius." Here at least she gives Anti-Christ his due.

Mrs. Montagu's *Essay* had to compete with innumerable other activities. She shared her contemporaries' delight in building. Part of her aptitude for hospitality expressed itself in magnificence. She offered her guests a choice of apartments decorated by the Adam brothers and Angelica Kauffman. At different times and in various houses were to be found a Chinese Room, a Cupidon Room, an

Athenian Room and, crowning them all, the famous Feather Room of Portman Square. Improvements also went forward at Sandleford, with Adam employed indoors and "Capability" Brown without.

Public events prompted long letters to absent friends and relatives. The controversial Stamp Act wrought havoc on both sides of the Atlantic. Writing to her husband in 1764, Mrs. Montagu reported that "our Colonies are in some sort of rebellion . . . it is imagined that there will be some warm work in the H. of Lords about the stamps and the resistance of the Colonies." Of the rapidly deteriorating situation Mrs. Montagu wrote at length two years later, saying, "this attempt of the Colonies to assert an independence on the Parliament of England is of a dangerous nature."

The Stamp Act was passed in 1765 when Pitt was ill and absent from Parliament. Upon his return he declared it an infringement of the colonists' rights and rejoiced that they had resisted. It was promptly repealed, leaving, however, unsettled the question of the right of Parliament to tax at will unrepresented and unconsulted colonists. Just as there were increasingly to be found in Boston, New York and Philadelphia loyalists who chose to throw in their lot with the mother country, so were there in England statesmen who were colonial sympathizers.

The most celebrated of these last was the Irishman, Edmund Burke. He was elected Member of Parliament for Wendover in 1766. Mrs. Montagu heard his maiden speech and thus described it to "Sylph" Vesey on February 22nd,* a date when a certain gentleman farmer of Virginia was marking his thirty-fourth year. "The stamp act was repeal'd by a majority of one hundred and eight and our friend, Mr. Burke, spoke divinely, yes divinely, don't misunderstand me and report he spoke as well as mortal man could do, I tell you he spoke better." Mr. Pitt followed and according to Mrs. Montagu rather overdid the rural simplicity of the colonists. Her letter continues, "He described the American planter sitting in his native innocence in his native woods and how cruel it was to disturb him there with a stamp duty." There were also, Mrs. Montagu reminded the Sylph, "the litigious man who goes to law or the mercantile man who sends commodities to sea." Granted these fledgling merchants,

* Washington was born on February 11, 1732. When the new calendar was adopted in 1752, there was an advance of eleven dates, February 11 becoming February 22.

"the pastoral part of the speech, though adorned with quotations from the Georgics did not greatly move the House."

Mrs. Montagu's admiration for Burke did not incline her to rejoice at the increased English taxes resulting from the repeal of the Stamp Act. Two months after her rapturous report of his eloquence, she joined Mrs. Boscawen in wishing "our ministers were shipped off to their friends in America. The country gentleman is to pay £10 a year for his coach. . . . I grieve for the gouty Squires and their fat wives who will not be able to let the coach and old Dobbin and Whiteface tug them to church, or to visit a neighbor while your American drives his gilded car and 6 bays tho' perhaps his Father was transported for felony." These very human desires to have it both ways were addressed to Mr. Montagu. His reply, quoted from Lord Bolingbroke, had an egalitarian ring. His Lordship had warned "that the time would come when six or seven millions of people would not be hewers of wood and drawers of water for two hundred thousand." This comment was an apt curtain raiser for the approaching decades of revolution in America, France, Ireland and in English industry.

During the summer of the same year Mrs. Montagu, leaving her husband to mathematics and coal, made an extensive tour of Scotland. Her companions were Dr. Gregory, professor of medicine at the University of Edinburgh, and his young daughter, Dorothea, who later became her ward. It will be remembered that Mrs. Montagu was, for reasons of history rather than temperament, deeply influenced by the Romantic movement. Her Scottish landscapes are in the vein of her Spa scenes, but gain from her (and our) not being nagged by chauvinistic bigotry. The rushing torrents, towering mountains and purple moors surrounding "Loughlomon" were all the more glorious for belonging to King George's three realms rather than those of Maria Theresa. It is hardly necessary to add that a volume of Ossian was carried in the coach, that Macpherson be invoked upon the "Classic Ground."

Her Scottish summer played its part in shaping Mrs. Montagu's career. At Edinburgh she met Lord Kames, whose *Elements of Criticism* she consulted in writing her Shakespeare *Essay*. Her delight in the landscapes of the highlands predisposed her to become, a few years hence, the patron of Dr. Gregory's friend James Beattie, Scottish poet and author of *The Minstrel* and the *Essay on Truth*. A recent visit of Thomas Gray to Scotland prompted her to write her theories upon her avocation of catalyst. Upon learning that Gray, although he was cordially received, was disposed to aloofness, Mrs. Montagu set down a conversationalist's creed. Writing to her sister-in-law, Mrs. William Robinson, she enunciated the following principles: "I agreed perfectly with him [Gray] that to endeavour to shine in conversation and to lay on for admiration is very paltry. At the same time when a man of celebrated talents disdains to mix in common conversation or refuses to talk on ordinary subjects it betrays a latent pride; there is a much higher character than that of a wit, a poet or a savant, which is that of a rational sociable being, willing to carry on the commerce of life with all the sweetness and condescension, decency and virtue will permit. The great duty of conversation is to follow suit as you do at whist; if the eldest hand plays the deuce of diamonds let not his next neighbour cast down the King of Hearts because his hand is full of honours. I do not love to see a man of wit win all the tricks in conversation nor yet to see him sullenly pass. . . ." Granted these admonitions, it is hardly surprising that Mrs. Montagu and Dr. Johnson were soon to quarrel.

During the approaching old age of her husband, Mrs. Montagu assumed increased responsibility for the collieries at Denton in Northumberland and at Allerthorpe in Yorkshire. At nearby Alnwick Castle, seat of the Duke of Northumberland, she met Thomas Percy, whose *Reliques of Ancient English Poetry* made an important contribution to enthusiasm for the British and Celtic past. She was doubtless projecting her dream of participating through patronage in the new reverence for "native wood-notes wild" when she wrote Mrs. Vesey that "there is you know a pre-established harmony between me and all poets. . . . Mr. Percy is a very agreeable well bred man and will make a good addition to our sect of blue stocking Philosophers."

Mrs. Carter, who had won recognition in the perilous regions of female publication, was naturally in Mrs. Montagu's confidence regarding the *Essay on Shakespeare*. To her she complained of the interruptions caused by domestic and business cares. A letter written during the summer of 1768 reads, "Between attending Mr. Montagu in his very infirm state, domestic Orders for the regulation of a family consisting of about thirty persons, letters of business, and my authorlike duties, I have sometimes a great hurry, and I have also some sick patients for whom I am obliged to make up Medicines, that being in some cases not to be trusted to another; poor Shakespear is last served."

Her pen was diverted from Shakespeare not only by such concerns, but also by the crescendo of public disorders that marked the approach of the American and French revolutions. These upheavals stimulated in England a growth in the political influence of the mob. John Wilkes, who had been exiled in France since his expulsion from Parliament in 1763, incurred in Paris debts of such magnitude that to escape his creditors he returned to England in the face of inevitable arrest. Five years out of office had not destroyed his demagogic genius. Judging quite rightly that the Ministry trembled before the threat of riots, his strategy called for his being returned to Parliament by popular acclaim. Predictably, he was imprisoned and equally predictably his arrest was protested by riots. Mrs. Montagu commented sarcastically on Wilkes's command of the adoration of his ruffianly following: "he will have 45 minced pyes sent him on Xmas day and 45 plumb cakes on 12th night and if he cannot find 45 Kings and queens, he may find the square of 45, of sluts and Varlets at his own lodgings. The Ministry design to keep him in prison till the meeting of Parliament after the holydays that they may make 45 blunders at the moderate rate of one per diem. . . ." And in another letter this fateful warning, "A mob that can read and a ministry that cannot think are sadly mixed."

Lady Mary and Mrs. Montagu both had family ties with the new world of novelists. The former was, we remember, second cousin to Henry Fielding, and the latter was cousin by marriage to "Yorick" or "Tristram Shandy," as Laurence Sterne was often called. He was, as a clergyman and a philanderer, a man who could be said, in extraclerical terms, not to let his right hand know what his left hand did. Probably for reasons of safety, he preferred as objects of his attention married ladies, one being "Sylph" Vesey and another the much younger Lady Percy, the Butes' daughter, to say nothing of Eliza Draper, whom he enshrined in *The Sentimental Journey.* Mrs. Montagu was alternatively indulgent to and critical of her "cosin's" "playing at romance and calling it love, playing at love and calling it friendship." In presenting him to her sister, Mrs. Scott of the Bath philanthropies, Mrs. Montagu took pains to forestall any objections to the roving ecclesiastical eye. "I will venture to say for him that whatever he may want in seriousness he makes up in good nature. He is full of the milk of human kindness, harmless as a child but often a naughty boy and a little apt to dirty his *frock*."

Notably lacking in this mood of amused tolerance was his wife, whose eccentricities have been pronounced by later authorities to be insanity. "Yorick's" conspicuous, if inconclusive, gallantries were sources of jealousy and shame that resulted in a hysteria thoroughly puzzling to Mrs. Montagu. With a splendid absence of the most elementary principles of psychology, she wrote to her sister that, "One would hardly think a woman unhappy from the persecution of her husband wd be eternally entering into disputes with strangers; yet this has been her case. . . . She is very absurd if, having a domestic enemy, she tries to have as many out of her family as she can make." It hardly seems necessary to point out that "Yorick" had given his unstable spouse every reason to fear strangers, especially female strangers.

This unhappy couple separated in 1762 and a year later Sterne died. His irresponsibility in marriage and in holy orders caused Mrs. Montagu to modify her previous indulgent attitude. The following judgment, written in 1768, reflects the tone of her *Essay on Shakespeare,* which was then nearing completion. "Poor Tristram Shandy had an appearance of philanthropy that pleased one and made one forgive in some degree his errors. However, as I think, there is but one way of a man's proving his philanthropy to be real and genuine and that is by making every part of his conduct a good example to mankind. . . ."

And then with a reference to Voltaire, who occupied her every bit as much as Shakespeare, she sounded a major theme. "There are but two kinds of people that I think myself at liberty to hate and despise, the first is of the class of soi disant philosophers who by sophistry would cheat the less acute out of their principles, the only firm basis of moral virtue; the second are witts who ridicule whatsoever things are lovely, whatsoever things are of good report. . . . Poor Tristram's last performance was the best, his sentimental journey would not have misbecome a young Ensign. I cannot say it was suitable to his serious profession." Mrs. Montagu's gravity was a dominant trait. In the months that saw the finishing of the *Essay on the Writings and Genius of Shakespeare*, it was naturally in the ascendancy.

Already sobered by the magnitude of her task, she was close to abandoning it because of the publication in 1765 of Johnson's edition of the complete works of Shakespeare. In his introductory volume appeared not only his *Preface to Shakespeare,* but also those of Nicholas Rowe and Alexander Pope. Mrs. Montagu's sentiments resembled those of a contemporary critic who embarks on yet another analysis of *Moby Dick*. After a flurry of letters to Mrs. Carter she decided to persist, feeling that, although "Both Mr. Pope and Johnson have written the prettiest essays imaginable on Shakespear. . . . I think they have done very little in shewing his excellencies in particular circumstances, and either general encomium or invective is to me not properly criticism." She would not have dreamed that she was betraying the pedant in her next line. "Both these writers aim to please rather than to teach."

Mrs. Montagu wrote her essay for a double purpose. It was not only her intention to teach Shakespeare but to teach that Shakespeare is superior to Racine and Corneille. This comparison is unfortunate and irrelevant; it serves to weaken a work that contains many pertinent observations and one excellent chapter, entitled *On the Praeternatural Beings*. The other chapters are *Dramatick Poetry, Historical Drama, Henry IV,* parts I and II, *Macbeth, Corneille's Cinna* and *The Death of Julius Caesar*.

The *Essay* appeared in April of 1769, the year of Garrick's Stratford Jubilee. Canny businesswoman as she was, Mrs. Montagu hoped that his popularizing of Shakespeare would attract readers to her book. The Jubilee, the first of all birthplace festivals, anticipated Disneyland, a rained-out Disneyland to boot. In September of 1769 the heavens opened. Scheduled fireworks fizzled; "Thou soft-flowing Avon" * rose; a pavilion built to host a masked ball was flooded; processions of Drury Lane actors in costume were drenched to the skin; only Dr. Arne's "Shakespeare Ode" performed in Stratford Church escaped the blight of rain. The Jubilee, though a fiasco, belongs to theatre history. It provided troubled England with comic relief that ranged from sneer to guffaw. Most important, Garrick suc-

* This was the first line of Thomas A. Arne's "Shakespeare Ode."

ceeded in making Shakespeare what he remains, a popular hero. It seems safe to imagine that many who attended the Jubilee turned with relief from such inanities as "The pride of all nature was Sweet Willy O" to Mrs. Montagu's dignified pages.

The *Essay* was published anonymously. It must have been most flattering to the self-made scholar to have her work mistaken for that of Joseph Warton, who is a significant figure in the history of Shakespeare criticism. For many months her anonymity was not penetrated. It was in December of 1769 that she confided to so close a friend as Lord Lyttleton. "I am sorry to tell you that a friend of yours is no longer a concealed scribbler. I had better employed the town crier to proclaim me an author; but being whispered it has circulated with incredible swiftness. . . . I am most flattered that a brother writer says the book would be very well if it had not too much wit. I thought there had been no wit at all in it; and I am as much pleased as M. Jourdain when his preceptor told him he spoke prose." This genuflection to Molière sounds a strange note in a work intended to exalt Shakespeare at the expense of French playwrights.

It is necessary in considering Georgian Shakespeare criticism to remember it is not until we reach the Victorians that our greatest poet attained the condition of infallibility. The Restoration theatre could take him or leave him alone; so dedicated a playgoer as Mr. Pepys dismissed *Romeo and Juliet* as "the worst that ever I heard in my life." Dryden did not hesitate to edit Shakespeare. Other playwrights distorted a tragedy such as *Macbeth* by the introduction of songs and "new cloathes and flyings for the witches."

The studies of Pope, Johnson and Mrs. Montagu were sincere efforts—if they seem superficial in the light of the accumulated material available today—to defend Shakespeare from the frivolity of the past, from attacks by French critics and, could they have known it, from the fawning of the future. The modern reader is no longer troubled by the fact that the theatre of the Bourbons is heir to Greece and Rome and that of the Elizabethans is not.

Our literary forebears never tired of comparing the classical tragedies of Racine and Corneille with the romantic and intuitive theatre of Shakespeare. The former observed the unities of Aristotle; the latter, by his own magic, unified tragedy and comedy, time, place and action. Pope, Johnson and Mrs. Montagu all dwelt on the fact that French tragedy was composed by rule; and the plays of Shakespeare, as contrasted with those of Ben Jonson, by instinct. Samuel Johnson wrote that "Shakespeare's plays are not in the rigorous and critical sense either tragedies or comedies, but compositions of a distinct kind; exhibiting the real state of sublunary nature which partakes of good and evil, joy and sorrow, mingled with endless variety of proportion and innumerable modes of combination." Mrs. Montagu, who was fond of placing Shakespeare against a primitive British past, asks, "Will an intelligent spectator not admire the prodigious structures of Stone-Henge because he does not know by what law of mechanics they were raised? Like them our author's works will remain for ever the greatest monument of the amazing force of nature which we ought to view as we do other prodigies, with an attention to and admiration of their stupendous parts and proud irregularity of greatness." Pope, who was adept in pinpointing that which "oft was thought but ne'er so well expressed," dismissed the controversy by writing, "To judge therefore of Shakespeare by Aristotle's rules is like trying a man by the Laws of one Country who acted under those of another."

The chapter in Mrs. Montagu's *Essay* devoted to Shakespeare's use of the supernatural deserves better from posterity than it has received. Here she emphasizes his indebtedness to the mythology of northern Europe, which had not, like that of the Aegean and Mediterranean, been reduced to a formula. The German forests and English moors more readily suggest the powers of darkness than do the sunlit slopes of the Parthenon. Allowing for inevitable religious prejudice, there is much to praise in the following Wagnerian passage: "A celebrated writer . . . has observed that the Gothic manners and Gothic superstitions are more adapted to the uses of poetry than the Grecian. The devotion of those times was gloomy and fearful not being purged of the terrors of the Celtic fables. . . . Climate, temper, modes of life, and institutions of government seem all to have conspired to make the superstitions of the Celtic nations melancholy and terrible. . . . The poet found himself happily situated amidst enchantments, ghosts, goblins; every element supposed the residence of a kind of deity, the Genius of the mountain, the Spirit of the floods, the Oak endued with fearful prophecy, made men walk abroad with a fearful apprehension 'Of powers unseen and mightier far than they.' "

Although the plays of Shakespeare abound in symbolic reference to Jove, Phoebus and Neptune, none of these divinities takes a hand in human destiny. Their uses are decorative. As Mrs. Montagu points out, when Shakespeare desired to put the supernatural to work he invoked the northern spirits of earth and air. Seen in this light, Caliban and Macbeth's witches are trolls; Puck and Ariel are leprechauns.

Mrs. Montagu, like most of her contemporaries, was handicapped in her judgment of Shakespeare by undervaluing the Age of Elizabeth. Brushing aside such luminaries as Spenser, Bacon and Donne, she assures her Georgian public that "Shakespeare wrote at a time when learning was tinctured with pedantry, wit was unpolished and mirth ill-bred. The court of Elizabeth spoke a scientific jargon. . . ." Was Mrs. Montagu thinking perhaps of a line such as "When first your eye I eyed" in concluding that Elizabethans cultivated a "certain obscurity of style"?

Dr. Johnson, in his justly more admired *Preface to Shakespeare,* does not do much better. Like Mrs. Montagu, he assumed that the Georgian present must in every way mark an advance over the English Renaissance, writing that "The English nation in the time of Shakespeare was yet struggling to emerge from barbarity." Of this chronological provincialism Macaulay was to be savagely critical. Johnson, he rashly asserted, had "ventured to publish an edition of Shakespeare without having ever in his life as far as can be discovered read a single scene of Massinger, Ford, Dekker, Webster, Marlowe, Beaumont or Fletcher." Like Johnson, Mrs. Montagu ignored the splendid theatre of those deprived times. It was her lofty, if mistaken, intention to pit Shakespeare against the Athenian unities and thereby confound that "foolish coxcomb," Voltaire. That she failed so to do was less because of her qualifications than because of the futility of the comparison.

Happier was her awareness of "something rich and strange" in her subject. She makes a nice distinction between learning and inspiration in conceding, as do all critics, that Shakespeare's intuition outpaced information. There is a prophetically romantic tone in the following: "Shakespeare seems to have had the art of the Dervise in the Arabian tales who could throw his soul into the body of another man and be at once possessed of his sentiments, adopt his passions and rise to all the functions and feelings of his situation." Although she herself welcomed aristocratic and scholarly restraints, she thought that Shakespeare's modest birth and learning might have provided a useful Bohemianism. He was, she reminds us, "born in a rank of life in which men indulge themselves in a free expression of their passions with little regard to exterior appearance. This perhaps made him more acquainted with the emotions of the heart and less knowing or observant of outward forms. Against the one he often offends, he very rarely misrepresents the other." And finally she considers Shakespeare's Englishness. Even though he leads us to the banks of the Tiber and the Nile, to Venice and Verona, he peoples these regions with the only people he knew, those of Elizabethan England. Mrs. Montagu is far from regretting that this is the case when she sets down these nationalistic sentiments: "Our noble countryman, Percy, engages us much more than Achilles, or any Grecian hero." Garrick's public was as impervious to classical mythology as had been Händel's. They preferred the Wars of the Roses to those of Troy because, continued Mrs. Montagu, they "knew the battle of Shrewsbury to be a fact; they are informed of what passed on the bank of the Severn; all that happened on the shore of the Scamander has to them the appearance of fiction." To this provincialism we owe such varied British creations as Falstaff, John of Gaunt, Bottom, Rosalind and Portia. "Small Latin and less Greek" proved a rewarding limitation.

The *Essay* tells us more about Georgian attitudes than it does about Shakespeare. For this reason it remains a period piece. It contains romantic stirrings, the new esteem for instinct and emotion over information, a respect for wonder—all these intuitive qualities conditioned by the conviction that the Age of Reason provided "the best of all possible worlds." And, most important, the *Essay* could not have succeeded without the recent esteem for women of intellect.

Succeed it did. It went through several editions and was translated into French and Italian. Garrick, whom Mrs. Montagu had praised in the *Essay*, promoted its sale which was, she noted, "very handsome in him as we have not always been the best of friends." Cowper commended "the learning, the good sense, the sound judgment and the wit." The author's elderly father, Matthew Robinson, was enchanted with his new "grandchild."

Predictably, the "ton" was inclined to think that one of their number was giving herself airs. The Dowager Countess Gower wrote to her cousin, Mrs. Delany, that Mrs. Montagu "has commenced author in vindication of Shakespeare who needs none. . . . I'll have it because I can throw it away when I'm tired."

Dr. Johnson was not disposed to welcome Mrs. Montagu to the burgeoning field of Shakespearean scholarship. He was excusably critical of her design to invoke the Bard against French deism. When Reynolds said that the *Essay* did her honor, Johnson's unchivalrous reply was, "Yes, Sir, it does *her* honour but it would do nobody else honour. I have indeed not read it all." Garrick broke in with, "But, Sir, surely it shows how much Voltaire has mistaken Shakespeare which nobody else has done." Johnson's succinct reply was, "Sir, nobody else has thought it worthwhile."

In terms of published criticism, the *Essay* is not equal to the prefaces of Rowe, Pope and Johnson. Nor could Mrs. Montagu rival her friend, Mrs. Carter, in scholarship. As a "female pen" she was outdistanced by both Hester Chapone and Hannah More. If, however, we consider Mrs. Montagu's self-imposed task as the product of informed and studious leisure, we will find much to admire in the patrician amateur who longed for citizenship in the Republic of Letters.

She never again wrote for publication. Having uttered her manifesto, she henceforth devoted her inexhaustible energy to the concerns of family, business, drawing rooms and protégés.

The prestige earned by her Shakespeare *Essay* had sobering effects. Already an influential hostess, Mrs. Montagu became, in the French sense of the word, formidable. Blue Stocking gatherings in the Cupidon Room or Chinese Room sometimes numbered seven hundred persons, who came and went from eleven in the morning until eleven at night. In her character formality had always predominated over spontaneity and earnestness over humor. As she grew older she became, as most people do, increasingly conservative. Her consciousness of having written a page in the annals of female scholarship led her to fall into a trap avoided by Elizabeth Carter, that of being headmistress to Johnson's London. Exclaimed Horace Walpole, to whom exasperation came easily, "Aspasia has both knowledge and wit with many virtues; but mercy on us! they are both indefatigably for ever at our service."

Despite her growing gravity, Mrs. Montagu remained capable of admiring in other women charms superior to her own. She wrote of Lady Hervey, who died at the age of ninety-one, "I have a great loss in Lady Hervey. In her society one tasted the rare pleasure of general conversation; polite and ingenious herself she communicated those qualities to her company, every one appeared better than in any other place. They were pleasing because they seemed pleased and that reserve which makes the most sensitive Nation in the world perhaps the least agreeable in society was laid aside. No person at her table or by her fireside had the arrogant vanity of shining alone, nor the pitiful pride of being afraid to speak lest they should not shine. They forgot whether they were or were not accounted witts and geniuses and remembered only they were her guests and as such to endeavor to be agreeable to her and the company." Both as a tribute to a friend and a definition of the spirit of the salon, it would be hard to improve on these splendid lines.

She was equally generous with Mrs. Vesey, whose gay parties, she must have been wistfully aware, pleased more than her semi-circular seminars. To her fey friend, evidently absent in Ireland, she wrote in 1772: "Come to England, get into your blue room, call all your friends around you, and let every melancholy remembrance be chased away. I often dream (with my eyes open) of this blue room. I see Mr. Garrick in one corner of it, Lord Lyttleton sitting close to the fire, Mr. Burke in the midst of your circle, Mrs. Carter on your sopha; the door opens, in trips a maccaroni, or stalks a minister of state or perhaps glides a fine lady: no matter who or what, the spirit of Vesey is mighty still; my dear sylph makes her company form a round O, and she sits in the Center and like the sun enlivens and illuminates the whole." Had Mrs. Montagu forgotten the Sylph's helter-skelter disposal of her guests?

Mrs. Montagu's fondness for the Celtic tradition expressed itself, from the early 1770s, in her patronage of James Beattie. She met the Scottish poet and clergyman through their friend-in-common, Dr. Gregory. In both his verse and prose he conformed to her preference for the romantic and the orthodox. His principal poem, *The Min-*

strel, not only follows in the vein of Macpherson's *Ossian* and Percy's *Reliques,* but also prefigures the "old unhappy far-off" school so soon to produce the Gothick utterances of Horace Walpole and Sir Walter Scott. As a defender of revealed religion, Beattie won equal recognition. Reynolds included him in an allegorical painting that challenges deistic error; he stands to one side holding his *Essay on Truth* while attendant spirits lead the viewers' eyes to condemn the former and reverence the latter. Mrs. Montagu delighted in forwarding both Beattie's poetic gifts and his ecclesiastical career. When Boswell, who was, where Dr. Johnson was concerned, on the defensive about Scotland and Scots, thanked the Sage for his kindness to a countryman, the reply was, "Sir, I should thank *you*. We all love Beattie."

As a patroness Mrs. Montagu was both efficient and tactful. She obtained for Beattie a royal pension of two hundred pounds, enabling him to "keep a horse and set his table with beef and pudding." She saw to it that he met not only his kindred spirit, Percy of the *Reliques,* but also Garrick, the Corsican hero Paoli, Lord Lyttleton, Mrs. Carter, the Duchess of Portland and Mrs. Delany. Nor was she above rejoicing that Boswell's friend Charles Dilly, the bookseller, acted very handsomely by Dr. Beattie in "an affair relative to a future publication." It was this aspect of Mrs. Montagu's career that prompted Fanny Burney to note that "Whatever her foibles, as a member of society Mrs. Montagu was magnificently useful."

Not surprisingly, the Beatties' visits to Sandleford, haunt of Mrs. Montagu's muse, lent ineffability to her increasingly florid letters. When on one occasion her visitors were delayed, she wrote to Mrs. Vesey that, "I have lost six weeks in which I hoped to enjoy his conversation in this quiet solitude where Philomel and he might have sung their alternate notes without having their harmony disturbed by the noise of folly and din of the busy world." The relationship of patroness and poet was, despite these rhetorical excesses, a sound one. Theirs was an age when art derived its support from extremely personal sources. It is to the credit of Mrs. Montagu and of Beattie that an arrangement frequently marked by arrogance on one side and flattery on the other was carried out in a manner that did honor to both.

The twenty-nine-year span between Mrs. Montagu in her early fifties and "His Honour" (as she called her husband when he annoyed her) now began to make itself felt. At the peak of her active life, she found herself responsible for a peevish old man who objected to her habitual comings and goings. Permitting herself a sister's license, she wrote Mrs. Scott an angry letter about "Mr. M's" objecting to her visiting Mrs. Boscawen. "Do you not admire these lovers of liberty!" she exclaimed. "What do the generality of men mean by a love of liberty but the liberty to be saucy to their superiors, and arrogant to their inferiors, to resist the powers of others over them, and to exert their powers over others." That Mrs. Montagu would employ so parliamentary a style in reporting a domestic difference reminds us that in 1772 a transatlantic domestic difference was approaching a showdown.

While her aging husband declined into senility, the death of her old friend, Lord Lyttleton, was hastened by the conduct of his ungrateful and disloyal son. Tom's dissipations were, even by the spacious standards of his time, impressive. Mrs. Montagu was in the unhappy father's confidence and wrote her husband, "I had a most melancholy letter from Ld. Lyttleton last post. He has reason to entertain some apprehensions that his son has sold the Reversion of the Estate and as he says sign'd and seal'd his ruin. . . . Poor Ld. Lyttleton will never again take pleasure in Hagley doom'd and destined to fall to some usurer. What a pity he built his fine house."

Mrs. Montagu viewed with understandable skepticism Tom's marriage in 1772 to a prosperous widow who bore the promising name of Aphia Peach. She wrote to Mrs. Carter that, "It was hazard enough to marry Mr. Lyttleton but I find she married him before the settlements were made. If Mr. L generously makes the settlements now the lady is in his power I shall have great hopes of his continuing in a proper course of life." So much for the times when a widow could be tricked out of her inheritance! The bride proved no match for her conniving husband who soon left her. Within a year of the imprudent marriage Tom's infamies had deprived Lord Lyttleton of the will to live. He died during the summer of the following year.

Georgian parents, following Hanoverian examples, assumed no responsibility for vexatious children. It was never suggested that anything but a natural depravity was responsible for debauchés as varied as Edward Wortley Montagu, Jr., Tom Lyttleton or the future Prince Regent. Pursuant to this myopia, the letters of condolence received by Mrs. Montagu do not attempt an explanation for, nor a solution to, the excesses of him who, when he is remembered, is referred to as "bad" Lord Lyttleton. The modern world has gained in candor what it may have lost in grace. It is difficult to believe that an intelligent woman today would be unaware of the irony inherent in the tribute to Lord Lyttleton père addressed by Mrs. Montagu to Mrs. Vesey. "He was my instructor and my friend, the guide of my studies, the corrector of the result of them. He made my house a school of virtue to young people and a place of delight to the learned."

Lord Lyttleton, in marked contrast to Mr. Montagu and Lord Bath, was his self-proclaimed disciple's senior by a mere eleven years. It may be because they were more or less of the same generation that their correspondence avoids the fulsome formality of that of Mrs. Montagu and Lord Bath. To few others would she have written, "Your Lordship asks why I don't write verses. Did you ever hear of a coal owner who was a poet." And in place of censorious reflections on the gallantries of Catherine the Great, she continued with "I forgot to tell your Lordship I begin to be reconciled to the Czarina. If she is not a good woman, she is a great Prince." Avoiding the temptation to preen herself on the success of her *Essay on Shakespeare,* she wrote to him, under whose aegis she had first appeared in print, that if she ever again turned author, "it will be of a practical treatise on sauntering."

Lord Chesterfield, whose disappointment in his son equalled that of Lord Lyttleton, died also in 1773. His famous *Letters to his Son* were promptly published and pronounced by the virtuous to mark him the Machiavelli of the drawing room. Mrs. Montagu was as vehement in her condemnation as Dr. Johnson, writing that, "As language grows delicate morals grow bad, for ugly things get pretty names."

Mrs. Montagu, who had not had Mrs. Delany's opportunity to observe Chesterfield's compassionate administration of Ireland, saw in him only what he continues to symbolize, grace at the expense of principle. Little dreaming that his counsels of insincerity would grant him a place as assured as that of Hogarth in the social history of their times, she predicted oblivion. Writing to Mrs. Vesey during the summer of 1774, she pronounced that: "As to Lord Chesterfield he was a Witt and a fine Gentleman, and a Witt while he is talking, and a fine Gentleman while he is bowing and making compliments, is in each capacity a very pretty mortal; but dead it is come to nothing, it is over, it is gone, and like the sky rocket after a short excursion in its brightness drops into night."

She was on surer ground in her analysis of the combination of sound advice and immorality that characterize the *Letters*. Always on the alert for coxcombery, particularly of a French kind, she continued. "Lord Chesterfields letters will do a great deal of harm in general, at the same time parts of his instructions might be useful; all he says on the importance and value of time, and his exhortations to indefatigable and continual application are excellent. . . . The course of study he points out and the objects of observation he recommends to Persons who wish to serve as foreign Ministers deserve the utmost attention from all who would fill such employments. But when he recommends adultery under the soft term of gallant arrangement, when he recommends the selfish system of a french bel esprit in morals, and the trickishness of a chef de parti in polititicks, he becomes a pernicious Preceptor."

Mr. Montagu died just after the outbreak of the American Revolution. His last illness was long and difficult, with the result that his harassed wife wrote more of the sick room than of Concord and Lexington. She was left an extremely rich widow and the mistress of all her husband's holdings. After settling her estate and legally adopting her young nephew, Matthew, she travelled north to take possession of her coal mines. Her letters describing her assumption of the role so frequently abdicated by absentée landlords give a vivid picture of her maternalistic conduct of industry and agriculture.

Because Mr. Montagu had been a generous patron of his miners and their families, his widow "thought it right to show the good people they would have a kind landlady." Never one to confine her hospitality to "ton" or talent, Mrs. Montagu caused the inkeeper to assemble "together sirloins of beef, legs of mutton, loins of veal, chickens, ducks and green peas which with ham, pigeon pies, tarts and custard fill'd up every chink of the table."

The approach of the Industrial Revolution is prefigured in Mrs. Montagu's offhand mention that, at seven years of age, boys commenced to work in the collieries. However, in terms of her times she was far more imaginative about the plight of the poor than were

many of her fellow proprietors; she did not share the prevailing belief that literacy unsettles the peasantry. Several years before she
assumed ownership of her husband's mines, she arranged "with a
schoolmaster to teach 50 boys to read and write" and "a dame to
teach the girls the arts and mysteries of knitting and spinning." Despite these philanthropies she continued to have qualms about the
source of her wealth, writing, "I cannot yet reconcile myself to seeing my fellow creatures descend into the dark regions of the earth;
tho' to my great comfort I hear them singing in the pits." She was
equally concerned about the above-ground employees at Sandleford,
preferring their prosperity to her own: "I hope though I am a farmer
that prices of wheat will soon fall for the poor labourers cannot earn
a subsistence for their families when bread bears such a price." And
in another letter a sinister light is cast on electioneering methods
detrimental to the voters: "we have a prodigious crop of barley and
there seems to be a great plenty of it everywhere. . . . I suppose the
coming election will raise the price of malt. I wish our poor people
ate more and drank less."

Once more free to travel, Mrs. Montagu visited Paris during the
summer of 1776. In her character of Blue Stocking and Shakespearean scholar, it was her intention to study at first hand the puzzling
French. Beside the usual retinue of servants, her party included her
companion and ward, Miss Gregory, and little Matthew "Montagu,"
whose French accent required attention. The visit was made at a significant time. The Declaration of Independence was shortly to re-
open hostilities between France and England, which ended permanently only with Waterloo.

Mrs. Montagu's attitude toward her hosts was ambivalent. She
envied the prestige enjoyed by the salon hostesses but she resented
their association with Godless influences. She had essayed and, in
large degree succeeded, in promoting coteries that imitated those of
Paris in all but deism. A great deal of thought had gone into this.
She had been at pains to inform herself not only of the villainies of
the two arch-infidels, Voltaire and Rousseau, but also to learn that
Diderot was "noisy and talkative," d'Alembert "dry and decisive"
and that Helvetius had "great simplicity." The time had now come
for her to join the English visitors to the Paris salons.

Mrs. Montagu's letters from France of 1776 give a striking picture of the luxury, brilliance and squalor that marked the approach of the revolution. Her trip from Calais to Paris was filled with incident. Public transportation was a service maintained by the crown. It involved exorbitant rates, rutted roads, spavined nags and rotting rope harness. Inns were infested with vermin. At Amiens accommodations were so primitive that by opening the wrong door she found herself out of doors in a chicken coop.

Mrs. Montagu lost no time in re-creating herself in her London capacity of great lady. After putting Montagu into a French school, she took a house in Chaillot, engaged an excellent cook and went shopping. "I have more books," she writes to her brother, "than I can read, and more clothes than I can wear, and more lace than I can want. It is surprizing what money I have spent out of a principle of economy; because they are cheap I have bought more shoes than a millipede could wear in 7 years. By my caps you would think I had more heads than the Hydra. I have 3 footmen and a coachman in new liveries with gold shoulder knots on each shoulder, fine scarlet and gold dress for my postillion and six horses in my coach when I go any distance." Perhaps her most startling concession to French fashion was in applying makeup so lavishly that English travellers said she looked as though she had scarlet fever. Thus housed and turned out in Parisian style, she prepared to receive the Enlightenment.

Her comments about her guests and her hosts are very perfunctory. Although she tells her sister and Mrs. Vesey of meeting the Marquise du Deffand and Mme. Geoffrin, the scientists de Buffon and de Bomare and the philosopher, d'Alembert, it is with the tenor of French society that she is concerned rather than personalities. She was not of the race of travellers who go abroad to form or confirm prejudice. She was quick to praise the "ease, politeness, and grace in ye manners of ye people," adding in another letter that, "The women in grace of person and of manner excell us; they possess in the highest degree whatever can attract admiration; the men have the most agreeable way of signifying that admiration, the style and manner of conversation is extremely agreeable. I am often in society with the most celebrated beaux esprits, and they really are very captivating. I have not spent a dull or insipid hour in company since I came to Paris. I have met with great civilities, and must say that their attention to strangers is very amiable, and has a generosity and nobleness in it which I love and reverence."

Such stimulating gatherings required passing through filthy streets where swarmed the sullen poor. Upon reaching her host's hôtel she submitted to the ordeal of stairways and corridors that did double duty for the imperfectly housebroken. The society reached by these malodorous approaches was handicapped by unbroken urban leisure. No punishment was more dreaded than to be exiled for *lèse majesté* to one's distant château. The French *beaux esprits* substituted conversation for action and debate for reform. In the early years of the American Revolution, they had lost their footing on the common ground of humanity and were rushing toward dissolution. Without sensing the horrors ahead, Mrs. Montagu felt that, despite its respect for intellect and accomplishment, something was amiss with French aristocracy. She wrote somewhat sweepingly that, "Here is no conjugal faith, paternal care, filial affection, brotherly love except among a few, nor is there any domestic order."

Just prior to her return she sent a more temperate impression of Paris to her brother Morris: "On Wensday I am to sup at the Marquise de Deffants, a Lady much celebrated for her witt and vivacity, and who has always a polite and agreable Society about her. I have not yet had time to see half the Pictures and other things that are to be seen here, but shall endeavor to visit them before I leave Paris. My great object has been to get well acquainted with the french character, and my great amusement the french Society. I shall be glad I have been at Paris even when I have left it. I find a greater difference from us in their sentiments, their tastes, their modes of life, than I had imagined. The only object (except of a very few of the very great) is pleasure, they have not found out that perpetual diversion without a certain mixture of business, and duties, and intervals of retirement, tires. The Ladies pass from the toilette to the spectacles, and from thence to parties at supper. They cultivate with great care all the little graces, and as it is every Womans ambition to be amiable, there is a good (deal) of jealousy of each others charms. The Men endeavour to be agreable, and each Sex succeeds very well. But the first object should be to gain esteem. An English character is indeed often a beauty disgraced to a certain degree by being a sloven in manners, a french one is frequently ugliness well drest and adornd. I am far from thinking the french Women lead happier lives than we do. Domestick tendernesses, and even domestick cares, are suitable to our Natures. The change we make in our amusements and mode of life by spending the summer in the Country is I think much in our favour. You are a very indulgent Confessor in finding such good arguments in favour of my dissipation of my money, but indeed the notice that has been taken of me here made it proper for me to live in a different style from those English who only go to see the plays and operas; I have passed my time very agreably, and my health is improved, tho I undergo a great deal of fatigue, having scarcely half an hour free from visits or notes."

The recognition accorded Mrs. Montagu as a Shakespearean critic was increased by her Paris sojourn. That this was the case is ironically owing to Voltaire himself. Upon the appearance of a new French translation of some of the plays, he penned another denigration of Shakespeare, whose works he described as an enormous dunghill. This production was read by d'Alembert at a meeting of the Academy held in August on the Feast of St. Louis. Many guests were present, among them Mrs. Montagu. It was entirely in the character of the aged polemicist to stage a studied confrontation with those who crossed his path. This time the familiar challenge to conflict backfired. Mrs. Montagu was immediately the center of academicians who vied with one another in apologizing for the great man's lowering of the exalted tone of their gatherings. Would she reply? Was she hurt? This time the advantage was with her; she pressed it. "Me, Monsieur?" she replied, "Not at all! Voltaire is no friend of *mine*."

Having thus ended her anti-Voltaire campaign, Mrs. Montagu returned to Sandleford, writing, "I am once more metamorphosed into a plain Country Farmeress. I have the same love for my pigs, pride in my pottatoes, solicitude for my Poultry, care of my wheat, attention to my barley and application to the regulation of the dairy as formerly." In conclusion she commented on the fact that the French aristocracy could not comprehend the pleasures of rural life nor of fostering agricultural economy. Something, however, of the influence of Paris was at work. Shortly after her return in October of 1776, she purchased from the Portman family a ninety-nine-year lease of number twenty-two Portman Square and, with "Athenian" Stuart as her architect, began to build her magnificent house.

She never travelled abroad again. Henceforth her life was to be occupied with educating her nephew, the concerns of farming and mining, writing and receiving innumerable letters, and entertaining guests who by the hundreds partook of her lavish hospitality.

The letters written during her later years were much concerned with the political upheavals in America and France. Her references to these events are, like her *Essay on Shakespeare,* indicative of the opinions held at the time. Lacking the instant history of radio and television, news travelled not only slowly but inaccurately. When the British took Philadelphia and Washington retired to starvation at Valley Forge, it was believed that the revolution had been put down. Mrs. Montagu was encouraged in this illusion by her belittling estimate of the American character. Writing to Mrs. Carter in 1777, she thus analyzed the insurgents: "You will think me perhaps a little severe in what I have said of the Americans, I speak of them in general; there are some individuals in all Countries as excellent as the weakness of human nature will allow: But where there has not subsisted a good form of government and a regular system of Laws and mode of manners the people in general never are of a good character. Many of the Americans are descended from Ancestors who fled from settled government and established religion to follow their wayward fancies; to these have been added a motley crew of Bankrupts, of offenders of all kinds, of schemers and visionary adventurers, or desultory wanderers. No general resemblance of character, no general object of pursuit, no traditional opinions or habits, if I may be allowed the expression, establishd any uniformity of conduct. Many causes of adhesion and cohesion were wanting in the Community. Considered therefore in a Social view they were not in good training." It seems not to have occurred to our columnist that the colonists' supposed lack of discipline hardly did honor to the Mother Country.

By the spring of 1778, England's dissatisfaction with Lord North's conduct of the war was increased by the arrival on American shores of French aid. Mrs. Montagu's regrets were as social as they were patriotic. Her visit to Paris had procured her many French correspondents and friends from whom she would now be separated. With pardonable flippancy, she wrote, "There are rumours of a French War but I believe it will not be declared before next Wednesday as I am that day to dine at Mr. de Noailles."

French intervention into what had begun as a family difference obliterated English confidence in prompt and easy victory. Soon it was being proposed that England grant the Americans the independence they demanded. Protesting these counsels of capitulation, Lord Chatham rose from his deathbed and addressed Parliament in an unforgettable scene.

Although Mrs. Montagu was not present, she wrote an impassioned account of what the Pitt family had told her of the Great Commoner's last speech. "The energy of his mind imparted force enough to his body to enable him to rise. He said he rejoiced that the Grave had spared him to this time, that he might declare himself against granting independence to America, and then he went on reprobating what had been said of the weakness and inability of this Country . . . but the sentiments were too great for utterance, the subject too important, too august he fell into a convulsion fit; he continued in the fit and the House in consternation. . . ." Thus melodramatically closed the gigantic career of William Pitt. He was carried home to die.

The author of the *Essay on Shakespeare* had, by virtue of her subject, repudiated the classical unities decreeing that violent actions shall take place offstage. Pursuant to this aesthetic, she felt it would have been better theatre for the patriot statesman to expire in the public performance of his office. With more grandiloquence than humor she thus rewrote the celebrated scene. "I have always admired the close of this great Orator's Periods but surely death wd be the most emphatick! And of all the figures in rhetoric a convulsion at such a time seems the finest."

Chatham's death signalled a low point in British morale. Mrs. Montagu concluded her heroics with "we are become a scoundrel nation worthy to be scorned and fit to be cudgell'd." Renewed warfare with France, with its threat of invasion of the Kentish coast, seemed in 1779 only too likely to fulfill her masochistic wishes. She could hear from Sandleford the guns of Portsmouth and trembled to think what this windborne roar portended. England's American fortunes declined on both sides of the Atlantic. The French alliance furnished, in addition to manpower, ports and ships. The Scottish sailor of fortune, John Paul Jones, commanded a French East Indiaman, renamed the *Bonne Homme Richard* in deference to *Poor*

Richard's Almanack. With this ship and an escort of the French navy, he menaced all the coast from Kent to Scotland. Directly in his path lay Mrs. Montagu's North Country holdings. She wrote to Mrs. Carter, who feared an attack on her native Deal, "I hope he will not victual his Fleet with my good oxen at Jarrow." Her trepidations were only too well founded. In September of 1779 Jones encountered the H.M.S. *Serapis* leading a convoy from the Baltic. A battle ensued, resulting, with heavy loss of life, in the capture of the *Serapis* off Scarborough. Mrs. Montagu's "Black People," as she called her miners, now demanded arms to protect themselves from the raiders. Her refusal to comply strikes an ominous note in regard to the industrial horrors of less than twenty years away. Not only was a female coal owner unqualified to play a general's part, but "it w'd be dangerous to teach them the military discipline and have arms that they might on improper occasions sieze upon." Improper occasions played a sinister role in late eighteenth-century history.

Among the most lurid of these were the Gordon Riots. They were fomented by Lord George Gordon in protest against Catholic relief measures that were under consideration by Parliament. We are accustomed to think of anarchists as products of poverty. In June of 1780 London was set ablaze by mobs led by a fanatical peer. Prisons were stormed, convicts set loose, distilleries invaded and the Bank of England threatened. Some three hundred persons were killed and many executed. By a shocking miscarriage of justice, the author of these atrocities was acquitted. Mrs. Montagu wrote from Sandleford that the mob rule formerly exploited by John Wilkes had established a perilous precedent; "those risings taught the mob to command and we their subjects to obey. Is Ld. George Gordon to murder as many men and burn as many houses as he pleases. . . . I shall most willingly allow blue flags and no popery to be put on my houses. I have learnt by sad experience that in this Land of Liberty one must illuminate and inscribe and wear the livery imposed not by the government indeed but by the ungoverned."

Unless bloodshed occurred in the neighboring streets or coastal waters, events of prime historical significance did little to change Georgian England's social patterns. The "ton" flocked to *The School for Scandal,* to the pleasure gardens of Ranelagh and Vauxhall and even to Bedlam, where lunatics were exhibited. Blue gatherings proliferated. Johnson, both at Streatham and his Literary Club, was at the top of his form, as were Boswell and Mrs. Thrale. Everyone read *Evelina* and, after its publication in 1778, carefully timid Fanny Burney was overnight metamorphosed into a stellar member of the Stratham coterie. In this capacity she met and recorded in her *Diary* the Queen of the Blues. The self-consciousness that accompanied her meeting persons of note must have been much increased by Dr. Johnson's facetious suggestion that she do verbal battle with Mrs. Montagu. "Down with her, Burney!—down with her! spare her not! attack her, fight her and down with her at once! You are a rising wit, and she is at the top. . . . So at her Burney—at her and down with her."

Fanny had shrewdly surmised that Streatham gave "the first of women in the literary way" an unwilling admiration. Her subsequent comments indicate that Hester Thrale and Elizabeth Montagu were rivals in hospitality and maintained a wary, albeit seemly, truce. "Mrs. Montagu is middlesized, very thin and looks infirm; she has a sensible and penetrating countenance and the air and manner of a woman used to being distinguished and of great parts." Fanny knew that the lady had been accused of "trying" for this same air and manner; "However" continued the journalist, "nobody can now impartially see her and not confess that she has extremely well succeeded."

Fanny Burney, whose skill in reporting conversation did not tarry far behind that of Boswell, is one of our few sources for hearing rather than reading Mrs. Montagu. Her talk was easy, friendly and quite removed from the stately periods of her letters. Upon Dr. Johnson's asking her if he might be expected to be invited to Portman Square, the hearty reply was, "Ay sure, or else I shan't like it: but I invite you all to a house warming. I shall hope for the honour of seeing all this company at my new house next Easter day: I fix the day now that it may be remembered."

Mrs. Montagu's majestic tastes in literature had thus far caused her to leave the reading of *Evelina* to others. As befitted the author of the *Essay on Shakespeare*, she was frankly proud that a work so commended should be a woman's. Learning that Fanny was even now writing her short-lived comedy, *The Witlings*, Mrs. Montagu offered to play patroness, saying, "if Miss Burney does write a play I beg I may know of it; or if she thinks proper see it; and all my influence is at her service. We shall all be glad to assist in spreading the fame of Miss Burney." What Fanny thought of being taken under Mrs. Montagu's capacious wing she did not reveal to her readers.

Mrs. Thrale's capsule description of her rival remains unequalled: "Yesterday I had a conversazione. Mrs. Montagu was brilliant in diamonds, solid in judgment, critical in talk." The theatre of these excellencies was soon to be the great house in Portman Square, which was even now nearing completion.

She possessed to a marked degree the delight in domestic and landscape architecture characteristic of her time and class. While "Athenian" Stuart, James Gandon, Robert Adam, Cipriani and Angelica Kauffman respectively erected and embellished Montagu House, "Capability" Brown improved Sandleford. Offsetting the financial hardships of war was a rise in the price of coal brought about by increasing urbanization. Thus Mrs. Montagu was able not only to spend lavishly but also to avoid the reigning curse of debt. As the work advanced she wrote of the "satisfaction of getting a receipt in full of all demands from the various artificers." Characteristically, she prided herself as much upon housewifery as upon scholarship. She added, "I own my taste is unfashionable but there is to me a wonderful charm in those words 'in full of all demands.' . . . The worst of haunted houses in my opinion are those haunted by duns."

In 1780 Mrs. Montagu celebrated her sixtieth birthday. She planned for old age as carefully as for her earlier projects. In future she would give herself over to the gratifications of house pride and to launching her nephew. She evidently knew that the new establishment in Portman Square laid her open to charges of having learned in Paris to give herself airs, for she wrote with unwonted self-justification, "I am sure such noble apartments will be a great addition to my pleasures. In the winter of the year and the winter of our life our principal enjoyments must be in our own house." As work progressed she confided that, "I am more and more in love with my new House. . . . My dwelling is so convenient and cheerful as a place of retirement, so ample for the devoirs of Society and so calculated for Assemblies that it will suit all one's humors and adapt itself to all one's purposes."

Her chief purpose was to create a setting that would please and perhaps dazzle. She built in accordance with the principle that would later be decried as conspicuous consumption. In a letter to her sister-in-law, she permitted herself ostentation that she would almost certainly have avoided with more critical correspondents. "Mr. Adams has made me a cieling, a chimney piece and doors which are pretty enough to make me a thousand enemies. Envy turns livid at the first sight of them."

Even so carping a visitor as Horace Walpole approved, writing in February of 1782 that he dined "at Mrs. Montagu's new palace and was much surprised. Instead of vagaries it is a noble simple edifice. Magnificent, yet no gilding. It is grand, not tawdry."

The county seats of the peerage furnished their owners with opportunities to make nature subservient to the exhibition of riches. It was perhaps because she derived her fortune from the land that Mrs. Montagu refused to distort the fertile fields of Sandleford. Here improvements were in the care of Lancelot Brown who, she wrote, had "not neglected any of its capabilities. . . . We shall not erect temples to heathen Gods, build proud bridges over humble rivulets or do any of the marvellous things suggested by caprice and indulged by the wantonness of wealth." "Capability" Brown died before the work was done, leaving Mrs. Montagu to carry out his plans. Eclectic hostess that she was, she feasted "all the work people employed under the direction of Mr. Brown in adorning and embellishing the pleasure ground."

The most colorful example of Mrs. Montagu's hospitality was her annual May Day party for London's chimney sweeps. Since coal had built her splendid house, coal's lowliest servants should be there received. Readers of Fanny Burney have their own reasons to be grateful for Mrs. Montagu's drop in drudgery's bucket. When in her old age Fanny wrote her *Memoirs of Dr. Burney,* she had attained a pomposity of rhetoric for which Macaulay holds Dr. Johnson responsible. Mrs. Montagu's compensatory cookout wrung from the "memorialist" (as Fanny styled herself) the following lofty lines: "Not all the lyrics of all the rhymsters, nor all the warblings of all the spring-feathered choristers could hail the opening smiles of May like the fragrance of that roasted beef and the pulpy softness of those puddings of plums with which Mrs. Montagu yearly renovated those sooty little agents to the safety of our most blessed luxury."

Mrs. Montagu planned her nephew with as much care as her house. Forewarned by the progress of such rakes as John Wilkes, "bad" Lord Lyttleton and young Edward Wortley Montagu, she took every precaution that her heir should follow in his aunt's sober footsteps rather than those of his frivolous mother. She preferred for him an English education, believing that the fashionable Grand Tour fostered fopperies and restlessness. His school was Harrow and his university Cambridge. The resources of these establishments were augmented by a private tutor, who assured attention to studies and avoidance of dangerous companions. By such means the childless aunt prepared the future Baron Rokeby to take his place in Parliament, to administer the lands to which he was heir, and to share in her concern for people of every condition.

She thus defined the social philosophy she desired for her nephew: "I have always pittied a certain set of people who some years ago called themselves the 'little world,' it is so much better to be of the general world. I would not have a man to confine his regards to witts, scholars, philosophers, politicians or fine gentlemen and ladies but to be able to converse with ease, and hearken with intelligence to persons of every rank, degree and occupation. The man who has only the graces of the drawingroom, and the tone of conversation of any particular set of men is little superior to what a monkey would be who had the articulate talents of a parrot."

The Queen of the Blues must have been sorely tempted to foster in her young nephew the precocity then so widely mistaken for intelligence. A short time before she adopted Matthew Montagu, she set down comments on child psychology that are at variance with the eighteenth-century belief that boys and girls are undersized men and women. It would be hard to improve on the following: "Minds ripen at very different ages. If the understanding is naturally slow, preceptors should be patient and not put it too much out of its natural pace. Some children apprehend quick; others acquire everything with difficulty. In the latter case, they should be encouraged, led and not driven." Recollections of Fidget's dancing days also modified the scholarly preferences of Minerva Montagu. Writing to her sister-in-law, Mrs. William Robinson, she reported Matthew's progress in horsemanship and dancing, adding, "I approve my dear neice's ambition to excel in dancing a minouet . . . a little ball, a frolick now and then is very good for young persons."

Matthew advanced from Harrow to Trinity College, Cambridge, in 1779. His school-leaving was marked by performing at Speech Day in the character of Medea. Fortified by this transvestite elocution, he was to win distinction in English declamation at Cambridge and eventually to second the King's Address to the House of Commons.

The great house in Portman Square was ready for occupany in December of 1781. As a finishing touch to its amenities, Mrs. Montagu ordered feather tapestries that metamorphosed brown tails of partridges, neck feathers of geese and the exotic plumage of macaws and peacocks into tulips and bluebells. It was a painstaking project requiring contributions from the cooks and gamekeepers of stately homes. Not until 1791 were the efforts of Mrs. Montagu and her stitching staff deemed worthy to be inspected by Queen Charlotte and an assortment of royal daughters. The chatelaine's response to this honor would not have been unworthy of Mrs. Delany; it was an occasion no "pen can describe, no paper contain."

On the eve of taking possession of her new home, Mrs. Montagu had reason (or thought she had) to withdraw her housewarming invitation to the Streatham coterie. A tempest in an inkpot intervened. The second volume of Johnson's *Lives of the Poets* appeared in 1781; it concludes with a sketch of Lord Lyttleton so belittling and perfunctory that it merits no place in a work containing the extraordinary *Life of Richard Savage*. Mrs. Montagu was doubly loyal to Lyttleton. He had been more than a friend. To him she owed being in print. As pannings go, Johnson's strictures on Lyttleton were mild but, in that they implied the professional author's condescension to the dilettante, they infuriated his protégée. Throwing both sense of humor and proportion aside, she likened her differences with the Doctor to Lady Mary's quarrel with Pope of sixty years earlier. She wrote at length of "the envy and the malice and the railing of such wretches as Dr. Johnson who bear in their hearts the secret hatred of hypocrites to genuine virtue and the contempt of Pedants for real genius. . . . I wish his figure was put as a frontispiece to his works, his squinting look and monstrous form would well explain his character. Those disgraces which make a good mind humble and complacent ever render a bad one envious and ferocious. Lady Mary Wortley Montagu says of a deformed Person who had satirized her, 'Twas in the uniformity of fate that one so hateful should be born to Hate.' "

It has been said that no quarrel is about what it appears to be about. Both Mrs. Montagu and Dr. Johnson set up for conversational suns around which docile satellites revolved. Each desired listeners, preferably of the reverent sort. Neither the Queen nor the Sage could bring the other to heel. If Lord Lyttleton had not detonated the drawing-room bomb, someone or something else would have done so.

Dr. Johnson, despite his intemperate bigotry, was not, as was Pope, vindictive. Still soothed by Streatham's hospitality, flattered by those who hung on his every word, and at the top of his literary fame, he could afford to play peacemaker, commenting wryly that "Mrs. Montagu has dropped me. Now Sir, there are people whom one should like very well to drop but would not wish to be dropped by."

The death, shortly after the appearance of *Lives of the Poets,* of Henry Thrale triggered the tumultuous dissolution of the Streatham coterie. It was one thing for erratic Dr. Johnson to be the stellar attraction of Thrale's overloaded table (he died of apoplexy induced by gluttony). It was another to be flung into a tête-à-tête with the still-young Hester who, thanks to Boswell, Fanny Burney and to her own *Thraliana,* is as well documented a widow as Queen Victoria.

The Thrale marriage was, like that of the Montagus, based on compatibility rather than passion. Here the resemblance ceases. Mrs. Montagu herself has told us that she was immune to the temptations of the flesh. Mrs. Thrale's capacity for romantic love had smouldered, unperceived by herself and her friends, through a perfunctory marriage, only to overwhelm her when she was in her forties. This Sleeping Beauty story has stimulated an entire literature of attack and defense.

The bridegroom-elect was her daughter's singing teacher, Gabriel Piozzi. As a musician, an Italian and a Catholic he offended against the prevailing marriage ethic, which had changed very little since Lady Mary's runaway romance. The leader of the opposition was Dr. Johnson. The comforts of Streatham were threatened, as were his theories of class, to which he gave the chilling name of subordination. Mrs. Montagu's hospitality to persons of every walk in life did not liberalize her views on suitable marriages. Her condemnation of unfortunate, infatuated Hester Thrale was as unyielding as that of her enemy, Dr. Johnson.

Hostility, like politics, makes strange bedfellows. Dr. Johnson, having needlessly deprived himself of the future Mrs. Piozzi's friendship, now desired to regain that of Mrs. Montagu. He was, as Boswell tells us "vain of the society of ladies." The death of blind Anna Williams, to whom, it will be recalled, Mrs. Montagu had earlier granted an annuity, provided means of reconciliation. Still lost in self-pity because "my mistress" had exchanged his querulous presence for that of her deplorable fiancé, he wrote to Mrs. Montagu and received a reply "not only civil but tender so I hope peace is proclaimed. I am now come to that time when I wish all bitterness and animosity to be at an end. I have never done her any serious harm nor would I;— though I could give her a bite! but she must provoke me much first. In volatile talk, indeed, I may have spoken of her not much to her mind; for in the tumult of conversation malice is apt to grow sprightly and there I hope I am not yet decrepit."

We owe to this reconciliation one of the most eloquent of Johnson's characterizations. In discussing with Boswell the attainments of Elizabeth Carter, Hannah More and Fanny Burney, he said of his recent opponent, "Sir, Mrs. Montagu does not make a trade of her wit but Mrs. Montagu is a very extraordinary woman; she has a constant stream of conversation and it is always impregnated; it always has meaning."

Mrs. Montagu's distaste for the supposed recklessness of her rival's eleventh-hour romance did not incline her to suspend her loyalty to the late Lord Lyttleton. A week after Johnson's death, which occurred in December of 1784, she shrewdly diagnosed his difficult temperament. "The news will inform you that Living Poets need not fear Dr. Johnson should write their memoirs after they are no longer able to refute calumny. I hear he dyed with great piety and resignation; and indeed he had many virtues and perhaps ill health and narrow circumstances gave him a peevish censorious turn. I am afraid Mrs. Thrale's imprudent marriage shortened his life." To Mrs. Montagu and her circle it seemed by no means preposterous that Mrs. Thrale at forty-three should sacrifice living-happily-ever-after to the last years of an elderly neurotic.

Cupid had further mischief in store. The following description of a day spent with her family at Sandleford glows with a warmth that was due to more than landscape or feather-work: "Our party consists of the fair Gregory, my nephew Montagu, his tutor, and your humble servant. If the weather is fine the young men take a ride in the morning, and about noon return to their Studies. Mademoiselle Greg drives me in a whiskey 'over the hills and far away.' We return before dinner long enough for the business of the toilette, and an hour of reading for the young lady, and the domestic regulations of Madame, and supervising the workwomen who are employed in a prodigious undertaking of embroidery in feathers; at four o'clock we sit down together to dinner with the good appetite, good spirits and good humour which fresh air, moderate exercise and excursions through the beautiful scenes of nature at this fine season of the year must naturally create; to this succeeds our pot of coffee, not laced with politicks, then tea is brought but with it comes not scandal, tittle tattle or calumny of any sort. We saunter together till within an hour of sunset, then I retire to my dressing room, the young folks still walk till nearly nine; they repair to their studies till 10, then comes supper mirth and laughter. I take my little supper in my dressing room by which I get some leisure time and leave my young people to indulge that innocent gaiety of conversation so becoming their time of life." Ignoring the fact that, *Mansfield Park* notwithstanding, a brother-sister environment seldom leads to the altar, Mrs. Montagu hoped her ward and her nephew would marry.

Dorothea Gregory's visit in 1783 to her Scottish relatives put an end to the matchmaker's dreams. Mrs. Montagu's fury upon learning that her "ungrateful" ward preferred a penniless clergyman to her nephew and heir does little credit to her excellent principles of friendship and patronage. She behaved, if possible, as badly as Dr. Johnson and, being of a commonsensical nature, with far less excuse.

Matthew's marriage to Elizabeth Charlton followed hard on that of Miss Gregory to the Rev. Archibald Allison. His choice of bride was calculated to mollify his possessive aunt. Miss Charlton was a ward in Chancery who lived with her grandmother. To the advantage of being an orphan she united a large fortune. Mrs. Montagu, who had longed for a parentless daughter-in-law in Miss Gregory, now found one in Miss Charlton.

Wedding customs have changed greatly during the last two centuries. Many, if not most, Georgians considered the sacrament of matrimony of too intimate a nature to admit of social celebrations. The wedding trip is also a recent ritual. In the eighteenth century the bride simply exchanged her home for that of the bridegroom, attended perhaps by one of her sisters lest she should be lonely.

Matthew Montagu and Elizabeth Charlton were married in London during the summer of 1785. Pursuant to the privacy principle, only close relatives were present. Mrs. Montagu described this occasion to her sister-in-law, Mrs. William Robinson, in a delightful letter that serves not only as social history but also as self-revelation. She opens upon a classical note: "Venus no longer sends her car and doves but a post chaise with 4 able horses and two brisk postillions as well." It was entirely consistent with the customs of the time and with Aunt Montagu's executive proclivities that she oversee the honeymoon, which was to take place at Sandleford. Her letter continues, "The decent dignity of the bride's behaviour and the delicacy of the bridegroom's did them honour and gave me great pleasure and," she concludes in a passage startling to today's mothers-in-law, "we are three as happy people as can be found in any part of the habitable globe."

As a substitute for Punch and his never-to-be bride, Matthew and the younger Elizabeth Montagu were an unqualified success. The devoted aunt early discovered that her nephew was of sound intelligence rather than brilliance and rejoiced that this was the case. Her comments about him suggest that she knew something of the impression she herself gave to others. Again writing to Mrs. William Robinson, she sounds what may have been a wistful note: "The most brilliant persons are not always the happiest or the most esteem'd; more rarely still the best beloved. Too much presumption in their excellencies, too little indulgence to the defects of others if it does not totally destroy our admiration certainly eliminates our affection and it is far better to be beloved than admired." If, as it was supposed, love had passed her by, she would have had it otherwise.

Mrs. Montagu was now sixty-five. The last fifteen years of her busy life coincided with one of history's most crucial periods. The world she was to leave in 1800 bore little resemblance to the one she had entered in 1720. Revolution had challenged the foundations not only of government, but also of philosophy, religion, science and the arts. Of the myriad upheavals transpiring around her, Mrs. Montagu's accounts are significant because they reveal the attitude of patrician England on the eve of the Napoleonic wars. She viewed "democratical" principles, as did her world, in much the same way that Wall Street views Karl Marx. Jefferson's momentous statement that government derives its just powers from the governed could not be reconciled to her maternal ethic of feasting chimney sweeps and miners. The horrors of the French Revolution were to be magnified in her orthodox eyes because they had atheistic associations. No good could come of the anticlerical machinations of the blasphemous encyclopedists. Being of the widely shared belief that the French were a frippery folk, she refused to take them seriously as revolutionaries. She wrote to her sister-in-law of the disorders already gaining momentum. "I cannot, by the best information form any conjecture how the fermentations in France will end. I rather think the spirit of liberty they have imported from America will be beat up into the froth of remonstrances and satires than have any solid effect." This comforting contempt was of short duration.

As the *Ancien Régime* broke down into scandal and bankruptcy, rumors proliferated. Mrs. Montagu wrote to her nephew in 1787, two years before the storming of the Bastille, that letters received from abroad gave "such an account of the situation of affairs and the temper of the people as makes one imagine that there will be some great revolution in France." The impending economic collapse received the sort of explanation that feeds on public demoralization. "The french King, I must not call him his most Christian Majesty," continued Mrs. Montagu, "is continually drunk, in this state his Queen . . . and other favorites of her Majesty obtained orders for immense sums . . . hence proceeded the enormous deficiency. . . ." Marie Antoinette was supposed, in addition to having personally squandered the national reserves, to surpass Catherine the Great in gallantry. This malicious lie was, like the let-them-eat-cake story, believed by otherwise intelligent people, including Minerva Montagu. She went on to declare "the affair of the Children's legitimacy very doubtfull and therefore a Revolution not improbable. Report assigns to each Royal Infant a different Father but if her Majesty is as bad as is reported they may all keep their usual title 'les enfans de France.' "

Mrs. Montagu's old age was marked by an increase of letters received over letters written. Among the most interesting of the former came from Matthew Montagu. One of them bears the intriguing date

of July 1789. It was evidently written before the 14th of that fateful
month. Had the Bastille already fallen the fledgling M.P. would
hardly have proposed to travel to France to assist the abolitionist,
William Wilberforce, in his campaign against slavery. His letter explains to his elderly aunt why such a reform must be international.
"The principal argument against the Abolition of the Slave Trade is
the danger of throwing into the hands of other powers what you are
about to relinquish and by that means transferring the advantage
without destroying the practice." It was the idealists' naïve plan to
settle in a Paris suburb (by which Versailles may be inferred) and
"there to live as quietly as is consistent with the great business." Mrs.
Montagu lost no time in pointing out that the French were too occupied in abolishing slavery within their own country to be concerned with the "peculiar institution" elsewhere.

Technology, like political and social change, was moving at a
pace too fast to be absorbed. Mrs. Montagu did not live to see her
"black people" subjected to the dehumanizing influence of the Industrial Revolution upon mining. These agonizing developments
were to confront her nephew and heir. There were, in addition to
industrial change, innovations in other fields. Eighteenth-century
balloonists were ancestors of today's aviators and astronauts. One of
them, Lunardi, caused as great a stir in England of 1784 as did Lind-
bergh in America of 1927. Mrs. Montagu's scientific imagination was
by no means fired by the balloon's faltering flight from fields adjacent to her mines. "Many hands," she scolded, "were by this means
taken off their labor. I must say for the honour of my Pitmen they
were not diverted from their duty either by curiosity or bad example." So much for the new ocean upon which mankind has learned
to sail.

Although Mrs. Montagu's attitude toward political and scientific
change was a backward rather than a forward glance, she kept abreast
of the innumerable literary developments that had, and were, taking
place around her. She was not among those to whom Jane Austen
addressed her famous defense of the novel in *Northanger Abbey*.
Somewhat surprisingly, she preferred Fanny Burney's *Cecilia* to *Evelina*. It was her habit to endanger her elderly eyes by reading in the
jolting carriage that bore her on her ceaseless journeys from Portman
Square to Sandleford and to the North Country. "Many a measured

mile and letterd post have I passed insensibly and unheeded by being engaged in some frolic with Tom Jones, or absorbed in the wonderful adventures of Robinson Crusoe. I can with great truth assure
you, I shall look on my long journey with much less apprehension
by having *Cecilia* for my fellow Traveller. If Cecilia has half the
sense and half the amiability of Miss Burney, I shall find improvement and delight in her company." When in 1786 "Cecilia Burney"
was imprisoned by Windsor's leaden magnificence, Mrs. Montagu
joined in mistaken rejoicing that her talents had been thus rewarded.

Factors of time and failing eyesight prevented Mrs. Montagu
from completing the transition from the poetry of Pope to that of
Wordsworth. Despite her pride in the affinity she believed to exist
between herself and poets, her correspondence contains only two
names to be found in the *Oxford Book of English Verse*. They are
those of Thomas Gray and William Cowper. If she read William
Blake or Robert Burns she was not impelled to comment.

Although the most important poets of the Romantic Movement
passed her by, their spirit did not. This sympathy with things to
come is evident not only in the Shakespeare *Essay* but also in an eloquent letter written to Sylph Vesey in 1777. It is an excellent example of the then rejection of classical values. Mrs. Montagu wrote, "I
. . . walked where Pope had walked and sat where he had sat; but
alas! I came back as prosaic as I went. . . . I admire and honor Mr.
Pope, he is a charming writer, and has every perfection a satirist and
moral writer can have but that something which marks a poet divine,
that lifts him 'above the visible diurnal sphere,' that gives him
visions of worlds unknown, makes him sing like a seraphim, tune his
harp to the music of the spheres, and raise enchantments around him,
was not in the said Mr. Pope; so tho' I pay him great respect I keep
my enthusiastick adoration for the great magicians who work supernatural wonders." Knowing nothing of *The Ancient Mariner,* nor of
the spells to be cast by Byron, Scott, Shelley and Keats, Mrs. Montagu found her wizards in Shakespeare, Milton and Spenser. She
shared with the poets of the immediate future a return to previous
romanticism. Long before the emergence of Wordsworth or of Matthew Arnold, she was in tune with the fervor of "Milton, thou
should'st be living at this hour" and of "Others abide our question.
Thou art free."

Of the women who appear in these pages, Mrs. Montagu had the widest scope. Lacking the bitter genius of Lady Mary, the gracious inventiveness of Mrs. Delany and the imagination of Fanny Burney, she became by virtue of efficiency, versatility and hard work a key figure of her times. She was challenged rather than inhibited by patrician England's traditional mistrust of clever women. Her immense fortune, augmented by her own business skills, was largely given over to providing a forum for literary London. Her mind and her more limited heart were as open as her purse and house. Although she commanded and relished admiration, she did not surround herself with sycophants, but numbered among her friends those who surpassed her as authors and scholars. The Age of Johnson was rich not only in platonic friendships but also in the loyal support which emerging authoresses proffered one another.

She had her detractors, especially among those who marched to the Johnson drum. People who take themselves seriously are apt to be laughed at, and Mrs. Montagu took herself very seriously indeed. It is hard to see how it could have been otherwise. Breaking new ground requires insistence that often leads to exaggeration. So few women, prior to the nineteenth century, ventured into print that those who did so constituted a minority, with the minority syndrome of self-consciousness.

Today's school jargon would term Mrs. Montagu an overachiever. She exploited to its limits each of her several abilities. She did not stop at what came to her easily; indeed, reading some of her more pedantic letters, we are inclined to regret that this was the case. To her activities as a coal owner and a farmer she brought not only compassion but also furnished practical, if paternalistic, answers to human needs. She espoused the reigning social approach to arts and letters that found its most skillful exponents in the "ruelles" * of the *Ancien Régime.* Under her aegis the salon in England reached its zenith.

A Sister of the Quill, Hannah More, who outdid Mrs. Montagu not only in publication but also in philanthropy, spoke of her as admiringly as had Dr. Johnson. "With Mrs. Montagu's faults I have nothing to do. From my first entrance into a London life till her

---

* The *Precieuses Ridicules* usually received in their bedrooms. The *ruelle* was the space between the bed and the wall.

death I ever found her an affectionate, zealous and constant friend as well as a most instructive and pleasant companion."

The revolutionary climate of her last years caused Mrs. Montagu to fear for the future of her adopted family. Three years before she died, she commended them to God's care. "When I consider the great blessings I enjoy in . . . my dear Montagu, his wife and lovely babes I blame myself for any suppression of spirits; but some times when I see the dear Family all gayly sporting before my windows, terrors of an invasion or of Civil dissensions seize me; and this I am conscious is criminal as well as painful for the mind and heart should in all circumstances only say Gods Will be done."

She barely crossed the threshold of the nineteenth century. Elizabeth Robinson Motagu died on August 25, 1800. With her husband and infant son, she is buried in the nave of Winchester Cathedral. Not far away lies Jane Austen, whom the Queen of the Blues would have been proud to welcome to the Feather Room.

5

THE PIONEER

Fanny Burney

1752-1840

FANNY BURNEY was by birth and environment well suited to serve as
a bridge between the lady letter writers of the past and the women
novelists of the future. Her forebears were sturdy West Country folk
who had their way to make. The patrician and prosperous Hester
Thrale judged the Burneys to be "a very low race of mortals," forgetting, perhaps, that she was indebted to just such a family for Dr.
Johnson, the bookseller's son who was the focal point of her tea-table
career.

As the Burneys prospered, producing in the process musicians,
authors and scholars, Fanny's social horizon was greatly enlarged. To
their house in St. Martin's Street flocked persons of fashion, talent and
notoriety. *Evelina*'s success transformed the shy girl into the shy
celebrity. Fanny's literary material came to include the "ton," the
Blue Stockings and eventually royalty itself.

Fanny's career as an author owes a great deal to Charles Burney's
activities in the performing and teaching of music, and especially to
his musicological writings. He was one of England's most gifted and
original musicians of the post-Händelian period. In his youth he had
come from Shrewsbury to be apprenticed to Thomas Augustine
Arne, his superior in composition and his inferior in virtue. Burney's
abilities and personal attractions destined him to unremitting activity. His were the keyboard instruments; he also composed and, just

prior to Fanny's immurement at court, had hoped to succeed Sir John Stanley as leader of the royal orchestra.

A significant part of Dr. Burney's career was concerned with drawing-room music. In his music room in St. Martin's Street was performed repertoire that has since been transferred to the public auditorium. He became, by virtue of his professional abilities and charm of manner, companion to persons of superior antecedents such as his first patron, Fulke Greville. In later years he purveyed all day and well into the night instruction to fashionable performers, among them the Thrales' daughter, Queeney. As befitted a musician-impresario with a following both patrician and talented, he emulated his literary and artist contemporaries by creating a salon of music.

Burney's attainments in teaching, performance and management, public and private, would have served to secure him a place in the annals of Georgian music. His major work, however, lay elsewhere.

Prior to the late eighteenth century, innumerable treatises on music had appeared. Scientists before the Christian era had emphasized the mathematical nature of sound. Samuel Pepys had frequented the Royal Society to hear discussions on vibrations and acoustics. During Burney's lifetime the encyclopedists, Diderot and d'Alembert, wrote about the physics of music. Nor was there any lack of books of more practical instruction. From the Elizabethan, Morley, to Burney's contemporary, Leopold Mozart, performers and teachers of performers had written on method and theory. It remained for Dr. Burney and, to a lesser degree, his rival Sir John Hawkins, to chronicle music in the light of cultural history. Dr. Burney's *General History* added a new dimension to music by admitting it to the humanities.

Charles Burney approached this monumental task by investigating the music and music-making of his own time. During Fanny's girlhood he absented himself for long periods to observe the *Present State of Music* on the Continent. Fortified by the success of the resultant two publications, he assembled with the help of his several daughter-scribes the *General History of Music* which remains his most important achievement.

Thus it was that the girl Fanny studied at two schools, both of them furnished by her own home and family. She studied conversation and personality from her father's guests; she absorbed the techniques of writing as she copied his manuscripts.

Fanny Burney

Fanny's environment, as befitted the family-dependent young lady of her day, was created by parents, brothers and sisters. She was the third of many children. Her own mother, Esther Sleepe, perhaps worn out by the rapid succession of six babies, died when Fanny was a child. Dr. Burney remarried. His second wife, the widow of Steven Allen of King's Lynn, contributed three young people to the Burney household. Two more children were born to the second marriage, bringing to ten the number of Fanny's companions.

As a training school for writing it would be difficult to improve on the Burney ménage. There was always a large cast of characters at hand. Then too, these were promising children. Fanny's elder sister, Hetty, married a first cousin, Charles Rousseau Burney. They were both virtuoso harpsichordists, and may well have been one of the earliest of husband and wife duos. The second child, James, in service at ten years old under Captain Cook, carried the thrust of empire to the South Seas. A younger brother, Charles, was destined for fame as a classics scholar. Among the Allen children who joined the Burney family, the most striking was Maria, a madcap adolescent to be loved and, with luck, restrained. Dearest of all was Susan, Fanny's younger sister who, with Nobody and "Daddy" Crisp, was to be the principal participant in epistolary confidences.

The children of the second marriage contributed to the intellectual traditions of the household. Dr. Burney's youngest daughter, Sara Harriote, became, like her half-sister, Fanny, a writer.

Mrs. Thrale, who saw no reason to account for her own literary interest, was puzzled by this busy clan. In her *Thraliana* she analyzed the spectacle of such industry. "The Family of Burney are a very surprizing Set of People; their Esteem and fondness for the Dr. seems to inspire them all with a Desire not to disgrace him; and so every individual of it must write and read and be literary."

With that engaging candor characteristic of her jottings, Mrs. Thrale concludes that money is not a major consideration with the Burneys. "He is the only man I ever knew, who being not rich was beloved by his Wife and Children . . . still I sh^d expect a rich Linen-draper to be better beloved in his own house—and nobody is so much beloved."

Nor was the affection inspired by Dr. Burney limited to the home circle. His popularity contributed to the success of the musical gatherings that played such an essential role in sharpening Fanny's powers of perception.

Her *Early Diary* * and her letters describe not only the celebrated singers and instrumentalists presented by Dr. Burney but also guests who rivaled the performers in interest. To hear Millico, Pachierotti and, in due time, the perilous Piozzi, there assembled in St. Martin's Street such luminaries as Prince Orloff, the discarded and possibly criminal lover of Catherine the Great; James Bruce, the Abyssinian traveler of dubious veracity; and that admired child of nature, the Polynesian Omai. One of the entries of the *Early Diary* has been transmitted almost intact to our times. It tells of the occasion when Hester Thrale brought Dr. Johnson, in his role of conversational virtuoso, to a Burney soirée. The Sage, in these, to him, uncongenial surroundings, failed equally at talking and at listening. Virginia Woolf retells the story in *Dr. Burney's Evening Party.*

The reading part of posterity owes a great deal to Fanny's inability to shine at these entertainments. Had she been as impressive a musician as Hetty, she would have been busy at the harpsichord. Endowed with Mrs. Thrale's powers of conversation, she would have vied with the company in the competitive talk that was the delight of the Streatham coterie and of Dr. Johnson's Literary Club. Shyness and mediocre musical gifts committed her to what was to prove a rewarding silence. Even her shortsightedness may have played its part in Fanny's talent for aural observation. Compelled to hear, rather than to watch others, she became expert in her ability to record dialogue.

The first pages of the *Early Diary* are given over to the earnest gush preferred by idealistic girls of many generations. She longed to fall in love, even if she fell "sola." She was edified by *The Letters of Frances and Henry.* Literary weeping was much in vogue and Fanny is pleased to report that during the second volume of *The Vicar of Wakefield* she was "surprised into tears" and "really sobb'd."

A visit with her stepmother to King's Lynn produced boredom that was, in its own way, as effective a goad to journalizing as Dr. Burney's musical parties. Even at sixteen Fanny proclaims herself (unlike her great disciple, Miss Austen of Steventon) committed to the life of London, Bath and other urban haunts of fashion. Lacking

* It was begun in 1768 when Fanny Burney was sixteen.

the cosmopolitan guests of St. Martin's Street, Fanny was beset by "tittle-tattle, prittle-prattle visitants." She was "sick of the ceremony and fuss of these fall-lall people." Where the immortal Jane would have come up with Mrs. Bennet or Mr. Woodhouse, Fanny was joining those authors who find that in a country town, "all the conversation is scandal, all the attention dress and *almost* all the heart, folly, envy and censoriousness." Despite this condemnation, Fanny was studying the ridiculous in personality and developing an aptitude for caricature that was to stand her in good stead when it came time to write *Evelina* and *Cecilia*.

A regularity of life safeguarded hours for writing. The *Early Diary* gives an interesting schedule for a country town day: "we breakfast always at 10, and rise as much before as we please, we dine precisely at 2, drink tea about 6—and sup exactly at 9." An undue attention to studies, as in the case of Mary Bennet, was considered, even by Jane Austen, to be pretension. Fanny took care to protect herself from such accusations. She tells Nobody that, "I make a kind of rule never to indulge myself in the morning—no, like a very good girl I gave that up wholly—accidental occasions and preventions excepted—to needle work by which means my reading and writing is a pleasure I cannot be blamed for by my mother as it does not take up the time I ought to spend otherwise."

This passage hints at Fanny's uneasy relationship with her stepmother. "The Lady," or "Precious," as the older Burney children referred to her, suspected, not without reason, that the close-knit offspring of Esther Sleepe were guilty of "treason." This uncongeniality could not have been caused by a failure of the second Mrs. Burney to keep pace with her new family in learning. When, many years later, Dr. Burney became again a widower, he wrote of his departed consort that "without neglecting domestic and maternal duties, she cultivated her mind in such a manner by extensive reading and the assistance of a tenacious and happy memory, as to enable her to converse with persons of learning and talents on all subjects to which female studies are commonly allowed to extend. . . ."

Perhaps Mrs. Burney found that Fanny's diary extended past the frontiers permitted to "female studies"; it seems more likely that she suspected her stepdaughter of letting off steam to Nobody. "The Lady" was very far from prefiguring such monsters as Jane Eyre's

Aunt Reed or David Copperfield's Mr. Murdstone. She must, however, answer to at least one charge of sadism.

About a year before the *Early Diary* opens, she made an apparent attempt to break Fanny's spirit. Deeming the girl's writings a combination of frivolity and vanity, she required Fanny to burn them herself. Susan stood by in tears. Upon the cruel pyre was immolated a childhood attempt at fiction called *Caroline Evelyn.* A decade later this destroyed story was to outdo the overworked symbol of the phoenix in the success of *Evelina.* It is pleasant to report that when the revised *Caroline Evelyn* brought unexpected celebrity to her creator, Mrs. Burney united herself with the public in astonished applause.

Fanny, warned by the loss of her first story, wrote in secret. During summer visits to King's Lynn, her place of concealment was a summer house that stood in Mrs. Burney's garden. In this retreat, Fanny, her stint of needlework completed, wrote to Nobody. She very early summed up what was to be her life's work. She wrote, on a summer Wednesday afternoon in this "sweet cabin," her pleasure in "writing down my thoughts at the very moment—my opinion of people when I first see them, and how I alter or how confirm myself in it—and I am much deceived in my *fore sight,* if I shall not have very great delight in recording *this living* proof of my manner of passing my time, my sentiments, my thoughts of people I know."

Mrs. Burney's cabin made another important, if less lofty, contribution to the future novelist's materials. Close at hand was the port of King's Lynn. The exquisite Georgian customs house which still stands at the quayside reminds us that this East Anglian harbor once trafficked on an international scale. To Fanny's ears, accustomed to the strains of Händel and Bach of Berlin,* rose the earthy, or more accurately, salty, talk of sailors and longshoremen. It was perhaps in this garden shelter that Evelina's somewhat incredible host, Captain Mirvan, took shape. When *Evelina* made Miss Burney the protégée of the "ton," wonder was expressed that so gently bred a young lady should write, in Mrs. Montagu's words, so "boisterous a book." Not all Fanny's listening had been done at Dr. Burney's concerts.

---

* This was Johann Christian Bach who, like Händel, had come from Germany to settle in London. He was one of J.S. Bach's composer-sons.

Fanny, deprived of her own mother and living in uncertain truce with "Precious," gravitated toward male authority. She might be said to be father-figure prone. There was her own charming father, whom she idolized. The success of *Evelina* was to add the paternal figure of Dr. Johnson to her lengthening list of mentors. It was, however, Samuel Crisp, whom Dr. Burney had met at the time of employment by Fulke Greville, who was to play the most important part in Fanny's transition from journalist to novelist.

Crisp had, in earlier years, written a tragedy to which not even Garrick could give wings. Stung by the failure of this venture, the frustrated dramatist retired to lick his wounds. He chose for his hermitage Chessington Hall, which was situated in Surrey, a jolting fifteen miles from St. Martin's Street. The young Burneys, especially Fanny, gladly suffered a drive over bad roads to reach Chessington, which was not only a second home but, in the production of *Evelina*, was to serve as a workshop.

Although Fanny's visits to "Daddy" Crisp were frequent, there was still the stimulus of distance to prompt letters. Crisp could not read enough of the girlhood doings of "Fannikins" and the other young people of her large family. For his delectation and her own she recounted day-to-day diversions and duties. It was to "Daddy" that many of her myopic observations upon the company and performers assembled by Dr. Burney were written. As befitted her father's daughter, she was transported by that vocal prodigy, Agujari. Just prior to the production of *Evelina*, she reports to the recluse of Chessington that, "At length, we have heard Agujari, we wished for you! —I can't tell you how *much* we wished for you!—The great singers of former years, whom I have heard you so emphatically describe seem to have all their talents revived in this wonderful singer!"

Agujari's antecedents were, as was often the case, uncertain. Fanny continues with a flourish of faulty Italian "Your Carestino, Farinelli-Senesino-alone are worthy to be ranked with the Bastardini."

The absent Mr. Crisp's replies were all that Fanny could have desired. In answer to her descriptions of fashionable guests and gifted exccutants, his enthusiasm was without bounds. "You have produced such an illustrious assembly of Princes and Generals, and lords, and ladies, and wits, and pictures, and diamonds, and shoulder knots, that I feel myself shrinking into nothing at the idea of them. . . ."

It will be recalled that the youthful Fanny was rewardingly shy. Mr. Crisp seems to have been aware that she preferred silent observation. He continues, "Nay, you yourself that made one among them, seem a little dazzled at their glare."

Crisp shows himself aware not only of Fanny's abilities but also her faults. He early accused her, with reason, of long-windedness. In the following passage he puts his finger on her propensity for a self-consciousness that was to plague her in life, and to bring her later writing to the point of near strangulation. "You cannot but know that trifling, that negligence, that even incorrectness, now and then in familiar epistolary writing, is the very soul of genius and ease; and that if your letters were to be fine-labour'd compositions that smelt of the lamp, I had as lieve they travelled elsewhere. So no more of that, Fanny, and thou lov'st me. Dash away whatever comes uppermost. And believe me you'll succeed better, than leaning on your elbow and studying what to say."

It would be interesting to have "Daddy" Crisp's opinion of Fanny's *Memoirs of Dr. Burney,* written in her old age when grandiloquence had claimed her for its own. Such was not the case in the months when *Evelina* was taking shape. Although Crisp was not aware of his Fannikin's furtive project, he sensed a ripening of her powers in a letter written about a year before *Evelina* burst upon the reading world. Late in 1776 he wrote to thank "dear Fanny for your conversation piece. . . . If specimens of this kind had been preserved of the different *Tons* that have succeeded one another for twenty centuries last past, how interesting would they have been! infinitely more so than the antique statues, basreliefs and intaglios. To compare the vanities and puppisms of the Greek and Roman and Gothic and Moorish and Ecclesiastic reigning fine gentlemen of the day with one another, and the present age must be a high entertainment to a mind that has a turn for a mixture of contemplation and satire, and to do you justice, Fanny you paint well; and therefore send me more and more."

Fanny was to write four novels of declining merit. *Evelina* is better than *Cecilia,* far better than *Camilla,* and infinitely better than *The Wanderer.* Ironically as the worth of her books deteriorated, their earnings rose. *The Wanderer,* which was, and remains, unreadable, brought in the largest sum. The commercial success of her later stories is, however, of significance because it indicates the advance of fiction, and of feminine fiction, in particular.

Fanny of the novels was a minor artist whose work inspired a major disciple. Among the list of subscribers to *Cecilia* appears the name of Miss J. Austen of Steventon, Hants. Although *Cecilia* does not fulfill the promise of *Evelina,* it is worthy of posterity's gratitude because its last chapter stresses a three-word phrase that fired Miss Austen's imagination. The phrase is PRIDE AND PREJUDICE.

Fanny of the diaries is in another category. Here we are in the presence of a splendid artist. Her literary talents and eventful life tended to foster the art of the biographer rather than the novelist. The fame that came to her through *Evelina* produced conditions more favorable for the development of the former skill than the latter. She became the protegée of persons she deemed, with reason, her superiors in rank and intellect. Her relationships with Johnson, Reynolds, Sheridan and the members of the court of George III supplied her with new and engrossing material.

The first of Fanny's many well-wishers was Dr. Johnson's "mistress," Hester Thrale, who, until the appearance of Gabriel Piozzi, devoted herself, in the words of the Sage, to soothing "twenty years of a life radically wretched." Learning that Fanny of over-night fame was the daughter of her daughter's music master, she lost no time in recruiting her for the Streatham coterie.

Fanny sensed in August of 1778 that a new and significant scene was opening before her. In the *Diary and Letters of Madame d'Arblay,* which succeeds the *Early Diary,* she rhapsodizes about her reception by the lively Mrs. Thrale. "London, August.—I have now to write an account of the most consequential day I have spent since my birth; namely, my Streatham visit.

"Our journey to Streatham was the least pleasant part of the day, for the roads were dreadfully dusty, and I was really in the fidgets from thinking what my reception might be, and from fearing they would expect a less awkward and backward kind of person than I was sure they would find.

"Mr. Thrale's house is white, and very pleasantly situated, in a fine paddock. Mrs. Thrale was strolling about, and came to us as we got out of the chaise.

"('Ah,' cried she, 'I hear Dr. Burney's voice! And you have brought your daughter?—well, now you are good!')

"She then received me, taking both my hands, and with mixed politeness and cordiality welcoming me to Streatham. She led me into the house, and addressed herself almost wholly for a few minutes to my father, as if to give me an assurance she did not mean to regard me as a show, or to distress or frighten me by drawing me out. Afterwards she took me upstairs and showed me the house, and said she had very much wished to see me at Streatham, and should always think herself much obliged to Dr. Burney for his goodness in bringing me, which she looked upon as a very great favour."

In her next paragraph Fanny gives way to the self-consciousness that Chauncey Tinker believes "she mistook for the virtue of modesty." Her writing abounds, unfortunately, in such fulsome insincerities. Mrs. Thrale permitted her guest a masquerade of humility by refraining from a "hint at my book, and I love her much more than ever for her delicacy in avoiding a subject which she could not but see would have greatly embarrassed me"—all this with frequent references to comings and goings of color, rushings from the room and delicious confusions.

At Streatham Fanny's propensity for the delineation of actual persons was to receive powerful stimulus. Her absorption in the frequenters of Mrs. Thrale's coterie succeeded to her interest in Dr. Burney's guests. That this was to be increasingly the case was perhaps to the detriment of her ability to create fictitious personalities as lively as are her portraits of those she met and knew. The more-than-life-size figure of Dr. Johnson dwelt, at Streatham, under the same roof. "Daddy" Crisp and Susan Burney thirsted for a closeup of the great man: "When we were summoned to dinner, Mrs. Thrale made my father and me sit on each side of her. I said that I hoped I did not take Dr. Johnson's place; for he had not yet appeared.

" 'No,' answered Mrs. Thrale, 'he will sit by you, which I am sure will give him great pleasure.'

"Soon after we were seated, this great man entered. I have so true a veneration for him, that the very sight of him inspires me with delight and reverence, notwithstanding the cruel infirmities to which he is subject; for he has almost perpetual convulsive movements, either of his hands, lips, feet, or knees, and sometimes of all together.

"Mrs. Thrale introduced me to him, and he took his place. We had a noble dinner, and a most elegant dessert. Dr. Johnson, in the middle of dinner, asked Mrs. Thrale what was in some little pies that were near him.

" 'Mutton,' answered she, 'So I don't ask you to eat any, because I know you despise it.'

" 'No, madam, no,' cried he: 'I despise nothing that is good of its sort: but I am too proud now to eat of it. Sitting by Miss Burney makes me very proud today!'

" 'Miss Burney,' said Mrs. Thrale, laughing, 'you must take great care of your heart if Dr. Johnson attacks it; for I assure you he is not often successless.'

" 'What's that you say, madam?' cried he; 'are you making mischief between the young lady and me already?' "

Fanny, the object of such tributes from such a source, was in an ecstasy of disavowed self-satisfaction.

During her Streatham visits, Fanny devoted her pen to the conversation of Dr. Johnson and Mrs. Thrale, and in so doing greatly advanced her journalistic skill. It is at her hand that we have Johnson's explanation for Garrick's appearance. " 'David, madam,' said the Doctor, 'looks much older than he is; for his face has had double the business of any other man's; it is never at rest; when he speaks one minute, he has quite a different countenance to what he assumes the next; I don't believe he ever kept the same look for half an hour together, in the whole course of his life; and such an eternal, restless, fatiguing play of the muscles, must certainly wear out a man's face before its real time.'

" 'Oh yes,' cried Mrs. Thrale, 'we must certainly make some allowance for such wear and tear of a man's face.' "

From Garrick, Johnson went on to an unflattering analysis of the character of Sir John Hawkins, Dr. Burney's rival in musicology. Unlike Dr. Burney, whom Johnson called "a man for all the world to love," Fanny learned, perhaps to her daughterly satisfaction, that Sir John was "penurious," "mean," possessing "a degree of brutality and a tendency to savageness that cannot be defended." He was, in short, "a most unclubable man."

Fanny, having written a clandestine book, was suspected by her Streatham companions of being embarked upon another secret manuscript. Mrs. Thrale had already suggested that Fanny write a comedy.

" 'Why, Madam,' Johnson ventured, 'she *is* writing one. What a rout is here indeed! She is writing one upstairs all the time. Who ever knew when she began *Evelina*? She is working at some drama, depend upon it.'

" 'Well that will be a sly trick!' cried Mrs. Thrale. 'However, you know best I believe about that, as well as about every other thing.' "

A few days later Johnson "was struck with a notion that Miss Burney would begin her dramatic career by writing a piece called '*Streatham*.'

"He paused and laughed yet more cordially and then suddenly commanded a pomposity to his countenance and his voice, and added, 'Yes *Streatham—a Farce*!' "

Johnson had guessed correctly. Fanny was writing her short-lived play, *The Witlings*. In her diary and letters she rehearsed the play-wright's craft.

"At tea-time the subject turned upon the domestic economy of Dr. Johnson's own household. Mrs. Thrale has often acquainted me that his house is quite filled and overrun with all sorts of strange creatures, whom he admits for mere charity, and because nobody else will admit them—for his charity is unbounded—or, rather, bounded only by his circumstances.

"The account he gave of the adventures and absurdities of the set was highly diverting, but too diffused for writing, though one or two speeches I must give. I think I shall occasionally theatricalise my dialogues.

MR. T.—But how do you get your dinners drest?

DR. J.—Why, De Mullin has the chief management of the kitchen; but our roasting is not magnificent, for we have no jack.

MR. T.—No jack? Why, how do they manage without?

DR. J.—Small joints, I believe, they manage with a string, and larger are done at the tavern. I have some thoughts (with a profound gravity) of buying a jack, because I think a jack is some credit to a house.

MR. T.—Well, but you'll have a spit, too?

DR. J.—No, sir, no; that would be superfluous; for we shall never use it; and if a jack is seen, a spit will be presumed!

MRS. T.—But pray, sir, who is the Poll you talk of? She that you used to abet in her quarrels with Mrs. Williams, and call out, "At her again, Poll! Never flinch, Poll"?

DR. J.—Why, I took to Poll very well at first, but she won't do upon a nearer examination.

MRS. T.—How came she among you, sir?

DR. J.—Why, I don't rightly remember, but we could spare her very well from us. Poll is a stupid slut; I had some hopes of her at first; but when I talked to her tightly and closely, I could make nothing of her; she was wiggle-waggle, and I could never persuade her to be categorical. I wish Miss Burney would come among us; if she would only give us a week we should furnish her with ample materials for a new scene in her next work.

This well-known dialogue was by no means Fanny's first nor last "theatricalising." Throughout many of the pages of her novels and diaries there is a suggestion of the art of the skit. Having been brought up in a family of musicians, she tended to see, and more particularly to hear, others in terms of performance. She was doubtless influenced by Garrick's inimitable characterizations, not only at Drury Lane but in the takeoffs with which he convulsed the Burney children when he visited them. Fanny possessed powers of mimicry "of amusing conversations and clever narrations with exact imitations of the voice and manner of those she described." * That *Evelina* should prompt her to write for the stage and that her mentors should urge her to do so was almost a foregone conclusion.

In *The Witlings* Fanny proposed to follow in Molière's footsteps. She too would satirize *Les Femmes Savantes*. She read her comedy to Mrs. Thrale, who was prompt to comment that "none of the scribbling ladies have a right to admire its general tendency." Was this for Fanny, herself the first of scribbling ladies, a tactful choice of subject? Dr. Burney thought it was not.

"Daddy" Crisp, having suffered theatrical trauma, was also pessimistic about Fanny's new project. In addition to cautioning her, in a general way, about the perils awaiting playwrights, he warned her against submitting herself to the counsels of her recent friends. Was he possessive about his Fannikins or, knowing her so intimately, did

---

* It was thus that Lady Llanover, in her edition of Mrs. Delany, accounted for the Duchess of Portland's condescending to meet Miss Burney.

he wish to arm her against her characteristic suggestibility? Hero worship came easily to her, entailing, as hero worship so often does, a surrender of independence. With Mrs. Thrale and Dr. Johnson to encourage her, and Sheridan to proffer the assistance of a master dramatist, what chance had Fanny of maintaining her own style? Crisp was usually sound in the advice he gave his protégée. He was never more astute than when he urged that *The Witlings* "be all your own till it is finished entirely in your own way; it will be time enough then to consult such friends as you think capable of judging and advising. If you suffer anyone to interfere till then . . . it won't be all of a piece."

Whether *The Witlings* was all of a piece we shall never know. Fanny was again forced to destroy her own work, this time by her father. She wrote to Dr. Burney that in obedience to his wishes the "poor Witlings" have sunk " 'down among the dead men.' " In this letter to her father we have Fanny at her most exasperatingly deferent. She cannot bear that Dr. Burney should "be hurt at the failure of my second," especially in the light of "the astonishing success of my first attempt."

This second literary holocaust is significant, in that it prefigures Fanny's obedience to Dr. Burney in the matter of her appointment to the dull court of George III. When she hesitated to make over her life to such regal drudgery as mixing Queen Charlotte's snuff, Dr. Burney and the aged Mrs. Delany (who had proposed the distasteful honor) were mortified at her reluctance. Fanny's inability to free herself from mistaken authority is tragically seen in *The Witlings* decision. How different from Jane Austen, who did not hesitate for a moment to tell the Rev. Stanier Clarke, librarian to the Prince Regent, which subjects she considered suitable for her talents! Had Fanny been capable of such clear-headed pluck, she might, like the greater Jane, have become a major artist of the novel rather than a major artist of the journal. Her instinct to conform, to cringe and sue for favor even where her well-intentioned father was concerned placed self-imposed limitations upon her creative powers and upon her literary future.

Fanny might deceive herself in matters of false pride and false modesty, but she could not deceive Mrs. Thrale. Although the mistress of Streatham first liked and then loved her new lion, she was never blind to her faults. She was capable of strongly critical comments which Fanny, euphoria notwithstanding, included in her diary. Fanny was accused of something very much like trying to have her cake and eat it too.

" 'Poor Miss Burney!' " said Mrs. Thrale with merciless acumen, " 'So you thought just to have played and sported with your sisters and cousins, and had it all your own way, but now you are in for it! But if you will be an author and a wit, you must take the consequences!' "

Mrs. Thrale in this disciplinary vein warned Fanny against affectation and "something worse."

" 'And what, dear Madam, what can be worse?'

" 'Why, an over delicacy that may make you unhappy all your life. Indeed you must check it—you must get the better of it for why should you write a book, print a book, and then sneak in a corner and disown it?' "

Why indeed, except that Fanny was, in Susan Burney's words, "such a prude."

Turning from Fanny's diary to Hester's *Thraliana,* the reader discovers that a clash of wills between patroness and protégée was always a possibility. The crisis about Mrs. Thrale's second marriage was several years away. Lacking Piozzi as a *raison d'être* for a broken friendship, the older and younger women might in any case have come to a parting of the ways.

Fanny, recently obscure, was touchy about accepting favors. Mrs. Thrale wrote in exasperation that Fanny "makes me miserable . . . so relentlessly and apparently anxious lest I should give myself Airs of Patronage, or load her with the Shackles of Dependence." Fanny was also touchy about doing favors, for her hostess dared "not ask her to buy me a Ribbon, dare not desire her to touch the Bell lest she should think herself injured."

The role of creditor is seldom easy. In the case of Mrs. Thrale and Miss Burney, the balance between favors given and received was subtle. Mrs. Thrale, Fanny's senior by many years, enjoyed wealth, wit, prestige and, for a celebrated span of twenty years, the presence at Streatham of Dr. Johnson. She introduced the deliberately retiring Fanny to the Sage and his circle. Fanny, on her part, had not only youth but creative and, more important, re-creative powers superior to those of her hostess.

Fanny, like Dr. Johnson, became a member of the Streatham

household. In addition to her sojourns there she accompanied the
Thrales to the correct watering places at the correct seasons. Bath
proved to her, as it was later to prove to Jane Austen, especially stimulating. Here was to be found Mrs. Montagu, Mother Superior to
the literary world of Georgian times. Fanny was "very glad at this opportunity of seeing so much of her; for allowing a little for parade
and ostentation, which her power in wealth, and rank in literature
offer some excuse for, her conversation is very agreeable and sometimes instructive and entertaining."

And now it was Fanny's turn to look askance at her patroness.
Contrasting her with Mrs. Montagu she continues, "of our Mrs.
Thrale, we may say the very reverse, for she is always entertaining
and instructive and sometimes reasonable and sensible; and I write
this because she is just now looking over me—not but what I think it
too!"

Christopher Anstey, who could not "forget he had written the
Bath Guide," was also present. It was at Bath that Fanny learned that
Hester Chapone, the ineffable writer of *Letters on the Improvement
of the Mind,* admired *Evelina.* Best of all was Fanny's encounter with
that most learned of "learned ladies," Elizabeth Carter. Fanny, at her
most perceptive, was instantly alive to the integrity of so sincere a
scholar.

"Mrs. Carter arose, and received me with a smiling air of benevolence that more than answered all my expectations of her. She is
really a noble-looking woman; I never saw age so graceful in the female sex yet; her whole face seems to beam with goodness, piety,
and philanthropy.

"She told me she had lately seen some relations of mine . . . who
had greatly delighted her by their musical talents—meaning, I found,
Mr. Burney and our Etty; and she said something further in their
praise, and of the pleasure they had given her; but as I was standing
in a large circle, all looking on, and as I kept her standing, I hardly
could understand what she said, and soon after returned to my seat.

"She scarce stayed three minutes longer. When she had left the
room, I could not forbear following her to the head of the stairs, on
the pretence of inquiring for her cloak. She then turned round to
me, and looking at me with an air of much kindness, said, 'Miss Burney, I have been greatly obliged to you long before I have seen you,

and must now thank you for the very great entertainment you have given me.' "

Fanny's response to praise from so disinterested an admirer was, for her, refreshingly simple. She continued, "This was so unexpected a compliment that I was too much astonished to make any answer. However, I am very proud of it from Mrs. Carter, and I will not fail to seek another meeting with her when I return to town."

Fanny was less inclined to cultivate the acquaintance of Lady Miller of Bath Easton, the impresaria of the famous vase. Horace Walpole has described the Millers in mocking detail, and Dickens is suspected of referring to the Muse of Bath Easton in the incident of Mrs. Leo Hunter's fancy-dress breakfast which was attended by the Pickwick Club. The vase was a seasonal institution. When Lady Miller arranged to meet Fanny it was not "vase time." At more propitious periods this vessel, hung with laurel and ribbons, stood in a bow window. It was stocked with *Bouts Rimés,* schedules like measure-treasure, love-dove, reason-treason and similar promptings to poesy. The Miller's guests drew from the vase their cues, improvised within the assigned rhymes and then the vase, in Lady Miller's account, became "the receptacle of all the contending poetical morsels which every other Thursday (formerly Friday) are drawn out of it indiscriminately and read aloud by the gentlemen present, each in his turn."

Lady Miller had succeeded in summoning to the vase Christopher Anstey, David Garrick and Anna Seward, the Swan of Lichfield. She must have wished to recruit "Evelina." An introduction was arranged and Fanny learned to her surprise that "notwithstanding Bath Easton is so much laughed at in London, nothing here is more tonish than to visit Lady Miller, who is extremely curious in her company, admitting few people who are not of rank or of fame, and excluding of those all who are not people of character very unblemished.

"Some time after, Lady Miller took a seat next mine on the sofa, to play at cards, and was excessively civil indeed—scolded Mrs. Thrale for not sooner making us acquainted, and had the politeness to offer to take me to the balls herself, as she heard Mr. and Mrs. Thrale did not choose to go.

"After all this, it is hardly fair to tell you what I think of her. However, the truth is, I always, to the best of my intentions, speak honestly what I think of the folks I see, without being biassed either by their civilities or neglect; and that you will allow is being a very faithful historian.

"Well, then, Lady Miller is a round, plump, coarse-looking dame of about forty, and while all her aim is to appear an elegant woman of fashion, all her success is to seem an ordinary woman in very common life, with fine clothes on. Her manners are bustling, her air is mock-important, and her manners very inelegant.

"So much for the lady of Bath Easton; who, however, seems extremely good-natured, and who is I am sure extremely civil."

Brightelmstone, as Brighton was then called, was visited by the Thrales every autumn. Consequently, to Brighton migrated the Streatham coterie of which Fanny was now a leading lady. Here she encountered a "foolish old beau," a certain Blakeny, whose name she charitably disguised. He was an elderly Irishman who possessed his countrymen's talent for playing himself. The author of the vanished *Witlings* could be relied upon to know good theatre when she met it. She wrote that she is "absolutely almost ill with laughing. This Mr. B—y half convulses me; yet I cannot make you laugh by writing his speeches, because it is the manner which accompanies them, that, more than the matter, renders them so peculiarly ridiculous. His extreme pomposity, the solemn stiffness of his person, the conceited twinkling of his little old eyes, and the quaint importance of his delivery, are so much more like some pragmatical old coxcomb represented on the stage, than like anything in real and common life, that I think, were I a man, I should sometimes be betrayed into clapping him for acting so well. As it is, I am sure no character in any comedy I ever saw has made me laugh more extravagantly.

"He dines and spends the evening here constantly, to my great satisfaction."

Following the destruction of *The Witlings,* Fanny commenced her second novel, *Cecilia.* It fails, for a number of reasons, to advance her stature as a writer of fiction. Like most creative persons Fanny needed privacy and leisure. The success of *Evelina* had deprived her of both, while furnishing her, as Crisp had foreseen, with a host of advisors. Dr. Burney, versed in the stage management of music, longed to play impresario to his now-famous child. He urged her to write ever faster, believing *Cecilia* superior to *Evelina* in both design and execution. Fanny's brother, James, the future Admiral, had an economic interest in the new novel because he was son-in-law to "Honest Tom Payne," the publisher. Susan Burney, now Mrs. Phillips, wrote frantic letters of advice. Even the hermit of Chessington failed to observe his own rules respecting Fanny's freedom of the pen. While Dr. Burney nagged his daughter to rush *Cecilia* toward publication, Crisp wrote that he was "not of your other Daddy's mind who would have it sent off to Mr. Payne just as it is. You have so much to lose, you cannot take too much care."

The bewildered and exhausted novelist suffered so from writer's cramp that she could hardly manage a letter to the concerned Susan Phillips. As the new work approached its completion early in 1782, she lamented that it was "too long in all conscience for the hurry of my people to have it produced. I have a thousand million fears for it. . . . Yet my dear father thinks it will be published in a month."

Although *Cecilia,* written under pressure, fails to keep pace with *Evelina,* it brought about, as had her first novel, another turning point in Fanny's dramatic career. The publication of her new book widened her circle of readers, increased her prestige and secured for her the friendship of the aged Mrs. Delany, whose fateful inspiration it was that Miss Burney should become a glorified servant to Queen Charlotte.

Cecilia appeared in 1782. In 1786 Fanny submitted to the wishes of her father and Mrs. Delany and entered into royal drudgery at the court of George III. The intervening years were troubled. It is interesting to speculate whether, lacking the changes and losses of this period, Fanny might have been spared five years of servitude.

Fanny's respect for the authority of the elderly has been noted. It was, until her marriage to a man younger than she, a decisive factor in determining her fortunes and misfortunes. In the period between 1783 and the end of 1784, she was to lose the three persons upon whom she most depended for advice in the conduct of her affairs.

Samuel Crisp died in 1783. In him, Fanny lost a venerable friend who respected her talents and corrected her weaknesses. His advice was usually sound. Perhaps he would have stood between Fanny and the bell that summoned her to dress Queen Charlotte.

Far more traumatic (and unnecessary) was Fanny's losing Mrs. Thrale through the then-supposed scandal of her second marriage. The *Early Diary* tells us how Hester had met and mocked Gabriel

Piozzi at one of Dr. Burney's elegant musicales. When she decided to make the Italian singer her second husband, Fanny's opposition to the match was as vehement as that of Dr. Johnson.

Posterity has found it easy to understand, and sometimes to sympathize with the possessive old man. Fanny's opposition has proved more puzzling. The Burneys were, like the Garricks, of humble origins. Like the Garricks, they had made, step by step, a secure niche in the cold stratification of Georgian society. Dr. Burney, the musician, and his daughter, the novelist, were imbued with a sense of professional worth. They set an equal value on becoming—as they did—members of the Polite World. They were an exception to the widely held view that players and singers were a low lot. Exceptions they should remain.

Undeterred by the objections of her daughters and of her old and young friend, the radiant bride turned the key on Streatham and, with her controversial husband, fled to the Continent. Dr. Johnson, his life possibly shortened by these blows, died shortly thereafter.

Fanny's patterns for visits to Chessington, to Bath, to Brighton and to Bolt Court, where resided Dr. Johnson, were suddenly at an end. A vacuum, intellectual and social, gaped before her. The friends to whom she had turned for counsel were no more. The stage was set for Mrs. Delany, charming, talented, and the confidante of royalty, to join the succession of Fanny's venerable mentors.

Some months before Mrs. Chapone introduced Fanny to her new best friend, she had learned from such august persons as Reynolds and Burke that "Swift's Mrs. Delany was among my unknown friends." In January of 1783, just prior to Daddy Crisp's death, Fanny and the Improver of the Mind "proceeded together to St. James's Place."

Had Fanny met Mrs. Delany during her *Evelina* period, she would probably have reported her own flutters rather than created one of the most winning of her many portraits. Fanny has proved herself in her novels and journals to be a spirited caricaturist. Unlike many humorists, she knew when to admire and, unlike the startled celebrity of ten years previous, she had learned to forget herself in another. Clearly, Fannikins was growing up.

"Mrs. Delany was alone in her drawing room, which is entirely hung round with pictures of her own painting and ornaments of her own designing. She came to the door to receive us. She is still tall, though some of her height may be lost: not much, however, for she is remarkably upright."

The development of Fanny, the artist, was hindered by her tendency to place herself in a parent-child situation, a tendency her early years at court aggravated. Mrs. Delany was of an age to be her grandmother. Happily she assigned her to this role.

"Benevolence, softness, piety, and gentleness are all resident in her face; and the resemblance with which she struck me to my dear grandmother, in her first appearance, grew so much stronger from all that came from her mind, which seems to contain nothing but purity and native humility, that I almost longed to embrace her; but I am sure if I had, the remembrance of that saint-like woman would have been so strong that I should never have refrained from crying over her." The embrace, or "salutation," took place with Fanny, apparently, dry-eyed.

Mrs. Delany, like Mrs. Carter, was grateful to "see one from whom I received such extraordinary pleasure." Then, with the "native humility" which Fanny admired, Mrs. Delany expressed her appreciation of a visit when there were no other guests; Fanny's account continues with Mrs. Delany's saying, "I hear so ill that I cannot, as I wish to do, attend to more than one at a time; for age makes me stupid even more than I am by nature and how grieved and mortified I must have been to know I had Miss Burney in the room and not to hear her!"

The intimacy between Fanny and her grandmother substitute quickly ripened. Upon Mrs. Delany's taking up her residence at Windsor, it became for the younger woman a dangerous association. It was at Windsor that Fanny's visits to her elderly patroness were now paid. It was here that the royal noose was prepared and tightened. Here George and Charlotte quizzed the future Second Mistress of the Wardrobe on her illusory ability to play the harpsichord, an accomplishment that might be expected of Dr. Burney's second daughter. Six months after meeting America's Last King * and his consort, Fanny embarked on a period of inappropriate service in an environment that was to prove both stultifying and lurid.

Until she entered Windsor, Fanny Burney's gifts for fiction and

---

* This is a reference to *America's Last King* by M.F. Guttmacher; it is a study of the king's derangement.

journalism hung in a delicate balance, with the latter skill slightly outweighing the former. Five years of menial chores irreparably damaged the novelist. Fanny's biographers have rightly lamented the reduction of her imaginative powers and in so doing have sometimes failed to do honor to her skill as a chronicler. At her hands, truth was not only stranger than fiction, it was better. We must turn to Saint-Simon for so vivid a picture of life at court. Her letters from Windsor and Kew with their descriptions of the mad King and his terrified family surpass in poignancy any of the "true pathetic" to be found in her novels.

Of Fanny's personal misfortune in her service at a court alternately dull and hysterical, there can be no question. She was lonely, overworked, bullied by a detestable colleague and frustrated by a myriad of major and minor obstacles. Queen Charlotte was of iron constitution and no imagination. Fanny, long before entering upon her duties, very accurately surmised the royal limitations in matters of sensitivity. The day after her interview at Windsor, she wrote the oft-quoted and prophetic "Directions for coughing, sneezing, or moving before the King and Queen." In the presence of her future mistress "you must not cough. . . . In the second place, you must not sneeze. If you have a vehement cold, you must take no notice of it. . . . In the third place, you must not, upon any account, stir either hand or foot."

For Fanny, who was by nature inhibited and self-conscious, these restraints were hardly therapeutic. Six months after she wrote to her sister, Hetty, this humorous description of preferred behavior in the presence of Royalty, she entered the Queen's service as Second Mistress of the Wardrobe. She learned that she had understated the case. There were many more disciplines to be rehearsed.

With certain notable princely exceptions, the court of George III and Queen Charlotte was virtuous and orderly. It was also boring.

The Princes and Princesses were numerous enough to span a full generation. When Fanny went to court in 1786, the Prince of Wales was twenty-four and his youngest sister, Princess Amelia, only three. The relationship between the future George IV and his parents conformed to the hereditary Hanoverian pattern of rivalry. The young George, despite dissipations and extravagance, had talents not shared by his dowdy parents. His musical abilities, his taste and his instinct for ceremony would have done a great deal to enliven an essentially bourgeois court. He was, during most of his adult life, estranged from his family because of his irregularities, among them his marriage to a commoner. Fanny was not long in learning how matters stood. She and the Queen read together "an account of a young man of good heart and sweet disposition, who is allured into a libertine life which he pursues by habit, but with constant remorse, and ceaseless shame and unhappiness. It was impossible for me to miss her object, all the mother was in her voice while she read it, and her glistening eyes told the application made throughout."

The King and Queen preferred a life of undeviating sobriety and routine. They had simple tastes. In their pursuit of domestic virtue they prefigured the character of their granddaughter, Victoria. Queen Charlotte woke early. She summoned the Second Mistress of the Wardrobe by "nothing more nor less than a bell." To be ready for the royal hooks and eyes, Fanny rose at six. It was usually not until after midnight that her duties left her free for a short night's sleep.

The activities of Windsor seldom varied. The Princesses did lessons and embroidered at their mother's side. The King hunted at the proper seasons, his equerries galloping dutifully with him. The hunters, returning to Windsor chilled and weary, were refreshed with barley water. The King and Queen enjoyed being read to. Garrick and Mrs. Siddons were engaged for special occasions and Fanny, as befitted a "female pen," was often asked to read from newspapers, sermons and plays. Since decorum demanded that no one sit in the royal presence, a standing lectern was used. A leaden silence was required of all assisting at these literary performances. Fanny lamented that "Nobody is to comment, nobody is to interrupt, and even between one act and another not a moment's pause is expected to be made. . . . But what will not prejudice and education inculcate? They have been brought up to annex silence to respect and decorum, to talk, therefore, unbid or to differ from any given opinion, even when called upon, are regarded as high improprieties, if not presumptions. . . . I now conceive the disappointment and mortification of poor Mr. Garrick when he read *Lethe* to a Royal audience. Its tameness must have tamed even him, and I doubt not he never acquitted himself so ill."

On pleasant evenings the King and Queen walked with their children and retainers upon the terrace. The public was encouraged to attend the domestic parade in loyal admiration of their sovereign paterfamilias. This ceremony somewhat parallelled the levees of Versailles. Here solicitations were made, eyes were caught and bows returned. Here, his daughter "in" his hand, Dr. Burney came to seek the post of conductor of the court orchestra. And it was probably here that Fanny sensed that their majesties had earmarked her for their service, and not her father.

The terracing over, a program of Händel's music was performed. To his regal strains, Fanny and her companions continued to stand. There were other physical hardships. Court attendants had to master the art of backing away from the royal presence; and they must never be detected in eating or drinking.

Such deprivations were difficult to sustain, especially during royal progresses to the stately homes of England. On such ceremonial visits the King, Queen, Princes and Princesses were regaled wth complicated Georgian fare while the exhausted equerries, ladies in waiting, and the Second Mistress of the Wardrobe stood fasting, hour by splendid hour.

Fatigue and hunger were to prove less severe trials than the emotional problems and disasters Fanny encountered during her five years at court. She was one of a group of arbitrarily selected persons who were as confined as travellers on a ship. Her day-to-day companions were upper servants of whom she was one, tutors, readers, chaplains, equerries and ladies in waiting. In detailing her life to her sisters, Susan and Charlotte, Fanny often retreated to camouflage. The Queen became the Magnolia. Other members of the royal family were the Rose, the Violet and the Lawrel (sic). Mrs. Delany's niece, Georgiana Mary Ann Port, was inevitably Miss P—. M. de Guiffardière, the Queen's French reader, was one of Fanny's minor trials. He pestered her with bantering gallantries which she deemed unsuitable for a married man who was a minister of the gospel. She was frequently "in wrath" at his insistence that she favor him with more of her attention. To describe his attitude toward her, or perhaps hers toward him, she referred to her tormentor as Mr. Turbulent.

The most ubiquitous of Fanny's associates was Mrs. Schwellenberg, Keeper of the Robes. In writing to Susan and Charlotte, Fanny called her superior, the Coadjutrix, La Présidente, and when she was more than normally odious, Cerbera. Mrs. Schwellenberg was a small-minded bully. She had long tyrannized over her colleagues. To have a celebrity at her beck and call was a new and heady experience. Her campaign against Fanny opened, quite literally, with a tempest in a teapot.

It was part of the duties of the Keeper of the Robes to preside, assisted by Fanny, at the tea table frequented by courtiers and guests. Here was a rich field for trifling humiliations. Within a few weeks of arriving at Windsor, Fanny learned that she had already lost ground. On July 24th she wrote, "Mrs. Schwellenberg and I meet in the eating room. We are commonly tête-à-tête. When there is anybody added, it is from her invitation only. Whatever right my place might afford me of also inviting my friends to the table, I have now totally lost by want of courage and spirits to claim it originally." Mrs. Schwellenberg had no intention of risking her third-rate authority by finding herself hostess to her assistant's celebrated friends.

Cerbera played a vicious part in the eventual undermining of Fanny's physical and mental health. She set to work to make a nervous wreck of the younger woman and very nearly succeeded. Yet, in the annals of Fanny's uneven literary performance, she emerges as one of her most skillfully drawn characters. With her broken English, her mean angers and her ignoble suspicions, she recalls Mme. Duval of *Evelina,* who seems, in retrospect, prophetic of the more powerful figure of Cerbera.

The grinding routine of garments handed and cups passed was varied at frequent intervals by royal birthdays. In August of Fanny's first summer at Windsor, little Princess Amelia had her third anniversary. Fanny described the solemnities in passages that were to delight Thackeray. He drew on her *Diary* for his chapter on George III in *The Four Georges,* adding to her words his imagined description of the terracing on August 7, 1786.

After telling us how simply the birthdays were kept, with no festivities other than new clothes, "unusually sumptuous" dinners and desserts and "a finer concert, by an addition of the musicians belonging to the Queen's band," Fanny gives us the "mighty pretty procession. The little Princess, just turned of three years old, in a robe-coat covered with fine muslin, a dressed close cap, white gloves and a fan, walked on alone and first, highly delighted in the parade. . . . Then followed the King and Queen, no less delighted themselves with the joy of their little darling."

Mrs. Delany was, of course, present for all such occasions. Princess Amelia "behaved like a little angel to her; she then with a look of inquiry and recollection" gave Fanny a child's honest stare. As befitted the sister of many younger children, Fanny was entirely at ease with infant royalty. " 'I am afraid,' " she said, "in a whisper and stooping down, 'your Royal Highness does not remember me?'

"What do you think her answer was? An arch little smile, and a nearer approach, with her lips parted out to kiss me. I could not resist so innocent an invitation. . . .' "

Fanny could hardly have guessed as she watched so happy a family scene that her tragic sovereign would, in two years' time, become the victim of "intellectual disease," in other words, insanity.* He felt himself to be in poor health during the summer of 1788; by November he had become a dangerous lunatic.

To treat his nervous symptoms, it was proposed that the King, with a small party, should travel to Cheltenham to try the effect of "the waters drunk upon the spot." Fanny was certain of being very comfortable because Mrs. Schwellenberg was not among the attendants. For a full glorious month she was to be "senza Cerbera." It was probably the only happy period of her term of servitude.

Not only was Fanny free of Mrs. Schwellenberg, she was frequently in the company of that interesting widower, Colonel Digby. He was Vice Chamberlain to the Queen, and appears in the *Diary* as Mr. Fairly.

Mrs. Digby had died almost a year earlier. It was now time to speculate upon whether Mr. Fairly would, or would not, marry again. Prior to the Cheltenham visit, he had asked Fanny what she thought of remarriage. He had been extremely happy with the first Mrs. Digby. Dared he risk a second attachment? Fanny's replies were models of discretion.

Court gossip had it that the widower would marry the Maid of Honour, Charlotte Gunning, for whom Fanny devised an inspired sobriquet, Miss Fuzilier. Fanny mistakenly inferred from Mr. Fairly's confidences that there was "no manner of truth in the report

---

* Recent medical research suggests that the supposed insanity of George III was due to physical rather than psychiatric causes. The question is discussed in depth in *George III and the Mad Business* by Doctors Ida McAlpin and Richard Hunter.

relative to . . . Miss Fuzilier." Encouraged by the Colonel's seeming as heart-whole as was proper for one recently bereaved, Fanny urged that where a "first blessing" was lost, it was reasonable to accept what "could come second, in this as in all deprivations."

The leisurely summer days at Cheltenham allowed Fanny plenty of time for comforting Mr. Fairly. She discussed with him such spirited topics as "Death and Immortality and the assured misery of all stations and all seasons in this vain and restless world." They read together from a work with the provocative title "Original Love Letters between a Lady of Quality and a Person of Inferior Condition." Mr. Fairly asked for, and received, Fanny's permission to write letters in her little parlor, using for his correspondence the writing desk presented to her by the Queen. Fanny happily added, "he writes very much, and his first pleasure seems receiving and answering his letters."

It was not surprising that the Second Mistress of the Wardrobe concluded that the Queen's Vice Chamberlain would "be wretched in singleness; the whole turn of his mind is so social and domestic. He is by no means formed for going always abroad for the relief of society; he requires it more at home."

Poor Fanny! By late summer the Cheltenham idyll had closed. She returned to Windsor still a spinster and once more a drudge. Her letters to her family made no attempt to conceal her unhappiness. They hint at a regret that not even the inevitable reunion with Cerbera could wholly inspire. "Melancholy—most melancholy—was the return to Windsor; destitute of all that could solace, compose, or delight; replete with whatever could fatigue, harass and depress! Ease, leisure, elegant society, and interesting communications were now to give place to arrogant manners, contentious disputation, and arbitrary ignorance! O Heaven!"

The Cheltenham waters failed to halt the advance of the King's insanity. Psychiatry during the self-styled Age of Reason was virtually nonexistent. Fanny, although aware that the King was daily losing ground, assumed that his symptoms were those of delirium, rather than madness. During October of 1788, she wrote that he was on "the eve of some severe fever." In November the storm broke; the benevolent King, so recently terracing with his large family, had become a lunatic with proclivities not only dangerous, but scandalous.

Fanny, in both *Evelina* and *Cecilia,* had experimented with melodrama. As the ceremonious tedium of Windsor gave way to days and nights of horror, it was her lot to live with it.

The Queen, who was not noted for imagination, was far more perceptive than Fanny in her diagnosis of the King's illness. She seemed to Fanny "almost over-powered with some secret terror" and "burst into a violent fit of tears." In the stolid, kindly Magnolia, it was, Fanny wrote, "very, very terrible to see."

Going to Queen Charlotte for her usual morning duties, Fanny abruptly learned that she had been "wholly unsuspicious of the greatness of the cause" the Queen had "for dread." Physical maladies had seemed to Fanny all that threatened the King "and great and grievous enough, yet how short of the fact." Shaken by her discovery, Fanny stood at the window watching the King's disordered departure for a drive with one of his frightened daughters, little imagining that she "should see him no more for so long—so black a period."

The King's condition manifested itself in all its fury at dinner that night. He seized the Prince of Wales and flung him against a wall. The Queen was beside herself and the Princesses wept at the sight of their father become an irrational monster. Mr. Fairly described to Fanny this nightmare scene. He then looked sharply at his colleague and asked, " 'Are you strong? Are you stout? Can you go through such scenes as these? You do not look much fitted for them.' "

Until this crisis Fanny, pride notwithstanding, had habitually derived moral support from her elders and supposed betters. Suddenly the situation was reversed. Her royal mistress was a sobbing, broken woman. Fanny's reply to Mr. Fairly would have done credit to anyone. For the self-protective "Evelina" it was heroic. "I shall do very well. For a time such as this, I shall surely forget myself utterly. The Queen will be all to me. I shall hardly, I think, feel myself at liberty to be unhappy."

The life of Frances Burney d'Arblay can, more than most lives, be divided into periods, each one being a story in itself. There is the shy girl of St. Martin's Street, the protégée of Streatham, the frustrated servant of the Queen, the forty-one-year-old bride of a penniless French nobleman, the English matron living in Napoleonic Paris and finally the aged Mme. d'Arblay who outlived not only her husband, but their only son. Thus Fanny, in addition to being in herself a literary turning point, lived a life of sudden change.

The illness of the King marked a new stage in Fanny's progress. She matured late, retaining adolescent limitations until she was nearly forty. In meeting the responsibilities so brutally thrust upon her and the other members of the royal household, Fanny departed permanently from her previous habits of dependence.

Nursing a psychotic patient requires skills hardly expected in courtiers. When the sufferer is a King, extramedical precautions must be taken. Soon the court was in total seclusion lest visitors should tattle of what they heard at Windsor.

In the case of George III, the normal need for discretion was distorted by the traditional father-son hostility of the House of Hanover. The Prince of Wales, like his grandfather, Prince Frederick, was an undutiful son. Largely to flout his father's simple-minded authority, he constituted himself a figurehead of the Whigs, the party of opposition. Health has always been a decisive factor in the affairs of state. At a time before tranquillizers, antibiotics or anesthesia, death frequently determined the course of history. The King's condition had to be concealed lest it prove useful to the enemies of his regime.

The harrowing duties of attending the King devolved upon equerries, pages and valets. They snatched what rest they could as the King's voice babbled itself into hoarseness. Even the weather was a trial. November of 1788 was a severe season. No fires were permitted in the King's apartments for fear that he would injure himself or others. Mr. Fairly and his exhausted companions went about their distasteful duties as chilled in body as they were in spirit.

The women who waited on the Queen were hardly better off. They, too, watched all day and all night lest their mistress be attacked by her disordered spouse. The better to protect her from being broken in upon, Charlotte was removed to more distant apartments, where she remained day after day with her daughters and attendants. Since she could no longer bear to hear the continuous drone of the King's voice, it soon became Fanny's duty to go to his rooms to learn how the night had passed. For many weeks the news was so "peremptorily bad and indubitably hopeless" that Fanny was constrained to soften the "relation in giving it to my poor Queen."

Frequently Mr. Fairly was Fanny's informant. He had, the *Diary* tells us, "some melancholy experience in a case of this sort, with a very near connection of his own." When other members of the household could not persuade the King to return to his bed, Mr. Fairly took him by the arm saying, " 'Your Majesty has been very good to me often, and now I am going to be very good to you for you must come to bed, sir: it is necessary to your life.'

"How fortunate," Fanny adds, "He was present."

In the state of siege forced upon Windsor, the members of the royal household were increasingly isolated. For Fanny this meant scoldings from Cerbera, who responded to the King's illness with "spasm and horror." It also meant the inevitable proximity of Mr. Fairly. Demure Fanny came, late in November of 1788, perilously close to letting her sisters know that she was in love with the Queen's Vice Chamberlain. She wrote that his "friendship offered me a solace without hazard; it was held out to me when all else was denied me; banished from every friend, confined almost to a state of captivity, harrowed to the very soul with surrounding afflictions and without a glimpse of light as to when or how all might terminate, it seemed to me, in this situation, that Providence had benignly sent in my way a character of so much worth and excellence, to soften the rigor of my condition, by kind sympathy and most honourable confidence."

Fanny chose an awkward moment for this (in her word) *éloge*. Shortly before she penned her tribute to Mr. Fairly's friendship, she reported a cryptic conversation to which she should have paid closer attention. Mr. Fairly hinted that his attentions to Miss Fuzilier were to be taken seriously. The King, he told Fanny, had accused him of a fondness for the company of "learned ladies."

" 'He gets,' " said the King, " 'To the tea-table with Miss Burney, and there he spends his whole time.' "

The significance of Mr. Fairly's next remarks was lost on Fanny. " 'I know exactly,' " he warned Fanny, " 'What it all means—what the King has in his head—exactly what has given rise to the idea—'tis Miss Fuzilier.' "

"Now indeed," continued the deluded Fanny, "I stared afresh, little expecting to hear her named by him. He went on in too much hurry for me to recollect his precise words"—and this from Fanny of the flypaper memory!—"But he spoke of her very highly, and mentioned her learning, her education, and her acquirements, with great praise, yet with that sort of general commendation that disclaims all peculiar interest. . . ."

This dialogue closed with Mr. Fairly saying, " 'since I have now got the character of being fond of such company I shall certainly . . . come and drink tea wtih you very often.' " He then hurried away with a laugh which Fanny told her sisters "he had all to himself."

Late in November it was decided to remove the King to Kew, where he could exercise out of doors away from the scrutiny of those accustomed to the terracing routine. Here was further hardship; Kew was intended only as a summer palace. No preparations for winter weather had been made. Mr. Fairly, whose "confidential favour with all the Royal Family enables him to let the benevolence of his character come forth in a thousand little acts and proposals," arranged to have bare floors carpeted and draughty windows and doors sand-bagged.

During the early weeks of the King's insanity, he had been under the care of physicians of the body rather than the mind. It was decided, as winter advanced, to call in Dr. Willis, a clergyman and doctor who, with his sons, treated patients suffering "intellectual" disease. The decision to take this step caused the Queen great distress, because Dr. Willis's psychiatric practice was well known. With him in attendance the nature of the King's malady would be crystal clear. Her fears were justified. Parliament deemed it a duty to be informed by his doctors of the King's prospects. Fanny was horrified. Early in 1789 she wrote, "Good Heaven! What an insult does this seem from parliamentary power, to investigate and bring forth to the world every circumstance of such a malady as is ever held sacred to secrecy in the most private families."

A royal family is, however, not a private family. The first of a succession of Regency Bills was the result of these inquiries. Many years passed before the Regency was at last enacted. That the King's final derangement was held off for so long was in large part due to the forward-looking methods of Dr. Willis and his two sons. They early predicted that their patient would recover and be in sounder health than before his crisis. They were reassuring, cheerful and steady. It was probably fortunate that they had not been conditioned, as had the court physicians, by the dehumanizing formality surrounding their King. When he shouted obscenities, horrified pages were commanded to stuff his mouth with handkerchiefs. When he behaved, he was rewarded with the sight of his daughters waving at Papa through the window. The unhappy King had never been treated as a fallible mortal to be pitied, encouraged and, if need be, punished.

George's recovery, which took place in February, was immeasurably hastened by the commonsensical Willises, whom Fanny described as "most delightful people." In the light of psychiatry's then morbid secretiveness, her next tribute strikes a note that does great honor to Dr. Willis and Dr. John; they were, she continues "all originality, openness and goodness." Openness, where a psychosis was concerned, was indeed original.

If Dr. Willis was open, Mr. Fairly was not. His tea visits, readings aloud and sentimental chats were Fanny's only solace during dark days. The fancies which came into being at Cheltenham revived. Cerbera, as was her wont, added her sadistic touch. With the bully's instinct for knowing where to place her blows, she accused Mr. Fairly of being "very onfeeling." The infatuated Fanny, to Mrs. Schwellenberg's satisfaction, flew to her hero's defense. "Equally amazed and provoked, she [Mrs. Schwellenberg] disdainfully asked me what I knew of him. . . . 'I know you can't not know him; I know he had never seen you two year and half ago; when you came here he had not heard your name.' "

"Two years and a half," I answered coolly, "I did not regard as a short time for forming a judgement of any one's character."

Mrs. Schwellenberg was quick to seize her advantage. Fanny was not only a matter of indifference to the Queen's Vice Chamberlain, she was socially beneath his notice.

This was too much for Dr. Burney's little girl. A few days later she prepared a revenge which almost tempted her to hint to Cerbera of an expected engagement.

Mr. Fairly went off for a week's respite from his arduous duties. He took leave from Fanny, but not from Mrs. Schwellenberg. Fanny, "looking forward to a friendship the most permanent—saw the elegibility of rendering it the most open." She "went back to Mrs. Schwellenberg," who characteristically chided her with being away so long. What a triumph to reply, "Mr. Fairly had made me a visit, to take leave before he went into the country.

"Amazement was perhaps never more indignant. Mr. Fairly to take leave of me! While not once he even called upon her! This offence swallowed up all other comments upon the communication.

"I seemed not to understand it; but we had a terrible two hours and a half! Yet to such, now, I may look forward without any mixture, any alleviation, for evening after evening in this sad abode."

It was just before Christmas of 1788 that Mr. Fairly went on his holiday. He returned on January 10th, having "been sent for express by her Majesty." Fanny wondered that she could have so long spared her Vice Chancellor, "wise, good, undaunted, vigorous—who has she like him."

To Fanny's well-controlled chagrin, she learned that her hero was leaving Kew. He would settle in London where he had many friends; he would attend the Magnolia only as she summoned him. He had had enough of "bustle, fatigue, cabal, and restraint." He had also had enough of Fanny, as she was shortly to learn.

Readers of Fanny's *Diary* have only a sprinkling of asterisks to convey that she had loved and lost. It must be remembered that the published *Diary* was issued after her death by her niece. It would hardly have been suitable to betray the confidences of a distinguished and eventually happily married aunt. Manuscripts in several libraries (among them the Berg Collection in the New York Public Library) supply the emotions hinted at by the editor's omissions. Since we are concerned with the Fanny of publication, the details of her disappointment do not come within our scope. Suffice it to report that by the time Colonel Digby (who was, as we recall, Mr. Fairly) married Miss Gunning in January of 1790, Fanny had recovered; Miss Fuzilier was henceforward Mrs. Fairly. Fanny had once more advanced in stature.

In February of 1789, Fanny's newly acquired pluck was put to the test. While walking in the gardens at Kew she saw three men she took to be laborers. It was the King and Dr. Willis and his son. Members of the household had been ordered, for their and his safety, to keep out of the King's way. Fanny may, in that outspoken age, have known of the erotic character of the King's illness; she knew, of course, that he was frequently violent. She took to her heels, hearing behind her the exhausted voice calling "Miss Burney, Miss Burney," while more and more footsteps joined in pursuit.

At Dr. Willis's command she stopped and turned to face her pursuers. The King advanced upon her with oustretched arms and, with a miraculous return of his "wonted benignity," kissed her.

Fanny was, by this chance encounter, one of the first to learn that her Royal Master was "so little removed from recovery." As the Willises had predicted, convalescence was assured. They were, Fanny rhapsodized, "surely sent by Heaven to restore peace and health, and prosperity to this miserable house!"

By February 16 the King and Queen were once more walking arm in arm; a few days thereafter the Regency Bill was withdrawn, and in March the King opened the House of Lords amid scenes of public rejoicing.

After events so shattering to the national morale, it was deemed desirable that the King should show himself restored in mind and body to his subjects. A royal progress occupied the summer of 1789. The King and court travelled, on roads lined with cheering citizens, to the southern and western counties, where the bracing climate of the New Forest and the seaside might complete recovery. Everywhere the royal party was acclaimed. Hospitality was proffered at great houses. There were ceaseless renditions of *God Save the King* by the loyal folk who rushed from field and shop to greet their sovereign. Fanny was frequently moved to tears. At Weymouth she was moved to her own demure laughter. Here a regal touch was added to the therapy of sea-bathing; "a machine," confided Fanny, "follows the Royal one into the sea, filled with fiddlers who play *God Save the King* as His Majesty takes his plunge."

On this triumphal tour Fanny, the sailor's sister, studied the phenomenon of tides. One of the stately homes to be honored by the royal visitors was near Plymouth. All was magnificence, with a "noble view" extending to Mount Edgecumbe and the neighboring fine country. George III, unlike King Canute, did not challenge the British Channel for, wrote the startled Fanny, "The sea *at times* fills up a part of the domain almost close to the house, and then its prospect is complete."

In matters of health and spirits, it was soon to be Fanny's ebb tide. Hope, loyalty and compassion had sustained her during months of suspense and anxiety. With Miss Fuzilier preferred to her by Mr. Fairly, suspense was at an end; so was hope. She must mask her disappointment as best she could, taking refuge in attempts to write tragedy in blank verse, an experiment that may have served to congest the prose style of *Camilla* and *The Wanderer*.

The King's recovery was an immense relief; it was also an anti-climax. The convalescent tour at an end, the diary dwindled and so did Fanny. Weeks passed with no or few entries. Symptoms multiplied. Even the Magnolia noticed that the Second Mistress of the Wardrobe looked ill, and went so far as to insist that she be seated while reading *Polly Honeycomb* and *The English Merchant,* a condescension that could never have occurred prior to the dreadful events of the previous year.

Late in May of 1790, Fanny was permitted to go with her father to yet another Händel performance. She seized this opportunity for a lengthy interview; a painful scene ensued. The deluded Dr. Burney, whose daughter's position at court was an immense source of pride to her family, was at last forced to face facts. Fanny had no regular holidays, nor leisure for her relatives, friends and writing. Under the accumulated pressures of royal drudgery, royal illness and the un-acknowledged sorrow of Mr. Fairly's fickleness, her health was threatened. She loved her "Royal Mistress, her merits, her virtues, her condescension." But, Fanny confessed, "I owned the species of life distasteful to me. I was lost to domestic endearment; I was worn out with want of rest, and fatigued with laborious watchfulness and attendance. My time was devoted to official duties; and all that in life was dearest to me—my friends, my chosen society, my best affections—lived now in my mind only by recollection, and rested upon that with nothing but bitter regret. . . . Melancholy was the existence where happiness was excluded, though not a complaint could be made! Where the illustrious personages who were served possessed almost all human excellence,—yet where those who were their servants though treated with the most benevolent condescension, could never, in any part of the livelong day, command liberty, or social intercourse, or repose!"

Even the ambitious Dr. Burney could not be deaf to such an appeal. " 'I have long,' " he cried, " 'been uneasy, though I have not spoken . . . but . . . if you wish to resign . . . my house, my purse, my arms, shall be open to receive you back!' "

It took Fanny more than a year to carry out her decision to leave court. Illness and fear inhibited her. She drew up "Memorials" only to postpone presenting them. She had a "daily intention to present my petition and conclude this struggle; night always returned with the effort unmade, and the watchful morning arose to new purposes that seemed only formed for demolition."

Fanny's resignation was finally presented in December, more than six months after the interview at the Händel performance. Protocol demanded that it pass through the meddling hands of Mrs. Schwellenberg, who was predictably "inflamed with wrath" and "petrified with astonishment."

It was another six months before Fanny's replacement arrived. On July 7, 1791, she began her last day of office. Everyone wept. Mrs. Schwellenberg softened to the unheard and inappropriate extent of suggesting that Fanny succeed to her post—"when it was vacated either by her retiring or her death."

For her five years of servitude, Fanny was significantly rewarded. She received a pension that was, a year later, to make it possible for her to marry the bankrupt and prospectless Chevalier d'Arblay. It was probably not too high a price to pay for many years of devoted love.

Lacking the disciplines and privations of her court career, the hyperdaughterly Fanny might never have married her foreign suitor. Dr. Burney disapproved, as would most fathers, of a husband who would have to live on his wife's pension and literary earnings. Nothing daunted, Fanny, liberated in more ways than one, married her Chevalier and set to work on the novel that was to build Camilla Cottage.

Fanny's *Diary and Letters* fills six volumes. Her tearful and rejoicing departure from court brings the reader to the end of the fourth. Because we are here concerned with the emergence of Fanny Burney, the authoress, we will take leave of her as she leaves Windsor. Her most significant writing was behind her. She had won for women novelists the right to publication. Her accounts of the trial of Warren Hastings and of the Battle of Waterloo have been deliberately omitted from this chapter, because they belong to the annals of legal and military history rather than the novelist's materials.

Fanny Burney's contribution to the surfacing of her sister "pens" is attested by the prompt appearance of Mrs. Radcliffe's "horrid" tales, Miss Edgeworth's amusing sketches of Irish life and the novels of that vaulting village genius, Miss Austen. Few minor novelists can be credited with such successors.

Her duties completed on July 7, Fanny went to take her last leave of their Majesties. The Queen wept. The King stood silent at the window. Fanny, the novelist-journalist, was at her most eloquent. "They were now all going—I took for the last time the cloak of the Queen and, putting it over her shoulders, slightly ventured to press them, earnestly, though in a low voice, saying, 'God Almighty bless your Majesty.'

"She turned round, and putting her hand upon my ungloved arm, pressed it with the greatest kindness and said, 'May you be happy.' . . .

"They then set off for Kew.

"Here therefore end my Court Annals; after having lived in the service of Her Majesty five years within ten days—from July, 1786 to July 7, 1791."

Thus Fanny wrote—the work was done. She went forward to women's common tasks, her uncommon task completed.

BIBLIOGRAPHY

D'Arblay, Frances. *Diary and Letters of Mme d'Arblay.* Edited by Charlotte Barrett. Preface and notes by Austin Dobson. 6 vols. London: Macmillan, 1904-05.

Blunt, Reginald. *Mrs. Montagu, Queen of the Blues.* 2 vols. London: Constable & Co., 1923.

Boswell, James. *Life of Samuel Johnson.* Edited by Birbeck Hill. Revised by L. F. Powell. 6 vols. Oxford: Clarendon Press, 1933.

Burney, Fanny. *Cecilia or Memoirs of an Heiress.* 2 vols. London: G. Bell, 1882.

———. *Early Diary.* Edited by A. R. Ellis. 2 vols. London: G. Bell, 1889.

———. *Evelina, or A Young Lady's Entrance into the World.* London: J. M. Dent "Everyman," 1956.

Burton, Elizabeth. *Pageant of Georgian England.* New York: Scribner's, 1967.

Clifford, James L. *Hester Lynch Piozzi (Mrs. Thrale)*. Oxford: Clarendon Press, 1941.

Climenson, Emily. *Elizabeth Montagu, Queen of the Blues.* 2 vols. New York: Dutton, 1906; London: Constable, 1923.

Curling, Jonathan. *Edward Wortley Montagu, The Man in the Iron Wig.* London: A. Melrose, 1954.

Davis, Fanny. *The Palace of Topkapi in Istanbul.* New York: Scribner's, 1970.

Delany, Mary Granville. *Autobiography and Correspondence of Mary Granville Delany.* Edited by Lady Llanover. 6 vols. London: Richard Bentley, 1861-62.

Doran, Dr. John. *A Lady of the Last Century.* London: R. Bentley and Son, 1873.

Hahn, Emily. *A Degree of Prudery.* New York: Doubleday, 1950.

Halsband, Robert. *The Life of Lady Mary Wortley Montagu.* Oxford: Clarendon Press, 1956.

Hemlow, Joyce. *Fanny Burney.* Oxford: Clarendon Press, 1958.

Hopkins, Mary Alden. *Hannah More and Her Circle.* New York: Longmans, Green & Co., 1947.

Johnson, R. Brimley. *Blue Stocking Letters.* London: J. Lane, 1926.

Kronenberger, Louis. *Kings and Desperate Men.* New York: Alfred A. Knopf, 1942.

Maxwell, Constantia. *Dublin Under the Georges.* London: Faber and Faber, 1956.

Montagu, Elizabeth Robinson. *An Essay on the Writings and Genius of Shakespear Compared with Greek and French Dramatic Poets with some remarks upon the misrepresentations of Mons. de Voltaire. The fifth edition, corrected, to which are added three Dialogues of the Dead, by Mrs. Montagu.* London: Printed for C. Dilly, 1785.

————. *The Letters of Mrs. Montagu.* Published by Matthew Montagu. 4 vols. London: T. Cadell and W. Davies, 1810-13.

Montagu, Lady Mary Wortley. *The Complete Letters of Lady Mary Wortley Montagu.* Edited by Robert Halsband. 3 .vols. Oxford: Clarendon Press, 1965-67.

————. *The Letters and Works of Lady Mary Wortley Montagu.* Edited by Lord Wharncliffe. Third edition with a new memoir by W. Moy Thomas. 2 vols. London: Bickers and Son, 1861.

More, Hannah. *The Works of Hannah More.* 7 vols. New York: Harper and Brothers, 1868.

Paston, George (Emily Morse Symonds) . *Mrs. Delany: A Memoir.* New York: Dutton, 1900.

————. *Lady Mary Wortley Montagu & Her Times.* London and New York: G. P. Putnam's Sons, 1907.

Pennington, Reverend Matthew. *Memoirs of the Life of Mrs. Carter.* 3rd ed. 2 vols. London: F. C. and J. Rivington, 1816.

Piozzi, Hester Lynch Thrale. *Thraliana, the diary of Mrs. Hester Lynch Thrale (later Mrs. Piozzi) 1776-1809.* Edited by Katherine C. Balderston. 2 vols. Oxford: Clarendon Press, 1942.

Plumb, J. H. *The First Four Georges.* New York: Macmillan, 1957.

Quennell, Peter. *Alexander Pope, The Education of Genius, 1688-1728.* New York: Stein and Day, 1968.

Scholes, Percy A. *The Great Dr. Burney.* 2 vols. London: Oxford University Press, 1948.

Stuart, Lady Louisa. "Introductory Anecdotes." In *The Letters and Works of Lady Mary Wortley Montagu,* edited by Lord Wharncliffe, vol. 1. London: Bickers and Son, 1861.

Thackeray, W. M. "The Four Georges." In *The Complete Works of William Makepeace Thackeray,* vol. 14. New York and London: Harper & Brothers, 1904.

Tinker, Chauncey B. *Dr. Johnson and Fanny Burney.* New York: Moffet, Yard & Co., 1911.

———. *The Salon and English Letters.* New York: Macmillan Company, 1915.

INDEX